LANGUAGE TRUTH AND MEANING

To Joe Collins
who made the Florida Congress possible

Language Truth and Meaning

*Papers from
The International Lonergan Congress 1970*, St. Leo College, 1970.

Edited by Philip McShane

UNIVERSITY OF NOTRE DAME PRESS

American edition, 1972
UNIVERSITY OF NOTRE DAME PRESS
NOTRE DAME, INDIANA 46556

First published in Ireland by Gill and Macmillan Ltd
2 Belvedere Place, Dublin 1
and in London through association with the
Macmillan
Group of Publishing Companies

Jacket designed by Des Fitzgerald

ISBN: 0-268-00478-1
Library of Congress Catalog Card Number: 72-3507

Printed and bound in the Republic of Ireland by
The Book Printing Division of Smurfit Print and Packaging
Limited, Dublin

Contents

List of Contributors

GARRETT BARDEN lectures in philosophy at University College, Cork, Ireland. He has written in various journals of anthropology and philosophy and is co-author with P. McShane of *Towards Self-Meaning*.

FR EMERICH CORETH S.J. is Professor of Philosophy at the University of Innsbruck and Director of the Institute for Christian Philosophy. His philosophical publications include *Metaphysik* (1961; English translation 1968).

FR JOSEPH FLANAGAN S.J. is Chairman of the Philosophy Department at Boston College. He has written a number of articles dealing with the thought of Bernard Lonergan and is presently completing a book on the philosophy of history.

DR ROBERT JOHANN professes philosophy at Fordham University. He is the author of *The Meaning of Love*, *The Pragmatic Meaning of God*, and *Building the Human*.

FR PATRICK A. HEELAN S.J. is Chairman of the Philosophy Department at the State University of New York. He is author of *Quantum Mechanics and Objectivity* and *The Observable: Observation, Description and Ontology in the Quantum Mechanics of Werner Heisenberg*.

FR MATTHEW LAMB is presently completing his doctoral studies at the State University of Münster, West Germany, and has published articles in various journals including *Continuum* and *Philosophy of Science*.

FREDERICK LAWRENCE is completing a doctoral dissertation on Gadamer and Lonergan for the Theological Faculty of the University of Basel. He is presently teaching philosophical theology at Boston College.

FR BERNARD LONERGAN S.J., author of *Insight* and of *Method in Theology*, recently Stillman Professor of Catholic Theology at Harvard University, is at present at Regis College, Toronto.

DR PHILIP MCSHANE edited *Foundations of Theology*, the first volume of papers from the 1970 International Lonergan Congress, and is author of several books including *Music that is Soundless: an Introduction to God for the Graduate* and *Plants and Pianos*.

DR SCHUBERT M. OGDEN is University Professor of Theology in the University of Chicago, having formerly taught at Perkins School of Theology, Southern Methodist University. His most recent book is *The Reality of God and Other Essays*.

DR DAVID M. RASMUSSEN is Associate Professor of Philosophy at Boston College. His most recent book is *Symbol and Interpretation*. He is editor in chief of the new journal *Cultural Hermeneutics*.

FR WILLIAM J. RICHARDSON S.J. is at present an Associate Professor of Philosophy at Fordham University. His writings include the major work *Heidegger: Through Phenomenology to Thought*.

FR BERNARD TYRRELL S.J. has just completed doctoral studies in philosophy at Fordham University with a dissertation *Bernard Lonergan's Philosophy of God*. Currently he is working on a book entitled *Christian Healing and Enlightenment*.

Introduction

PHILIP McSHANE

THIS second volume of papers written for the First International Lonergan Congress at Florida in 1970 has the unity of topic expressed in its title but there are considerable variations in treatment. Some articles aim at directly presenting an aspect or application of Lonergan's view, a second group of articles are critical of points within Lonergan's position, and a third are comparative, relating Lonergan's approach to recent efforts to elaborate a more sophisticated theory of meaning and of the *Geisteswissenschaften*. This third type of article should especially be valuable in broadening the context of the chapters in Fr Lonergan's book, *Method in Theology*, published in March this year, which deal with subjects such as Meaning and History. The first two types of article, on the other hand, should be of value in helping the reader to raise the existential question as to where he or she stands in relation to what I might call the prior context[1] of *Method in Theology*.

Here I yield to the temptation to extend my introductory comments further than I did in volume one. What I add is not meant as a critique of the present papers—this I leave to Fr Lonergan—it aims rather at fostering an authentic orientation towards personal growth in both meaning and mystery on the part of the present readers of both this volume and *Method in Theology*.

I recall now two questions relevant to that orientation that were asked of Fr Lonergan during the general interview at the Florida Congress. One question related to the danger of neglect of *Insight* and its complex methods, due to more immediate interest in *Method in Theology;* the other regarded the nature of the shift to interiority as axial in Jaspers' sense.[2] For Fr Lonergan *Insight* was clearly the way into the ongoing interdependent processes outlined in *Method in Theology*, and its challenge could not be bypassed.[3]

To the question of the axiality of the well-defined shift to interiority his answer was affirmative.

Now it seems to me that such an affirmation of axiality should demand serious self-questioning of the contemporary philosopher or theologian. If I may be personal, the task of shifting adequately into that novel horizon is one I find decades-long. Again, from conversations with Fr Lonergan during his visit to Dublin in 1971 I found that his own growth was much slower than one might be inclined to assume—that, for example, his precise self-appropriation on the level of judgement was an achievement of the process of writing *Insight*. And so, while it is true that the verbal expressions of the minds of great men shorten our labours, that like pygmies we stand on their shoulders, there can be an element of illusion regarding just how much shorter our labours are to be, just how authentically we stand.

I recall here a lesson drawn from zoologists' long efforts to understand thirst:[4] 'The philosopher may learn a lesson from this for his own field. If the understanding of animal thirst is a remote goal of the zoological enterprise, the philosopher should hardly consider the understanding of human understanding or human thirst for understanding as some youthful achievement prior to doing his own thing.'[5] To move thoroughly into the horizon of interiority requires the precise exercise of a generalised empirical method far more delicate than the empirical method of zoology, an exercise which must be patiently prolonged if it is to succeed.

To assimilate Lonergan calls for a like exercise in interiority. I think any who have spent long years getting hold of their own acts of insight, and still longer years getting hold of the act of judgement (the stumbling block for so many of Lonergan's readers), will understand well enough my repugnance for exposing his doctrine in the context of the present essay. I think they will agree also that unless his readers are ready to undertake a parallel labour (not necessarily so prolonged inasmuch as they may be less tardy of intelligence) they have little chance of understanding what Lonergan is doing or talking about. This is rather bluntly said, I am afraid, but is there not room for a measure of bluntness at this stage? If we wish either to praise or to blame we must first understand. Lonergan's position is that the way to understand him is to carry out for ourselves the performance of appropriating conscious activity. He has said as much in *Insight*, he has repeated it for years in his lectures, and his claim is ignored, sometimes as much by disciples as by opponents, both of whom turn more readily to the objective products of his thoughts than to their own operations.[6]

What I am concerned with here is the specification within philosophy and theology of a general, but undeveloped[7] and unexploited,[8] theory of adult growth. I am concerned about the deepening of the ongoing collaboration for which we came together in Florida. I am concerned about the possibility of an increasing number of thinkers of our time being able, intelligently and with feeling[9] commitment, to echo the words of Husserl on his forty-fifth birthday: 'How I would like to live on the heights. For this is all my thinking craves for. But shall I ever work my way upwards, if only for a little, so that I can gain something of a free distant view? I am now forty-five years old, and I am still a miserable beginner.'[10]

The intention of truth in mythic consciousness

GARRETT BARDEN

BESIDES the significance of particular mysteries and myths both have a basic meaning, the account of which cannot in principle avoid the discussion of the relations between itself and the critique or interpretation of particular myths. The myth's emergence is grounded in a particular mythic consciousness but if the radical meaning of myth is to be reached then the fundamental contours of that consciousness have to be discovered.[1] The study of literature supposes some unity in the many disparate expressions to be investigated[2] but even when this supposition is explicitly acknowledged, its validity and consequently the source of the unity are unquestioned. Expressions are linked to one another but they are linked most fundamentally in their source and so a discussion of the radical meaning of literature, of myth and mystery, of ritual and dance, must be genetic.

Human science may be adequately understood only when human knowing is conceived as a dynamic structure and its operator specified. Mythic consciousness is to be grasped by understanding its mode of operation and the manner in which the intention of truth is uttered within its confines. This intentionality which reveals the straining of intellect includes both wonder and precise question, the unlimited desire of intellect and the absolute quality of the judgement which closes the movement that the question began, and which at once prepares and clears the field for the new question that will begin the process anew.

The interlocking of these two aspects of intentionality divides the universe into the known and the to-be-known, corresponding to the questions already answered and those that remain unsolved.[3] It grounds one's presence to oneself not merely as a knower but as one who knows progressively; it is this presence to self as a developing subject that reveals the division. The to-be-known is not confined to the basic question on transcendent being; it includes more commonly the pedestrian and unavoidable experiences of simply not understanding e.g. how the television works, the principles governing the internal combustion engine etc. Commonplace examples are deliberately chosen to stress that on the theoretical level the unknown includes simply all that is not understood. The realm of the to-be-known is revealed and generically defined by the fact of unanswered questions.

Questioning is the image on which the insight into oneself as wondering subject emerges but there are other images of thinking, wondering, understanding, judging which have to be linked with the theoretically significant image. One may think of Rodin's Thinker or more crudely of the image on the dust cover of *Insight*, one may imagine oneself solving a difficult problem, one may recall posture and movement, but these images are not the relevant images for introspective psychology. That these images perform a different role from that of the scientific phantasm seems obvious but it is much less clear what their role is. An objectification of self takes place in the theoretic enquiry into the nature of the subject[4] but there are other objectifications of self in art and imagination. Yet there is the one subject and so there will be a correspondence between the objectifications despite the fact that these will not be subject to the same patterns of emergence and laws of development.

One's self presence as questioner reveals the to-be-known and on this image may emerge the fundamental insight into one's nescience; there are questions which one has not answered; there are others one cannot yet raise; one is ignorant and the boundaries of one's ignorance are unknown. Corresponding to this intellectual fact, which is itself not static but fluid, there is on the psychic level a consonant psychic orientation which has to include some cosmic dimension.[5] This psychic image, which utters the orientation, is neither the theoretic phantasm nor yet the artistic image—although the art image may well present this feature of human living; one thinks of some of Klee's works for example— but a sense of the uncanny and the unfamiliar that at times invades one's consciousness. Whether this affect invades and elevates the commonplace[6] or whether it is attached to some unusual image or event is not of radical importance. Whatever the case there will be a division between the familiar and the strange, the domesticated and the untamed. The content of the different realms will differ from culture to culture and the recognition of this variability has led some to doubt the fact of the basic division.[7] The division has become a commonplace in anthropological writing under the title Sacred-Profane but the basic inadequacy of the theories is that there is usually an attempt to generalise content illegitimately and to impute to others affective stances that belong exclusively to the investigator. The division between familiarity and strangeness does not, however, determine how this division will be subsequently elaborated and objectified. Evans–Pritchard notes that witchcraft was familiar to a Zande but this fact does not mean that it was familiar in precisely the same way as growing groundnuts was familiar.[8] Similarly, the ancestors or exemplars are familiar to the Ngatatjara but they are the familiar denizens of another realm. There occurs in expression a taming of the uncanny which is thus trapped and rendered less dangerous. As we shall suggest this is a function of the medium regardless of the particular interpretations.

The psychic image becomes symbolic 'when it stands in correspondence with activities or elements on the intellectual level'[9] without losing its psychic affect. A symbol has an obvious feature which has in the past tended to dominate discussion although there are signs of the eclipse of this position. This is the cryptic aspect of symbolism: the symbol is an image which stands for something other than itself: arbitrariness or presumed naturalness were secondary considerations. On this position the image was a veil which concealed the reality for which it stood, as a message in code disguises itself.[10] But a symbol has too a revelatory character; it is the expression of the subject within a certain modality, a manifestation of the subject in which he is already meaningful to himself. So the dreamer is never totally meaningless in his dream although, awake, he may enquire into the genesis of the plot and imagery in an effort to reach a theoretical grasp of the inter-relations between various elements of his total existence.[11] Similarly, a sense of awe or guilt or joy in all its nuances and resonances may be correlated with one's culture and one's history but the theoretical understanding of the affective event is not the affect and the crucial fact is that the affect is already embodied in a meaningful image.[12] The subject becomes present to himself in the symbol which obscurely utters his psychic intentionality in harmony with basic intellectual reach.

The obscurity of the symbol expresses the generic obscurity of the primitive subject but a further stage is reached when there is no longer simply the link 'between levels but an interpretation of the image is offered'[13] and the intention of truth begins to penetrate the symbol. The image is no longer merely the affective symbol of human ambiguity and human desire; by the interpretation there occurs a transformation of the image into a statement on the nature of man, of society, of the cosmos, which takes up the symbol with its burden of affects and meanings to transform it into an objectification of what is considered to be the case. Thus the world is expressed and contained for the audience whose possibilities of self-knowledge are now socially, publicly, traditionally embodied in the statement. To the questions: what is man? what is society? what is the nature of the universe, the order of the world?, the answers are already available, and, indeed, scarcely avoidable.

Available answers may satisfy some but in so far as the answer is incorrect it remains in principle vulnerable. Vulnerable answers may be exposed but the correct questions must first emerge, and though this is in principle possible, it is not always probable. Perhaps wonder about the nature of man is pervasive but it cannot be specified and formulated in a sufficiently penetrating question until the questioner is sufficiently intellectually developed and detached. The image is interpreted certainly but psychic equilibrium and affective resonance have not been lost; the wonder which prompted the interpretative element is but one component in the total subjective orientation of the subject into the to-be-known and the unfamiliar. Wonder may be the source of questioning but it is subjects in their concrete existence who ask questions which will, accordingly, not be purely theoretic but will include the affective movement towards content or the flight from anxiety fed by uncertainty.[14] The traditional answers to traditional questions are the expression of such undifferentiated subjectivity; the newly invented answer, however, does not escape this fate. Conversely, even if the available expression is an adequate expression of a correct theory it will mean nothing to one who is not sufficiently detached to raise the theoretic question and sufficiently developed to grasp the fact that he can appropriate the answer only after an immense theoretic labour. The affective elements in his present orientation clamour for an immediate home. Thus, as one would have expected, among the Ngatatjara the biblical story of creation is accepted as a narrative of exactly the same kind as a popular scientific account. One does not have to go as far afield but the point is that expressions from a literary context which has developed different and contrasting modes of expression for different modes of meaning are necessarily reduced to one mode in a context where different modes of expression and meaning are not evolved.

Adequate understanding of self requires the prior development of the subject but self presence is prior to such development, and wonder in which one is present to self is prior to both theory and detachment and clear differentiation; so the early specifications of the generic wonder are themselves very general; little is known and there is little appreciation of the lack. So even the theoretical elements in the total orientation remain weakly defined; there is little grasp of what kind of answer would suffice and so an answer which is affectively resonant and which has behind it the authority of tradition is acceptable.

The question has remained inchoate; the intention of truth is but one feature in the total subjective orientation and so the judgemental character of the statement may not be prominent. The statement is considered to be true but there is no realisation of the criterion of truth, of the way in which the statement has to fit into the context of the totality of true statements, of principles of contradiction and coherence. The statement is accepted as true because it is obvious; it is obvious because it is unquestionable; it is unquestionable because it is expressed. There are other grounds for its obviousness and these must be explored if the relations between the apparent order of everyday and the seeming arbitrariness of the products of imagination are to be pinned down. Practical activity has built into it a correction to the premature and mistaken judgement, although the control is neither infallible nor wholly safeguarded from enveloping error. Events force some correction on practical ideas and one cannot persistently ignore this control and survive. However, the operatively intelligent acceptance of the check is prior to the theoretic discovery of the nature of the control and its implications. To learn by trial and error is a spontaneous activity; to enquire about the nature of the spontaneity and to elucidate the structure of the judgement and the characteristics of evidence belongs to a more delicate enquiry. One may, and commonly does, learn by trial and error without ever coming to note the role of either direct or reflective understanding in the activity. Human intelligence and reasonableness is revealed in practical activity; the actor's understanding of his own intelligence and reasonableness demands a shift in viewpoint that itself requires the slow development not merely of the individual but of the community. Before this immense development occurs the actor fails to distinguish accurately between the various elements in the particular intelligent and reasonable act. Doubtless he imagines, understands, judges, feels, decides; doubtless these activities are distinct, but he does not know that they are distinct and so fails to grasp the implications of his intelligent enquiry and reasonable assent. This subject is conscious in his activities but since these are undistinguished by him, he is present to himself as an undifferentiated subject.

The undifferentiated subject does reach correct conclusions in particular cases but he neither asks nor knows about the manner in which these conclusions are reached. Malinowski's contention that the savage was as reasonable or rational as the civilised person is of course grounded in this basic fact, but what Malinowski failed to grasp, and what his successors have failed to grasp, is how the intelligent and reasonable practical person could surround himself with a mythic universe. The failure, as will gradually appear, is rooted in the more serious failure to grasp the implications for the interpreter himself of the attempt to understand a viewpoint.[15] It is necessary to go beyond the mere assertion of rational activity to an understanding of the nature of this activity, for the interpreter is faced with precisely the same problem in his own development; he is intelligent and reasonable; he may be able to use these words but he does not necessarily know exactly what intelligence and reasonableness are. The assumption that these activities are understood by everyone blocks enquiry and leads to unrecognised mutual misunderstanding between interpreters.

Operatively the pragmatic success of his activities reinforces the judgements of the undifferentiated subject; contrary instances are the occasion of further questions but the kind of questions that emerge, their range, how far one is willing to push the investigation, depend not exclusively on the practical issue but on the existential context of the subject. Mythic consciousness may penetrate even practical activity in that it places severe restrictions on the emergence and range of enquiry. It appears that the particular event is

2

not to be understood except by placing it within the habitual context of the actor. Further, when one leaves the realm of obvious and admitted practicality the criterion of success changes radically. There is little or no possibility of corroborative or corrective events and so a new operative criterion holds sway: the real becomes what is expressed and what is communally accepted. Naming confers social status ensuring that the thing named may be dealt with by the members of the linguistically constituted universe, for language is a complex, flexible and developing image in which the community presents itself to itself; so a merely imagined entity—provided that it is not communally known to be merely imagined—is domesticated, brought within the scope of social and communal meaning, once it is named. Descriptive statements which by way of a certain exclusiveness have always had a constitutive aspect now become less reservedly constitutive of the social universe. The intention of truth persists but the grasp of the subject's own responsibility recedes as the statement gains in social acceptance until finally not only does one's own judgement seem irrelevant but the very idea of basic enquiry is submerged. We are faced then with a situation which Durkheim incipiently recognised in his notion of collective representations; but unlike Durkheim I have tried to relate the representations to their source in the community of meaning subjects.

In many contemporary studies myth is linked to dream[16] in which the intention of truth is not very evident, and in many of these theories and for a variety of reasons the truth of the myth is considered as an irrelevancy. A position which would include the intention of truth as a fundamental element in mythic consciousness must have something to say about theories which seem to ignore this. First of all, then, ancient dream analysis and the dream analysis in some contemporary primitive cultures assume the truth of at least some dreams. Dreaming was simply another way of reaching the truth. From my own researches among one particular group of Australian aborigines I discovered that dreams were uncommonly well remembered, at least in their general outlines. Almost any one of them would be able to list about twenty or thirty different dreams that he had had recently. For the most part these dreams were considered interesting or entertaining but only some were thought to be of immense moment. For instance, an old woman dreamed of the crucified Christ and when this became publicly known it was followed by an increase of Christian enthusiasm. Dreams of a sufficiently high energy, somewhat like an oracle, are imbued by the waking subject with the intention of truth despite the admitted obscurity of the expression. For the modern analyst the dream is true inasmuch as it is the obscure expression of the dreamer but its most basic meaning is its function in the maintenance of psychic equilibrium and in this it is properly preconceptual.[17] The value of the psychic expressiveness of dream symbolising is slowly being discovered and there is the suggestion that mythic symbols fulfil an analogous though social function.[18] Properly there is no intention of truth in dreaming although the force and colour of the dream may so engage the dreamer that on waking he remains uncertain of the status of his dream; but this uncertainty supervenes in waking consciousness. Within the confines of dreaming consciousness its reality is literally unquestioned to provide a predeliberate context wherein some of the tensions of waking life may receive expression and release and wherein the psychic orientation of the dreamer in the face of living may be obscurely revealed.[19]

Perhaps something analogous occurs in myth but a distinction must be made between the myth as believed and the myth as performed. As the dream achieves its end while it is being dreamt, so the expressive aspects of myth are realised when the myth is being told in a special and appropriate context.[20] Within the context the truth of the myth is assumed; the intention of truth is not focal during the performance but the assumption dominates the entire event. The expressive function cannot be achieved unless serious questioning is either held in abeyance or lulled into acquiesence by suitable rhetorical devices which allow the question in innocuous form, as, for example, at a political rally.

A myth is performed in a context in which its truth is assumed; it is, therefore, also believed. In art there is a shift in conscious orientation which is variously described as the suspension of disbelief or the entry into a virtual world but this is not the case with myth. The statement may evoke enthusiasm, loyalty, religious fervour, but it must also convince. Mythic consciousness is therefore subject to a critique which dreaming consciousness escapes and its ambivalence emerges most notably when one recognises that conviction may be achieved by the power[21] of the expression to evoke enthusiasm and loyalty: then, as Eliade remarks, the myth is true because it is sacred—when the term sacred includes all the pre-rational affects associated with the imagery. As the dream overawes the waking subject, so the affective elements in mythic consciousness override the demands of intellect. A spurious and premature conviction is achieved and the subject is blocked in his position by the pressure of tradition and the lure of symbol.

It follows that there is a dialectic within mythic consciousness: the intention of truth vies with the affective imagination. So far I have suggested that the intention of truth which would issue in reasonable affirmation is overcome by the affective power of the image to rest in a less than reasonable conclusion about the nature of man, society and universe. But a reverse influence is also discernible: the intention of truth issues in a definite statement and thus at once limits the flexibility and range of imagination while conferring the status of reality on a restricted imaginative scheme.[22]

We have been working towards an idea of the notion of the real in mythic consciousness for which 'the real is the object of a sufficiently intense flow of sensitive representations, feelings, words and actions'.[23] What is meant is that such a sufficiently intense flow will be constituted as real; what is not meant is that mythic consciousness has an idea of reality other than the projected constitutive image. Mythic consciousness is opaque to the mythic subject from which simple fact follows the notable conclusion that the theoretic grasp of a particular mythic consciousness, or of mythic consciousness in general, is not identical with that consciousness' grasp of itself. Not only is the theoretic grasp different, it is assignably different; the theoretic understanding will locate this particular instance of mythic consciousness within the framework of a theory of human knowing and so will inescapably rest on and emerge from a general cognitional theory. In so far as it fails to do so it will remain no more than descriptive. In so far as the theorist cannot do this he is himself in need of development; for the correct theory of human knowing is not on paper but in a mind and the prerequisite for its emergence is the interpreter's reflection on his own activity and his eventual grasp of the interrelations between the elements in the process of knowing. Until he succeeds in this undertaking—or at least until he begins to glimpse its outlines, its intricacies and its necessity—not only will he fail to go beyond description but he will completely overlook the need, the possibility and consequently the manner of doing so.

For him description will be final and attempts will be made to defend this stand; there is an irony in Lonergan's remark[24] about the primitive's inability to conceive other men with a mentality different from his own; for the whole of the difficulty lies in the conception, not in the initial acknowledgement or description of the fact of their existence.

Since both wonder and imagination are dynamisms it would be a mistake to conceive mythic consciousness as static. The communally accepted expression of that consciousness in myth may remain unchanged over several generations but the reason for the conservatism is as much in the power of the accepted expression linked with linguistic criteria of reality as in any lack of dynamism in consciousness. When an expression constitutes the reality which it describes it cannot have the basic uncertainty of an hypothesis and its breakdown involves not only a change of mind but a change of heart and the collapse of the affect-laden universe in which the community lives. Yet the myth possesses its own vulnerability; from the side of intellect there is the possibility of the emergence of questions which would undermine the basis of mythic questions; from the affective side there is the possibility that with the revolutions of history the old images may no longer inspire and so may become affectively irrelevant to changed personal and social conditions.

What would be unquestionably regarded as a 'myth' is a story having to do with the unfamiliar affectively awful sphere of human consciousness, but mythic consciousness, as has been hinted, is not restricted to this domain. We must attempt a generalisation and the clue is the notion of reality. A mind may be dominated by myth but only because more basically it is dominated by mythic consciousness. Commonly mythic consciousness is confined by scholars to its manifestations in the primitive mind; the significance of Fr Lonergan's position for human science is that it locates mythic consciousness in the philosopher himself. As the reader of *Insight* is constantly reminded, the issue is 'a personal appropriation of one's own dynamic and recurrently operative structure of cognitional activity'.[25] Such an achievement demands a development of and in the subject; it involves a critique of self which will in effect be an effort on the part of the subject to break the bonds of his own involvement in mythic consciousness which can be understood correctly only in so far as the break is successful. In

this venture the central issue is the criterion of the real; the movement from mythic to critical consciousness will consist in a radical
shift in one's meaning of the real. The mythic subject understands,
frequently in particular cases he understands correctly, but he
doubts that understanding correctly is knowing.[26] For the mythic
subject the real is known in judgement but it must also be imaginable and imagined.[27] The shift from mythic to critical consciousness
is not made by repeating a series of correct propositions, not even
by the ordinary procedure of affirming these propositions. The
appropriation of consciousness that is required if the developed
is to be sustainedly successful requires a long and diligent scrutiny
of one's own activity of knowing not only in order to discover that
by the real one means what one affirms in judgement but also to
discover that when one is off one's guard what one tends to mean
by real is a mixture of affirmation and imagination. The way of
development is through 'the discovery (and one has not made it
yet if one has no clear memory of its startling strangeness) that
there are two quite different realisms, that there is an incoherent
realism, half animal and half human, that poses as a half-way
house between materialism and idealism and, on the other hand,
there is an intelligent and reasonable realism between which and
materialism the half-way house is idealism.'[28]

This incoherent realism may be formulated as a theory of reality
like materialism or idealism, but before its formulation it is the
notion of the real operative in mythic consciousness, as before its
formulation as a theory the intelligent and reasonable realism is the
notion of the real operative in critical consciousness. The startling
discovery that one has to make is not merely that a formulated
theory is false, but, much more importantly because the discovery
demands an intellectual conversion, that one's habitual mode of
operation is inadequate. Precisely because development consists
not merely in changing theories but in shifting modes of operation
and modes of consciousness the mere affirmation of correct propositions and the denial of false propositions is not sufficient; the
issue is not the proof of propositions but the development of the
subject which occurs only through the slow emergence and survival
of the developed modality of consciousness.

The apparent immediacy of data instils the notion of an obvious
reality. One senses the real world in which one acts; it is apparently
immediately present and familiar; one acts within it; one learns by

solving the practical problems that it sets and by one's mistakes; it is a fundamentally unquestionable world and one resents attempts to question it. Sensitive immediacy presents the world in which one lives; the success of one's living guarantees its reality; to any question of the criterion of reality one's spontaneity has swift recourse to the familiarity of sense. One is intelligent; one learns and devises plans; one asks questions and arrives at answers. The intertwined guarantees of sense and intelligence become operative criteria of reality. One senses, understands, judges but without accurately adverting to the distinctions between these activities. One does not ask about intellectual criteria of the real; one may not advert to any problematic. The real is obvious as is sense which becomes linked with affirmation as a further guarantee. It is not difficult to discover how this confusion arises and why it is so difficult to eradicate. When one knows a triangle, one sees it as one saw it before but because the knowing is not a second vision which discredits the first, because it goes beyond seeing but includes data, the obviousness, the familiarity and the reassurance of sense incline us to assume and demand that the real be also imaginable. All this occurs before any theory of the nature of the real emerges; but a theory in line with this response is also possible. Such a theory would hold that it is from sense that our cognitional activities derive their immediate relationship to real objects[29] but while it grows out of mythic consciousness it is still not an accurate account of that consciousness for the intention of truth is already spontaneously operative even if it has not yet attained a sufficiently directive and critical role. For the intention of truth is not knowing, it is merely intending; the intention is satisfied only when truth is reached but the movement from intending to knowing is susceptible to deflection from the interference of other desires and interests.

The mythic subject *qua* mythic is incapable of reaching an adequate account of the criterion of reality. If he acknowledges that the real is reached only in judgement and discovers the proximate and remote criteria of judgement in his own acts and habits, then by that discovery he moves from being a mythic to becoming a critical subject. He has made an immense existential leap. In so far as he remains confined within the purview of mythic consciousness any attempt to discover the criterion of the real must remain within these boundaries and he has little effective choice but to latch on to the commonest and most striking component in human knowing, sense.

The great shift from mythic to critical consciousness involves development of and in the subject; it is an experimental issue which will 'consist in one's own rational self-consciousness taking possession of itself as rational self-consciousness'.[30] The possibility of the development resides in the intention of truth operative in both modes for if the development is to occur the question which initiates the transition must first occur. And it will have to occur within mythic consciousness. The history of philosophy will be, accordingly, a dialectical movement of successive attempts to interrogate mythic consciousness with the constant possibility of breaking its boundaries and the inverse possibility of making its boundaries more secure. More significantly the history of the individual philosopher will be a dialectic for he must slowly discover himself as continually liable to mythic consciousness and must make the attempt to go beyond it. The culture as the public embodiment of common meaning is subject to a similar movement for it can embody the meaning of minds enmeshed in myth and so will perpetuate the confusion, or express with greater or less adequacy the meaning of authentic subjects and so invite continued development.[31]

The pressures against development are various and powerful. Within the subject there is the warm familiarity of the present to contrast with the unknown demands which a new position might make on him; social pressures against such a programme are equally clear for the ramifications of change are so great and so unexpected that it is often safer to risk the discomforts with which one knows how to live and deal, than the unsuspected shifts that might result from any but the most superficial changes. Even if one does clamour for change it is much more convenient to have a definite, if unanalysed, image of the desirable than to embark on a process of questioning that might lead to demands that one would prefer not to meet, to consequences that one would gladly avoid. In such a mêlée appropriate symbols are devised to support each side and soon the very question of questioning is relegated to the background and emotive images carry the day. There are more subtle ways of blocking the programme. One may profess interest in the question but note that it belongs to another discipline; one may devote a seminar to its discussion but only in order to satisfy the remnants of one's scientific conscience. Still, the blocking procedure must not become apparent and so a symbol of scientific detachment will have to take the place of scientific enquiry. For the basic feature of all obscurantism is not merely that the question is ignored but that the ignoring of the question is justified. One cannot admit distortion in oneself for this is an invitation to development, a revelation of the possibility of mythic consciousness, of an inauthentic tradition and most significantly of personal inauthenticity. The first inkling of one's own lack of development is already a beginning and invites complementary adjustments and advances. Unless these are forthcoming 'either the initiated development recedes and atrophies in favour of the dynamic unity of the subject, or else that unity is sacrificed and deformed to make man a mere dumping ground for the unrelated, unintegrated schemes of recurrence and modes of behaviour.'[32]

Thus the transformation of the subject involves more than solely theoretic change; the sources of distortion in the subject include his desires, his hopes and his fears. He tends to construct a universe in which he can live without too much pain; the unfettered implementation of the intention of truth, the unrestricted questioning, might shed unpleasant light on this universe and so is to be avoided. With greater or less deliberateness there occurs a flight from understanding with its resultant rationalisations, which may be undertaken by the subject himself although it is safer and less likely to lead one dangerously close to self-discovery if one accepts whichever of the available more or less well-developed and attractive myths and slogans is most appealing.[33]

The achievement of the transformation, far from being a conclusion, is a beginning which reveals ever increasing horizons of development. Yet it is a precarious achievement and the subject is always liable to fall back into the inauthenticity of myth.[34] Retrogression is not likely to be one's previous position for the rejected development must be in some way included and rendered harmless by the new myth. So, for example, the introduction of Christianity among some Australian aboriginal groups resulted in a transformation of the mythic context to include whatever could not be wholly ignored within a new mythic universe. Incorrect positions are vulnerable but they are replaced not by correct positions but by new errors which stifle the disturbing question; so it is that mythic consciousness remains under vastly different guises.[35]

The communal acceptance of a myth tends to block intellectual development despite the fact that the myth is at the same time the product of the uncontrolled desire to understand. Whichever of these aspects dominates at any time it remains the case that the myth tends to determine the general nature of the universe and to suggest the type of questions that are acceptable. Myth delineates a horizon, or, more accurately, the objective pole of the horizon the subjective pole of which is mythic consciousness. Metaphysics equates with the objective pole of the total and basic horizon but the subjective pole is the enquirer freed from the distortions of mythic consciousness. The dialectical development of the incarnate subject from mythic to critical consciousness indicates a corresponding opposition between myth and metaphysics.[36] The unavoidable intentionality of truth reveals the subject's orientation from mythic to critical consciousness; the embodiment of that intention in myth grounds the dialectical relationship, of which the mythic subject cannot be aware, by which 'myth looks forward to its own negation and to the metaphysics that is all the more consciously true because it is also the conscious rejection of error'.[37]

Mythic consciousness is not aware of this dialectical relationship because it fails to understand the development role of the intention of truth and the need to discover the criterion of reality implicit in that intentionality. To grasp this lack in mythic consciousness is to go beyond that consciousness and from that grasp some conclusions concerning the procedure of human science seem to follow. To correctly understand another's mythic consciousness, his viewpoint, and his expressions, is to link that consciousness, that viewpoint and those expressions dialectically and genetically to the possibilities and finalities of human intelligence. To be able to do this, of course, requires the prior self-development of the interpreter; if this development has not occurred the interpreter cannot go beyond a merely descriptive account of the alien viewpoint and expression; indeed, since the data confronting the interpreter are not merely given but have a meaning, even an accurate description may not be possible.

This suggestion meets with strenuous opposition in contemporary anthropological circles for it smacks of an attitude which is deplored under the title of ethnocentricity. Since this is a common and long-established interpretative stance, it is as well to pay it some attention. There appear to be at least two meanings associated with it. On the one hand there is the claim that the interpreter is not competent to judge the theories, ideas, dogmas, decisions, judgements and culture of another people. On the other hand there is the rule that the interpreter should not assume in others an intellectual, psychic and cultural context identical with his own. Although these two meanings are distinguishable they are not always distinguished in the interpreter's mind and many authors overtly subscribe to both meanings.[38] In the history of the growth of anthropological theory the two meanings emerged together and this to some extent accounts for contemporary confusion.

The first meaning seems to involve an acceptance of a theory of the relativity of truth and so excuses the interpreter from learning from the author he is studying or from attempting to discover the source of the author's errors. He does not learn from the author since, by definition, the author's truth will be different from his own; he finds no need to discover the source of the author's error since, again by definition, the author is not in error. What he must ignore is the intention of truth in himself and in the author.

None the less the interpreter writes from a viewpoint and commonly—if his viewpoint is that of the majority of contemporary human scientists—this will include a distinction between the empirical and the non-empirical into which, since he writes for an audience who share his viewpoint, he will divide the universe of the author. He will define the first or empirical realm as that in which judgements can be verified according to his own rules and the non-empirical will be the residual sphere in which judgements which cannot so be verified occur. He may note that this division does not occur in the author's mind and that the division rests on the inevitability for him of his own viewpoint but because he is not interested in the truth of the author's meaning he fails to advert to the underlying question of the reason for and the conditions of the possibility of the different viewpoints of which he is obscurely aware.[39] Further, because the distinction between empirical and non-empirical is too familiar to the majority of interpreters for them to advert to its obscurity, to its likely mythic dimensions, and to its basic inadequacy, the relations between the supposed empirical and non-empirical components in the author's meaning remain unanalysed and the very question concerning these relations is rarely raised. In fact Frazer's position is hardly transcended and the issues raised by a Lévy-Bruhl are skirted rather than dealt with.

The second meaning is quite different, it is rather a rule of procedure which manifests the obscure recognition that viewpoints differ, that expressions emerge from viewpoints which form the context of particular meanings and which have to be dialectically related to each other. It would note that the empirical is not distinguished from the non-empirical in one viewpoint exactly as it is in another; and that the distinctions in both instances are to be explained. In short, the relativity of the first position is not pushed far enough; having adverted to differences it is content with an incoherent abandonment of truth; it fails to advance to a critical appropriation of self which would reveal the sources of difference and provide an all-embracing viewpoint not intrinsically dependent on particular cultures, one which would allow for the comparison of viewpoints which anthropology is traditionally supposed to provide. Needless to add, this is a development of the second position; contemporary anthropological meaning on this question is obscure and inchoate; yet, even the verbal recognition of the problem indicates to the critic a possible source of development.[40]

Although it is difficult to discover another's viewpoint it is not difficult to advert to different expressions and it is no more than tedious and time-consuming to collect and catalogue these expressions. It remains that the expressions are merely expressions and that their collection is no more than the first step in the interpretative process; indeed, since the data for human science are already meaningful it may not even be the first step. Now implicit in the first position concerning ethnocentric interpretation seems to be the claim that the interpreter should efface himself before the manifest authority of the text. But in this case there is no understanding, for meaning is in a mind. If by self-effacement is meant that the interpreter should not work out elaborate theories on the nature of meaning, that he should not try to appropriate his own intelligence and rationality, that he should make no effort to become a critical subject, then he remains a spontaneous subject who cannot but understand the text in the light of his own unanalysed viewpoint. He may understand but his understanding is uncontrolled. He may try to eschew prejudice but he will have no clear idea of what prejudice is; he will confuse content and context, statement and operation and cannot but fail to reach the source of the expression he is trying to fathom. The call for the rooting out of prejudice implicit in the criticism of ethnocentricity, if it is to be anything more than a pious metaphor, or the mere exchange of one set of prejudices for another, must reasonably develop into a demand for the achievement of critical consciousness.[41]

I have considered myth as an interpretation of the world, as revealing what is the case. The interpretation is expressed in an image which, within mythic consciousness, is not clearly distinguished from idea and judgement. The image is imbued with affectivity and linked not only to the intellectual development of the subject but also, more spectacularly, to his psychic and social role. Because human expression is always an image the affects associated with psychic and social achievement may be linked with almost any human expression. The reader may consider the affective charge of words associated with accepted or rejected positions in any theoretical expression. Sentences which were originally the expression of verified theories become dominantly the affect-laden image of positions accepted or rejected for other than intelligent reasons. The words remain the same but the original meaning is lost to be replaced by an unauthentic affective commitment to a tradition which is no longer expressed in the words but has become the words. Language is corrupted, the dynamism of intellect is ignored and decadence is accepted as authentic.[42]

The understanding of self is also the constituting of self; the appropriation of one's rational self-consciousness depends on the development of the subject. This is not to suggest that knowing exercises a constitutive effect on its object[43] but to note that 'before man can contemplate his own nature in precise but highly difficult concepts, he has to bring the virtualities of that nature into the light of day.'[44] The persistent effort to understand the subject contributes to the subject's development and so reveals the virtualities of the thing to be understood. The being of the subject is becoming; its development is a progressively differentiated consciousness of self which allows for a clearer and more accurate knowledge of self which in turn opens the way for an even more refined consciousness of self as intelligent, reasonable and free.

The mythic subject is confined within an undifferentiated consciousness and his image of self expressed in myth is necessarily of an undifferentiated opaque subject. Although he is intelligent, reasonable and free in principle he neither adverts to, nor under-stands, his intelligence, his reasonableness or his freedom. If he is to develop, he will do so by going beyond this initial subjectivity; he will be the same numerical subject but qualitatively different. As he develops, the original image of self embodied in myth cannot but change its function for it does not express the subject with the same adequacy. The continual becoming of the subject is 'anticipated immanently by the detachment and disinterestedness of the pure desire [to know]'[45] and the original image will embody this immanent anticipation. The intention of truth has here another function: besides attention given to the truth of the statement, besides the fact that myth circumscribes a horizon of being, there is a third fact that mythic consciousness will express, and myth will in some way embody the expression of the desire for totality. Expressive of the to-be-known, as has been seen already, it is expressive too of the desire to achieve that state.

As human knowing is a dynamic process operating the passage from ignorance to knowledge through wonder, so the becoming of the subject is a dynamic process which includes biological and psychological development but also, as its specifically human element, the free self-constituting of the subject himself through conscious experience, understanding, judgement and decision. Once more the operator is wonder and the intention of truth be-comes an immanent quest for perfection; it becomes the intention of goodness. Within undifferentiated mythic consciousness dis-tinctions between image, grasp, affirmation and decision are blurred; the expression of that consciousness does not critically distinguish between what is to be known and what is to be done. Myth may be expected to enshrine an ideal to be achieved.

The subject is born into a human world constituted by the common meaning of the community and he lives and develops in it. The truth of this world is not exclusively that it is a correct interpretation of what is but also that it is correctly constituted—that it is, in fact, a suitable human environment. The subject will be bound to this world by ties of tradition and sentiment but he cannot rest utterly content in it unless it likewise satisfies his intelligence. Unless one assumes a necessary harmony between sentiment and intelligence one discovers here a fundamental tension in human living; the manner in which sentiment and immediacy conquer or corroborate intelligent assessment and rational decision throws light on the nature of rationalisation and on the place of symbol in concrete living.[46]

Even critical knowledge of self does not eliminate a symbol of self and if one's critical knowledge is to become habitually and spontaneously operative in living then the symbol must support the critical position. Rationalisation seems to occur by moving from one symbolic world to another with different and perhaps contrary affects from which flow different activities and with which different ideas are consonant. For the product of mythic consciousness expresses both the supposed truth of the universe and the value to which the intention of goodness is linked. The dynamic unity of the subject does not allow for a simple waiving of the notions of truth and goodness (the terms and to some extent the concepts may be, of course, expendable) but demands that these notions be apparently constitutive of the symbolic universe. Human activity is never merely animal for it is concretely constituted by a meaning that cannot escape these notions.

Genuineness, opposed to rationalisation, is the attempt to order sensitivity. Such ordering implies some apprehension of the starting point, the term and the process, and in so far as the apprehension is mistaken, the different components in the development are operating at cross-purposes and development is in fact hindered; there may even result a breakdown of the subject.[47] The apprehension of the starting-point is an understanding of the subject as compounded of laws and schemes on a variety of harmoniously to-be-linked levels.[48] The process of rationalisation reveals that for critical self-knowledge to become effective 'the content of systematic insights, the direction of judgements, the dynamism of decisions . . . [must] . . . be embodied in images that release feeling and emotion and flow spontaneously into deeds no less than words'[49] while the anticipatory grasp of the fact of laws operative on the psychic and lower levels reveals that the lower level events set limits to the appropriate way of life that is to be attempted. The symbolic, complex, obscure image of self that is the immediate context of spontaneous action must be developmentally included in the complete development of the subject.[50]

The contextual image of self in all its detail is proper to each person but it has its public contours in the shared meaning that constitutes the community.[51] Thus the image becomes less responsive to the immanent dynamism of intellect and less susceptible to any change that a particular individual might demand, for it has passed from the fluidity of the immediate to the relative stability of the socially expressed and approved. The individual is born and becomes adult within the meaningfully constituted society; 'the choice of role between which one can choose in electing what to make himself is no larger than the accepted meanings of the community admit; his capacities for affective initiative are limited to the potentialities of the community for rejuvenation, renewal, reform, development. At any time in any place what a given self can make of himself is some function of the heritage or sediment of common meaning that comes to him from the authentic or inauthentic living of his predecessors and his contemporaries.'[52] In so far as the individual's meaning is absorbed into the common store it can either expand or contract the communal horizon, it can either interrogate or reinforce the tradition. The problem of human intellectual development, the problem of the fundamental conversion *ex umbris et imaginibus ad veritatem*, the problem of the transformation from mythic to critical consciousness thus attains a social dimension. Human community is constituted by meanings which are either critical or mythic and so the field of conflict is shifted from exclusive concern with the individual to concern with the authenticity of the tradition. But the basic problem of human development recurs with each person and in each generation so that even an authentic tradition can be distorted and corrupted, so that the possibility of myth is always with us as is the possibility that one who would have power in society might exploit it. So philosophic development has to be extended from scattered individuals into education in order to give the common maxim that education trains the mind some concrete, existential and understood validity. What is asked for is a control of meaning.[53]

Control of meaning is not to be restricted to the control of one's critical activity, for the achievement of critical consciousness by no means eliminates the ordering of the total subject which must include his affectivity. To the signs and symbols associated with the proper development of the subject Fr Lonergan gives the name 'mysteries'.[54] Mysteries are linked to the symbol of self which forms the immediate context of everyday living: they are 'dynamic images which make sensible to human sensitivity what human intelligence reaches for or grasps'.[55] A reflection on the experience of prayer may elucidate the idea. Speculative theology or philosophic efforts to reach God are not immediately relevant to the stimulation of religious feeling,[56] but if one's knowledge of God's existence and one's imperfect understanding of one's faith are to be operative in spontaneity they must be linked with images that engage one's sensitivity. Prayer is such an image; it is not the experience of God, nor is it any sensitive awareness of God; it is a sensitive engagement of the psyche associated with one's knowledge and belief. It is a complex image compounded of speech, song, gesture, light, space, time. The total image is evoked in the praying subject not merely by what seem clearly his own gestures of tongue and body but also through his sensitive integration of the song and gesture of others, of the architecture, decoration and acoustics of the place. It is an image which gathers up all the senses with music, incense, dance; it includes such cryptographic features as ritual gestures of blessing, washing, fasting; it invests, in many traditions, the surrounding world of water, sky, earth with a religious relevance until all things tell of the glory of God. This many-faceted and subtle image is linked with the person's knowledge and belief. But what is to distinguish mystery from myth? Clearly it is not the dynamism of the symbol on the psychic level but the nature of the link between image and interpretation. The mystery can be distorted into myth when the imaginative integration is allowed unduly to interfere with the proper finality of intellect. The transition from mythic to critical consciousness involves the transformation of the subject; the transition from myth to mystery involves the transformation of the subject for mystery is the transforming sensitive integration of the subject associated with the pure desire. Again, just as myth includes an interpretation that looks in fact to its own demise with the subject's growth, so mystery includes an interpretation that looks to its own completion on the purely theoretic level. So the mysteries of Christ look to the fruitful understanding of theology and their ultimate completion in the supernatural vision of God. It follows that images which are descriptively similar are, from an explanatory viewpoint, now mysteries and now myths, for what is involved in the advance from myth to mystery is not 'any rationalist sublation of both mystery and myth, but simply a displacement of the sensitive representation of spiritual issues'.[57]

Since advance in self-knowledge implies the transformation of the subject there is the further conclusion that earlier symbolic

3

sequences will no longer serve as adequate expressions of the later subject; subjective development implies and includes a transformation of the dynamic image of self and its consequent communal contours; so an earlier image may express a cruder subjectivity than a later form. Conversely, in times of decline, an earlier dance may express a more excellent subjectivity and so issue a challenge to the later decadence.

As an individual and a community come to distinguish with increasing exactitude between sensitive and intellectual activities there emerges the possibility of art in the strict sense. Or, rather, the artistic elements and virtualities inherent in the imagining of which we have been speaking begin to emerge and develop in their own right.[58] Art liberates the intelligent control of imagination from the intention of truth as involved in mythic consciousness and separates it from the link with interpretation involved in mystery. The artist, as Collingwood hints and Langer develops, makes a virtual universe. Mysteries are linked obscurely to the unknown sphere anticipated by intelligence as well as to the sensitive integration of the already known but they are linked too to interpretations of man and society that are held to be true. Myth is the unanalysed expression of an undifferentiated consciousness that does not clearly distinguish between the grasp of reality, the constitution of society and the imaginative representations of both. Art is expressive of the possibilities of the imagining subject and for this reason can take over and transform discarded myths, e.g. the tale of Gilgamesh is not true in a historical sense but it is expressive of human longing and may be incorporated into an aesthetic pattern of experience and its theme can become a commonplace, under various transformations, of world literature. Art becomes an objectification and a revelation of imagination: its truth is not that it states theoretically what is the case, not that it mythically confuses image with explanation (though some theories of art, whether by artists or others, may do this), but that it presents a satisfying image.[59] Professor Frye notes that literature makes not true but hypothetical statements but the statements of literature are not statements of hypotheses; rather that intentionality is excluded and the intention of truth remains not in the movement towards absoluteness of judgement and the totality of true judgements, but in the consistent attempt to symbolise human straining for being. Thus art's meaning and its validation lie in the artistic deed; art liberates from the bonds of practicality in an expressive revelation of the freedom of the subject; its proper meaning occurs not in critical analysis but in the momentary engagement of the subject in the artistic event.

The irrelevance of truth in artistic meaning is not an invention of the critic to facilitate his analysis; it is immanent in the event and points to a difference in the relation between image and subject in art, myth, and science. This difference grounds Mrs Langer's theory of art as constitutive of a virtual universe. That theory has no more than a verbal meaning inasmuch as the reader does not attend to his or her own artistic meaning sufficiently to allow him or her to grasp the relation between image and subject in the event. Only when this introspective analysis has been undertaken by a sufficient number of theorists can the technical term 'virtual' be used with any confidence; until then the term is likely to have as many meanings as it has users and a measure of specious agreement is reached with no better basis than the conventions of contemporary language. Mrs Langer writes that the kind of knowledge that occurs in art has hardly been examined; this lacuna will remain as long as critical attention is directed almost exclusively to an examination of the image while the actual meaning of the aesthetic subject, although at times assumed thematically and necessarily operatively assumed, remains at best on the periphery.[60] It is accepted that although anyone can look at the expression of a theorem in the calculus, only those who understand the calculus can attain its meaning; it is less generally accepted—although no less true—that although anyone can look at or listen to an artistic image, only those capable of artistic meaning can fathom it. Yet if one reflects on one's own and others' development, it becomes clear that the ability to move into the aesthetic mode is acquired. No doubt children are imaginative; no doubt this imaginative virtuosity should be encouraged and developed for it can grow into and add to aesthetic experience since it includes aesthetic elements and is the condition of the possibility of artistic development, but it is not yet artistic meaning.

The artistic image constitutes its own context within which certain responses are appropriate. The spontaneous ease in making these responses is not an addition to artistic meaning; it is a component in that meaning. Artistic meaning is complete in itself; it has a relevance to practical affairs but its relevance is not immediate. Rather it is mediated by the intentions, insights, judgements and decisions of the unique subject whose self is partly constituted by his artistic meaning. Immediately artistic meaning is the transformation of the subject; it frees him not merely from practical concerns but from the confines of his practical self. Art presents symbolically the range of human subjectivity and possibility and can thus break through the boundaries erected by practical living and distorted intelligence. This is the far-reaching significance of artistic meaning; the artistic subject is the same person as the practical subject; so all art is political but not confined to any political theory or practice. Art reveals possibility but not an immediately practical possibility; what is most basically revealed is the fact of possibility.

I have been attempting to analyse the role of the intention of truth in mythic consciousness. To do so I have to concentrate on the act of meaning rather than on the expression of meaning and I have been led to suggest that exclusive concern with expression leads inevitably to the overlooking of the intention and of the notion of dialectical development and the differentiation of consciousness that flow from it. I have concentrated on the intentionality inherent in mythic consciousness to discover in myth a truth that is meant; but what is meant? What is meant is the subject and what the expression provides is a context in which he is obscurely objectified. Myth provides an interpretation of the world—of other men, of society, of earth, sea and sky—because its prime meaning is to provide a human context of which the measure is man. So Gilbert Durand can order the manifold of images in relation to three dominant human reflexes and Mircea Eliade can discover in myth a common stem of expression that is pre-logical, pre-conceptual and pre-philosophic. Nor is this expressiveness the objectification of some abstract, a-cultural, a-historical subject, but the objectification and release of the subject immersed in the conflicts, tensions, desires, fears and hopes, in the successes and failures, of his community and time.[61] As the dream is dialectically related to waking consciousness to constitute with this the total existential context of the actor, so myth and ritual are dialectically related to both dream and everyday affairs to form the total social context within which the community operates. But, as I have suggested, myth takes up both dream and practicality to constitute the total social horizon and 'to penetrate, surround and dominate both the routine activities of daily life and the profound and secret aspirations of the human heart'.[62]

The position adopted here on the radical meaning of myth and mystery may be contrasted with other theories. I have noted a pre-conceptual aspect to mythic meaning and quite clearly this usage calls to mind the ideas of Lucien Lévy-Bruhl. Perhaps the major difference between his position and mine is that he inclined to confine mythic consciousness to primitive man and to the religious sphere and to consider that the break between primitive and civilised mentality was absolute while on the position taken in this paper mythic consciousness is by no means confined to primitive peoples but is properly studied by an introspective scrutiny of self. Although its most obvious and spectacular expressions are associated with religion it is not confined to this domain. Further, there is a genetic and dialectical relation between mythic and critical consciousness which is acted out in the development of both individual and community. Lévy-Bruhl was fascinated by logic—by the movement from premises to conclusions—and in his early writings tended to consider the lack of logic as the key to primitive mentality. Later—and this is particularly true of the Herbert Spencer Lecture of 1931 and the posthumously published *Carnets*[63]—he recognised the possibility of the logical operation being correct while the premises were mistaken. In contrast I suggest that logical operations may or may not occur in mythic consciousness, that the reflective discovery of logic is certainly a development but it is not the crucial transitional move (though a necessary condition) from one mode to another. The pre-logical elements of myth do not strain towards logic but have their own mode of ordering. In Lévy-Bruhl there is little or no emphasis on development or progress whereas the notion of human development, both individual and social, is central to the theory set out here.

Commitment to a theory of development, besides being extremely unpopular in many circles, inevitably starts the ghost of Frazer and other evolutionists. But where Frazer thought of myth as primitive science with excrescences to be pruned away until one had reached a purely rationalist position, the suggestion outlined here is that myth is to become mystery and that development consists in the achievement of critical consciousness and the displacement but not the abandonment of the sensitive representation of spiritual issues.

I am in agreement with Frazer with respect to the affirmation of the possibility and the fact of intellectual development but must part company with him when it comes to an analysis of the nature of the starting-point, the term and the process of that development. Although Frazer may have admitted the development of the individual, this was not his central concern, and his notion of development stressed content to the detriment of any adequate consideration of performance. Frazer gave his attention to the contrast between ideas about the universe, whereas I have noted the source of world views, the development of that source, and the unescapable orientation to development immanent in the source. Thus, where Frazer would be refuted simply by uncovering his ethnocentric bias, the theory set out here can be refuted only by showing that the intention of truth is absent in mythic consciousness, or in the performance of the subject.[64]

Later research led to the discovery that, as Malinowski puts it, savages are as rational as we are in the conduct of everyday life. Evans-Pritchard noted that a sort of practical logic and matter-of-factness was operative in some magic. This discovery tended to discredit Lévy-Bruhl and to render evolutionism irrelevant. Yet there are serious gaps in the theories incorporating the discovery. If a single subject is eminently rational in one context and not so in another, then a theory of his mentality must attempt to relate the opposed contexts. The weakness of contemporary theories is that they make no attempt to do this unless one considers that a theory of the relativity of truth relates the contexts by the bald assertion that there is no conflict. I have tried to link the contexts by indicating that within mythic consciousness the criterion of reality, even within a totally pragmatic context, is never merely the rational 'Yes' but the object of a sufficiently integrated and intense flow of sensitive representations.[65] Now, the sphere of common, domesticated, imaginatively integrated reality provides the sufficiently intense flow, and the immediacy of practicality provides sufficiently imaginatively acceptable instances and contrary instances. The sphere of the unknown, symbolising the unknown, obscure subject, provides sufficiently forceful images but contrary instances are merely unacceptable images. I have suggested that the breakthrough comes not simply with technological achievement but with a new self-knowledge that ushers in a new criterion of the real.[66] Against contemporary theorists I have reintroduced an evolutionary perspective but I have done so by shifting the ground of the methodological inquiry from the study of the mentality of any particular person or people to the study of the inquirer's own mentality with its inherent dialectic tension. 'Prior to all writing of history, prior to all interpretation of other minds, there is the self-scrutiny of the historian, the self-knowledge of the interpreter. That prior task is my concern.'[67] Accordingly, my analysis of mythic consciousness is not an analysis of the mentality of primitive people, nor is it a generalisation which has its source in the analysis of my own mythic consciousness. The data to which the reader should refer is that of his own consciousness. No doubt in my efforts to reach understanding there are particular antecedents; I am a single subject with a single history, but these antecedents and this history are not the only instances of mythic consciousness attempting to become critical, and so the reader must attend to my images not as mine but as his, or in so far as they lead him to discover the data on which insight can emerge.

Attention to mythic consciousness has revealed a self-developing subject. But this development occurs on many levels and the control of meaning refers not to the exclusion of any level or the smothering of dynamism but to 'advance in self-knowledge . . . increasing consciousness and deliberateness and effectiveness in . . . [the] choice and use of dynamic images, of mottoes and slogans',[68] and to a reflective level of meaning where not merely do we know well enough what we mean, but we can say exactly what we mean and we can know the place of that meaning in human finality. What is required is not a retreat from the complex manifold of new meanings in the sciences and technologies. What is required is not an effort to embrace all these meanings in popularised form. What is required is an understanding of the source of these meanings and images, for science and technology embody meaning in images. Only thus can the complex manifold become ordered both intellectually and imaginatively. That ordering may seem a very abstruse affair that can be left to philosophers and artists, but, on second thoughts, one may agree that this is not the case. For the manifold is oppressive and some kind of ordering will be produced which will promise to be less oppressive than the manifold. Nor is ordering difficult for it is not difficult to produce and perpetrate yet another myth. There is, then, a demand for order and it falls first to the philosopher to discover the source and to disseminate his discovery. The temptation of the philosopher is to note that within the manifold he seems to have no place, to overlook the demand and the method of ordering, and to climb on some bandwagon already included in the manifold. And if this is true of the philosopher it is even more true of the Catholic theologian. The Catholic tradition is part of the manifold of contemporary meaning even if it is a decaying part, an antique. But Catholic meaning is not part of the manifold; it is, as a matter of fact, the world order. The theologian's task is to come to a fruitful understanding of that order as it orders contemporary man. When one considers man as he concretely is, he is oriented to mystery as that mystery is revealed in Catholic faith. Naturally, this is not accepted with the manifold because of the nature of the manifold, and it cannot be accepted by any of the myths that offer to order the manifold. The theologian's temptation, like that of the philosopher, is to insert himself into the manifold or to attach himself to some popular myth; but to yield to this temptation is to accept a popular, easily understood, fundamentally transient and irrelevant importance and to overlook one's place in the slow growth of a critical control of meaning which is the providential movement of human history.

Immediacy and the mediation of being: an attempt to answer Bernard Lonergan

E. CORETH

THE philosophical thought of Bernard J. F. Lonergan, as it is represented above all in his main work *Insight*, is too profound and rich in content to be given its due in a position paper of brief scope. I will have to limit myself to several aspects. For that, however, Lonergan himself offers me a point of departure since some years ago he made a thorough critique[1] of my *Metaphysik*.[2] I am sincerely grateful for his kind and understanding evaluation of that philosophical exploration of mine. Yet I wish to accept the friendly challenge that is contained in the critical remarks, particularly at the end of his discussion.

He holds the view here—over against me—that metaphysics is not the absolute basic and total-science because it does not coincide with the fundamental total-horizon but has to do only with being as the 'objective pole' of our horizon; it fails, however, fully to grasp and explicate the 'subjective pole' of this horizon. Therein Lonergan sees, so it seems, not simply a defect in my exposition of metaphysics, but a legitimate self-delimitation of metaphysics as such, in so far as it is concerned with being. Metaphysics, thus, does not reach the concrete and universal total-horizon; nonetheless, it presupposes it. Therefore it is first necessary to make explicit the 'subjective pole' of the total-horizon on which the concrete, socially and historically determined person—as 'incarnate inquirer'—finds and questions himself. From this it follows also that the method of metaphysics is but one method among many other methods and must therefore be considered and grounded in the further horizon of a universal doctrine of methods that needs, however, to be established transcendentally.[3]

With this in mind as well as Lonergan's work as a whole, if I ask myself where—despite all the surely very far-reaching agreement in our thought—the decisive point of difference between the two conceptions lies, the answer, it seems to me, is in the respective understanding of being. And it lies above all in that the function of being is differently applied within the method of a transcendental reflection and explication. Since Lonergan confronts my *Metaphysik* in the aforementioned article with the position of E. Gilson, permit me to say aphoristically: for Gilson being is the immediate; for Lonergan it is what is mediated or to be mediated; whereas for me—admittedly in terms of Hegel—it is at once 'immediate and mediated', i.e., it is mediated or self-mediating immediacy. This tension and movement of being is the condition of the possibility of all human inquiring and thinking. It is the task of metaphysics, however, through transcendental retrieval to thematise and make explicit the mediation of immediacy.

To make more clear how this is meant, we want in the following: (I) to begin with the meaning and distinctiveness of transcendental thinking. That in turn raises (II) the question concerning the relation between subject and object. Therein is disclosed (III) what I wish to call the mediation of immediacy of being and what metaphysics, as foundational, is to demonstrate and explicate through transcendental reflection.

I. THE TRANSCENDENTAL QUESTION

1. The transcendental problem arises patently from the basic question of all philosophy. The basic question, however, is the question about the basis (ground). The early Greek philosophers already ask about the *arché panton*, the ground of everything, and thereby assign philosophical thinking its task for all time: to question everything for its ground, to get at the foundation of everything. It has to interrogate every subject or subject area, to rise above it with a view towards its ground, also to reflect upon all the findings and methods of individual sciences for their presuppositions. To this extent philosophical thought is by its very nature a movement of rising above or transcending; it is—in this broadest sense—a transcendental occurrence.

The transcendental question—in the narrower sense which the word has since Kant—necessarily appears the moment cognition becomes conscious that it has *a priori* conditions. There is no pure immediacy of the 'given' or 'appearing' object, because every cognition of an object presupposes the subject that knows, which in its own performance mediates to itself the content of the cognition and makes that content its object. If then the performance of the cognition is questioned about the preceding conditions of its possibility, which are in such a way constitutive of the performance that they can be reductively exhibited from it, then that is a transcendental reflection. This reflection can start with everyday or scientific inquiring and knowing; it can also lead other modes of human self-realisation back to their *a priori* conditions in order to grasp them in their very nature. This does not predetermine whether these preceding conditions lie alone in the immanence of the subject or transcend the subject itself. Here is the starting-point for the possibility of a metaphysical deepening of the transcendental question. In any case that question will first arrive at its goal when it is able to grasp and to ground the performance in the ground of its very nature.

From this it follows that the transcendental reflection on our cognition—on the performance of inquiring and judging—raises the fundamental claim to furnish the prime-foundation of cognition. This claim lies in its very nature. It was already raised by Kant, after him by German idealism and by every transcendental philosophy that understands itself, down to the present. The nature of such reflection is basically misunderstood if a transcendental method is indeed applied, say for grounding the metaphysics, but if another theory of cognition not transcendentally founded is presupposed for it, which is only thereafter to be transcendentally 'deepened' or 'supplemented'. Questions about the theory and critique of knowledge surely retain their meaning and validity, but only upon a basis transcendentally secured. For this reason the transcendental method is not one possible method alongside other scientific and philosophical methods. Rather, it assumes a fundamental priority because it interrogates everything with a view towards its 'prius', in order to understand it 'a priori'; it must reflect critically upon everything—including every method —and must transcend it with a view towards its presuppositions.

2. Lonergan, I believe, agrees with this too. For he demands that also a general doctrine of methods be grounded transcendentally, i.e., that every particular method of scientific or philosophical knowing must be transcendentally led back to its preceding conditions.[4] Thereby every individual method in its function is at the same time relativised and integrated into a whole. Only from the transcendentally mediated total-horizon of the human world

of cognition with the multiplicity of its functions and dimensions do the meaning and limits of the individual, functionally limited method arise. For Lonergan such a transcendental doctrine of methods is, however, still not metaphysics, nor yet a methodology for metaphysics, but something that fundamentally precedes metaphysics.

In response I wish to say: every cognition—whether it wants to be or not—is cognition of being. Every method of cognition is thus a method of cognition of being. And every grounding of cognition is a grounding of cognition of being. It can only take place in that cognition reflects upon itself, criticises itself. In this critical reflection on cognition itself, it is not simply—according to the famous objection that Hegel already advanced against Kant's critique of cognition—that the cognition which is to perform the reflection is again being presupposed. But that is possible, provided that all cognition is cognition of being only because the cognition itself is being—performance of being or occurrence of being— towards which the cognition directs itself. And are not all such ascertained structures of cognition once again structures in which being manifests itself as being-in-itself, a self-luminousness? We are not going to escape being, not in a doctrine of cognition or of methods either. Certainly one can extrapolate and do a purely formal analysis of the modes of cognition, but the question is whether one thereby transcendentally reaches and discloses the fundamental occurrence that takes place in knowing as such, and thus also in all modes of knowing no matter how diverse in method. If transcendental reflection wants to get to the bottom of the performance of cognition in order to understand it in terms of its ground, then it must lead cognition back to being and ground it on the basis of being. In doing that, it itself already becomes metaphysics. That is to say, cognition, reflected transcendentally upon its ground, discloses itself as occurrence of being which has always been taking place, as the condition of its possibility, in the horizon of being; therefore transcendental philosophy is itself already metaphysics, provided it fulfils its own essential intention, just as metaphysics can be nothing other than transcendental philosophy.

3. By its very nature transcendental reflection, whether we understand it metaphysically or not, demands a fundamental prime-foundation of cognition. But the question is, whether and how it

can carry out this task. Here arises a further, it seems to me even weightier, consideration. For it remains presupposed that first something must be 'given' and 'appear' if we want to question it transcendentally. That holds, furthermore, for every other question: something 'given' and 'appearing'—a phenomenon in the broadest sense—awakens our questions; it remains presupposed in the questioning and is at the same time transcended through the questioning. Thus, for a correct, appropriate formulation of the question it is important that the phenomenon first comes into sight correctly, i.e., as it 'shows' itself. All philosophical thinking has characteristically a phenomenological base or nexus. That is not a discovery first made by 'phenomenology', but basically something self-evident for every serious and rigorous questioning and thinking, even if exact phenomenological analysis and description only discovered its scientific method since Husserl. The transcendental method too does not thereby exclude a phenomenological element, rather it necessarily presupposes it. If the question previously arose whether metaphysics presupposes a transcendental grounding that itself is not yet a metaphysics, then the question now arises whether transcendental philosophy, be it understood formally or metaphysically, presupposes a phenomenological moment that is only subsequently reflected transcendentally.

Nevertheless, basically no contradiction exists between phenomenology and transcendental philosophy. They are two mutually related phases of the same methodological process. On the one hand, the transcendental question, wherever it may take its starting point, presupposes a phenomenological moment. That, for instance, Lonergan's *Insight* far surpasses my *Metaphysik* in careful phenomenological analysis—in his case, the analysis of various modes and methods of cognition—I gladly concede.[5] It remains admittedly an incontrovertible deficiency of my effort that in it—above all, lest the book grow any more voluminous—the phenomenological element does not get its due. Yet I wanted by no means fundamentally to skip over it; that would be a misunderstanding. On the contrary, I consider it a necessary methodological element, demanded by transcendental reflection itself, inherent in its very nature. The immediacy is that which must be mediated; there is no mediation without immediacy.

However, there is also no immediacy without mediation. For that reason, on the other hand, every properly understood phenomenology that is aware of its problematic, points beyond itself and insists upon the transcendental question. There is no pure phenomenon, no pure and subject-free objectivity of the 'thing itself'. There is no pure immediacy of what appears and what is to be received because every objective content which comes to us as givenness is already mediated through the performance of the subject. The way in which we see the object, against which background and in which context we understand it, which questions we direct at it, and which answer—from our perspective—we expect from it, all this helps determine the object as it discloses itself to us and becomes 'phenomenon'.[6]

That means, however, that it is not only a pure *a priori* that conditions and determines our mode of knowing the object—be this *a priori* understood with Kant as pure transcendental subjectivity, or metaphysically as pure transcendental openness of spirit for being. That kind of pure *a priori* has always mediated itself in concrete experience and historical event. Conversely this does not mean a pure *a posteriori* over against a pure *a priori*; that would again be pure objectivity over against pure subjectivity. Rather, the concrete background of the experience and of the historical event itself becomes the preceding condition of knowing and understanding newly encountered contents. There is never a pure thinking by a transcendental subject but always only concrete man in his world, in society and in history, the person who is shaped through his own experiences and decisions, who finds himself in a historically concrete situation with which he must come to terms, who understands and questions himself, however, again in terms of a socially and historically shaped language and thus interprets and attempts to ground himself. To that extent I fully agree with Lonergan's designation of the concrete person as 'incarnate inquirer', who must form the point of departure for philosophical reflection.

II. SUBJECT AND OBJECT

1. Yet Lonergan understands this point of departure in the concrete person in a way that nevertheless strikes me as questionable. According to him there opens up from that point, as his 'subjective pole', a further total-horizon which is proper to metaphysics. For metaphysics can abstract from the concrete person as the inquirer, consider him simply formally, and restricts its task

to the interpretation of the 'objective pole'.[7] Here the question arises for me whether a subject-object dualism is not thereby reintroduced and held anew. And is it not precisely in a transcendental metaphysics that this dualism must be overcome by being transcended and comprehended on the basis of a common originating ground? This cannot succeed as long as 'being' is again understood as objectivity after all. Thereby one reverts to a level of problematic that already Kant and German idealism criticised as 'dogmatic metaphysics' and whose conquest was a central problem until Heidegger. Only a transcendental-metaphysical interpretation of being is able to do justice to this problem. It must lead the concrete dialectical happening between subject and object back to the ground of its possibility in order to reach being—not as the essence of objectivity, but as that which reveals and mediates itself in this dialectical happening as its ground.

Perhaps, however, to do justice to Lonergan's conception, we must go back to the way in which he introduces and defines the concepts 'Subject' and 'Object'. The Object is that about which—within a context of correct judgements—a correct judgement can be asserted. To that extent the concept of objectivity is included in every context of correct judgements.[8] Disregarding this context, we can thus say even more simply: Object is that which can be asserted in true judgements. As subject Lonergan then understands an Object, about which it is true that it affirms itself as knower.[9] It is, then, an Object, i.e., something about which a true judgement is possible, but about which in particular the judgement is true that it affirms itself as knower. Nonetheless, the question here is whether the subject is thereby reached at all and accurately defined. Is it not already the 'subject as Object', i.e., the subject already made the Object of knowing and of judging, grasped as Object, consequently objectified, no longer the 'subject as subject', i.e., in the original performance of its knowing that precedes objectifying reflection?[10] The cited definition of the subject presupposes, first of all, that this 'something' that affirms itself as knower, and thus makes itself the Object of its own affirmation, simply knows itself already before, i.e., exists in the original performance of cognition that precedes reflection and makes it possible, and therein experiences itself; the subject as subject is presupposed. And secondly, the true judgement that our 'Object' affirms itself as knower presupposes again a subject that performs this cognition and makes the true judgement. The subject in its self-realisation—the 'subject as subject', not yet the 'subject as Object'—is not thereby reached but presupposed. Over against it stands the Object as the content of actual or possible knowing: as the 'other'. Does this not introduce anew or presuppose an opposition between subject and Object without guiding it back to, and understanding it through, a preceding ground?

2. To be sure, the resolution of the subject-Object opposition has in the present been widely turned into a cheap slogan. It is only valid if the 'resolution' is understood in its full range of meaning.[11] The duality of subject and Object in the sense of the fundamental phenomenon that I relate myself—as knower, striver, and doer—to 'something other' will always continue to exist and is not to be resolved. The phenomenon is grounded in the fact that 'I' am not everything, but a finite subject within a reality that transcends me. Nonetheless, the opposition between subject and Object, so absolutely fixed by modern thought, must be overcome: i.e., the pure subject that understands itself in rationalism as 'autonomous reason' and in idealism as 'absolute reason' and that places itself vis-à-vis an equally pure, subjectless Objectivity—the idol of modern science. Indeed there is only an occurring dialectic of mutual conditioning and intertwining between subject and Object. Man is only 'subject' because he has always been Object of his world and his history, with which he must nevertheless come to terms on his own. And the contents to which we relate in knowing and striving only become 'Objects' in so far as they are grasped and understood by us, that is to say, in so far as they enter our concrete horizon of experience and understanding and are realised out of that horizon.

An absolutely fixed subject-Object dualism cannot account for the concrete relationship between subject and Object but makes that relationship in its essence impossible. It becomes a rigid opposition that excludes every mediation. The mediated occurrence, however, in which the subject mediates itself in the Object and the Object in the subject, is possible only on the basis of an enveloping unity which differentiates itself in this occurrence and at the same time preserves its unity—one could show how herein the analogy of being is fundamental or rather is presupposed as the condition of this occurrence.

If we grasp everything as something that is, and if—starting, say, with inquiring or with judging—we are able to exhibit being as the last and unconditioned, all-embracing horizon, in which we realise ourselves in the 'other' and toward which we reach out beyond all individual entities, then 'being' means not only the being of objects, nor only the realm of possible objectivity. It also means the being which we ourselves are, i.e., which we ourselves realise and experience as the being that sets everything that simply is or happens into its actuality. What 'being' means, discloses itself in fact primarily, with greater immediacy, in the actuality of one's own self-realisation (self-performance). Here being does not reveal itself as object, but as spiritual, self-illuminated, self-conscious realisation: as being and knowing in the identity of performance.[12] At the same time, however, in so far as I ask about being and thus have not taken hold of being totally in the performance of my knowing, there appears a difference between performance and being. More precisely, it is the difference between the being of one's own self-realisation and the being which transcends me and my performance, for which—in asking about 'other'—I must therefore first reach out.[13] This is a tension which is essential to the finite spirit and lies, in the horizon of being, at the basis of the total dynamic of his questioning and progressing cognition.

3. If after exhibiting the horizon of being in my *Metaphysik* I moved back to self-consciousness—more precisely to the knowing of being in self-realisation of spirit, then the reason for this lay not in a critique of cognition but in a metaphysics of cognition. That is to be noted here because this point has occasioned several misunderstandings.[14] After the horizon of being has been exhibited in its unconditioned and unlimited character in terms of the performance of inquiring, a critique makes no sense and has no further validity. The question has already become obsolete, whether it is a matter of the horizon of absolute being-in-itself or a matter after all only of a horizon of relative being for me. The categorically unconditional validity of cognition of being must no longer and can no longer be secured by reference to an immediate experience of being by consciousness. If it is referred to nevertheless, that has, for one thing, a methodological-systematic reason. After being in its totality has been exhibited as total-horizon, we must proceed to a differentiation in the knowing of being. We do not know only about 'being' and nothing but being—that would be, with Hegel,

'the night in which all cows are black.'[15] We know rather, even if in the comprehensive horizon of being, about a differentiated multiplicity of existents. The first fundamental distinction that is established in every performance of inquiring and knowing is the duality between me and the other, between subject and Object, but, as indicated, in an occurrence of mutual mediation. This leads, secondly, to the further question, how the subject as such is constituted, what is an intellectual act of inquiring or knowing, for which being is disclosed or illumined in so far as it is performed in the horizon of being. The question about the origin of the projection of the horizon remains patently valid, even required. But this question receives its answer only from the innermost nature of such a performance, in which an identity of being and knowing is revealed, but at the same time a distinction between being and knowing.

If then we refer back to self-consciousness (as knowledge of being through one's own self-realisation) which is presupposed as condition and involved in the performance of all inquiring and knowing about 'other', and if we have even designated it as experience of being and certainty of being, then—against the background of the preceding mediation—that is an already mediated and thus grounded certainty. This certainty is only possible within the (already exhibited) horizon of being, in which I relate myself to other entities and distinguish myself from other existents, thereby experiencing myself, however, immediately as an existent. Again in Hegel's words, it is a 'mediated immediacy', i.e. one that does not exclude a mediation but presupposes it and nonetheless is a genuine immediacy of cognition of being, an immediacy, that is, whose transcendental condition has become visible.

III. IMMEDIATE AND MEDIATED

1. This leads to the last but perhaps most important point of difference, because it is metaphysically the most significant. With reference to Lonergan's 'Metaphysics as Horizon', I may risk repeating the formulation: being is for Gilson the immediate and for Lonergan the mediated. Gilson represents an immediate realism, in which we grasp being intuitively in all the contents of experience.[16] He speaks of a 'seeing' or 'beholding' (*voir*) of being in what is given to the senses; it is the immediacy of an intellectual intuition.[17] I do not wish to contradict this thesis absolutely, in

any case not as unconditionally and unqualifiedly as Lonergan does. For there is an intuitive element in intellectual cognition; otherwise intellectual cognition would not even be possible. There exists an immediacy of spiritual insight, despite any and every mediation; otherwise a conceptually rational mediation would not be possible either. Yet whether it can be designated accurately with Gilson as intuition of being or even of the concept of being, seems highly questionable to me; I would reject it.[18] But even if we had such an intuition, it would be nonetheless conditioned *a priori* and made possible through the characteristic nature of the human spirit capable of such intuition. Even if we perceive being *a posteriori*, this presupposes *a priori* the possibility, or the making possible, of this occurrence. The question thus remains valid, even philosophically required, which *a priori* conditions are presupposed in the performance of an insight, even if an immediate insight. Only in this way can its essence, its validity, and its range—even perhaps its limits—be mediated. It would certainly not be legitimate to stop before this question, or even to demand a regional and partial surcease, thus excluding the question of a mediation and invoking the immediacy of an intuition. By this I wish to say that even when being has been immediately given to us, there remains the task of mediating this immediacy transcendentally. Thus, the immediacy would in no way be sublated, but conceived out of the grounds of its essence in its very possibility. My objection to Gilson, then, is directed not so much against his appeal to immediacy, but against his exclusion of mediation.

2. For Lonergan, on the other hand, being is the mediated. He rejects decisively the immediate and uninitial realism of Gilson. Towards this end he investigates very carefully, as is well known, the mathematical, the empirical-scientific, and the everyday (common sense) modes of knowledge, in order to elaborate their common basic structures. They are manifested within the dynamism of the cognitional process as such, in the constant transition from perceiving, through understanding, to judging. Only after long preparation—which it is neither possible nor necessary to reproduce here—does he reach a foundation of metaphysics. In this connection the notion of being (*seins begriff*) is decisive for him as well as for the entire Aristotelian tradition. Hence, it will be of central significance for us to see how and in what sense he introduces the notion of being.

Lonergan distinguishes being as that which has been known or is yet to be known, as the object of real or possible knowledge; it is simply the knowable.[19] Such an operative definition, gained as it is from the performance of knowing,[20] 'assigns, not what is meant by being, but how that meaning is to be determined. It asserts that if you know, then you know being; it asserts that if you wish to know, then you wish to know being . . .'[21] Such a definition has its value and validity in so far as it indicates the function that belongs to a concept—in this case to the concept of being—in the performance of our cognition, which question it answers, which intention it fulfils. In this case it is the fundamental and universal function of all questioning and knowing: namely wanting to know something. But if so functional a definition is not continually defined in terms of content—again, out of the performance of the cognition itself—then it remains a tautology. The assertion: 'If you know, then you know a being' would accordingly only declare: 'If you know, then you know that which you know.' Just as tautological would be the proposition: 'You know an Object': it would mean 'You know that which you know'. Since according to Lonergan the concept of the existent means the 'objective of the pure cognitional striving', then being means pure objectivity and the latter means pure knowability.

All these assertions will only make sense if the concept of the existent is given ongoing definition in terms of content above and beyond its functional definition. One must make explicit the sense of the original meaning which had always been already intended—even if only implicitly—in the performance of such assertions. This is disregarded by the definition that solely indicates the function of the concept. The concept is able to fulfil this function in the cognitional process, however, only through the sense of its meaning which is intended in or along with it. To that extent such a functional definition points beyond itself and demands a definition in terms of content; otherwise the function dissolves too and the concept becomes meaningless. By a definition of content I obviously do not mean an externally empirical definition, but rather, in the rigour of transcendental method, the sense of a meaning which has always been presupposed and intended in the performance of inquiring and knowing as the conditions of its meaningful possibility. But what do we mean when we inquire about something or know something; when we inquire about the 'existent' or know the 'existent'? In what way is something knowable and what in it is knowable? In what is the 'virtually unconditioned' grounded, with which we affirm the existent in judgement? Do these questions not necessarily lead to being? And do we mean by being only the very essence of objectivity, that is, of knowability? What do we mean by being?

Lonergan characterises my conception over against the thesis of Gilson in the following manner: in Gilson being is 'seen' or 'beheld' in the sensory appearances. For me, on the other hand, being is that about which one inquires in view of the sense data. Far from being beheld in the sense data, being is that which is intended in that we go above and beyond the sense data. For inquiring goes beyond the already-known to the not-known, in order to reach it in knowledge. The already-known is the sensory givenness; the not-known or not-yet-known, which we want to know and about which we must inquire, is being.[22] This characterisation is surely correct but, in my opinion, not yet sufficient. It seems to me almost more appropriate for Lonergan's position than for me. For I understand as being not only the final but also the first, not only that which we aim at in all our inquiring and striving and yet never attain, but also that which we always have already and which we perform in all our inquiring and knowing. It is not only the mediated—in an occurrence of mediation that can come to no conclusion because it also has no beginning—but also the immediate, which we have always known and yet never fully understand, about which we must therefore always keep on asking. But we can only inquire about it because we have incipiently always known it. It is an original knowing as condition of the inquiring. It must continue to define and unfold itself, without ever being able to overtake being so as to comprehend it; it does not dissolve the inquiring.

How could we ask about being if we did not already know about being beforehand? How could we reach out for being, if we had not always been already with being? How could we project the horizon of being, if we did not know ourselves as existents in being? The performance of asking and knowing cannot reach being, if it were not itself—as performance—being that realises itself and in its performance knows itself. Nor could we, however, inquire about being as that which we do not yet know but want to reach in coming to know it, if being would not transcend both us and the performance of our questioning and knowing. The tension and movement which here show up in being I once designated as 'dynamic identity'.[23] I do not know if Lonergan would contest what is meant by that. In his work, it seems to me, it is not sufficiently taken into account. Therefore, the most profound and decisive point of difference that divides our conception can, I believe, be termed as follows: for Lonergan being is only the final, not also the first; it is only the goal of the mediation, not also its beginning, and hence not also that which in it—in dynamic identity—mediates itself and continues to define itself. In brief, let me say: Gilson lacks the mediation of the immediacy of being; Lonergan lacks in the mediation the immediacy of being.

3. This raises, once more, however, the question about the nature and task of metaphysics and with this we return to the initial problem. If metaphysics is to be understood on the basis of its very nature and to be grounded critically, then this can occur only through the transcendental retrieval of the conditions of its possibility. It is not a crucial issue for me whether the transcendental grounding should already be called metaphysics or not. With Lonergan one could speak of a transcendental doctrine of cognition and methods that precedes metaphysics.[24] But if this doctrine transcends all other individual scientific and philosophical methods through reflection upon them and aims at a categorical prime-foundation of cognition, then it must become metaphysical—appropriately—in the sense that it grounds and justifies cognition as cognition of being, in the sense that it discloses the horizon of being as the total-horizon within which our cognition is performed and all particular modes and methods of cognition are articulated.

Transcendental reflection demands, nonetheless, a phenomenological nexus. Again it is not a crucial issue for me whether this phenomenological element is to be considered as mere presupposition or as an internal, intrinsic moment of the transcendental method. On the one hand, every transcendental recovery, and also a transcendental-metaphysical one, demands a phenomenological nexus; on the other hand, that nexus is not given as pure immediacy but points beyond itself and insists upon the question of its preceding contingency. Therefore it seems to me correct not rigorously to separate these two methodological elements but to understand the phenomenological element as the internal moment of the transcendental reflection.

It is more important, however, that thereby the final total-horizon is reached and interpreted. Lonergan insists—and I agree with him completely—that the point of departure be the concrete person as the 'incarnate inquirer'.[25] Hence the horizon of concrete experience and understanding must be disclosed, the horizon in which man in his world, in community, and in history understands himself and verbally interprets himself. That requires a phenomeno-logical-hermeneutical explication of the 'world of man'.[26] Such an explication, however, can never comprehend the complete and concrete fullness of content because every man has his own 'world' which takes shape from his own experiences and decisions and which never completely coincides with the 'world' of another. One is therefore able to extract only the essential moments of content that universally belong to the 'world of man' and constitute his horizon of understanding.

This shows, however, that the 'world' in this sense of the horizon of concrete experience and understanding does not by its very nature form the final horizon in which man realises and under-stands himself.[27] For the world is always factically limited—while at the same time, however, fundamentally open. We inquire further, we have further experiences, grasp further meanings in content and reference. The world of understanding is constantly expanding towards a final and unconditioned horizon which, how-ever, intrinsically constitutes the total understanding of the world and relationship to the world of man, as condition of his possi-bility. We can call this last horizon 'being as totality'. This horizon can only be grasped 'abstractly', because we are never capable of comprehending the totality of being in the concrete fullness of its content; and it can only be thematised 'analogically' in terms of our experience of the world, in the language of our understanding of the world, transcending the latter, however, analogically. From this it follows that, on the one hand, the 'world' always and necessarily points beyond itself to 'being' as the final and uncon-ditioned horizon of our performance of the world, but that, on the other hand, the thematic interpretation of 'being' is just as necessarily bound in turn to the 'world' as the concrete, historical and linguistic horizon of understanding. One can speak here of a dialectical relationship of reciprocal condition and mediation between 'world' and 'being': more precisely, between a pheno-menological-hermeneutical interpretation of 'world' and a transcendental-metaphysical explication of 'being'.[28] Every element is referred to the other and conditioned by the other; only through the mediation of the other can it fulfil itself.

From this it does not, however, follow that—according to Lonergan—a fuller and further total-horizon discloses itself from the 'subjective pole' of the horizon, viz., concrete man, a horizon within which metaphysics selects as its 'objective pole' an abstract and limited partial-horizon. Neither 'world' nor 'being' can be reduced simply to a subjective or an objective pole; both are determined in terms of content through the concrete occurrence of mediation between subject and object. 'World', however, is the immediate horizon of experience and understanding of concrete historical man. Limited and open at one and the same time, the 'world' constantly awakens our further inquiry in reaching out toward the final, absolutely embracing total-horizon of 'being'. If we succeed, at least in terms of basic structures, in thematising being and in making it explicit—as the constitutive condition of the world of man—then we have reached the final and unconditioned horizon of all human inquiring and knowing, striving and acting, but also of all special modes and methods of knowing employed by the individual sciences. To that extent—so it continues to seem to me—metaphysics, thus understood, is the basic-science that goes to the final ground of everything, and the total-science that embraces everything in terms of its final ground.

Knowing and language in the thought of Bernard Lonergan

JOSEPH FLANAGAN

A CENTRAL difficulty in discussing Lonergan's thought is that the scholastic tradition out of which his ideas emerge is not a very familiar context for most of his readers. This difficulty is significantly increased by the fact that Lonergan is attempting a rather fundamental reorientation of this scholastic tradition. Within any tradition one usually discovers, according to his own perspective, an authentic and an inauthentic version and Lonergan, particularly in his early writings, made just such a distinction in the scholastic tradition. It would be quite helpful, therefore, in presenting Lonergan's thought, if the reader had some idea of the position that Lonergan is opposing in his attempt to reorient the scholastic tradition. For this reason, I intend to construct a strawman opponent called the 'logician' who will represent all that is 'evil' in scholastic thought, and with this rhetorical device I hope to highlight what I think are some of the major factors in Lonergan's thought.

This paper has two main sections. In the first I will discuss Lonergan's theory of knowing which, as he maintains, determines a thinker's position regarding the question of objectivity and reality. In the second, I will discuss how Lonergan's theory of knowing grounds his theory of language.

I. TRADITIONAL LOGICAL ACCOUNT OF KNOWING

In the scholastic analysis of knowing it was customary to conceive the cognitional process as involving two principal acts—understanding and judging. I shall discuss these acts first as Lonergan's opponent the logician conceives them and then present Lonergan's own version of knowing.

First Act: Understanding

The first cognitional act, understanding, would be explained something like this: I notice something; I wonder 'what' the thing is; and suddenly, I realise, it's a flying-saucer. The recognition occurs simultaneously with the emergence within my mind of the concept, flying-saucer, and, since the concept in my mind corresponds with this particular, visible instance of flying-saucers, I can assert quite confidently: it certainly is a flying-saucer. Notice that no account is given of how 'knowing' itself takes place except to state that you grasp singular, visible objects by having in mind invisible concepts. To account for the production of this interior concept the logician postulates an inner power that he names 'agent intellect'. This 'inner power' illuminates, immaterialises and transforms sensibly impressed images into luminous inner words called 'universals' which are universal because their meanings are applicable in the same way to successive individual instances of x, y, z. Lonergan has caricatured this account of the formation of inner words as a metaphysical sausage machine with sensations and images going in one end and concepts popping out the other end.

The existence of the agent intellect, then, is postulated or deduced from a spoken or written word like 'hippie' which of itself does not refer to this or that hippie but to any instance of hippie. And since we do not see 'universal hippie' but only think him, we must account for this fact of 'thinking universals' by postulating a power that can metamorphose singular 'seeables' into universal 'thinkables'. The evidence, then, for the existence of this 'force' is in our speaking and writing which manifests universals of all kinds and classes, and from that evidence the logician argues back to the 'agent intellect'.

Second Act: Judging

This machine-like model of understanding can be extended and slightly complicated by the logician to explain the second and consummative cognitive act through which we reach truth: the act of judging. Like understanding, judging also can be explained by the same silent and impersonal power of the 'agent intellect' which not only generates concepts for thinking but can also combine these concepts into propositions, and metamorphose the propositions into premises that lead to universal, necessary conclusions to which all men can, and eventually must, give assent. The agent intellect accomplishes these transformations by a process called 'reasoning' which precedes and leads to conclusions which are then uttered in declarative statements of fact.

The first step in this mental process of combining concepts into the larger unit termed 'proposition' parallels the grammatical operation of putting words into sentences. The mechanical explanation of this process is as follows: confronted by its own inner words the agent intellect, now referred to as 'reason', compares these separate units of meaning, divides them into subjects and predicates, and then moulds them into inner sentences (propositions). The propositions are then compared and arranged in a syllogistic pattern leading the mind to its natural goal: the conclusions. In other words, the mind once it is confronted with inner words and sentences moves towards its own natural term—judgement or conclusion. As the first mental act 'pops out' concepts or definitions, so the second act of judging generates conclusions.

The explanation can be reversed. The logician's mind interiorly confronted by a universal necessary truth, to which it has concluded, may wonder what is the basis of the conclusions that it is about to utter publicly and assertively. This demands a 'look back' to the premises grounding the conclusions. As the mind reasons forward to its goal, so it can now reason backward (reflect) and recover the process. Conclusions are backed up by premises which are primarily persuasive because of the form or pattern interrelating the premises, and implicitly containing the conclusion. The patterns can be reduced to four figures and nineteen syllogistic moods, all of which are various 'ways' of 'causing' conclusions. But there are even more fundamental causes or reasons for concluding to particular propositions and these are the 'first causes' of the mind or, as more commonly named, first principles. Operating, then, in the light of its own first principles, the 'agent intellect' guides the intellect as it reasons its way through the premises and arrives safely at the conclusion. The system is completed by pointing out that these ultimate principles—contradiction, identity, and excluded middle—are axiomatic, self-proving sources of truth, and so the intellect, moving forward from understanding to judging by composing and dividing concepts into propositions, illuminates itself through first principles which all correct conclusions can be reduced to and deduced from. *Per accidens* someone may doubt the validity of these first principles but *per se* any ordinary, rational animal will be thoroughly satisfied with the way these principles move his intellect to judgements, and guarantee their ultimate validity. Such an account of knowing safely removes from judgement any arbitrariness, and gives one a method of reaching and preserving truths without fear of becoming too subjective.

This explanation accounts for the whole process of knowing without even mentioning whether or not these successive steps take place consciously or unconsciously, whether they are your concepts and conclusions or Julius Caesar's. Such an account of knowing 'applies to' all the rational animals without indicating whether their agent intellect is five years old or fifty. One gets the impression from such an account that a computer could be programmed to perform all the necessary operations and, thereby, free us from the unfortunate interference of any human variables.

In review then, knowing begins with sensible stimuli that 'press' the mind into action, stirring up feelings and imaginative presentations which in turn solicit the ever vigilant agent intellect into its first act of probing into the multiplicity of images and searching out the latent intelligibilities. Suddenly these silent, unconscious forces produce an inner word which is not only applicable to this sensible image but also transcends all similar sensible instances, and so is universal in itself, and reveals the intellectual soul as transcending material conditions of particular places and times— a 'mind for all seasons'. Successive inner words are composed and divided into interior sentences through the agent intellect which now initiates the syllogistic patterns designed to lead us to conclusions that are verifiable by the light of first principles.

Third Act: Deciding

A similar logical and mechanical account can be given of the process of deciding. Those conclusions that the intellect stamps as universal, necessary truths can be selected as principles of conduct, which then confront the human will as rational commands, guiding it in the formation of true moral decisions. Conclusions are thus transformed into moral laws backed up by basic principles by which the will naturally seeks the good revealed by the light of the mind. In this case the principles beget the laws that generate decisions that govern behaviour, and the relation between concrete behaviour and moral law is again the logical relation of a universal principle to a singular concrete decision. Again all subjective errors and variables are safely eliminated.

Endowed with such a mind we can generate concepts and conclusions, building up a body of knowledge whose certitude is guaranteed by its logical coherence and, more ultimately, in naturally known first principles. We can go on and generate a moral code that is based on these naturally known first principles expressed in 'natural' laws that should govern human conduct.

Thus in a very abbreviated and somewhat exaggerated view we have a traditional manualistic description of the knowing and deciding—a metaphysical monster that we have conjured up for Lonergan to slay.

Lonergan's Theory of Knowing

Instead of characterising knowing and deciding in terms of the products of these activities, namely, concepts, conclusions, and decisions, Lonergan turned his account of knowing around and focused on the questions that initiated the acts of understanding, judging and deciding. Understanding was correlated with the question 'what is it?' He tied judging to the question 'is it really so?' And deciding was characterised by 'ought it to be so?' The result was a complete transformation of the traditional logical model.

Consider the state of mind you are in when questioning as opposed to answering. Questioning puts you in the paradoxical position of knowing and not knowing. You know, otherwise you would not question, and yet if you already know, questioning would be superfluous. With this focus on questioning we can introduce the interesting personal experience of tending towards an answer that we can call the 'known-unknown'. Between knowledge, the product of knowing, and ignorance, a lack of knowing, there is the state of mind where you synthesise all that you already know, and then utilise this 'known' to attack the unknown. This gives us the category 'known-unknown'—a very concrete, and dynamic way of conceiving knowing.

Furthermore, when you focus on questioning as it pressures for understanding you are much more likely to discover the central event in knowing which lies between the question and the concept— the moment of insight. Insight is the magic moment when you reduce a stubborn complicated problem to magnificent simplicity with one swift stroke. You may have spent the whole previous day wrestling with a problem and suddenly, next morning when you are not 'putting the question', all the parts fall into place—the mind clicks. A common enough experience, yet the logician's account of understanding does not identify this sudden flash as understanding, but passes over it and focuses rather on the subsequent phase that occurs when you start 'concept-forming', when you are trying to formulate the insight and confront your mind with its discovery. Once the mind is confronted, then, in the logical account, one knows. The phase of knowing that initiates the process by questioning, the phase of knowing that is present in the inner flash, and the phase of knowing when the mind consciously conceives itself are all overlooked. Knowing occurs only when you are confronted with concepts. At this point you become conscious and knowing occurs. For Lonergan, on the contrary, the whole process from start to finish is conscious.

Insights are very familiar experiences, they do not have to be believed since everyone occasionally experiences them, and experiences them consciously. All you have to do to verify insight is to catch yourself in the act of 'doing' insight. It is your performance, and it can be so experienced provided you learn the art of 'self-appropriation', the art of catching self right in the midst of understanding. Concentrate on your conscious state of putting the question, raising your mental pressure, demanding insight, closing in on an expected meaning, etc. These are not unconscious activities. We could describe each act in great detail. The point is that if you have done the understanding, made your own meaning, then concepts come alive, they lose their impersonal, static character and become conscious products of your own conceiving, understanding and questioning. Otherwise concepts belong to their original authors and remain for you an abstract set of words that one can memorise but not understand.

Further, once one isolates insights within one's own experience, then the content of understanding is discovered to be, not some concept appearing in the mind, but understanding itself as consciously and deliberately conceived. What you mean when you write and speak are not words and concept but your own understanding of these words. Meaning does not have its source in printed or spoken words, nor even in mental words, rather mental words are formed and subsequently expressed because you actually *do* understand—a personal and conscious performance that is quite frequent and obvious.

There is, then, a conscious knowing that is pre-conceptual, and it is insight. Insight, in turn, has its source in the mounting tension that you feel when you are 'putting the question', and taking aim at a known-unknown.

Judging as Insight

Turning now to the second phase of knowing we can make a similar criticism of the product-oriented and mechanical model of judging that pops out impersonal conclusions. Lonergan's first step in transforming the logician's computer-like account of judgement that we have previously described is to correlate judging with the question from which it emerges and to which it responds. The 'judging question' may take a variety of forms but the simple question 'is it so?' sufficiently identifies the experience. Central to his explanation of judging is the specification of precisely what judging contributes to the knowing process. At first glance it seems that the main event in knowing is the insight that discovers meaning, while judging merely nods approval or disapproval to the meanings that understanding proposes for judicial action. The logical account of judging would admit that whether a proposition is or is not so, does make considerable difference. But the logician never explains just what is this difference, and how judging 'makes' the difference, except by the vague and ambiguous claim that propositions are true if they correspond to reality. Such correspondence supposes some sort of mental picture-taking that mirrors internally our 'real' external surroundings. The problem can be put another way.

To judge, one must have a standard to judge by; if you ask 'is it so?' apparently you do not know if it is so. But, if this is the case, then how will you as judger be able to conclude knowing with the claim that your answer really is so unless you already have the answer in your possession? The logical solution to the problem is, as we have seen, to assert the presence of a few first principles that we all inherit as part of the natural human equipment. All true propositions can then be referred to and measured by these universal reasons. Such a solution obviously relieves us of personal responsibility for the truth or falsity of our assertions. Lonergan, however, does not let the subject off so lightly.

Lonergan locates the specific contribution that judging makes by insisting on the question which initiates the judicial review that will gradually conclude with a judgement. This insistence on the question which initiates the process, again allows him to open up the process and draw attention to the insight that grounds the conclusion or assertion. However, the judging insight is considerably more difficult to specify than the insight of understanding. Since judging requires the slow careful reviewing of the evidence, Lonergan refers to it as a reflective insight, contrasting it with insight as understanding or direct insight. By focusing on judging as a 'slow-motion' insight he is able to point up what is most unique in the specific contribution that judging makes to the knowing procedures, namely, the person himself.

Just as we contrasted the logical account of insight with Lonergan's, by insisting that for him it was a conscious event, so also the same contrast holds for judging. In fact, judging is even more conscious, and it is conscious in a different way. It is you who do the experiencing, understanding and judging but the 'you' who is performing differs qualitatively in each successive phase. (If we were to go on and analyse the act of deciding or preferring we would find this act also presences you in a different and more personal way.) Recall that we characterised understanding as 'doing' as well as receiving, and we insisted that the catching on was your own. Now judging is even more of a personal performance, more of a 'self-constituting' activity. To speak of knowing then as an act of constituting is to speak of different phases and styles of consciousness and constituting which can be experienced and verified, provided one carefully appropriates how his personal presence varies as he himself shifts from one of these activities to the next. In other words, the total process of knowing combines one and the same self in three successive phases, each of which can be analysed as 'temporally' distinct and concretely simultaneous. It is not the purpose of this paper to deal with these qualitative differences. We wish only to point out that Lonergan specifies judging as a conscious, self-constituting activity, and thereby locates a new dimension in the cognitional process by which he can specify what judging adds to the understanding.

The second significant problem in judgement to discuss is its contextual aspect, and to explain more concretely how previous judgements enter into and form the background of present judgements. Before we do this, however, it would be well to sum up the points we have made.

Implicit in our analysis is the following argument: knowing and deciding combine four activities all of which are conscious and constitutive: experiencing constitutes you in a context to be questioned, understood, judged and decided; in understanding you transform the context and constitute yourself in an experienced, understood but not yet 'judged and decided' context. With each conscious activity you subsume and incorporate your previous state into a new kind of knowing attitude, and finally you emerge within a deciding context in which your 'doing' of your knowing transforms itself into personal behaviour. In the first phase of experiencing, it is you who are constituted, but in the last three it is you who do the constituting; and it is not just the activities that are being constituted, it is your 'self' and your world which is being generated and constituted. You slow the process down when it comes to judging and deciding because the constituting takes on a more intimate and personal tone. There is commitment involved in the judicial phase, and it is you that are being committed. More significant, as the process repeats itself, it is not only knowing and deciding that recur but you and your world recur and emerge into being. Not only does it take time to make a judgement but it also takes time to make you into a person; time enters into the very process of personhood; just as it takes time to learn to walk and talk, so a similar temporal process is involved in making a human person. To support these statements we would have to develop a section on Lonergan's theory of consciousness but within our own context we wish only to focus on the key element in the argument, namely, how does understanding transform experiencing into 'understood experience' or, how does present understanding transform itself into fuller understanding which in turn forms and reforms experiencings?

The problem can be formulated: are successive cycles of knowing and deciding added onto one another or do they coalesce into and constitute a fuller, more extensive unity that transforms you and your experiencing? To rephrase the question more exactly: how do concepts coalesce into propositions, and how do premises coalesce into conclusions? If these questions are answered, then, the more difficult question can be handled: how does the subject constituted through last year's knowing and deciding, coalesce and

5

contextualise himself within this year's version of self? Lonergan's answer is: insight.

Concepts do not coalesce but insights do. One can have three successive acts of understanding into the meaning of force, mass and acceleration, or one may interrelate these concepts back and forth until all three understandings cumulate into a more comprehensive view that controls the meaning of each individual concept within a single, systematic meaning. The ability of a physicist who masters concept variations in a series of different equations is understanding the same meanings in successively different contexts. This cumulation of insights can be specified as an increase in combinatory power of understanding. One grasps how concepts link to one another in all sorts of various ways, and how these combinations explain and comprehend more and more data. More questions get answered by the same concepts which, while retaining their original identity, may change in meaning as the context changes.

Take the case of the child who has just 'caught onto' and learned a new grammatical operation. He has, for example, just discovered how to 'subjunctivise' meanings, or he has learned how to change declarative expressions of meanings into subjunctive ones. This implies that he can take his present vocabulary of meanings which he has been able to express only in declarative forms and transform these declarative meanings into subjunctive expressions. Thus the context of meanings that he is able to intend has been significantly extended. Notice the child has not added any new words, rather he has learned to operate on his present context of words and restructure them with a new set of subjunctive forms.

Earlier we stressed how insights allow us to formulate, consciously and deliberately, what the insights mean; now we are focusing on a different function of insight: the ability to combine a set of concepts of 'meants' in different ways and under different conditions. This ability derives from a substantial increase in understanding which is not only able to generate new concepts but can reason and operate on prior concepts, combining them into new and unexpected phrases that will transform their meanings and yet maintain their original identity. For example, the power to add may develop into the power to subtract, multiply and divide, and with each new operation the 'combinatory power' of your intellect leaps to a higher and more impressive mastery over the domain of numbers. Such examples could be extended with more precision and detail but our present concern is only to stress that words, concepts or numbers do not change but our ways of thinking with them and structuring them do. Insights cumulate into successively higher and more impressive powers that operate through concepts over wider and wider areas of experience.

If we shift now from direct insights to reflective insights the same point can be made in a different way. Just as concepts do not coalesce but acts of understanding do, so premises do not 'dissolve' and fuse with one another but reflective insights can and do so fuse. Each successive step in a syllogism involves you in a single act of judging 'understanding', and while the successive steps expressed in the premises remain quite distinct, your act of judging the major premise cumulates into your succeeding act of judging the minor premise, and then unites into the single, comprehensive, reflective insight that grounds all the steps leading to the conclusion. Judging re-enacts the understanding, but not for the sake of understanding, but for the sake of understanding correctly. In addition to 're-understanding', judging also re-experiences, it reviews all the conditions under which the original questions emerged; this is why judging takes time, before you judge correctly you must revert to the original situation as it was 'being experienced' and as it was 'being understood and experienced'. This means that judging reverses the flow of experience and goes backward into the former experience before understanding occurred and transformed the experience. These are the activities and 'cares' that distinguish understanding and judging or direct and reflective insights.

But judging is not just a question of combining propositions and reasoning to conclusions. Just as direct insights rise to higher unities increasing their combinatory power over concepts, so reflective insights cumulate into higher and more comprehensive structures that combine more and more conclusions into what we term a framework that allows you to subsume and transform more and more experience and understanding in reaching judgements. Such cumulative reflective insights can be called a context, and within such a context you have certain powers of operating: powers of understanding and judging your experiencing in certain definite patterns. For example, the Newtonian physicist who has mastered all the operations necessary to handle with ease the various formulas and equations of mechanics, will be able to meet any objection or problem which these operations are capable of answering. These operations give him a considerable range and combination of meanings for explaining how the solar system operates. But if one were to ask him an 'Einsteinian' question, one that presupposed the ability to deal with a fourth, temporal dimension and a non-euclidian space, then he would be unable to operate on such a question at his present level of understanding. Such a question would be beyond his present range of competence, and could not be handled by just a slight increase in his 'thinking power', but would, instead, involve a major shift in his context of judging—a new and more comprehensive set of knowing operations would be needed. Or, if we substitute the term horizon for context we can say that such a question would be beyond his horizon, not his horizon of hearing or seeing but beyond his understanding and judging horizon. The Newtonian physicist does not have the operations for dealing with the 'Einsteinian experience'.

In his interesting introduction to Einsteinian physics, *One, Two, Three—Infinity*, George Gamow takes the reader through a series of imaginative gymnastics trying to break down and transform the ordinary way of imagining the physical universe, and to develop in the reader new imaginative horizons within which he can perform the acts of understanding that are necessary to understand the Einsteinian version of our universe. You can move successively from the ordinary view of the world into the Copernican, Newtonian and Einsteinian world-view, provided you can master the successive groups of operations, which form the meaning limits of these successively wider and more comprehensive horizons. The limits or vanishing points of the final horizon will not be as visible or noticeable as the previous horizons, since it is only by going beyond your present horizon that you discover that it was a horizon, i.e. that it was a limited viewpoint.

Past judgements do not pass away, or rather, the individual judgements may pass but the power to re-make them continues in *your* present, reflective, operating powers. Reflecting, then, can mean reviewing a past experience as understood and judged in the past, but it can also mean making the same judgement, reaching the same past conclusion under new conditions and circumstances and within a different horizon. Reflective insights contextualise and transform past experiences into present situations, or they can reverse themselves and make present situations operative in understanding past situations. The past is not 'over'; it can be re-presenced, re-enacted, and you perform the re-presencing and re-enacting.

Horizon, then, specifies the present limit of your world, but it includes the past experiencings, understandings and judgings that have cumulated and united to give you your present set of knowing and deciding powers with which you can shape and structure every successive, past, present or future experience that happens to fall within their structuring range. Other past or present experiences, other types of questions do not concern you and fall beyond your past, present or future concerns.

Occasionally one arrives at a moment of major decision and may consider reorienting one's entire horizon in a way that would reject most of one's past structures. More frequently, however, past insights continue to cumulate and direct our present feelings, questionings and imaginings in ways that are consistent with our present 'intendings'.

Horizon can be further clarified by contrasting how different orientations and structures of knowing may develop in one and the same person or in different people. Consider the cast of the judge and juror in a murder trial. Both operate within the same physical surroundings and within the same 'hearings and seeings', and both intend to formulate and express a correct verdict. Yet judge and juror operate from quite different sources and viewpoints which may be complementary, but more frequently are somewhat at odds. Thus, while both consider the same evidence, the horizon of each reaches into his experience in a way which limits it before it even reaches the questioning phase. So the judge operating within his legal horizon judges that certain evidence is not even admissible for questioning; he insists, for example, that this statement must be struck from the record, that article is not able to be introduced as evidence, that objection is overruled, etc. The juror, on the other hand, operating within a knowing context that has been structured by concrete, practical concerns, frequently finds judgements made within the judge's specialised legal horizon rather short-sighted and narrow. The juror does not see why legal questioning is restricted, and he may think that his own ordinary and familiar method of questioning does not impose such restrictions, although his own horizon with its practical, concrete concerns sets very definite limits to the types of questions he will entertain.

The common-sense person frequently finds questions that cannot be answered within short periods of time to be unimportant and not worth asking. Within the common-sense horizon, interest quickly disappears when the questions become technical or theoretical. Interest is what controls questioning even as questioning controls answering, and theoretical interests are beyond the knowing horizon of the ordinary man; he does not care for or value such experiences. This difference in horizon may become a conflict of interest and values, and then, you not only have two persons operating from different experiential structures but their horizons come into conflict with and oppose each other.

This completes the contextual aspect of Lonergan's theory of judging. As a final consideration in understanding his theory of judging, it would be helpful to explain the technical term that Lonergan worked out to specify his theory: the 'virtually unconditioned'.

In the logical context of knowing, there are very few conditions that have to be given before one can reach a conclusion and know its truth. We have outlined the conditions already: a human substance with an external and internal sensory apparatus, and some sort of receiving centre or switchboard for organising stimuli and forming images that the 'agent intellect' illuminates and immaterialises, and thereby generates concepts, propositions, premises and conclusions in the light of a few, natural, first principles. In such an explanation there is no concern for the linguistic, historical and cultural conditions of the person who is performing the knowing. No mention is made as to whether the subject is awake and conscious of what he is doing, nor the amount of time it takes to do it, nor the context within which he is performing, i.e. the historical, cultural setting. Lonergan, on the other hand, thinks that such cultural conditions do enter into and influence the judicial process. He insists on the conditions under which the judgement was made, i.e. was the subject awake, was he sober, intelligent, how old was he, what historical and cultural conditions were being experienced when the statement was being verified for its 'unconditionality'. Logical unconditionality is absolute and it tends to forget the conditions that surround judging except for the few we mentioned.

When Lonergan classifies judgement as 'virtually unconditioned' he intends to emphasise that human judgements may be absolute but only within very limited contexts. To specify this 'absoluteness' one must be aware of the limits within which one is operating. For example, compatriots of Columbus and Copernicus would have been completely correct in judging and asserting that the earth was flat and circled by the sun, if they had reviewed the conditions under which they were concluding. From where I am standing the earth is flat, and the sun, as I observe it, does drop behind the mountain. Similarly, Newtonian scientists did not realise they were formulating and asserting laws that also had their conditions —namely, that bodies fall at fixed velocities only when certain conditions are given but the conditions as structured in Newtonian laws are the ideal conditions of a vacuum which are not the conditions given in our physical universe but only approximate them. The Newtonian scientist would have been correct if he had stated that bodies actually fall at velocities approximating the conditions of a vacuum.

Human judgements, then, are limited, finite judgements, which means that they fall into a context of understandings and experiencings which provide conditions and set limits within which the assertion uttered is absolute. Human judgements are never simply absolute but only virtually absolute, namely, in virtue of such-and-such conditions of this person's experiencing, understanding and judging, etc. And the limits are not only applicable to judging but also pertain to reasoning, understanding and experiencing; we never simply reason but always reason about something or question something. Experience is also quite finite; it is in this place and at this particular time. As we have already pointed out, questioning itself is not open-ended in the way that the logician tends to think it is, but merely tends to be unrestrictive in the measure that we know the restrictions under which we are operating.

This completes our explanation of Lonergan's theory of knowing. In another context it would be advantageous to continue at this point with an analysis of his theory of deciding but for our purpose, we have established a sufficient context for explaining his theory of language.

II. LANGUAGE

In discussing Lonergan's theory of language we will follow the same method as we did in explaining his theory of knowing, first presenting a 'logical' theory of language, and then contrasting it with Lonergan's theory.

The logician starts his analysis of language from a grammatical perspective and classifies words as nouns, verbs, adjectives, etc.; these grammatical parts come together to form wholes; sentences, paragraphs, etc. Such structures are further analysable into more basic and parallel logical structures which lie behind and correspond to these more common grammatical structures. For example, behind and parallel to the spoken words are the inner concepts which the logician divides into subjects, copulas and predicates; these logical elements or parts combine to form the structure called proposition which is the logical counterpart of the sentence. Propositions in turn combine through syllogistic structures to produce the deductive series that form the logical counterpart of spoken or written paragraphs.

More significant for the logician than this correspondence between logical and grammatical structures is the parallel between logical and mental structures. Going behind the logical structures the logician uncovers the structure of the mind itself. As already noted, behind the concepts he finds the first mental operation: understanding. Behind the composing and dividing of propositions is the second mental act, judging; behind both is the agent intellect which illuminates and immaterialises sensible and imaginative presentations, and reasons out conclusions with the aid of a few, natural, first principles. The analysis of language, then, yields a grammatical, logical and mental or, more technically, a metaphysical, structure.

From the parallel between such structures it is easy to see how the logician works out his philosophy. Thus, if one asks the logician what words mean, the answer is obvious: they mean things. If one takes the next logical step and asks, what things, the answer is equally obvious: visible, palpable things. Language lets us point to and talk about these things, and by interrelating words in sentences we can interrelate all these things. Through nouns we can specify the 'what' or 'meant' we are referring to; with adjectives we can qualify and characterise these 'whats', with verbs we can put them in motion, and with adverbs and prepositions we can structure things spatially and temporally. Thus, the structure and events in the visible world find their parallel in the grammatical world.

The logician, however, can carry his philosophy much further and strip the grammatical universe from all its subjective and 'secondary characteristics'. He eliminates all the grammatical details of place and time, and he reduces to the single copula, is, all the variety of motions, times and moods that are expressed in verbs. Nouns are reduced to a few general classes of things, each of which is subdivided by certain specifying qualities. And so the things of the visible universe, including minerals, plants, animals and men, are reduced to their primary and more essential forms. But there is still a final stage in the logician's philosophy where he becomes the metaphysician.

The metaphysician further simplifies this logical world by converting the logical subjects into metaphysical substances; predicates turn into accidents, and all activity is converted into appropriate human, animal and plant operations which are then hierarchically arranged at various levels of being. Persons become substances with only accidental variations, who think with concepts and reason logically by the power of first principles to conclusions which are grammatically expressed in sentences with appropriate gestures and in various grammatical moods.

But are the sentences true? Are the claims people make really valid? Yes, if they correspond to real things. What a person means is things, and his meaning is true if what his mind conceives, thinks and concludes, fits in with and corresponds to the visible, multi-coloured universe.

Thus we have constructed for Lonergan a symbolic dragon which with him we can now proceed to slay. In taking up the sword it would be well to keep in mind where the dragon is most vulnerable. The logical theory of language focuses on the correspondence or supposed parallel between visible, grammatical, logical and metaphysical structures, hence it is this supposed parallel that will provide the central point of attack.

Lonergan does not deny that there is a correspondence between the visible things in the universe and the spoken or written words, a second correspondence between the way that things interrelate and the way that words interrelate within sentences, a third correspondence between grammatical and spoken structures, a fourth correspondence between grammatical and more inner and loftier logical structures, and a fifth correspondence between logical structures and our inmost personal conscious states that form the ultimate structures underlying all the previous structures. What Lonergan denies is that there is any one-to-one correspondence between these successive structures. Therefore, in place of an isometric relation he proposes an isomorphic one. However, since this contrast supposes a considerable context of meaning it would be well to attempt to communicate the insights whose content gives meaning to the term 'isomorphic structures'.

Between your interior state and its verbal or written articulation there is similarity and difference, there is continuity and discontinuity. To state just what you mean clearly and precisely may involve a wide variety of expressions many of which may not be necessary for some readers but may not be enough for others. Thus, one can take spoken or written words as providing a multiplicity of experience which you as author are making available for your listeners as a source that will stimulate or move them to a wondering phase, and, if they are alert and you are intelligent and lucky in your selection of phrases, the 'inner light' of some of their minds may flash on, and they will catch on, and under the power of this understanding they can consciously, carefully and deliberately conceive for themselves your meaning which in turn can be expressed in similar or quite different phrases and paragraphs. And so, while words and concepts may line up back to back for the logician, they do not match up so neatly with insights. Insights may 'cover' phrases, but they may also cumulate and unite so that they correspond to sentences or paragraphs. Thus a single insight if it follows from considerable questioning and mental pressuring may take much more than a paragraph to express, and it may have to be broken up into a series of smaller insights, and spaced out over several chapters hoping to lead the reader into a series of cumulating insights with the intention that the reader will end up with the central unifying insight which the author had before he started to write. The reader who does so understand frequently feels the whole thing could have been said much more simply and directly or in a quite different sequence or with a better choice of phrases or by adding and subtracting points that would have provided the reader with better clues. Once you have in your mind what the author has in his mind, then you can forget the way the author argues his case, and rephrase it, hopefully, with more significant and adequate expressions.

Another example of the discontinuity or break between written words and mental words can be seen in the reader's practice of underlining. If one picks up a book that one has underlined it can be marked off to show where merely verbal experience became 'suddenly' intelligent verbal experience; if one picks up the same book after years of dealing with the subject one finds that one's insights have shifted and particular phrases and words have picked up in meaning while others have lost significance. What determines meanings, then, is not words but insights—direct and reflective ones. And not only do insights correct themselves over a period of time so that previous underlinings now seem irrelevant or incorrect, but the author in his own attempt to express his insights finds them shifting and growing so that he has to go back, rewrite, and change the sequence of expression. The central meaning that the author intends to communicate may be quite vague in his own mind as he sits down to write. If he is writing about something quite familiar, then the changes that come while writing will be less significant and will not usually change what he intended to say but merely provide more effective ways of stating it. The written statement, then, does not contain meaning but only an experiential source of meaning which must be *made* meaningful by the reader himself by performing for himself the meaning that the author previously made for himself. Words have a meaning because they express insights and decisions; in themselves words are only multiple markings on a paper—an experience—that become meaningful when experienced intelligently.

Again, words do not mean, rather the author means and the reader means. Thus the principal critique of the logical theory of meaning and language is that the truth of a statement is not to be found principally in the sentences and conclusions expressed on the page but by knowing what the author meant or intended when he phrased his insights; by knowing what were his understanding, judgings and decidings that guided his choice of phrases, sentences and paragraphs (sentences, etc. are only instrumental acts of meaning). From this viewpoint one may discover that the author did not have too many insights, he was not sure of what he was attempting to communicate, and the phrasing and paragraphing primarily reveal a lack of meaning, a lack of understanding and judging. Meaning, then, has its source in knowing; knowing has its source in acts of feeling, understanding, judging and deciding, and these acts have their sources in the respective questions that initiate the intelligent, transforming movement that generates in the author and reader the four successive phases of knowing and deciding. Questioning also has a source, and it is within a context of prior wondering, questioning and answering which structures your present horizon of past, present, and future knowing.

Focusing again on the expression of meaning one might wonder why in writing *Insight*, Lonergan chose to express himself in the 'chapter' form, and not in the dialogue form as Plato did, or the 'disputed question' form as Aquinas did. The question can be broadened. Why doesn't Lonergan use the literary mode of expression that Camus used? Could Lonergan have expressed the meaning he intended in *Insight*, in the literary form that certain Existentialists have employed? The answers to these questions turn on a distinction between principal and instrumental acts of meaning.

Principal acts of meaning refer to understanding, judging, reasoning, reflecting, deliberating and deciding, while instrumental acts of meanings are the expressions in gesture, speech and writing which carry and embody these principal acts of meaning. Meaning, then, refers primarily to the successive phases of knowing and deciding, and secondarily to the various styles of expression, i.e. artistic, linguistic, literary and theoretical modes of discourse. This distinction has some interesting implications and will permit us to heighten our contrast between a logical theory of language and Lonergan's.

The logician tends to think that the function of language is to speak the truth about oneself or one's world, and one does this if one's spoken and grammatical structures of meaning correspond to what is meant. And obviously what one means is the visibly coloured world around us. Naturally the logician is baffled when it comes to forms of language and styles of expression like poetry and novels which do not make any truth claims, or hardly any. If the novel or the play does not follow syllogistic patterns, if it does not attempt to prove any proposition, then such styles of expression as it employs are merely subjective statements based on one's life of feelings, and such expressions vary considerably from person to person. Lonergan, on the other hand, would specify the various forms of expression as instrumental acts of meaning, and to understand their function one must relate them to the principal acts of meaning that the author intended.

The algebraist primarily intends to express his understanding, and so he stylises his structures of expression in ways that will maximise the conditions for understanding on the part of his listener or reader. He expects that his reader will experience, judge and decide but he aims to bring all these separate phases to focus their intent on understanding, i.e. he intends the reader to orient his experiencing, understanding, reasoning, judging and deciding for purposes of understanding, and only understanding. The point we are making is quite general, and so several other examples are needed to clarify our own intention.

The fellow who writes murder mysteries intends to structure his stories to communicate insights, but he presents experience to his reader in ways that will 'hide' the intended insight until the last chapter. The mystery writer expects to feed his reader with clues that will allow understanding, but he also attempts to lead his reader into misunderstandings which means that the reader will be expected to judge his misunderstanding and self-correct, etc. The logician is quick to point out that mystery thrillers do not involve understanding and judging because they do not involve *logical* understanding and logical judging. The logician cannot conceive that one would understand and judge, just for the fun of it; understanding and judging, then, for the logician, must be expressed in logical as well as grammatical form. Mystery thrillers, therefore, are from the logician's viewpoint, emotive not cognitive.

Another example is the advertiser who, like the preacher, aims and structures his message in imperative forms that will harass his audience into action. Unlike the preacher, however, most advertisers try to arrange their words in a way that will discourage questioning on the part of the listener. They intend their listeners to react to their message but they prefer them to react without understanding, and so they select their phrases and arrange their meanings in ways that tend to block and repress critical wonder.

If we now consider the instrumental meanings employed by the mathematician, Euclid, and the mystery writer, Earle Stanley Gardiner, we can answer our earlier question on Lonergan's style of expression. Both Euclid and Gardiner intend to communicate insights to their respective readers, but they are insights of quite different kinds, and are embodied in quite different patterns of expression. The difference between mathematical and literary patterns of meaning is, for our present context, like the difference between common-sense and science, and will serve to explain why

Lonergan chose to express his principal meaning in the first chapter of *Insight* with mathematical and scientific examples.

Lonergan makes it quite clear in his analysis of common-sense patterns of knowing that hunters and housewives, each of whom have their own specialised horizons of common sense, enjoy and perform any number of acts of understanding. But when you are attempting to introduce your reader into an original and very specific 'principal meaning' of understanding, then you select the phrasing and examples that will most clearly embody your meaning. And the geometer has a style of expression that features insight in clear, exact concepts. There may be difficulty in getting Euclid's point, but there is little argument as to what his point is, once you have got it—the hermeneutic literature on Euclid could fit in your watch pocket. In other words, there is no problem about Euclid's principal meaning, because of the way he instrumentalised his meaning.

Recall that logicians embody their meanings in expressions that do not take readers into account. The reader of a logical treatise has no historical or cultural background, he is completely anonymous. Aristotle constructed a logic that would be meaningful both to Egyptians and to Athenians, both to twentieth-century American professors and to second-century Romans. Euclid did the same with his geometrical forms and theorems. His geometry was intended and expressed without any particular audience in mind. In other words, when we speak of a technical, formal or abstract language we are speaking of a language that is designed without concern for the background of the reader or listener. This is why there is, relatively speaking, no hermeneutical problem in deciphering such languages.

A second point is that technical languages, while involving all four phases of meaning on the side of the author, nevertheless in their expressions tend to focus on just one phase. Thus, mathematical expressions primarily express understanding precisely as understanding. The mathematician consciously and deliberately conceives understanding by abstracting from the historical and cultural conditions under which and within which he is understanding. And, because he abstracts from these conditions, the tendency is to consider logical expressions as bloodless, skeletal presentations which are withdrawn from the much richer historical and cultural milieu of their author. Lonergan attempts to refute this pejorative meaning of abstract by insisting on the enriching side of abstraction, which is the prior insight that allows you and gives you the 'power' to abstract. Unless you have enjoyed the enriching moment of insight that Euclid tried to express, you will not understand why Euclid formulated his meaning the way he did. But if you do catch on, the bloodless, abstract expression seems like a perfect way of phrasing it.

If we shift now from mathematical examples to ones taken from the science of physics we can point out a shift of emphasis from understanding to judging. The mathematician judges; he is quite concerned about knowing whether his meanings are correct, but he is not concerned with applying his formulas to concrete, sensible events. The field within which the mathematician judges is primarily imaginative, and not sensible, whereas the physicist wants to check whether or not his formulas are verifiable under certain specifiable concrete and sensible conditions. Physicists must test their propositions, and they realise that their propositions are only hypothetical until actually proven. Thus the patterns of knowing in physics and their instrumental expressions tend to emphasise the significance and contribution that judging makes to knowing.

If we shift now to common-sense patterns associated with everyday living, we find that, in this orientation of knowing, the knower is actually not interested in knowing but in doing. Housewives and hunters understand and judge but they do so, not 'for the sake of' knowing, but for the purpose of doing. Thus common-sense expressions are not formulated as laws that explain astronomical events but as maxims and proverbs that tell you how to run a house prudently, how to catch game skilfully and how to behave morally.

Examples of the precise 'nature of' insight are best taken from mathematics, and not from common-sense modes of understanding and judging. Common sense supposes insights but it does not emphasise them in its expressions as geometry and physics do.

And so, before taking up common-sense examples which stress neither understanding nor judging, Lonergan specifies the principal acts of meaning—understanding and judging—with examples taken from mathematics and physics. Then, he proceeds to take up the common-sense pattern of knowing which orients knowing to the practical concerns of everyday living and so features the intentional life of the person as it structures behavioural patterns.

From these rather general observations the reader can anticipate how Lonergan could work out a history of different styles of expression.

One can distinguish in an author what he meant 'principally' and the 'instruments' that he chose to express this principal meaning. The reason, then, for developing new word meanings or even a whole new technical language is that what you intend to mean 'principally' demands it. Your meaning cannot be adequately formulated in the present modes of expression: they will not carry your meaning. If you use present modes of expression with their past and present meanings your reader will miss the point of your rather remarkable and original insight. Lonergan proposes, then, that the interpreter should expect that styles of expression will change in the course of history and that the *general* direction of the change will be towards more adequate ways of expressing the primordial pattern of meaning: experiencing, understanding, judging and deciding. For example, the significant difference between Plato's choice of the 'dialogue' and Aquinas' choice of the 'disputed question' style of expression is that the latter emphasises precisely and rather decisively what and how the question is to be judged. Between Plato and Aquinas changes in theoretical meanings had brought about a need for new ways of expressing meanings.

We are now in a position to answer our previous questions as to why Lonergan chose to express himself the way that he did. In the Introduction to *Insight* Lonergan makes it quite clear that his principal meaning in any one of the first ten chapters will be found in chapter eleven. His central or principal meaning in each successive chapter, then, keeps shifting, cumulating and building toward eleven. In chapter eleven Lonergan asks his reader to make a judgement on his own acts of experiencing, understanding and judging, i.e. do you, in fact, experience, do you 'insight' directly and reflectively: this is what Lonergan asks his reader. The key to the question, then, is to grasp just what these acts of experiencing, understanding and judging are, and how they combine into the one act called knowing. To specify what he means by understanding, then, Lonergan selects examples from mathematics since such expressions feature insights precisely as insights. To clarify the contribution that judging makes to knowing, Lonergan selects examples from physics and particularly from 'statistical' physics, and these expressions highlight how judging is verified under concrete conditions. By contrasting classical and statistical physics Lonergan can demonstrate that the 'classical' judgements made by physicists like Galileo and Newton tended to overlook the fact that their laws were verified under very specific conditions. Science can be absolute only in very limited contexts, and the context must be reviewed, reflected and judged. Chapters one to ten, then, provide the experiences in which one can understand and judge precisely what it is to understand and judge both in science and in the street. Thus the first ten chapters, if understood, can be understood and verified as the ground for affirming in chapter eleven that you are in fact a knower under specified, limited and concrete conditions. The ability to mean and to control the meaning that Lonergan intends in chapter eleven directly depends on the extent to which the reader has appropriated his own operations of experiencing, understanding and judging. These appropriated operations are the 'principal' meaning that Lonergan intends to present to the reader in *Insight*. His modes of expressions and his examples are the instruments he uses to carry this central meaning.

At this point it would be well to summarise our intent. Recall that our central intent was to communicate the isomorphic relation that holds between visible, spoken, grammatical, logical and cognitional structures, and on the other hand, to break down the logical view which would line up these structures in a parallel, isometric fashion. We first attacked the supposed parallel between inner and outer words, and inner and outer things, in which view knowing projects itself through concepts into propositions, and through words into sentences and through sentences into things. Now we propose to attempt to reverse this supposed correspondence by a different approach to the nature of grammar and logic.

The parallel that the logician proposes between grammatical, logical and mental structures leads one to suppose that children must already have embedded in their minds certain logical structures that back up and ground the grammatical forms with which they 'syntax' and speak their meanings. We propose a different and somewhat opposite view.

Before children learn how to add they usually learn how to count; the power to add supposes that one already has the power to number. Adding considerably increases the child's mastery over numbers, even as the successive operations of subtracting, dividing and multiplying combine to give him a unified set of powers by

6

which he can interrelate and generate such new, numerical forms as sums, products, remainders and quotients. We have already referred to this increase in power as insight increasing its own understanding and reaching a new and higher level at which it can express itself in new combinations of meaning. Using the same model one can give a similar dynamic account of the process of learning to speak.

The child usually learns how to speak before he learns to speak correctly; and so speaking precedes and conditions the performance of higher and more difficult grammatical operations. And just as each successive arithmetical operation enhances and broadens one's mathematical horizon by increasing one's combinatory powers, so each grammatical operation permits the child to increase his power and control over his expressions. For, as dividing is an operation that generates quotients according to a set of rules, so grammar is a set of personal operations enabling us to generate and structure meaning in verbal and written utterances called sentences, paragraphs, etc.

Using the same model we can now develop our argument and compare the difference between logic and grammar, and their respective structures, to the difference between arithmetic and algebra. To move from arithmetic to algebra is to master a whole new set of operations and rules which not only expand the arithmetical horizon but significantly transform it. The tendency is to suppose that both arithmetical and algebraic operations work within the domain of numbers, and so the algebraic operations merely permit us to structure our number horizon in a new and more complex way. However, this is not the case since algebra does not deal with numbers except in an indirect way, rather it deals with the relations between numbers or, more specifically, it deals with the operations by which we operate on numbers. And so acquiring the algebraic set of operations will not only enhance your arithmetic horizon; it will significantly transform it, and allow you to move into a whole new horizon of meanings. It is not our intent to explain this transformation but to point out that the shift from grammatical operations to logical ones is like—is isomorphic to—the shift from knowing how to group numbers arithmetically to knowing what arithmetic itself is.

To move from the ability to write and speak correctly to the ability to think logically involves acquiring a whole new set of operations such as defining, proposing, deducing, etc. And these logical operations do not just enhance and extend your present powers of expression and your present meaning horizon but rather transform it and permit you to generate a new horizon of meanings. We can illustrate this more concretely with the classic example of Socrates.

The Athenians all knew how to identify brave deeds, and how to differentiate the just, temperate man from his opposite, but when questioned by Socrates as to just what bravery and justice were, they found themselves tongue-tied. They were like students who knew how to add and divide, who could do what the rules commanded, but when they were asked, what is dividing, they could only state what they did when they divided. Similarly, the Athenians could only point to the brave, just man and describe what he did. The Athenians had no concepts of justice and bravery if by concept you mean a meaning that is fixed and limited by the logical operation of defining. The Athenians were able to control their meanings by all the various syntactical operations and structures that one possessed if one knew how to speak the Greek language correctly. But Socrates was attempting to introduce new controls for correcting meaning; he wanted to exercise a control over meaning that neither Greek grammar nor rhetoric would provide. Just as the arithmetician does not know what arithmetic is unless he is able to operate on arithmetical operations and thereby grasp their meaning with algebraic operations, so the Athenians could not produce the meanings that Socrates intended unless they could exercise a much higher control over meaning than grammatical or rhetorical operations permit.

A culture that has dictionaries possesses a tool that permits its people to exercise control over the various combinations of meaning that are common to their language. But a person who actually owns the power to define and deduce in nineteen different syllogistic ways is able to control grammatical and rhetorical forms of meaning, and to transform these meanings into logical structures that are isomorphic with grammatical structures. But just as the algebraist does not deal with arithmetical numbers, so logic does not deal with grammatical objects.

Logicians write and speak with concepts, plumbers write and speak with words, and there are no concepts 'in back of' the plumber's words if he does not possess the logical power of conceiving and defining just what he means by his spoken and written words. In this case the plumber lacks the 'power' to conceive and explain his understanding and judgings, which does not mean that he has no control over his expressions, but only that he has no logical control and is not interested in acquiring such controls because his knowing is controlled by doing. The plumber's method of measuring his way of knowing is pragmatic, not logical.

We cannot argue here all the details of these distinctions, but the main points are the distinction between a technical language and ordinary language, and recognition that the difference between these languages is not just one of degree but is constituted by quite different operations of understanding and judging.

Just as the algebraist can generate meanings that the arithmetician would not think of, so the logician can generate a new dimension of meaning that the grammarian would not understand if his understanding was not reoriented in the direction of, and in pursuit of, the logical ideal which the Greeks introduced into the field of meaning.

This distinction between a technical and a grammatical mode of expression is obviously artificial since ordinary language expressions involve more than just grammatical structures; but with this limitation in mind, we can clarify the contrast between grammatical and logical structures, and between technical and ordinary languages.

A further example may assist us. Consider the interpreter who has mastered the grammatical structure of the Caribou Eskimo language. Behind this structure lies a basic set of operations and if the interpreter is to operate it he will require definite powers of understanding and judging to give him the ability to recognise definite patterns of meanings in the Eskimo's speech. Suppose that in addition to possessing these powers and operations he also has the ability to think and judge logically. Such an interpreter could, then, analyse the Eskimo writings grammatically and logically, but supposedly Eskimoes have never had their Socrates, and have not bothered to acquire and master logical ways of thinking, deciding and behaving. What advantage would a logical method of interpretation of a non-logical expression serve? The logician might find that there are some actual patterns of expression that suggest syllogistic patterns with which he is familiar but more likely such structures would be quite latent or implicit. If the interpreter claimed that truth, reality and goodness can only be reached by knowing through logical operations and syllogistic structures, then, he could write off the Eskimoes' thinking as illogical, false and unreal. But Lonergan's reply would be that both grammatical operations and logical operations involve experiencing, understanding, judging and deciding but that neither set of operations equal or correspond exactly to this more basic structure of knowing and deciding. One develops a logical mode of understanding and a logical mode of expression for very precise purposes which involve an ideal orientation and concern in knowing which the Eskimoes simply do not have. This does not necessarily make the Eskimoes less intelligent, less prudent, or less responsible. It would if the logical mode of judging exhausted and perfectly expressed your powers of reflecting. But as Lonergan points out in his analysis of judging, the deductive inference pattern expressed in the formula: if A, then B, but A, therefore B, is a very general form or structure of judging, general enough to comprehend most grammatical and logical forms of judging but by no means general enough to catch the richness and subtlety of our own judicial act as it actually occurs. You can sum up and pour a whole life of understanding into a single act of judging and deciding, and no logical expression will ever capture the way you did it, and can still do it.

Similarly, neither the grammatical nor the logical operations and structures will exhaust the operations and structures of knowing and deciding. For before you were even speaking, you were wondering and meaning. Children embody meaning in their faces and fingers long before they use words to carry their understanding or meaning. Gesturing, singing and dancing can be as expressive of meaning as sounds patterned into words and sentences. And each of us responds to such meanings with wonderings of our own which we in turn incarnate quite naturally and spontaneously in our own facial and bodily gestures. We frequently communicate wordlessly and silently. Before one means with words, one is fumbling for words, and the meaning may already be in the face and gestures, which may be more meaningful than the words which follow. Speaking a word, naming an object, gives you, as Helen Keller realised, a heightened and intensified experience of your own power to intend and mean, a power to dispel the obscurity and opaqueness of a specific unknown that may be occupying your curiosity and raising your 'mental pressure'. Speaking lets you space out your meanings into smaller units that can be combined and re-combined into endless varieties and patterns of meanings. With the fixity and limits of words you specify from a large number of possible meanings 'what' you mean; from an insight you can conceive and form a meant, and then *mean* with it. 'Meants' are words you conceive, and with which you mean. Outer spoken words are from inner ones, and inner ones are from insights. Understanding and judging provide the conditions for you to mean and to pattern sounds into meaningful words.

Speaking, then, is a way of expressing or carrying meaning. Speaking lets you develop grammatical controls within the field in which you are meaning, and so gives you the power and operations to specify where you are, what time it is, how fast you are walking, where you are going, when you will get there, etc.

It is possible to put one's meaning into words or into paint but in order to express oneself in colours one must master the controls that this medium demands. There are no grammatical nor logical controls for aesthetic meanings. Even when the artist expresses himself in words he does so in ways that neither grammarians nor logicians can understand if they limit meanings to grammatical and logical structures.

There is a basic structure of meaning and it has its source in the four phases of meaning that characterise your way of being in the world. And it is this basic and primordial structure of meaning that grounds and constitutes all the various operations of controlling meaning, and all the various styles and carriers of meaning. It is to the appropriation of this foundational pattern of meaning that Lonergan invites the reader in *Insight*. Science, common sense, art, symbols, etc. are all expressions of this primordial pattern, and therefore in so far as one has 'appropriated' this structure one owns a method of meaning which will ground all the other methods including grammatical, logical, scientific, etc. And with such a method one can discover the correspondence between these various cognitional structures since each one of them is an expression of a more basic pattern of knowing that specifies how the form of logic is like the form of grammar, i.e. how logic is isomorphic with grammar.

Lonergan and Dewey on judgement

ROBERT O. JOHANN

THE purpose of this paper is to explore the relationship of the cognitional theories of John Dewey and Fr Lonergan. Its thesis— one that has come as no little surprise to me—is that despite many obvious differences in language and approach, as well as basic disagreement on many specific questions, the two men have remarkably similar views about some basic points of cognitional theory.

In order to make my point, I shall first indicate a number of elements in the position of each philosopher that would seem to put them poles apart. It was my awareness of these elements, plus my growing conviction that whatever its shortcomings, Dewey's thought was basically on the right track, that made me conceive this paper originally as an opportunity to criticise Lonergan's 'excessive intellectualism'. However, once I began to get inside Lonergan's ideas—and let me say at the outset that I do not claim more than a beginner's acquaintance with the extraordinary range and depth of his thought—I found it more and more difficult to disagree with him. Even more surprising, Lonergan's 'excessive intellectualism' began to give me insights into what Dewey was about that I had never had before. And it worked the other way too. I became progressively convinced that my new-found appreciation for Lonergan's intellectualism—it now no longer seemed so 'excessive'—had its roots in the fact that I was approaching him from Dewey's angle of vision. Parts of Lonergan that I had read years ago, and that at that time had turned me off, now made wonderful sense. Indeed, as each man passed through the filter of my own limited understanding and was translated into my own idiom, I found I could say 'yes' to both of them. On the basic matter of cognitional theory, instead of moving in different directions, they actually converge.

This, then, is what I shall try to bring out in the second part of my paper. Since the nature and role of judgement is crucial in cognitional theory, I shall try to show how Dewey and Lonergan are in basic agreement about it. Finally, since my view of each of these men is from where I stand in my own philosophical development, I would like to say a few words about where that is. This will take the form of indicating at what points Dewey and Lonergan might learn from each other, but will actually be an indication of how I have learned from (and possibly misunderstood) both. If it does nothing else, it will at least place my own biases and predilections on the table and possibly throw some light on why I say about the two men what I do.

Apparent Divergence

Some of the central themes in Dewey's thought (and some of the reasons why I was originally drawn to it in preference to that of Lonergan) are the following:

(a) *Reality is more than something to be known.* One of the things Dewey was always lashing out against was what he called the 'intellectualist fallacy', the assumed ubiquity of the purely cognitive relationship, the point-for-point identity of the real with objects of knowledge. This identification, he felt, was at the root of all the sterile dualisms that have plagued philosophy, the unbridgeable chasms between mind and body, fact and value, phenomenon and noumenon, the world of science and the world of everyday life. When knowledge is taken as that alone by which we have genuine access to the real, and when the object of knowledge *par excellence* 'is a mathematico-mechanical world (as the achievements of science have proved to be the case), then how can the objects of love, appreciation and devotion be included within true reality?'[1] The answer is that they cannot. Hence the widespread subjectivism today in the whole area of morals and regulative meanings, a subjectivism which it was one of Dewey's chief concerns to fight. And the way he did it was to drop the assumption from which the problem stems. 'The assumption of "intellectualism" goes contrary to the facts of what is primarily experienced. For things are objects to be treated, used, acted upon and with, enjoyed and suffered even more than things to be known. They are things *had* before they are things cognised.'[2] Indeed, for Dewey, things in their concrete reality can only be had, only be matters of immediate qualitative experience. What knowledge provides is not a grasp of things *in themselves* but only the *order* of their interrelationships. '. . . Physical science makes claim to disclose not the inner nature of things but only those connections of things with one another that determine outcomes and hence can be used as means. The *intrinsic* nature of events is revealed in experience as the immediately felt qualities of things.'[3]

Turning briefly now to Lonergan, we get quite a different picture. 'Being (or reality) is the objective of the pure desire to know.'[4] It is the term of the unrestricted intention that directs and structures cognitional process and it lies at the end of that process, not at its beginning. For we only *have* what we are *given*, and what we are given is the content of experience, either direct or introspective, a matter of sense or consciousness. However, 'by our senses we are given, not appearance, not reality, but data. By our consciousness, which is not an inner sense, we are given, not appearance, not reality, but data'.[5] What we can be said to *have*, therefore, is neither being nor reality but only the data from which, through the mediation of insight and rational reflection, a judgement of being can be constructed. It is only in the exercise of judgement, the culmination of the knowing process, and not otherwise, that being is attained. Thus Lonergan can define being as the 'to be known by the totality of true judgements', and that totality 'is the complete set of answers to the complete set of questions'.[6] The correlation of being with inquiry and its identification with the term of inquiry, the content of reflective understanding, could hardly be more explicit or emphatic.

(b) *Knowing is not something final and complete, but is essentially instrumental in character.* A recurrent theme in Dewey's writings is not only the primacy but also the ultimacy of gross, qualitative experience. Experience is 'primary as it is given in an uncontrolled form, ultimate as it is given in a more regulated and significant form—a form made possible by the methods and results of reflective experience'.[7] The object as known, i.e. the product of regulated inquiry, is not the thing in its existential sufficiency, but the thing as means. Objects as known are 'means of control, of enlarged use and enjoyment or ordinary things'.[8] The objects of primary (or everyday) experience and of secondary (or scientific) experience are thus not competitors. The latter are essentially intermediary, i.e. ways and means of having the former in a more secure and regulated fashion. 'When the secondary objects, the refined objects, are employed as a method or road for coming at [directly experienced things], these . . . cease to be isolated details; they get the meaning contained in a whole system of related objects; they are rendered continuous with the rest of nature and take on the import of the things they are now seen to be continuous with'.[9] This is what Dewey means by the essentially instrumental character of knowing and its products. He does not mean that a person may not pursue knowledge as an end in itself. As he remarks, 'the pursuit of knowledge is often an immediately delightful event; its attained products possess aesthetic qualities of proportion, order and symmetry but', he continues, 'these qualities do not mark off or define the characteristic and appropriate *objects* of science. The character of the object is like that of a tool, say a lever; it is an order of determination of sequential changes terminating in a foreseen consequence.'[10] Thus cognitional process, along with its products, is essentially a transitional affair between two states of direct *having*, i.e. between having things simply as given and having them as meaningful and significant, between having them haphazardly and having them in a way such that intellect is at home with them. This is not to downgrade inquiry or the knowledge in which it terminates. It is simply to insist that knowledge arises and functions within a context, that it has its meaning in terms of its bearing on that context, and that the context in question, which is the final context of all man's intentional activities and that alone in terms of which they make sense, is the inclusive affair of our everyday common life, not as known but as lived (i.e., what Dewey means by 'experience'). It is this 'context of non-cognitive but experienced subject-matter which gives what is *known* its import.'[11]

For Lonergan, however, it is quite the other way around. It is not experience which includes knowing, but knowing which includes experience. Instead of cognition being a phase (and an essential one) in the intelligent reconstruction of experience, experience itself becomes but one stage (however essential) in the construction of knowledge. Human knowing, he insists, is a dynamic structure whose functional components are experience, understanding and judgement. All three are required. 'Without [experience], there is nothing for a man to understand; and when there is nothing to be understood, there is no occurrence of understanding. [But even] the combination of the operations of sense and of understanding does not suffice . . . There must be added judging; a judging, indeed, that is based on both. For to pass judgement on what one does not understand is, not human knowing, but human arrogance. [And] to pass judgement independently of all experience is to set fact aside.'[12] Thus, whereas for Dewey, it is the place and function of knowing within experience that gives knowing its import, for Lonergan it is the place and function of experience within knowing that gives experience its import.

To be perfectly fair, Lonergan does say things, especially when he speaks about 'rational self-consciousness' as distinct from 'rational consciousness', that have implications for a theory of experience. But since, as far as I can see, this implicit position is not only more in accord with Dewey's doctrine than are his explicit statements, but also is seemingly in conflict with these same explicit statements, I shall reserve comment on it for the third part of this paper. Suffice it to say here that Lonergan, in contrast with Dewey, sees knowing as something final and complete precisely because he sees it as that by which being (or the real) is attained and the pure and disinterested desire to know (that radical intention which defines man as man) is fulfilled.

(c) *Finally* (and briefly, for much more could be said) *truth is a forward- not a backward-looking relationship*; it is not a matter of the mind's conformity with the antecedently real, but of the mind's at-homeness (correspondence) with consequent reality, i.e. with what is had as a result of its own transforming activity. At the core of Dewey's theory of inquiry is his position that knowing is not simply beholding, but is temporal and transitive. He completely rejects the notion that the process of inquiry is something purely mental, making a difference in the knower but not in the to-be-known. Thus, describing experimental inquiry—and for Dewey all genuinely scientific inquiry is experimental—he says that it has three main characteristics:

The first is the obvious one that all experimentation involves *overt* doing, the making of definite changes in the environment or in our relation to it. The second is that experiment is not a random activity but is directed by ideas which have to meet the conditions set by the need of the problem inducing the active inquiry. The third and concluding feature, in which the other two receive their full measure of meaning, is that the outcome of the directed activity is *the construction of a new empirical situation* [italics mine] in which objects are differently related to one another, and such that the consequences of directed operations form the objects that have the property of being *known*.[13]

Inquiry, therefore, involves the effective ordering of an existential situation to the end that it make sense, i.e. be actually commensurate with intelligence. 'What makes any proposition scientific', says Dewey (and here scientific is equivalent to warranted and true), 'is its power to yield understanding, insight, intellectual at-homeness, in connection with any existential state of affairs, by filling events with coherent and tested meanings.'[14]

Far then from denying the correspondence theory of truth, as is sometimes thought, Dewey insists on it. His idea of correspondence, however, is not a relationship that is pictorial and static, but one that is functional and dynamic. The relation is not like that of a photograph to its subject-matter but, in Dewey's image, more like that of a key fitting a lock.[15] The truth of a proposition is its functional correspondence to an otherwise problematic situation. It is grasped as true when it is grasped in this functional role of making sense of what would otherwise remain indeterminate and unsettled.

In this matter, I think the difference between Lonergan and Dewey is more verbal than real. Despite the fact that Lonergan explicitly rejects the idea that knowing is 'simply taking a look' and despite the fact that what he has to say about judgement fits in beautifully with Dewey's ideas on that subject (as I shall try to show), he seems content merely to define truth as correspondence without nuancing this last notion sufficiently to avoid misunderstandings. Thus, for example, when he simply says that 'all marshalling and weighing of evidence, all judging and doubting are efforts to say of what is that it is and of what is not that it is not',[16] so that truth may be defined 'as the conformity or correspondence of the subject's affirmations and negations to what is and is not',[17] one can easily get the impression that for him the subject matter of inquiry is already, antecedent to the inquiry, actually commensurate with human intelligence and that the sole function of inquiry is to construct a mental (or intentional) reproduction of what is already there. And this, as we have seen, is precisely what Dewey rejects.

Manifest Convergence

In order to bring out the basic similarity of the ways in which Lonergan and Dewey understand cognitional structure, I have chosen—because of the limits of time and space at my disposal—to focus on their respective views of judgement, and even more particularly of judgement in concrete situations. There is, of course, a much larger question that begs for attention—namely, how does each of these philosophers understand the relation between metaphysics and cognitional structure? There is more than a surface likeness between Lonergan's way of translating metaphysical statements into cognitional statements and Dewey's insistence that traditional ontological categories are forms accruing to things as a result of their subjection to critical inquiry.[18]

Dewey defines inquiry as 'the controlled or directed transformation of an indeterminate situation into one that is so determinate in its constituent distinctions and relations as to convert the elements of the original situation into a unified whole.'[19]

In this definition, what Dewey means by 'situation' is 'not a single object or event or set of objects and events' but the *contextual whole* which is man's environment and within which he has to act.[20] Precisely as a whole, it is not something known, but something had. (For knowing involves understanding, and understanding involves relating one thing to another; the whole however cannot be related to anything outside itself, but is rather that within which all distinctions and relations are instituted.) Now this whole, this situation can be 'had' by the rational agent (whose situation it is) in different ways, e.g. either as making sense or as not making sense. To speak of a situation 'had as making sense' is to speak of one in which the rational agent, who is called to act in the light of meanings, the significant connections of things with one another, is at home. It is one whose distinguishable constituents are grasped as hanging together, adding up, cohering—one, therefore, grasped as commensurate with intellect and to which intellect, accordingly, is a 'yes'. This is Dewey's 'determinate' or 'settled' situation. By contrast, the indeterminate or unsettled situation, the one had as not making sense, is the one with which intellect neither is nor can be at home. Called to deal with things in the light of their significant connections, he finds himself involved in a situation whose elements, however much 'had' in their immediacy, are not had in their relationships, are not had as hanging together, but are had precisely as indeterminate in their significance. 'Thus', Dewey remarks, 'it is of the very nature of the indeterminate situation . . . to be *questionable*',[21] and correspondingly, we might add, it is of the very nature of the determinate situation to be unquestionable. Both, for Dewey, are immediately 'had' qualitative states of affairs, the one as provoking inquiry, the other as terminating it, and inquiry itself is the intermediate process by which the one is transformed into the other.

Without going into an analysis of the 'pattern of inquiry' as Dewey sees it—suffice it to say that even in its details it bears a strong resemblance to Lonergan's analysis of cognitional structure —let us turn now specifically to judgement as concluding inquiry. Judgement, for Dewey, is 'the settled outcome of inquiry'.[22] Again, 'the final judgement arrived at is a settlement'.[23] To illustrate what he means in detail, Dewey resorts to an analysis of the settlement of a legal case, the judgement of a legal case, the judgement of a court of law, which he says is a literal instance of judgement in the sense defined.

The occurrence of a trial-at-law is equivalent to the occurrence of a problematic situation which requires settlement. There is uncertainty and dispute about what shall be done because there is conflict about the *significance* of what has taken place, even if there is agreement about what has taken place as a matter of fact—which, of course, is not always the case. The judicial settlement is the settlement of an *issue* because it decides existential conditions in their bearing upon further activities: the essence of the significance of any state of facts.[24]

To put it in the language used above, judgement is the determination of the significance of existential conditions, which conditions had up to then been indeterminate in their significance.

Now there are for Dewey, two aspects to this determination (or active settlement), one material and the other formal. As he expresses it, the matter of the final settlement or judgement is the changed situation itself,[25] the situation whose elements, as a result of the process of inquiry, are now so distinguished and related to one another as to form a unified whole and make sense for a rational agent. The formal aspect of the judgement, on the other hand, is the agent's *acceptance* of the changed situation as making sense; it is his assent to it, his 'yes' to it. Both these aspects are essential to final judgement. Without the material aspect, the newly determinate situation, there is nothing for the agent to assent to and so put an end to inquiry. Without the formal aspect, the agent's 'yes', he is still in the position of entertaining other possibilities, he is still inquiring, and the situation remains unresolved.

From Dewey's standpoint, therefore, final judgement may be defined as the rational agent's 'yes' to a situation newly (i.e. as the result of inquiry) had as determinate (or unquestionable). The 'yes' is based or grounded on the situation as now making sense, i.e. as commensurate with intelligence; the situation, on the other hand, is had as one calling for a 'yes' and precisely because it is so commensurate. The judgement is warranted precisely to the extent that it is a 'yes' given to a situation had as calling for a 'yes'.

The similarity of Lonergan's position to that of Dewey as just outlined can be shown by an analysis of what the former has to say about reflective insight into concrete situations as grounding concrete judgements of fact. Lonergan notes that 'human judgements and refusals to judge oscillate about a central mean.' If the precise locus of that divide can hardly be defined, at least there are many points on which even the rash would not venture to pronounce and many others on which even the indecisive would not doubt. What, then, he asks, 'is the general form of such certitude of ignorance and such certitude of knowledge?'[26]

Lonergan answers this question in terms of his position that knowledge is a grasp of the virtually unconditioned. Since what he says cannot be presented in summary fashion any better than he himself presents it, I shall quote the brief text in full. Such certitude of ignorance and such certitude of knowledge is had when

there occurs a reflective insight in which at once one grasps

(1) a conditioned, the prospective judgement that a given direct or introspective insight is correct,

(2) a link between the conditioned and its conditions, and this on introspective analysis proves to be that an insight is correct if it is invulnerable and it is invulnerable if there are no further questions, and

(3) the fulfilment of the condition namely, that the given insight does put an end to further, pertinent questioning and that this occurs in a mind that is alert, familiar with the concrete situation, and intellectually master of it.[27]

The language, to be sure, is different. But what is Lonergan saying here if not that a 'yes' to a situation intellectually ordered (i.e. understood) in a certain way is warranted to the extent that the situation so ordered is had as one precluding further, pertinent questioning (i.e. as itself unquestionable) and calling for a 'yes'. To give one's 'yes' to a situation before it has been so settled and determined in its significance as to preclude further questioning is to be 'rash'; to refuse one's 'yes' once the situation has been so settled is, in Lonergan's terms, to be 'indecisive'. Thus, and this is the crucial point for both Lonergan and Dewey, the matter of judgement as final—that, namely, to which the 'yes' of judgement is essentially correlative—is an immediately 'had' qualitative state of affairs, i.e. a state of affairs resulting from the very process of inquiry and had (not known) as an unquestionable basis for further intelligent activity. For as Lonergan explains in the paragraphs preceding the one quoted, the conditions for the prospective judgement are not fulfilled when it is simply a case of no further questions occurring to me. 'The mere absence of further questions in my mind can have other causes.'[28] The rashness of my temperament and my eagerness to satisfy other drives may prevent their emergence. On the other hand, 'it is too much to demand that the very possibility of further questions has to be excluded. If, in fact, there are no further questions, then, in fact, the insight is invulnerable; if, in fact, the insight is invulnerable, then, in fact, the judgement approving it will be correct.'[29]

This is what Lonergan says, and Dewey would agree. But Lonergan could have said more and, if he had, his position would be even more explicitly in line with Dewey's. For not only is the exclusion of the very possibility of further questions 'too much to demand' in the sense of not being really necessary. It is 'too much to demand' quite literally in the sense of demanding the impossible. For if knowing is a matter of warranted judgement, and if judgement is warranted to the extent that it is a 'yes' to a situation that is settled and determinate in its significance (i.e. to a situation calling for assent), then the settled (or unquestionable) character of the situation, to which the 'yes' of judgement is correlative, cannot itself be something known. It can only be something immediately experienced and, in Dewey's sense, qualitatively had. In other words, just as it is only the immediately experienced unsettledness of a situation that provokes inquiry and the temporary suspension of assent, so also it is only the immediately experienced settledness of a situation that terminates inquiry and grounds the giving of assent. This means, of course, that immediate, qualitative experience is not something occurring only at the beginning of inquiry, it also occurs at its close. Nor is its role limited (as it is in Lonergan's explicit theory of experience) to providing the data for inquiry; it also (as Dewey contends) supplies the inclusive context within which alone the process of inquiry itself has meaning and import.

That Lonergan himself is not unaware of this is suggested by his remarks (in the same section of his work from which we have already quoted) to the effect that reflective insights such as ground judgements must be seen as occurring *within* an ongoing, 'self-correcting process (that not only "tends to a limit" but that) reaches its limit in familiarity with the concrete situation and in easy mastery of it'. Lonergan calls this 'the process of learning'.[30] For Dewey, this inclusive, self-correcting process is precisely what is meant by experience. Experience is a self-correcting process, a process of learning, precisely because it is not simply had by the rational agent, but had qualitatively in ways that are proportionate and correlative to the agent's own active interventions. As Dewey never tired of saying, human experience is not simply a matter of doing nor simply a matter of undergoing (or having), but a combination of the two. It is only because man has the sort of experience he does *in connection with* his own *doings* that learning occurs. It is through immediately experiencing the qualitative results of his various dealings that these acquire significance for man, and he learns to cultivate some and avoid others. The inherent connection within the experiential process of doing and having (undergoing) is what makes it essentially self-correcting. And formal inquiry, as Lonergan and Dewey are concerned with it, is simply the thematised and systematic exploitation of this connection in the interest of a richer, more meaningful experience.

Mutual Enrichment

Now unless I have completely misunderstood either Lonergan or Dewey or both, it seems to me that each of them has something to teach the other. If it serves no other purpose, a brief statement of what this might be will at least indicate what I have learned from both and where I presently stand in relation to each.

As I remarked earlier when contrasting Dewey's theory of knowing as instrumental in character with Lonergan's conception of it as something final and complete, there are things which Lonergan says about 'rational self-consciousness' that seem to imply a theory of experience in connection with knowing that is more in accord with Dewey's own. Thus, writing on cognitional structure in the issue of *Continuum* that was devoted to his thought, Lonergan comments on the various levels of one's presence to oneself as follows:

To heighten one's presence to oneself, one does not introspect (which can only yield the subject as object); one raises the level of one's activity. If one sleeps and dreams, one is present to oneself as the frightened dreamer. If one wakes, one becomes present to oneself, not as moved but as moving, not as felt but as feeling, not as seen but as seeing. If one is puzzled and wonders and inquires, the empirical subject becomes the intellectual subject as well. If one reflects and considers the evidence, the empirical and intellectual subject becomes a rational subject, an incarnate reasonableness. If one deliberates and chooses, one has moved to the level of the rationally conscious, free, responsible subject that by his choices makes himself what he is to be and his world what it is to be.[31]

I have included this long quotation because it indicates a number of things pertinent to our theme. First of all, it is clear that these ascending levels of self-presence are not at the outset objects of knowledge or judgement but of immediate qualitative experience. Secondly, the experience of oneself as a rational subject, i.e. as a knower, which—as Lonergan is at pains to explain in the same article—is the composite experience of oneself as experiencing, understanding and judging, is not final but only a step (however essential) towards a more inclusive level of experience, that, namely, of oneself as a rational self-conscious subject, which itself is final. This does not mean, to be sure, that all these various levels of direct experience, including the final one, cannot themselves be subjected to inquiry and judgement terminating in knowledge, so that the subject not only knows (i.e. experiences himself as a knower) but knows his knowing, and not only acts responsibly (i.e. experiences himself as responsible) but knows himself as such. It does mean, however, that this knowledge too, no less than that had of other things, is not an end in itself but is for the sake of actually behaving responsibly and for having the kind of self and world that results from such behaviour. As Lonergan himself puts it later in the same article, 'authentic living *includes* objective knowing, and far more eagerly do human beings strive for the *whole* than for the part'.[32] But if this is the case, then it ought to be true for Lonergan no less than for Dewey that it is the place and function of knowing within experience (our direct doings and undergoings) that gives knowing its import, rather than the other way around. If knowing is only a part of authentic living, then it is this inclusive process of concrete living that provides the context of inquiry and knowledge, and it is their bearing on this context, precisely the sort of living they make possible, that makes inquiry and knowing meaningful activities. In my judgement, therefore, Lonergan's explicit theory of experience suffers from being elaborated wholly within the context of inquiry rather than being portrayed as itself the inclusive context within which all significant activities, including inquiry, take place and have their significance. This more comprehensive view, which his own ideas seem to call for, he might profitably borrow from Dewey.

But Dewey also has much to learn from Lonergan, especially from Lonergan's anthroplogy. The particular point I have in mind is Lonergan's conception of man as animated by a pure and disinterested desire to know. The reason why Dewey needs something like this is connected with his view of the immediately had qualitative context as precisely that which regulates the ongoing course of inquiry. In his article on qualitative thought,[33] the main point is that only the progressive and qualitative reconstruction (through the process of inquiry) of the immediately had context can give the inquiring mind the assurance it is on the right track and ultimately home. It is only the progressive transformation of the situation, initially had as unsettled, into one that is had as settled and determinate, that can guide inquiry on its way.

This, I think, is true. But I also think it can be true only if man, the inquirer, is not merely sensitive and responsive to these qualitative aspects of the situation, but is initially and innately a kind of pure appreciator of sense and meaningfulness. In other words, Dewey's qualitative context can function as a guide to inquiry only if man is animated and constituted by a kind of pure and unrestricted appreciation of objective sense, only if man is originally and natively a radical 'yes' to objective sense. For, without such an original and native orientation on the part of the inquirer, the qualitative transformation of the situation could only be a matter of indifference and not guide at all.

If, then, we take Lonergan's pure desire to know as the unrestricted desire to make objective sense—for that is what knowing as an active process comes down to—we can see it as a function of, and derivative from, the original orientation. It is precisely because man is innately a lover of sense that he feels called to say 'yes' to it when he finds it and seeks to make it where it is lacking. In this light, 'being' or 'the real', Lonergan's objective of the pure desire to know, becomes the terminal pole of man's basic orientation, of his radical intentionality. It would be defined as whatever is had, or can be had, as meaningful and significant, i.e. as making sense (which, for a number of reasons like those sketched by Lonergan, includes absolutely everything).

I think ideas such as these, although perhaps abhorrent to Dewey's temperament, are not only implied by what he actually says but need to be developed and incorporated if his own cognitional theory and doctrines stemming from it (especially his ethics) are to be complete. And my point here is that anyone interested in thus completing Dewey might profitably turn to Lonergan. Thus, in my view, each of these towering thinkers complements and reinforces the other at crucially strategic points. Or so, at least, it seems from where I stand.

The logic of framework transpositions[1]

PATRICK A. HEELAN

I. The Crisis of Classical Scientific Objectivity

Recent studies in the history of science have raised some disturbing questions about both the notion and the validity of objectivity in science. Classical scientific objectivity comprises a constellation of properties which, it is claimed, characterise genuinely scientific truths. Among those properties is that of being open to testing and inspection, in principle by all men wherever they may be and at whatever epoch of history. Secondly, there is the property of expressing what is so, independently of human interests, initiatives, bias, social circumstances and historical environments. Thirdly, there is the property of picturing an object, not as that object is related to man but as it is in itself, absolutely as it were, or as related to the rest of nature, a nature that is thought to possess an essence independent of the contingent historical meaning that man (*Dasein*) has conferred upon it. These three properties are summarised in truth-invariance relative to communities of knowers separated in space and time, and truth-invariance relative to those transformations and substitutions in the purely physical world that define the content of a scientific law or theory.

These three properties of science distinguish it from common sense and other cognitive claims. Unlike common sense or even philosophy, science is international, cosmopolitan and has, it is said, one universal language. So pervasive is this belief about the one language of science that it seems to be part of the meaning of the term 'science'—the enterprise, namely, of constructing the unique, perfectly objective and permanent description of nature. Such a view of science was supported during the first three hundred years of its existence by the classical philosophies of Bacon, Newton, Descartes, Spinoza and Kant, and has been ratified by Einstein, Heisenberg and the scientific community in general.

Recent studies of the ongoing historical character of the scientific enterprise, notably by Butterfield, Conant, Kuhn, Agassi, Feyerabend, Hanson, Sellars, Wartofsky and others, attack the assumptions of one language, continuity of meaning, and cumulative growth implied by the classical notion of science. Newer theories have displaced older ones, sometimes—as in the case of phlogiston—without even leaving a trace. Sometimes a newer theory is found to be inconsistent with the older one like Newton's Laws of Motion, which replaced Kepler's. Or a new theory like relativity mechanics may suppose a change in the meaning of the basic scientific terms used both by the new mechanics and the old it replaces. In either case, truth-invariance relative to human communities separated in space and time is abrogated. The current crisis of scientific objectivity, then, has arisen out of the need to re-examine the goal of one scientific language implied by traditional usage in the meaning of the term 'science', in the light of the historical facts of transpositions of scientific frameworks and of the process of radical criticism of frameworks now seen to have been operative in the scientific enterprise.

The crisis of scientific objectivity has been met in a variety of ways. It is claimed, for example, that there is a basic set of scientific facts (usually called 'observational facts') that remain invariant in time under changing theoretical interpretations. Such a theory does not picture the world as it is: its role is purely formal, or cybernetic, or calculational. Scientific realists, like Peirce or W. Sellars, take a different view. For them the scientific enterprise, at any moment of time, is merely tentative and provisional but is *en route* towards the goal of what has been called the 'Peircean scientific framework'. In this view, the merely phenomenal manifest framework of common sense (the Aristotelian sediment in common language) is replaced by a more and more adequate scientific framework in which alone ultimately will be expressed the true and perfect and objective description of the world: definitive science.[2]

I propose first to argue against the view that the process of continuity and growth in the history of science takes place in a domain of observational facts given immediately and indubitably in experience without the involvement of the subject (Section II). I shall then consider three ways in which successive or alternative scientific frames can be logically related (Sections III, IV and V), and finally, I shall discuss the questions raised by Sellars and Peirce with regard to the manifest and scientific image of the world (Section VI).

II. The Myth of the Given

A basic observational fact is conceived as one to which the knower contributes nothing but the recognition, immediate and indubitable, that such is the case, and the descriptive predicates themselves, it is claimed, do not involve the knower; it is further held that such a fact is invariant under changing theoretical interpretation.

To show that there are no such primordially given facts, it is sufficient to point out in the first place that there is no experience which is not an experience of a certain kind and that, consequently, the descriptive framework is antecedent to the possession of the given of human experience. A descriptive framework expresses the dimensions possessed by the cognitive expectations of a subject interrogating his experience in a certain embodied way. Bernard Lonergan in *Insight* uses the term 'heuristic structure' for the meaningful structure of inquiry that is presupposed and operative when a conceptual frame is being used.[3] Prior, then, to the conceptual frame is a heuristic structure that guides, criticises, corrects and refines the descriptive frame in time until it articulates perfectly the horizon of reality made accessible to the embodied knower through the functioning of the heuristic structure within its characteristic mode of human behaviour. There is then no object of experience that does not involve in some way the subjectivity of the knower. Whatever is given in experience is given in terms of a descriptive frame which is itself the product of a heuristic structure. It may be that certain heuristic structures are given in such a way that all men share or can be made to share in the same univocal set in which case some kinds of objects could be indubitably given. This is a supposition that has to be investigated and *prima facie* there are reasons both pro and con; but whether or not there are such and which ones are such, will be decided not by immediate inspection but only after a laborious examination. There is, then, no immediate, intuitive access to a domain of scientific facts, and consequently there are no epistemologically privileged scientific facts.

Moreover, the contrast between the observational, on the one hand, as epistemologically certain and descriptive of reality, and the theoretical, on the other hand, as tentative, provisional and not descriptive of reality, cannot any longer be sustained. Certainty is found in the use of both types of predicates, and both are used descriptively of the world. If what is observed is a motion, then whatever we understand a motion to be, whether a trajectory in a curved space-time manifold or the outcome of an Aristotelian desire, what we have observed is either a trajectory in a curved space-time manifold or the product of an Aristotelian desire. Our certainty at having observed a motion is our certainty of having observed either a trajectory in a curved space-time manifold or the product of an Aristotelian desire. The theoretical explanation of motion becomes an ingredient of our observations of motion. Observational language, in fact, becomes laden with theory. That there is in principle no aspect of observational language that is free from the intrusions of theory is the well-known theme of a certain group of authors led by Toulmin, Hanson and Feyerabend.[4] In brief, we might summarise their conclusion and ours, that *observational* and *theoretical* are not characteristics of predicates but of predications of uses of predicates: a *theoretical* use being inferential, mediate and circumspect vis-a-vis realistic intent; an *observational* use being non-inferential, immediate and realistic in intent.

III. *Progressive Development of a Tradition*

The question arises in what sense can two different frameworks describe or explain a common domain of facts? Common facts require common descriptions, common descriptions imply common meanings, and common meanings suppose one common framework. Perhaps the example of Kepler's Laws and Newton's Laws gives the clue to one possible answer.

A sufficiently complex heuristic structure can start a tradition of inquiry that manifests itself in and through a historical family of conceptual frameworks: for example, the movement to give a mathematical account of motion that started in the Middle Ages with Bradwardine and others, continued through Kepler and Newton and found its most developed expression in Einstein's general theory of relativity. The theories of motion it generated cannot be opposed and contrasted with some alleged basic descriptive account that remained historically invariant but must be opposed and contrasted with one another, for although they used the same vocabulary or linguistic tokens, and range over what is claimed to be a common domain of facts, they make different and mutually inconsistent predictions. Newton's Laws, for example, yield different results from Kepler's Laws with regard to a multi-planetary system like the Solar System, since Newton accounts for orbital perturbations through interplanetary gravitational forces but Kepler does not. Two theories, however, cannot be simultaneously held if they yield inconsistent results in a domain where the difference is significant. Thus, in the historical sequence, Newton's Laws came to be accepted in place of Kepler's as giving a correct account of planetary motion. The framework transposition exemplified is one where both frameworks are concerned with the same type of problem and involve (what appears at least to be) a common set of descriptive predicates (the kinematical variables). Everything Kepler's Laws did (in the domain of its validity) Newton's Laws did better and more accurately but not vice versa. Let L_K represent Kepler's frame and L_N Newton's frame, then let us define a logical relation called 'implication' symbolised by '$\longrightarrow$', such that in the example just discussed $L_K \rightarrow L_N$ but not necessarily vice versa: 'whatever problems can be solved in L_K can also be solved in L_N but not necessarily vice versa.' The sequence of historical frameworks L_1, L_2, etc., that constitute the development of a tradition, then, are a linearly ordered set under the implication relation '$\rightarrow$' where $L_i \rightarrow L_j$, provided i is less than or equal to j.

Taking as a model the relationship between the laws of Kepler and Newton, it appears with regard to the question when two frameworks can describe or explain a common domain of facts that an older framework is a sub-framework of a newer one that preserves the common range of facts invariant in the transposition.

IV. *Incommensurable Frameworks and Multiple Mutually Exclusive Horizons*

A different problem arises where conceptual frameworks using the same linguistic tokens, employ nevertheless incommensurable categorisations. This is the realm of conventionality in theory and observation. There can be no common domain of facts described or explained by such frameworks.

An example might be the description of geometrical relationships between things that appear as everyday objects. In ordinary language those relationships are based upon a rule of congruence (a rule for deciding when two lengths are equal) that involves measurement by transported rigid rulers. This rule of congruence gives a Euclidean space to everyday objects—the space to which we ordinarily belong and which carpenters, architects and others use in the exercise of their profession. We have in fact become so accustomed to the Euclidean character of our everyday world that we are ready to believe that God made the world to be Euclidean. But the everyday world is Euclidean only in so far as man uses a ruler or some equivalent form of length measure. Other rules of congruence exist that yield different geometrical descriptions of the world. For example, it has been shown by Rudolf Luneburg that a binocular visual comparison of lengths under standardised conditions gives a kind of visual space that turns out to be Lobachevskian (a constant curvature space of negative curvature).[5] Objectivity (in the sense of intersubjective validity) for the new spatial experience is gained by involving a sufficiently large sample of normal people in structuring their spatial affirmations in this way and teaching them to speak the language appropriate to the description of objects in visual space. That such ordering of space is in fact more than a laboratory experiment, is suggested by post-impressionist painting. In a study of Van Gogh's painting, I have postulated a close relation between the space represented and the artist's awareness of the anomalous (non-Euclidean) structure of binocular visual space, and I have proposed an explanation for the widely-recognised 'distortions' of Van Gogh's space on the mathematical principles appropriate to the new space.[6]

A mathematical analysis of the visual forms which ordinary rectilinear physical objects, like tables, chairs, floors, walls, ceilings, etc., would have in the perception of an observer habituated to constituting his space in this way can be computed from the geometrical formulas. Such an observer would notice for instance, that the floor space tilts upwards towards the horizon, that distant objects are brought forward, that nearby objects protrude towards the observer and appear in inverse perspective and that the straight lines are bent in certain predictable ways. To people habituated to a Euclidean interpretation of their perceptual experience these anomalies appear as *perceptual illusions*. Some of these illusions have been noticed in the course of experiments on human perception—for example, with points of light in a dark room; others are in common experience such as car headlights at night or the heavenly bodies in the night sky. The peculiarities I have mentioned are found represented in the pictorial space of Vincent Van Gogh's paintings and to a certain extent also in those of Paul Cézanne. These painters, who were not geometers, learned, it seems, to speak a new spatial language, a language based upon a binocular experience of length congruence. This new linguistic proposal was not an arbitrary one, if my interpretation is correct. It was rooted in a geometrisation of space by visual means, resulting in a new kind of space which seems to have replaced classical Euclidean space as a form of the real world in the linguistic usage of the two artists mentioned. So then, classical Euclidean space— the space in which we cope with practical survival problems— became presumably for Van Gogh and Cézanne a domain of mere appearances; reality for them was non-Euclidean.

Meaning, language and conceptual frameworks, then, though conventional, are not arbitrary, since they grow out of human experience. There may, however, be no way of inferring all the untapped possibilities of human experience, past, present and future, and actual experience may be the only profile of human potentialities we can concretely get to know.

One might argue that a conceptual framework must conform to some set of basic facts established as such, say, by a Supreme Intelligence, all antecedent to human experience. But unless the Supreme Intelligence is conceived of as a supremely intelligent man (contacting the world therefore through a sensitive body) its description of facts cannot in general be normative for human experience.

The example I have used of two incommensurable geometrical frameworks, Euclidean and Lobachevskian, illustrates two possible forms of the human experience of space. These two frameworks cannot, however, be combined into one description without incoherence. They are two separate incommensurable spatial descriptions and not different aspects of one thing. The root of their incommensurability lies in the fact that they are embodied in two mutually exclusive sets of heuristic behaviours.

Let me introduce some new terms and specify more exactly the meaning of some terms already used. *Heuristic structure*:[7] a heuristic structure is the anticipation of a known unknown; that is, it is the structure of systematic inquiry guided by a set of canons and embodied in a pattern of human exploratory behaviour. A heuristic structure gives meaning to the descriptive language in which the inquiry is formulated. When the form of the unknown has been explicitly sketched out, we find it lies on the circumference of a closed set of semantically linked descriptive predicates called a hermeneutical circle. *Horizon*:[8] a horizon is the set of possible objective (in the sense of intersubjective) facts attainable by and through a heuristic structure equipped with a descriptive language. (*Descriptive*) *language*: a language is the set of descriptive statements[9] which in the formal mode map the material facts belonging to a horizon. The mapping is a 'picturing' of facts in language, a 'projection' of a horizon of factual human experience onto a domain of public signs (sentences). I take a descriptive language, then, to be the open set of descriptive factual statements that can be constructed using the limited linguistic resources of a descriptive language, namely, names (or other referring expressions), descriptive or explanatory conjugates, and the logic of sentences, predicates and quantification. *Linguistic context*: the necessary and sufficient conditions subjective and objective, for the use of a descriptive language.

The two cases we have considered are the replacement of one horizon by another more adequate than the first within the same tradition of inquiry, and the co-existence of multiple though mutually exclusive horizons standing for a variety of valid projections of human experience, constituting, therefore, different and incommensurable traditions.

V. Complementary Frameworks and Complementary Horizons

A third kind of framework relation is what I shall call 'the complementarity of horizons'. The term 'complementarity' is taken from quantum mechanics and expresses that peculiar relationship discovered in quantum mechanics, for example, between the two descriptive languages of (exact) position and (exact) momentum. The term was applied by Niels Bohr to the contextual character of description in quantum mechanics: given certain conditions, position language was the appropriate one, given other conditions, momentum language was the appropriate one. The conditions that constitute the linguistic context are related to measurement. Thus the theoretical inability in quantum mechanics to measure exact position and exact momentum simultaneously makes it impossible to have one linguistic context in which both (exact) position and (exact) momentum language can be used. However, if we are willing to admit the use of inexact position and momentum predicates (the inexactitudes to be governed by Heisenberg's Indeterminacy Principle), then the complementary languages of exact position and exact momentum appear as limiting cases of a more general quantum mechanical descriptive language of inexact concepts. Complementary languages, then, are context-dependent descriptive languages which, although conditioned by mutually exclusive linguistic contexts, do not constitute incommensurable traditions, and serve, in some sense, as expressions of lower restrictive or limiting viewpoints within a higher more comprehensive viewpoint. The broader and more inclusive descriptive language of the higher viewpoint stands to the lower complementary languages in a way that will be stated more precisely and formally below.

The paradigm case of complementarity is exact position language L_A and exact momentum language L_B in quantum mechanics. Both L_A and L_B have their necessary and sufficient conditions: L_A that the quantum system be in contact with a position-measuring environment (instrument plus suitable boundary conditions); L_B that the quantum system be in contact with a momentum measuring environment. Precise position language L_A is the linguistic projection of precise position measuring contexts A; precise momentum language L_B is the linguistic projection of precise momentum measuring contexts B. Let it be noted that L_A and L_B are subsets of a broader, more inclusive quantum mechanical kinematic language $L_{A \oplus B}$ in which the space-time description of a quantum system can be formulated, even if the environment should exclude the possibilities of a precise position measurement or a precise momentum measurement.[10] Precise position language L_A, precise momentum language L_B and the language of the higher viewpoint $L_{A \oplus B}$, constitute, with suitably defined complements, what is called a non-uniquely complemented lattice of languages. Let us then define the condition under which two languages are complementary: L_A and L_B are *complementary* in $L_{A \oplus B}$ if and only if L_A, L_B and $L_{A \oplus B}$ constitute part of a non-distributive lattice of languages under a partial ordering to be defined more accurately below. What I have done here formalises, in my view, the significant element of what is meant by 'complementarity' in physics.[11]

Let us suppose that there exists a language L'_A which is a development of L_A, and L'_B which is a development of L_B, and that L_A, L_B, L'_A, L'_B, $L_{A \oplus B}$ and L_O (the common lower bound of the lattice) constitute the kind of non-uniquely complemented lattice sketched in Figure 1 below.[12]

The relationship represented by the arrow is a transitive reflexive relation and is called a 'partial ordering' or 'implication'. Whenever any two elements of the lattice, say L_X and L_Y, are in the partial ordering relation, symbolised $L_X \rightarrowtail L_Y$, then we say that L_X *implies* L_Y. Moreover, a least upper bound (l.u.b.) $L_X \oplus L_Y$, and a greatest lower bound (g.l.b.) $L_X \otimes L_Y$ of L_X and L_Y are defined in the following way: $L_X \oplus L_Y$ is the l.u.b. of L_X and L_Y if—and only if—both L_X and L_Y imply $L_X \oplus L_Y$ and $L_X \oplus L_Y$ is the lowest such element in the diagram with that property. $L_X \otimes L_Y$ is the g.l.b. of L_X and L_Y if and only if $L_X \otimes L_Y$ implies both L_X and L_Y and $L_X \otimes L_Y$ is the highest such element in the diagram with such a property. From these definitions it follows that $L_X \rightarrowtail L_Y$ if and only if $L_X = L_X \otimes L_Y$ and $L_Y = L_X \oplus L_Y$. Moreover, every element of the lattice has a complement represented by a prime with the properties such that $L_X \oplus L'_X = L_{A \oplus B}$, $L_X \otimes L'_X = L_O$, and $L''_X = L_X$. The lattice in Figure 1 is non-distributive, since

$$L_A \oplus (L'_B \otimes L_B) = L_A$$
$$(L_A \oplus L'_B) \otimes (L_A \oplus L_B) = L'_B$$
$$\text{but} \qquad\qquad L'_B \neq L_A$$

This kind of lattice differs from a Boolean lattice where the operations of sum and product are distributive.

The elements of the lattice are not descriptive kinematic sentences of quantum mechanics, but a set of six distinct descriptive quantum mechanical languages, each treated as an indivisible element of the lattice. The partial ordering (symbolised '$\rightarrowtail$') between two languages L_X and L_Y relates higher or lower viewpoints by a new form of implication, one that relates languages and not sentences: $L_X \rightarrowtail L_Y$ if and only if whatever 'can be said' in L_X 'can be said' in L_Y. The l.u.b., then, of two languages L_X and L_Y is the lowest language L_Z such that whatever 'can be said' in L_X or L_Y 'can also be said' in L_Z. This corresponds to the lowest higher viewpoint which comprises both lower viewpoints. The g.l.b. of any two languages L_X and L_Y is the highest language L_W such that whatever 'can be said' in it, 'can also be said' in L_X and L_Y. The attention of the reader is called to the fact that the phrase needs some form of commentary. What is formulated in L_X connotes the more restricted character of meanings in L_X: what is formulated in L_Y connotes the more comprehensive character of meanings in L_Y. It would appear from the above that the passage from L_X to L_Y seems not to involve strict univocity. However, since equivocity would destroy the relation of implication, what might be at issue here in the nature of implication is some form of analogy. As I am here concerned with formal structure, I shall put aside for more detailed consideration elsewhere, the problems raised by the issue of analogy.

A logic that relates languages rather than sentences I shall call 'a context logic', for each language has its unique context, the set of necessary and sufficient conditions for its valid use; thus a logic of languages is also a logic of contexts, a context logic.

The lattice of six distinct languages taken in the material mode can be re-interpreted in the formal mode as a logic for propositions in a meta-language I call 'the meta-context language'. The meta-context language describes linguistic contexts and names the languages appropriate to the context. In this meta-context language, the logical sum ('p or q') of the two sentences 'p' and 'q' is mapped on the l.u.b. of the two sentences, that is, on '$p \oplus q$'; the logical product ('p and q') is represented by the g.l.b., that is, by '$p \otimes q$'; negation ('not–p') is complementation. The partial ordering of 'p' and 'q' ('p $\rightarrow$— q') is implication. The correct locus of the non-classical logic of quantum mechanics for example, is, contrary to the received view, not in a quantum mechanical object language which is most probably subject to classical logic, but in that language I have called 'the meta-context language of quantum mechanics'.

Because of the difficulty in grasping intuitively the character of a non-distributive lattice, it may be helpful to illustrate the structural relationships by recourse to a biological example. Let us suppose a number of biological populations of the same species, where genotype distributions play a role analogous to descriptive languages. Two stable populations A and B of the same species exist in different environments isolated from one another, say by a broad impassable river. Each population has the same set of genotype but distributed according to different statistical curves G_A, say, and G_B. Let us call the set theoretical union of the two populations 'the Boolean union of the two populations' and write the corresponding distribution of genotypes $G_{A \cup B} = G_A \cup G_B$. Such a union has a minimal scientific significance, however, since it refers to two geographically separated populations with different environments and subject to different natural selection pressures. The kind of union which is of scientific interest is the union achieved when the geographical barrier between the two populations is removed, say, by building a bridge across the river, and each population is able to range over the territory of the other. In this case, new selection pressures arise, genes are exchanged and new hybrids are formed. The exchange of genes, hybridisation and natural selection work in the course of time to produce a new steady-state distribution of genotypes in the expanded stabilised population $A \oplus B$, which now occupies the whole territory. Even though presumably all the genotypes of populations A and B persist in the united stablised population $A \oplus B$, the distribution $G_A \oplus B$ is not a Boolean union of the original distributions G_A and B_B, but constitutes a l.u.b. in a non-distributive lattice involving G_A, G_B and $G_{A \oplus B}$ as elements of the partial ordering.

The extension of context logic from descriptive languages, say, to philosophical languages is also possible. Bypassing the difficult problem of defining what constitutes a philosophical language, let me simply postulate that to every coherent philosophical *corpus*, C, there is a unique philosophical language L_C. I shall suppose that there are criteria for deciding when a set of sentences constitutes a coherent philosophical *corpus*, and will consider the Aristotelian and the Platonic-Augustinian tradition as differing and subsequently synthesised in the philosophy of Aquinas. The Aristotelian would be represented by a historical sequence of philosophical languages L_{Ai} where i indicates the members of the sequence. Similarly, the Platonic-Augustinian tradition would be represented by a historical sequency L_{Bj} of philosophical languages.

Now it is the contention of Gilson, Geiger, Fabbro and others that Aquinas synthesised both of these traditions in an original way.[13] Let me try to formulate this thesis using the notions of context logic sketched out above.

Taking a scissors to the *corpus* of Aquinas' writings, let us cut out all those passages that have an Aristotelian flavour. To these, we shall add a sufficient number of passages also of the *corpus* but of a neutral character to constitute a coherent body of philosophical writings. Then this subset of the Thomistic *corpus* taken in itself apart from the rest of Thomas' writings would constitute objectively speaking and independently of the subjective intention of the author, an Aristotelian *sub-corpus* which could be artifically carved out of the same Thomistic *corpus*. Let L_A be the Aristotelian sub-language and L_B the Platonic-Augustinian sub-language of these *sub-corpora*. Then L_A and L_B are sub-languages of Thomas' unabridged philosophical language $L_{A \oplus B}$. The Gilsonian thesis would then claim that $L_A \rightarrow - L_{A \oplus B}$; and $L_B \rightarrow - L_{A \oplus B}$, where L_A and L_B are the lower viewpoints relative to $L_{A \oplus B}$, the higher viewpoint. The Gilsonian thesis, however, would make the additional claim, that Thomas created an original synthesis of the two traditions transcending both and each enriching the other with new insights. In other words, the synthesis fulfils the condition that $L_{A \oplus B} \neq L_A \cup L_B$ (that is, $L_{A \oplus B}$ is not the set theoretic union of the sentences of the original languages) since more 'can be said' in $L_{A \oplus B}$ than 'can be said' in L_A or L_B. L_A, L_B and $L_{A \oplus B}$ obey the relations of the context logic discussed above where L_A and L_B are the lower viewpoints and $L_{A \oplus B}$ is the higher viewpoint. $L_{A \oplus B}$ is then a philosophical language in equilibrium, more or less, with the critical philosophical experience of Aristotelians, Augustinians and Thomists.

Other examples of language pairs that may well fulfil the partial ordering relation of complementarity are physics and biology in relation to biophysics, mental and physical languages in relation to ordinary language, aesthetic and functional language in relation to the philosophy of value, and so on.

The relationships exemplified by complementarity are logical relationships and as such do not involve a historical or genetic ordering of the elements. Some of the examples, however, suggest that a genetic and historical relationship may in certain cases parallel the logical one; that is, the logical arrow '$\rightarrow -$' may sometimes coincide with the direction of historical evolutionary development. Indeed the fulfilment of the logical relation may even turn out to be the most reasonable criterion to judge 'true' (authentic) evolutionary development from the 'merely apparent' (or inauthentic). Just as in the biological analogue, $G_A \rightarrow - G_{A \oplus B}$, and $G_B \rightarrow - G_{A \oplus B}$, the arrow follows the passage of time in the evolu-

8

tionary biological situation, so in the Thomistic synthesis of the Aristotelian and Augustinian traditions. $L_A \rightarrow\!\!\!- L_{A\oplus B}$ and $L_B \rightarrow\!\!\!- L_{A\oplus B}$, the arrows also follow the passage of time and consequently bear an evolutionary interpretation in the history of philosophy.

The passage from two disjoint and in some respects mutually antithetical traditions to a synthesis can be described in the following way, which I should like to propose as a logical analysis of a progressive dialectical development. At time t_0, two groups of speakers representing the Aristotelian and Augustinian traditions, enter into dialogue with the disinterested desire to know. Let L_{A_0} be that member of the sequence of Aristotelian languages spoken initially by one group, and L_{B_0} be that member of the sequence of Platonic-Augustinian languages spoken initially by the other group. During the course of the subsequent dialogue, L_{A_0} comes to be replaced by L_A, and L_{B_0} by L_B (both replacements in the same tradition) in such a way that a new language $L_{A\oplus B}$ is formed satisfying the complementarity relationships: $L_A \rightarrow\!\!\!- L_{A\oplus B}$, $L_B \rightarrow\!\!\!- L_{A\oplus B}$ but $L_{A\oplus B} \neq L_A \cup L_B$. $L_{A\oplus B}$ is spoken by all—a language in which Aristotelians, Augustinians and Thomists can all share, each understanding the other while maintaining the separateness of their respective traditions. It is the non-Boolean character of the complementarity relation that guarantees that the synthesis $L_{A\oplus B}$ is richer than the antitheses L_A and L_B taken together but in mutual contextual isolation. $L_{A\oplus B}$ is the outcome of a progressive dialectical development involving two complementary traditions represented by L_{A_i} and L_{B_j}.

An illustration of progressive dialectical development in the history of science is given by the history of theories of optics. A summary of the history of optics especially useful for my purpose is given by Mario Bunge in his volume *Scientific Research II*.[14] Table 1 below is taken from that work. I have added the bottom line which assigns alphabetic symbols to the language frameworks of optical theories. The alphabetic order corresponds roughly to the order of historical appearance. Let us introduce a partial ordering relations (symbolised '$\rightarrow\!\!\!-$') of the following kind: $L_X \rightarrow\!\!\!- L_Y$ if and only if all the optical problems solved in L_X can be solved in L_Y but not necessarily vice versa. The set L_A, L_B, etc. when ordered by this relation takes the form schematised in Figure 3 of a non-distributive lattice ($L_A = L_B$, L_C, L_D, L_E, L_F)

on top of which is an incomplete non-distributive lattice (L_F, L_G, L_H, L_I, L_J, L_K, . . .) that would become complete if a synthesis could be made of L_K and L_H. Primed complements, being to some extent artificial constructions, are not represented in the figure. Moreover, besides the complementary relationships represented by the alternative paths from L_A or L_B upwards, some of the paths themselves, e.g., $L_I \rightarrow\!\!-\ L_J \rightarrow\!\!-\ L_K$, manifest the type of linear ordering characteristic of a progressive development within the same tradition (as outlined in Section III). In this example, the analogical relation 'whatever can be said in L_X can be said in L_Y' turns into the more specific 'whatever problem can be solved in L_X can be solved in L_Y'. Figure 2 illustrates the combined linear and partial orderings which characterise the transformation systems outlined in Section III and V.

The possibility of extending the notion of complementary traditions from two to three or more complementary or mutually antithetical traditions is suggested by the observation that the property of forming part of a non-uniquely complemented non-distributive lattice is not restricted to just two complementary traditions but could involve three or more. The structure of such a lattice with eight elements is represented in Figure 3 below.[15]

We are then led to the proposal of defining a progressive dialectical development as one that involves various historical traditions so ordered as to constitute a non-distributive lattice by a partial ordering of the analogical kind that can exist between traditions where the partial ordering also follow the direction of the passage of time.

VI. The Manifest and the Scientific Framework

The fourth relationship concerns the 'manifest framework' in which we describe objects by means of perceptual predicates referring to the contents of the intuitions of colour, continuous extension, solidity, etc. and scientific frameworks in which postulated and inferred entities play an explanatory role. The question I want to raise is: Which of the frameworks describes what the physical world is really like? Which of Eddington's two tables is the *real* table—the solid, continuous, coloured table or the discontinuous swarm of agitated colourless molecules?[16]

I am for the moment concerned with only two points: (i) assuming that the scientific framework describes what is really the case, does this imply that the predicates of the manifest framework are merely appearances in the sense of *phenomena*? And (ii) is it plausible that the history of scientific frameworks is the history of a movement towards the unique perfect scientific description of the physical world (towards the Peircean framework)?

(i) Concepts articulate distinctions made by a human subject within a patterned way of life, and consequently every concept relates an object, directly or indirectly, to man, who as *Dasein*, constitutes his world around him by his purposeful, exploratory activity. This purposeful exploratory activity can relate the object to the subject in either of two ways. Firstly, it may reveal an object in its direct relation to man's bodily sensibility, his needs and his purposes. This is the horizon of things-to-subjects-for-subjects— and is the home of what Lonergan calls 'experiential conjugates'.[17] Secondly, it may reveal the object in its relation to macroscopic instrumental contexts. These serve the dual purpose of being physical relata with respect to the scientific description and of producing signals which serve as a communications channel for the scientist to read. What I have just described are the scientific horizons of things-to-instruments-for-subjects, where public sign-facts describable in experiential conjugates become the media through which cognitive entry is made into the new horizon of signified scientific facts.

On this account both the experiential and the scientific frameworks yield true descriptions of what is the case, but in relation to different patterns of heuristic behaviour. Relative to the scientific horizon, the sign-fact located in the experiential framework is one of the characteristic modes under which scientific fact appears: in that sense, a sign-fact in the experiential framework is not one of the realities of the scientific horizon, but the appearance of a reality (in that horizon). It is not a mere appearance, however, since within the horizon of the experiential framework, a horizon of things-to-subjects-for-subjects, the sign-fact has its own reality.

But we might ask, are Lonergan's experiential conjugates identical with what Sellars means by *predicates of the manifest image*?[18] Sellars characterised the manifest image as the residue of Aristotelian thinking present in ordinary language. This residue takes a naïvely realistic non-relational stance, what Lonergan calls that of the 'already-out-there-now-real'. Its predicates consequently are used in actual fact as if they had not the structure of thing-to-subject conjugates, even though if Lonergan's analysis is correct, this structure should be attributed to them. This is a case where what is meant by ordinary language does not coincide with what should be meant if a correct insight into the heuristic structure of perception and other related predicates has been obtained.

To consider Sellars' argument that, since one and the same object (e.g., a table) cannot have at one and the same time the opposing characteristics of continuity and discontinuity, solidity and relative emptiness, colour and absence of colour, then if one, the scientific set, is noumenal—and this is Sellars' option—the other, the manifest set, must be phenomenal. The latter is Sellars' conclusion. The argument is based on the assumption that the only alternative to the manifest image is the scientific image. There is a third possibility, however, namely, that perceptual and other related (Aristotelian) predicates are to be understood, not as part of an already-out-there-now-real, but as part of a horizon of things-to-subjects-for-subjects. The correct opposition, then, is not between the manifest and the scientific images, but between two notions of the real: an already-out-there-now-real and the content of virtually unconditioned factual judgements formulated on the basis of experience, insight and reflexive understanding. Adopting the latter criteria of the real, both perceptual (Aristotelian) predicates and scientific predicates can be realistically and descriptively attributed. Each, moreover, as was pointed out in Section II can be used in a mediate and inferential way, that is, 'theoretically', or in an immediate and non-inferential way, that is, 'observationally'.

(ii) Finally, is it plausible that scientific description is moving towards the ideal of a unique, perfect and definitive description of the physical world?

On the one hand, the doctrine of complementary frameworks which shows how it is possible for rival frameworks to come together in a synthesis which contains each and is larger than both, renders plausible the view that the outcome of a historical dialectic between complementary scientific theories might well be cumulative, leading to successive syntheses in the sense proposed above in Section V, rather than to a discontinuous non-cumulative sequence of historical 'paradigms'. On the other hand, the discussions of Sections II and IV strongly suggest two things: the contingency of human patterns of life, and (consequently), since a human pattern of life is used to explore and so to constitute a

World, the conceptual framework we use to give meaning to a pattern of life is to some degree contingent and conventional. These considerations render implausible the claim that science, cumulative and progressive as it may be in the sense of the preceding paragraph, is moving towards a unique and definitive goal independently of the path the history of science takes to reach it.

Is scientific progress indefinite? Among the answers attempted is that of Lonergan who does not give a categorical answer to the question.[19] On the one hand, he admits there is in science always a further decimal point to be conquered in the conquering of which a framework transposition may take place. But with respect to radical theoretical revision, he makes the following statement: 'theories can be revised if there is a reviser. But to talk about revising the revisers is to enter the field of empty speculation in which the name, revision, loses its determinate meaning'. There is, then, in his view, an upper limit to revision built into the heuristic structure of human inquiry: the basic structure of human inquiry cannot itself be revised. It cannot be inferred from this that the deployment in time of the disinterested desire to know moves along a uniquely determined trajectory of evolutionary development. Lonergan's logic of scientific growth which defines growth by the relation between higher and lower viewpoints, does not restrict the higher viewpoint to the next in a predetermined succession of viewpoints. Since real novelty and creativity are not ruled out, they are a part of what a philosopher and historian of science might look for in his close acquaintance with the history of science and culture. It is consistent with Lonergan's doctrine in *Insight* that the history of science should turn out to be the creative development by man of evolutionary sequences of complementary frameworks, a view put forward and held by T. S. Kuhn and P. Feyerabend in their most recent publications.[20] Science, then, like music, would be in a certain sense a human composition; music exploiting the potentialities of a man-made sound, science exploiting the potentialities of man-made physical interactions with nature.

Perfect science, like perfect music, may not be the least upper bound of all lattices, but merely the l.u.b. of all surviving historical lattices. One might well find among the 'blind alleys' of science, or in certain esoteric theories, incommensurable traditions dropped because they were not able to be synthesised in the dominant historically developing lattice. Or one might find a variety of lattices developing historically side by side, though incommensurable in principle with one another.[21]

From the foregoing, it is clear that there are a variety of logical models at hand to understand inter-framework relationships and especially developmental transpositions between frameworks in history. The task of using these models in limited or extensive analyses has yet scarcely been begun.

TABLE I. STAGES OF OPTICS

(From M. Bunge, *Scientific Research II*, p. 47)

Typical facts and laws	Ray optics (HERO)	Hydrodynamic aether theory (DESCARTES)	Corpuscular theory (NEWTON)	Longitudinal wave theory (HUYGENS)	Transversal wave theory (FRESNEL, CAUCHY, GREEN)	Electromagnetic theory (MAXWELL)	Electromagnetic theory without aether	Electromagnetic theory with curved space	Electromagnetic theory with electron theory	Quantum electrodynamics and nonrelativistic Q.M.	Quantum electrodynamics and relativistic Q.M.
1. Rectilinear propagation	x	x	x	x	x	x	x	x	x	x	x
2. Reflection	x	x	x	x	x	x	x	x	x	x	x
3. Refraction	x	x	x	x	x	x	x	x	x	x	x
4. Extremal travel time	x	x	x	x	x	x	x	x	x	x	x
5. Dispersion	x	x	x			x	x	x	x	x	x
6. Superposition					x	x	x	x	x	x	x
7. Double refraction				x	x	x	x	x	x	x	x
8. Decrease of speed in transparent media					x	x	x	x	x	x	x
9. Diffraction				x	x	x	x	x	x	x	x
10. Interference				x	x	x	x	x	x	x	x
11. Doppler effect				x	x	x	x	x	x	x	x
12. Polarisation					x	x	x	x	x	x	x
13. Radiation pressure			x			x	x	x	x	x	x
14. Anomalous dispersion									x	x	x
15. Invariant speed light							x	x			x
16. Change of frequency in gravitational field								x			
17. Light scattering									x	x	x
18. Blackbody spectrum										x	x
19. Photoelectric effect										x	x
20. Compton effect										x	x
Alphabetic designation	L_A	L_B	L_C	L_D	L_E	L_F	L_G	L_H	L_I	L_J	L_K

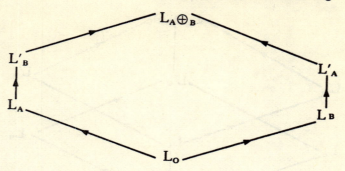

Figure 1. A non-boolean lattice for two complementary languages L_A and L_B.

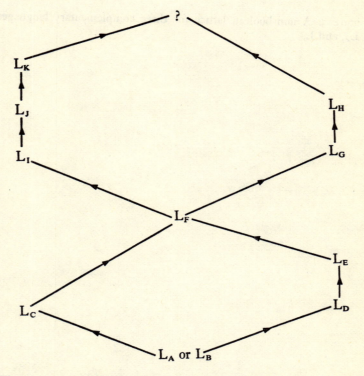

Figure 2. A combination of partial and linear orderings of optical theories in their historical sequence, taken from Table 1.

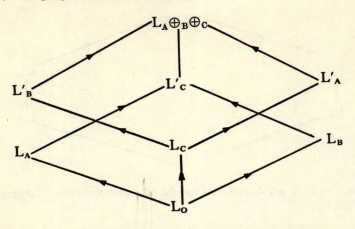

Figure 3. A non-boolean lattice for three complementary languages L_A, L_B, and L_C.

Wilhelm Dilthey's critique of historical reason and Bernard Lonergan's meta–methodology

MATTHEW LAMB

I. THE PROBLEMATIC AND ONGOING COLLABORATION

Introduction

The present paper discusses, however briefly and inadequately, two interrelated problems. First there is the more specialised problem concerning the relation between Dilthey's critique of historical reason and Lonergan's meta-methodology.[1] Frederick Crowe already suggested this relation in his account of Lonergan's earlier and later works. If '*Insight* could be defined with respect to Kant as a correction and completion of his work, so the new phase (of Lonergan's thought) can best be defined with respect to Dilthey'.[2] Certainly the interest of the later Lonergan in horizon analysis, the dimensions of meaning and historical consciousness finds a deep resonance in the life work of Dilthey. More important still, in the measure that Lonergan was able to correct and complete the critiques of Kant, to that degree he may well be in a position to carry out a critique of historical reason which Dilthey *de facto* never succeeded in completing. For, if Dilthey was convinced that the Kantian shift to the subject posed the basic philosophical problem of his day,[3] he was no less emphatic on the need to correct the Kantian critiques, especially in the light of historical consciousness.[4] In general one might say that Kant's articulation of the categories was too static, and his distinction between pure and practical reason too dependent on the noumenal thing-in-itself, for his method to handle the complexities of history.[5] Dilthey's advances in the development of a method apt for history were notable but, as we shall see, they were continually hampered by uncritical presuppositions on the connection between knowing and reality. It appears as though Dilthey was unaware of the significance of his own attentive, intelligent and critical per-

formance in seeking to explicate the related and recurrent contexts
or patterns (*Zusammenhänge*) in human historical life.

Before taking up these problems in the second section of this
paper I should like, in the present section, to reflect on the significance of this confrontation for an international congress on ongoing
collaboration. Certain insights of Dilthey into the currents of
thought in his day grasped problems whose further developments
today are demanding reflection on the foundations of collaboration,
especially in terms of the relations between scientific and historical
consciousness. The historicality of the modern scientific revolution
has to be incorporated into the foundations of collaboration. This
problematic suggests why the later Lonergan's writings are best
defined in reference to Dilthey rather than to Heidegger or
Gadamer.[6]

The idea for this congress grew out of the need experienced on
all sides today for inter-disciplinary communication and collaboration. The problems of contemporary man and his world are far
too vast and complicated for any one mind or specialised community of research effectively to handle. If the polarisations in the
political and academic world are any indication, collaboration is
not a luxury but an urgent necessity. Yet the pressure of the need
seems matched only by the difficulty in satisfying it. Communication and collaboration call for some commonly shared ground of
understanding and language, some commonly accepted norms of
verification and evaluation, if communication is to be something
more than simultaneous monologues, and collaboration more than
the juxtaposition of efforts. Two questions immediately arise. How
would it be possible to reach a normative understanding helpful
for collaboration across such widely diverging fields of specialisation as those represented at this congress: the arts, the natural and
human sciences, philosophies, theologies? Is it not hard enough
to attain some type of collaboration among the many specialisations
and trends within each of these fields themselves? Secondly, how
could norms be established for a truly *ongoing* collaboration?—
norms which positively foster creatively new developments within
the fields themselves and within the overall collaboration, norms
which would be open and critical? In a sense, these two sets of
questions are interrelated. The efforts at inter-disciplinary collaboration within specialised areas of research eventually lead to wider
and wider circles of collaboration as, for example, in the problem

and planning orientated think-tanks and general systems-analysis research centres. The many variables in such wide collaboration, along with the indeterminacy of the future, require in their turn an open ongoing type of team-work.

A Fundamental Problem

Now these questions associated with ongoing collaboration are by no means foreign to the two thinkers under consideration. Although unaware of the extent such communication and collaboration would assume in our day, Dilthey's desire to explicate a critique of historical reason might well be considered as an attempt to uncover the conditions of the possibility of such collaboration. As early as 1859 he jotted down in his diary what was to become the programme for his life work:

The Kantian investigation of the categories and Fichte's attempt at their deduction would be continued on in the work of someone who would analyse the movement of the human mind according to the unity of its world, according to the necessity of its external and internal coming-to-be, according to the similarity of its foundational goal, etc. Such realities do not have any logical necessity, nor do they originate from such; they spring rather from a primal dark drive of human nature. If they are correctly studied as an inner movement of the mind, they are concomitant with the *a priori*. They are not objectified (*vorhandene*) thought-patterns in the mind, but are the movements constituting the essence of human reason . . .
A new critique of reason must proceed from:
　1. the psychological laws and motivations from which art, religion and science simultaneously originate.
　2. the critique must analyse systems as natural products, as crystallisations the primal form of which are schemata; schemata which follow from the basic regularities studied in 1.
　3. Such a critique will not lead to scepticism, rather it will find in the necessary and general performance-patterns of the human mind the basis on which to handle sense perceptions scientifically.[7]

This short passage reflects many characteristics of Dilthey's later thought. First, there is the sweep of his interests. No aspect of human historical activity could be dismissed; the arts, the sciences and religions—all are objectifications of life and reveal something of man's historical nature.[8] Secondly, such an openness to all historical manifestations of mind is possible only in a genetic fashion[9] inasmuch as attention is turned from the products of human historical activity to the sources and emergent processes of this activity and its products. Thirdly, this switch of attention cannot be realised by logical deductivist means. The contingency of history itself precludes strict logical necessity, so that the methodological exigence calls for an explication of the pre-logical dynamisms, of the movement of mind itself in history. For the human mind is not some supra-historical entity; the essence of human reason is constituted by its activity.[10] Fourthly, the endeavour to get behind a mere induction of all the historical thought-forms or products, while at the same time not falling into a logical deductivism, seemed possible for Dilthey in terms of an exposition of the psychological laws and dynamics operative within all of the various fields of human history. This was not, however, a clear-cut psychologism. Dilthey differentiated his own position on a descriptive and analytic psychology from an explanatory-reductionist tendency in empiricist psychologisms.[11] His thought did not achieve the clarity on this matter that Husserl's did, whose work Dilthey would cite approvingly in later writings; this in part was due to Dilthey's concern with meaning and its sources as expressions of historical life rather than with the logical functions of meaning.[12] Finally, the references to sense perceptions and the 'dark drives' of human nature foreshadow a type of extroverted perceptualism from which Dilthey never succeeded in freeing his thought. His move from a psychologism to a more phenomenological descriptive analysis of the intentionality patterns or structures of conscious historical activity could not of itself remedy this defect, either in Dilthey's treatment of the objectivity of knowing or in his quest for the normative in the *Geisteswissenschaften*.[13] Dilthey did not criticise the perceptualist notion that the empirical natural sciences have their normative moment in the empirically given. Although he did not grasp that the empirical given is but one element in the process of verification[14] he saw that the empirical experience grounding the *Geisteswissenschaften* was an inner rather than an outer experience. While the natural sciences could than be content with hypothetical constructs, testing their validity against the empirically given, the *Geisteswissenschaften* could not claim that the inner experience was mediated by hypotheses.[15] We do not hypothetically experience our own self-awareness. Not wishing to follow either the idealists (who overlooked the radical conditioning of all ideas by history) or the empiricists (who could not account for the constitutive character of consciousness) Dilthey hoped to avoid both extremes by relating historical objectifications to inner experience.[16] Convinced of the irreducible nature of consciousness or inner experience, some of his arguments against reductionist psychologies anticipated the phenomenologists, and he articulated this inner experience as the basis for the *Geisteswissenschaften*. Any historical expression can be meaningful for us since it is an expression (*Ausdruck*) of an inner experience (*Erleben*) which we can understand (*Verstehen*) by re-experiencing (*Nacherleben*) the expression. The basic structures of inner experience are similar in all men.[17] Dilthey thus set about investigating the recurrent patterns in this experience and, especially in his later work, relating a vast range of historical objectifications to those patterns.[18]

I believe the achievements and shortcomings of Dilthey can be very instructive for any attempt to work out the foundations of an ongoing collaboration. Certain basic configurations of the problems he faced reveal an affinity to those now compelling us towards interdisciplinary collaboration. The consequences of historical processes which he sought to clarify and interrelate have, in the sixty years since his death, gained a momentum he scarcely could have foreseen. I should like to illustrate this by a series of configurations which indicate both the urgency of an ongoing collaboration and its possible foundations.

First, Dilthey was keenly aware of the implications of the scientific revolution initiated by the Enlightenment. In societies and cultures previous to this revolution, myth, religion or philosophy had the essential functions of providing each particular community and society with world-views and normative value-orientations which offered at least the outlines of an all-embracing meaning. In the West these functions found a classical perennial expression in Greek metaphysics, within which the natural and human sciences had a sub-altern or sub-cultural status. The hypothetical, experimental and explanatory thrust of modern science had effectively dismantled these metaphysical world-views, reducing their adherents to sub-cultural minority status, without supplying any comparable alternatives.[19] This accounts in part for the increasing alienation between science and social historical life.[20] These concerns find a reflection in several currents of contemporary thought. On the surface, there are the discussions about the two-culture problem.[21] More profoundly run the arguments on value-free science; the dilemma that, on the one hand, the sciences methodologically avoid the larger issues on the meaning of life while, on the other hand, the sciences are in need of some immanent norms if they are to avoid irrational and unscientific manipulation by economic-political group and national bias.[22]

Secondly, Dilthey saw how in the eighteenth and nineteenth centuries philosophy, demoted from its metaphysical primacy, retreated from the fields taken over by the sciences and began concentrating attention on the sciences themselves. This took the forms of a theory of theories, a logic of scientific activity, cognitional theory.[23] The tendency of philosophy as 'Besinnung über das Denken' could then take the form of a science of 'innere Erfahrung' or 'Geistes-wissenschaft'.[24] Today an analogous move is noticeable within the sciences themselves. They seem to be reaching what Boulding and McLuhan refer to as a 'break boundry'.[25] This can be approached from several angles. The insight of Heisenberg's Quantum Mechanics into the constitutive role of the human scientific observer is paralleled by the praxis of the natural sciences in the formation of new physical and chemical elements and compounds, experimentation in genetic manipulation, the cybernetical alterations in fields ranging from neurology through engineering and industrial production to information systems and aesthetics.[26] The natural scientists are beginning to look to the human sciences for the scientific norms capable of guiding the increasing transformation of nature into a man-made world.[27] For their part, the human scientists—especially the sociologists and political scientists—are developing a growing interest in the philosophy or science of the sciences.[28] Here the break boundry phenomenon is revealed in the convergence of scientific and historical consciousness,[29] the sciences enlarging the sphere of human power and control, thereby provoking reflection on the—till now—haphazard and uncontrolled overall development of the sciences themselves, and the relation of scientific activity to the other forms of human conscious activity.

Thirdly, at this point the methodological efforts of Dilthey provide interesting insights. The problem is how one could adequately handle such totalities as sciences, societies, history, in such a manner that one would move from inductive descriptions of past and present components of the whole to the functional patterns which could serve as norms to order present and future components towards the progress rather than the destruction of the whole. In the light of Hegel's efforts and failures, Dilthey realised the impossibility of any deductive thematisation of the whole.[30] On the other hand, he could not accept a purely empirical, hypothetical mediation of the whole via the individual sciences, for this approach is unable to account for the constitutive character of consciousness in such mediations and so cannot discover the vital sources of its own conscious activity, whereby it could relate the components it analyses to their historically developing totalities.[31] For Dilthey the 'Besinnung über das Denken' was part of a 'Besinnung über das Leben' that could reveal the basic functions or structures constitutive of the multiplicity of historical 'Lebenserfahrungen'.[32] Such a *Lebensphilosophie* would overcome the scepticism generated by historical consciousness by fully accepting the consequences of that consciousness;[33] it would be 'die Wissenschaft des Wirklichen'.[34]

These problematic configurations are reflected today in the growing awareness of the limitations imposed on any purely systematic mediation, even in terms of scientific activity itself. This finds expression in the discovery by Gödel of the inherent limits of any formal-deductive systematic totality; in the questions raised by the persistence of a system in General Systems Theory; in Kuhn's analysis of the limitations of paradigms in scientific discovery; in the debates between Structuralism and Marxism; as well as in those between the logical orientation of the Popper school and the hermeneutic-dialectic trend of the Frankfurt school.[35] Common (in varying degrees) to each of these discussions are the problems of totality, of its logical systematic mediation, of the sources of this mediation and their relation to other forms of mediation and evaluation in social historical life.[36]

Finally, Dilthey realised that the limitations of systematic mediation meant that any 'Besinnung über das Leben' must take into account the artistic and religious mediatory functions in society. There could be no Hegelian sublation of the artistic or religious imagination through systematic logical thought.[37] He saw a certain transcultural dimension operative within religious interiority both in terms of the ability of historical religions to assimilate divergent world-views and in terms of the transcendent

9

in Schleiermacher's dialectic.[38] His own studies on literature had convinced him of the 'typical' significance of the artistic as creator and carrier of meanings constitutive of world-views.[39] Contemporary theologies, especially in the West, indicate a massive effort at a critical confrontation of man's religious traditions with the insights and challenges of the secularist, atheistic, scientific and revolutionary hallmarks of modern reason.[40] Of paramount importance here is to what extent (if any) these religious traditions must contribute to the dialectic of survival and progressive emancipation on which the future of man depends.[41] For its part, a comparison of the contemporary artistic imagination with its historical predecessors typifies the direction of the dialectic. The art forms of previous ages conformed to certain easily recognisable patterns, e.g. Romanesque, Gothic, Baroque. The freeing of the individual imagination in Impressionism and Expressionism and the shift towards psychic automism in Surrealism has liberated the artistic and poetic imagination from set patterns. The creative variety and polyvalence of art-forms today seem to insist that pattern has value only to the extent that it reflects the process itself; meaning must somehow contain its own controls.[42]

This very brief sketch of parallel problematics in Dilthey and our present situation suggests two interrelated sets of provisional conclusions. The first infers the need for broad inter-disciplinary communication and collaboration. For the emergence of historical consciousness which Dilthey recorded in philosophy and the *Geisteswissenschaften* has today spread to almost every field of scientific activity. This demands that the constitutive character of scientific consciousness thematise and appropriate its own open and dynamic processes so that, on the one hand, the historical totality of the scientific revolution can responsibly constitute its own present and future by promoting projects germane to those processes (thereby avoiding irrational manipulation by group and national biases), and, on the other hand, so that the scientific revolution be in a position effectively to appreciate and scientifically mediate other totalities in history, such as the artistic or religious. The collaboration such a programme requires is possible only if history itself, in its spontaneous and reflective manifestations, is grounded in certain open and dynamic structures of conscious intentionality.

The second set of provisional conclusions asks to what extent

Dilthey's critique of historical reason could provide guidelines for elaborating the foundations of such a collaboration. Positively, there is his recognition of the irreducible nature of inner experience: the vital self-presence in world (conscious intentionality) which cannot be fully and completely thematised. This did not lead Dilthey to retreat into a vague romanticist hermeneutic; with the conceptual tools available to him he tried to work out the basic functional patterns or structures operative in history and the scientific mediation of history. If he did not succeed in overcoming historicism nor in articulating a dialectic based upon *Verstehen*, then a fundamental problem in our confrontation with his thought is to what extent he did not adequately criticise presuppositions common to both idealism and empiricism, to what extent the per-ceptualism he allowed the natural sciences (and which could not account for the constitutive character of those sciences discussed in the second configuration above) was simply 'interiorised' in his handling of 'innere Erfahrungen', and if this, in turn, kept him from adequately relating science to life.

Towards a Solution

The significance of a confrontation between Dilthey and Lonergan lies in the ability of meta-method to carry through the starting point of Dilthey to a thematisation of interiority, which is then capable of returning to the worlds of science and spontaneous history in a methodological manner.

Those familiar with the criticisms of Dilthey by Gadamer or Habermas might find the above formulation of the fundamental problem in Dilthey somewhat puzzling, although it bears some resemblance to theirs. With Gadamer it would criticise a Cartesian-ism in Dilthey's conception of natural science. But there is no question of maintaining that modern science in its concrete per-formance is seeking a Cartesian certitude.[43] I do not blame Dilthey for seeking to relate inner experience to scientific method. If he did not succeed, I would suggest it was for a reason analogous to why Heidegger never carried through his penetrating reflections on 'der Ursprung der Wissenschaft aus der eigentlichen Existenz'.[44] For there is more than a passing similarity between Dilthey's conception of interiority and Heidegger's notion of truth in *Sein und Zeit*.[45] In an age of fragmented consciousness, we not only need to follow the Heideggerian recall to the sources of authentic existence, but also must seek to mediate the meaning of this disclosure in all fields of human historical activity. If understanding is 'die ursprungliche Vollzugsform des Daseins, das In-der-Weltsein ist', we cannot afford to overlook its presence in the vast sweep of the modern scientific revolution.[46] Otherwise we would be only seeking an escape from the concrete dimension of contemporary being-in-the-world.

With Habermas I would admit an implicit positivism in Dilthey's notion of scientific objectivity.[47] But the criticism is made from a horizon of self-reflection where the desire to know—Habermas' 'Wille zur Vernunft als ein emanzipatorisches Erkenntnisinteresse'—is appropriated in its basic open and dynamic structures. It is these structures which ground the secondary structures operative in Habermas' transcendentals of 'Arbeit, Sprache und Herrschaft', and would allow him to articulate his own performance in inferring these structures from the concrete historical-social process, thereby avoiding the reductionist relativism he criticises in positivism, pragmatism and historicism without falling into the equally unacceptable counter-position of idealist dogmatism.[48]

I believe, then, that a confrontation of Dilthey and Lonergan is not without relevance to an understanding of later thinkers whose criticisms of Dilthey remain more or less within the limits defined by *Anschauung*, not as a figure of speech but as a stance towards the real. For the fundamental problem in Dilthey formulated above concerns the bifurcation of the phenomenal and noumenal which is by no means absent in more recent philosophers.[49] Only by overcoming this bifurcation would we be in a position to handle the long-range problems of our present historical situation. The emergence of modern science and historical consciousness in the Enlightenment, their increasing differentiations and contemporary convergence, forces into the open the need for a basic dialectic to liberate historical man from a basic alienation. As basic, the alienation and dialectic were always operative but the classical forms of culture, with their arbitrary standardisations of man and his historical activity, rendered their thematisation impossible. The dissolution of those classical forms faced modern man with the dilemma of recognising his own radical historicality and simultaneously finding the critical norms with which he could counteract the repressive irrationality in himself and society. The various forms of the phenomenon-noumenon dichotomy, in both their epistemological and their ethical implications, at bottom accepted this dilemma in trying to circumvent it.

The significance of Lonergan's meta-method, it seems to me, consists in his destruction of both the dilemma and the dichotomy through its thematisation of the basic horizon of historicality.[50] The invitation to a self-appropriation of this basic horizon is not to reach above or behind history nor autocratically to impose some pattern on it, but to discover in one's self the open and dynamic structures of one's own constituting of history and, through collaboration with others, gradually to articulate the complications, concretisations, amplifications and differentiations of this basic horizon in the historical process itself. To appropriate the empirical, intelligent, critical and existential structures of conscious intentionality is the exact opposite of boasting an Archimedean lever that would permit one immediately to pry into all problems. For such an attitude would be an inattentive, unintelligent, uncritical and irresponsible forgetfulness of one's radical historical finitude and so evince the absence of self-appropriation. The acceptance of this historicality methodologically means adopting a moving viewpoint which, through collaboration, could work out the concrete dialectics operative in all the patterns of historical experience—whether those be common-sense, artistic, political, scientific, philosophic or religious.[51] It is the appropriation of the dialectic of the basic horizon (men in their constitution of history either are or are not attentive, intelligent, critical, responsible) that breaks through the phenomenon-noumenon bifurcation. For it exposes the inadequacy of all forms of positivistic relativism without appealing to a Kantian faith in the 'intuitus originarius' of God, or to a Hegelian absolute knowledge, or a Marxian 'Träger der Geschichte'. Meta-method is not a Husserlian *Epoche* with its *Weltvernichtung* in an effort to attain transcendental subjectivity, only to be asked by Heidegger in what sense the absolute ego is also factual I; nor is it a Heideggerian *Daseinsanalyse*, the brilliance of whose ontological difference is confronted by Richardson's query of how *Da-sein* is related to ontic individuals, or Being-as-history to ontic history.[52] Meta-method attains its universality not by abstract or other variations of the noumenal-phenomenal bifurcation, nor by stripping objects of their peculiarities, but by envisaging subjects in their necessary concrete constitution of history.[53]

The basic dialectic, then, cannot do without the relative dialectics in history, any more than the basic horizon of meta-method could do without the relative horizons of particular methods.[54] Its function is rather to coordinate these relative dialectics and liberate them from the bias generated by their alienation from their own sources. This is especially necessary today as we become more aware of the interrelated complexities involved in historical-social revolutions and transformations, and the inability of the relative horizons of the past with their dialectics to cope with them. Politically the absurdity of the arms race and the threat of total nuclear destruction has ruled out national sovereignty or class warfare as ultimate criteria. This admission, however, must not fall into a resignation in the face of politico-economic colonialism and exploitation. Economically the scandal of increasing poverty in the midst of affluence and the concentration of capital reveal the limits of free enterprise theories, while the momentum towards a post-industrial society proportionately narrows the applicability of dialectics based upon ownership of the means of production.[55] In the sciences the point was made by Norbert Wiener that to live successfully in an increasingly man-made world 'we must know *as scientists* what man's nature is and what his built-in purposes are' (italics mine).[56] Dispelling the myth of the ivory tower and value-free science is not enough. A revolution within scientific consciousness whereby it would explanatorily appropriate the trans-cultural sources of its own historical activity is needed so that its constitutive re-shaping of nature and man be guided critically and responsibly towards goals consonant with those sources, i.e., towards the humanisation and education of society rather than its mechanisation and obfuscation.[57] These dialectical problems are reflected on the level of philosophy where, on the one hand, the growing recognition of a tyranny in tolerance and a new irrationalism under the guise of pluralism is matched, on the other, by an equal abhorrence of any restriction of freedom or arbitrary imposition of particular systems. In terms of meta-science the same problem occurs in the recognition of the limits of logical systematic analysis and, at the same time, a reaction against vague unverifiable appeals to the pre-logical.[58] Unless I am mistaken, these political, economic, scientific and philosophical dilemmas signal the relevancy of meta-method whose basic dialectic is grounded in the open and dynamic sources leading every man to desire and claim a measure of attentiveness, intelligence, reasonableness and responsibility in his constitution of history—whether the latter be in the realm of common sense, politics, economics, science or philosophy. For Lonergan the *fundamental alienation* of man is from these sources of his own historicality.

Hence the fundamental problem mentioned concerning Dilthey's conception of knowledge and history is by no means unrelated to an explication of adequate foundations for ongoing collaboration. From the *Wirkungsgeschichte* of Dilthey's thought we know that he did not establish such foundations, although his efforts at grounding the *Geisteswissenschaften* intended this. It will be argued in this paper that his failure did not come from his *desire* for scientific objectivity nor from his *attempt* to relate this objectivity with the certainty of inner experience—as Gadamer maintains[59]— but from his uncritical conception of this *Lebensgewissheit* as the mere givenness of self-presence. It is not that Dilthey cast doubt upon all previous traditions but that he failed to criticise the notion of interiority as irreducibly 'vorstellendfühlend-wollend' which he simply took over from his tradition. Thus one might say that Dilthey did not have enough of the Enlightenment's 'Vorur- teile gegen Vorurteile' and, paradoxically that it was this lack which contributed to his failure to overcome historicism.

Since such an interpretation of Dilthey is not quite in vogue I have had to give a rather long summary of the main features of his critique of historical reason, documented with copious footnotes. It is important that the positive aspects of Dilthey's approach be not overlooked simply because of his inability to carry through his intention of reconciling scientific and historical consciousness. The section on Lonergan's meta-method will then be very short, indicating how his notion of interiority embraces both the spon- taneity of common sense and the methodical quest for scientific objectivity. The destruction of the phenomenon-noumenon bifur- cation will be briefly treated, along with some suggestions on how one might structure certain areas of collaboration in the light of the foundations he provides.

II. HISTORICALITY AND METHOD

The following presentation makes no pretence to completeness. Both the limits of this paper and the unfinished status of Dilthey's and Lonergan's thought on the subject make any such claim quixotic. The first part will treat certain main themes in Dilthey's critique of historical reason, hoping to give at least an outline of its structure. The second will discuss certain key aspects of Lonergan's meta-method, indicating their divergence from Dilthey's position. The inevitable lacunae in the second part will, no doubt, be filled by other contributors to this volume.

A. *Dilthey's Critique of Historical Reason: the Starting Point*

Dilthey saw the central task of his generation as the confrontation of empiric scientific consciousness and historical consciousness. The latter had broken the last chains of metaphysical or religious absolutes which the former had not already destroyed. Man was free. But the 'kraftlose Subjektivität' of Romanticism had shown that the relativity of historical consciousness must discover its universal grounds if man could, on the strength of his past, recognise the real norms for his progress into the future.[60] Scientific consciousness was not degraded. Yet he saw that the momentum and clarity of method in the natural sciences was not matched by the *Geisteswissenschaften*, a lack of clarity that could be traced to the latter's historical development.[61] So long as the human sciences merely copied the natural sciences they could not fully handle what they should *if they were to be empirical*, i.e., if they were to deal adequately with the *experience* present in any human historical reality.[62] 'Alle Wissenschaft ist Erfahrungswissenschaft'.[63]

Dilthey never had a fixed expression for the experience central to the human sciences and history. The experience was awareness (*Bewusstheit*), consciousness (*Bewusstsein*), self-presence (*Selbigkeit*), interiority (*Innerlichkeit*), mental fact (*geistige Tatsache*), spontaneity (*Lebendigkeit*); in his earlier writing it is usually referred to as inner experience (*innere Erfahrung*), while in the later the term, lived experience (*Erleben*), is more frequent.[64] Without this inner presence of self (*Innewerden, Für-michdasein eines Zustandes*) there could be no history, no science, no art, no religion.[65] This is historical life (*Leben*) whose spontaneity (*Lebendigkeit*) is historicality (*Geschichtlichkeit*).[66]

Philosophy in its historical forms had not sufficiently grounded itself on this 'ganze, volle, unverstümmelte Erfahrung'.[67] Yet this was the source of all philosophies, so that Dilthey's grounding of the human sciences was tantamount to a philosophy of philosophies.[68] And since historicality embraces all historical reality, such a philosophy would be the science of reality.[69] But do not the natural sciences also know reality? The critique of historical reason, then, should try to establish the relation between the natural and human sciences, elaborate the structures of its inner experience, ground the presuppositions of this elaboration and, finally, infer the categories and methods consonant with the structures of inner experience. I shall sketch each of these respectively, adding a section on the unresolved dilemmas in Dilthey's position.

The Natural and Human Sciences

For the natural sciences the empirical method of observation and hypothesis formation found their verification, their relation to reality, in the external experiences of the outer world.[70] Dilthey wavered in his criticism of the Kantian thing-in-itself and there are statements, such as the following, which imply a capitulation to the noumenon-phenomenon bifurcation:

A truth of the external object as a correspondence of the image with a reality does not exist, for the latter reality is not given in any consciousness and so escapes any comparison. How an object appears apart from any consciousness cannot be known.[71]

Dilthey holds that there is only one generic experience differentiated by its direction into inner and outer.[72] The natural scientist's object is always mediated by some type of sense perception: 'An object independent from the self is present to us only through the senses. Thus only sense impressions can be joined into an object.' For Dilthey 'the indispensable correlate of the object is one's own self'.[73] There is, then, a priority of inner experience, though the natural scientist need not reflect upon this in his actual performance.[74] Dilthey was not about to follow Kant's notion of this priority as that of transcendental apperception. Kant's refutation of idealism tried to show how inner experience is possible because of outer experience,[75] which coincided with the necessary relation of empirical consciousness to transcendental consciousness, or consciousness of self as originating apperception and prior to all experience.[76] Thus for Kant the 'Ich, das denkt' and the 'Ich, das sich selbst anschaut' is similar to the relation we have to any object of intuition and inner perception, so that the inner perception knows the subject as appearance and not 'an sich'.[77]

Dilthey's reasons for rejecting the Kantian critique might be reduced to two. First, it did not correspond to either the anticipations of the natural scientists or to the convictions of common sense. Secondly, and more profoundly, it failed to grasp the unmediated reality of inner experience. Kant's *a priori* is 'rigid and dead' because the real conditions and presuppositions of consciousness must account for historical experience.[78] Now inner experience, the self-presence interior to all and any historical activity, is immediately *real* and certainly *there*.[79] It is this inner fact which introduces the difference between natural and human sciences. In both scientific realms are to be found methods of comparison, analysis, explanatory construction; in both, hypothesis formation plays an important role.[80] The natural scientist classifies and compares the objects he experiences, he analyses their various components; in doing this he is *experiencing* the reality of the objects, they act on him in terms of impression and resistance not originating in his inner experience.[81] This is what grounds the consciousness of the reality of the outer world.[82] When the scientist moves on to explanatory constructions on the cause-effect relations between objects he is involved in *Denkzusamme-hänge* that cannot exceed the status of the hypothetical.[83] For this is to move beyond the experience of reality: 'Leaving the domain of experience, one has only thought concepts to deal with—not with reality itself'.[84] The extrorsive movement of the natural sciences away from experience implies that they cannot know the reality of the objects in themselves.

The reality the human sciences are concerned with is quite otherwise. In so far as these sciences merely take over the explanatory-constructive methods of the natural sciences they lack the proper control for the verification of their hypothetical constructions.[85] Historical-social realities are expressions of human interiority or historicality.[86] The direction of the human sciences must, therefore, be introrsive. The 'objective reality' of these sciences is not to be attained by constructive-hypothetical-explanatory methods but by descriptive-comparative-analytic ones.[87] In grounding the human sciences one is not going behind inner experience or historical life for 'Leben erfasst hier Leben'; Kant's treatment of this inner experience or *Leben* as mere appearance was a 'contradictio in adjecto'.[88] Just as man experiences the certainty of his own self-presence, so the reality of historical life is experienced (*erlebt*) and understood (*verstanden*) rather than explained (*erklärt*).[89] The task, then, is a *Selbstbesinnung* that is at once psychological and historical, that would proceed to describe and analyse the functional relationships and structures operative in individuals (*Lebenseinheiten*) and how the larger acquired patterns or contexts (*erworbene Zusammehänge*) are related to, and differentiate, those structures.[90] There is a basic circular character in this procedure: the historicality of the individual leads to an understanding of the larger contexts of history and these in turn lead to a fuller grasp of the individual.[91] In this circle there are many hypothetical components, but in so far as the descriptive-analytic elaboration of inner experience adequately represents the historicality of this interiority it has secured a certain basis in this inner experience itself.[92] As the word 'Selbstbesinnung' indicates, the descriptive-analytic elaboration is not primarily a purely logical exercise at all; like the elaborated, the elaboration must be experienced and understood.

The difference between the natural and human sciences parallels that between outer and inner experience. The former are extrorsive seeking correlations in nature, the latter are introrsive seeking the correlations, meanings, values, goals, constitutive of man and all human historical reality.[93]

Recurrent Introrsive Structures (*Erleben*)

If the reality of the outer world can be experienced in the complex interactions of impression-resistance,[94] still the reality itself cannot be certainly known.

It is just the opposite with whatever I experience in myself; as a fact of consciousness it is there for me because I have become it interiorly. A fact of consciousness is nothing else than that which I innerly experience. Our hoping and acting, our wishing and willing: this inner world is as such its own reality . . . these mental facts are as reality there and enjoy the full status of the real.[95]

This is important for grasping the nature of the self-reflection needed to thematise properly the reality-itself of inner experience. The inner perception of this experience does not objectify the experience:

Every external perception rests on the distinction of the perceiving subject from the perceived object. On the contrary, every inner perception is primarily nothing else than the inner awareness of a state or happening. A state exists for me in so far as it is conscious. When I feel sad, the feeling of sadness is not my object of perception; rather, in so far as I am conscious in this state or condition, it exists for me as a conscious state. I become it interiorly.[96]

Thus the observation which is to elaborate the inner recurrent structures of interiority (*seelischen Strukturzusammehänge*) is aimed at a heightening of awareness (*verstärkte Erregung der Bewusstheit*).[97] Dilthey is concerned to have the reader experience (*erleben*) his descriptions of the inner structures. Space does not permit an adequate summary of this procedure. In Figure One I have outlined the main functions in the basic structures and the interested reader can refer to the sources.

The fundamental correlation is that between 'Selbst und Aussenwelt'.[98] Dilthey had studied the action-reaction (stimuli-response, input-output) theories and remarked on the growing complexity of interiority (the functional processes between stimulus and response) as one ascended from lower to higher animal forms.[99] But the biological and neurological studies are merely helpful, not central, to his descriptive-analytic elaboration of the 'status conscientiae' in man.[100] From his teacher, F. A. Trendelenburg, Dilthey took over the classic distinctions of interiority (*Seelenleben*) in terms of cognitive, emotive and volitional faculties. But even more than Trendelenburg, Dilthey dropped the notion of faculties and transformed them into dynamically interrelated functional structures.[101] These three main functions explicate the totality of interiority (at least in generic fashion) and all human activity 'even in the realm of intelligence, must be related to the totality of interiority as the performance of willing-feeling-imagining men'.[102] Because 'This totality is life' one can assert that reality-as-such is related to it.[103]

In Figure One I have tried to present schematically the more important related and recurrent functions and structures according to Dilthey. He had studied the physiology of the spinal cord and brain but I have reduced this to a mere indication of the sensory-motor systems.[104] The many two-headed arrows indicate the continual complex interplay between the three spheres of imagining (cognitive), feeling, willing. The interplay is presented as circular by Dilthey. He saw the difficulties in relating the cognitive and volitional structures and attempted a solution through the mediation of the emotive.[105] This may be accounted for in part from Dilthey's recognition that the awareness in the feeling of sorrow, etc., is not to make the feeling into an object—an insight of capital importance for his notion of inner experience.[106] 'A bundle of instincts and feelings; that is the centre of our inner structure.'[107] The thought processes as elementary logical operations make possible a certain self-determination which, through distinct valuations and volitional purposes, liberates man from the tyranny of stimuli.[108]

The upper section of Figure One schematises the main developmental structures of interiority, the functions present in its articulation into the acquired patterns (*erworbene Zusammehänge*) constituting individuality.[109] Physical development, environment and, especially, the socio-cultural differences of history (*geistige Welt*) are the outer conditions leading to different constructions of reality, different ideals, values, purposes in the myriad articulations of interiority.[110] This is especially seen in the finalistic selectivity (*Zweckmässigkeit*) whereby different individuals go about realising both subjective (*Lebensfülle, Trieberfüllung, Glück*) and objective (*Selbst- und Arterhaltung*) purposes. [111]

Each of these structures and functions is realised differently in different individuals, societies, cultures. But the variety of realisations does not lead to a sublation of its own presuppositions; history does not sublate the basic structure of historicality.[112] If men were to cease being cognitive-emotive-volitional, there would be no history. Because the basic structures are both experienced and of this inner experience they share the latter's certainty and universality.[113] In one stroke, so to speak, they ground both the relativity of historical consciousness and the universality of scientific consciousness. Historicality implies a certain unity-indifference: the basic structures of interiority in their realisation constitute individuality: 'at the same time, however, they unite the individuals with other human beings'.[114] History does not sublate a certain fundamental similarity between men;[115] if there were a total heterogeneity there would be no possibility of any understanding at all.[116]

The Experience of Interiority and its Representation (*Ausdruck*)

In the grounding of the human sciences in a descriptive-analytic psychology the inner experience is self-mediating. From 1900 until his death in 1911 it was this self-mediation that especially interested Dilthey. His psychological and historical *Selbstbesinnung* leads to a philosophical one as 'a consciousness concerned with every instance of consciousness, a knowledge related to all knowing'.[117] If self-presence in its spontaneous historicality is not an awareness of the subject-as-object but as subject,[118] then how would a method based on the self-mediatory subject-as-subject attain objective knowledge? For Dilthey confessed both his own personal desire and that of the human sciences in general to attain 'an objective knowledge of the interrelationship of human experiences in the human-historical-social world'.[119] He had claimed, against Kant, that we do *experience* the reality of the external world through the emotive and volitional functions of interiority. He tended to agree with Kant in so far as the more complex cognitive functions are able to know the object as a reality-in-itself only hypothetically. But the reality-in-itself which the human sciences seek to know is within inner experience, and so Dilthey had to explain how the cognitive functions attain an objectively valid knowledge of this inner reality. He did this by working out the notions of objective comprehension and possession, relating them to the basic structures of interiority.

In Figure Two I have schematised these notions. Here I shall limit myself to discussing some important aspects of objective comprehension as mental (*psychisch*).

Objective mental comprehension is a unity of diverse operations (attention to mental facts, observation of them, relating them to their conceptual contexts, judging this relation) aimed at grasping cognitively the experiences.[120] This experience is inexhaustibly varied and complex, as history demonstrates. Dilthey was extremely cautious on the subject of an objective knowledge; he saw clearly the mistakes of Hegel in trying totally to mediate historical life conceptually.[121] This historian or philosopher will never know 'the essence of life'; there would always be 'the inexhaustibility of experience'.[122] Yet 'the mind must be capable of achieving by itself a grounded knowledge', and such a self-mediation should be understood as systematic knowledge representing the myriad aspects of historical life. There is no *one* super-science of history.[123] The many scientific efforts at understanding build a 'second-order world of mind', a world of theory, which strives to represent the world of spontaneous history as adequately as possible.[124] The notion of representation guarantees that the normative would not be in the mediation but in the self, not in the concepts and judgements of theory but in inner experience. A fundamental error in all metaphysical systems, Hegel's included, was to maintain that their worlds of theory had an objectivity independent of spontaneous history (*Lebendigkeit*).[125]

Dilthey's cognitional theoretical grounding of the human sciences, then, did not have its starting point and norm within the world of theory—as Kant's did in terms of the natural sciences and mathematics—but in the spontaneous historical world.[126] The human sciences themselves sprang from the praxis of life, they are a complex of historical and systematic contexts, so that there is a continuous interaction between 'Erlebnis und Begriffe'.[127]

Concepts and general judgements mediate historical events and the comprehension of these events as a context. Such concepts and judgements arise first of all out of the praxis of life. However, the gradual progress in the understanding of the contexts of history becomes dependent upon the development of those sciences analysing the individual contexts which, as cultural systems, are spread throughout the course of history . . . Finally, historical understanding and the systematic Geisteswissenschaften are not only grounded on conclusions drawn from the facts of historical-social life, but they also presuppose certain insights into the development of interiority or consciousness life.[128]

The key to the self-mediation of the basic structures of interiority lies, therefore, in determining how the mediating concepts and judgements function as representations, first within spontaneous historical life and then in reference to an objective comprehension of interiority.

The experience of comprehension (*Auffassungserlebnis*) is a structural unity through the relations of its components among themselves and to their objects. Elementary understanding grasps *what* someone is experiencing in his expressions; spontaneous interiority achieves a partial transcendence in its expressions, an objectifying of itself, especially in linguistic expressions.[129] In this spontaneous knowing we are not aware of the acts themselves but of their contents which determine the object.[130] The latter does not change as the various acts bring its various aspects to consciousness: 'without the object having to undergo change, our awareness as the manner in which the object is present to us changes, when we move from an intuition to a memory to a judgement on the object'.[131] This accounts for the structural unity among the representative acts, also proving the normative element as 'Angeschaut oder Erlebt'.[132] The reality itself of the object is intuitively related to the subject in true judgements. Judgements do not grasp the thing itself but representatively determine its essence.[133] 'Die Sache selbst' is 'intuitiv gegeben' and the representative functions of concepts and judgements are not clearly distinguished.[134] As long as the experienced is not fully represented there exists the drive to ever more adequate knowledge, wherein the move from experience to the universal occurs, so that the realisation of all the relations contained in the experienced or intuited would be 'der Begriff der Welt'.[135]

Turning to the objective comprehension of inner experience itself, or the self-mediation of *Geist*, one finds similar functions or acts unified by the object, in this case interiority. The only difference here is that the reality is already there:

Inasmuch as the comprehension of inner experience has a relation to an object (i.e. the inner experience itself) it is similar to the comprehension grounded in sense intuition. . . . The comprehension of psychic contexts or states is as much an endless task as that of comprehending external objects. Yet in the former it is a matter of gradually thematising what is already contained within conscious experience. Thus the reality of the psychic object is always present and, at the same time, must be ever more adequately thematised in concepts.[136]

Attentive observation must be careful not to destroy the spontaneity of inner experience.[137] The definitive establishing (*festigen*) of the object is attained in the positing of judgements which refer to the inner experiences and determine their essence within a context of representations. 'The judgement knows (*meint*) the inner experience. By its very nature as a sign it is a conditioned representative context, which is related to the inner experience.'[138] What is known in judgement, then, is not so much the inner experiences as such, but its *Wesenbestimmung*:

What is known in judgement is a content (*Sachverhalt*) transcending the inner experience; and it is related to a psychic context in the mode of a determination of its essence, or at least in the mode of a relation to such an essential determination. Such essential determinations (*Wesenbestimmungen*) are not adequately or completely reduceable to inner experience. They tend only to analyse such experiences, to bring them clearly into consciousness, to summarise them.[139]

As judgements, the conceptual constructions of interiority are representative. Historically they are manifold; Dilthey gives four—an objective universal, an empirical, a causal and a religious—besides his own conceptual construction of interiority as structurally dynamic. 'Each of these constructions is based in the nature of the object (i.e. interiority as objectified) and in the manner in which it is there. . . . Each of these objectifications of inner experience grasps some aspect of the psychic reality.'[140] These differing, at times contradictory, conceptualisations of interiority made possible entire historical epochs, thereby expressing an aspect of interiority and, through such conceptual expressions, affected (*einwirken*) the interiority itself. As the conceptualisations, so the other modes of objective comprehension of interiority, attentive observation and judgements, all express in their own way some reality in so far as they are concerned with inner experience. 'For in this entire discussion we are dealing *only* with representations of the experienced.'[141]

Dilthey's elaboration of the objective comprehension and the self-mediation of interiority, therefore, could arrive at no inherent justification of his own conceptualisation of inner self-presence as imagining-feeling-willing. Or rather, its verification implied the verification of all other conceptualisations as well. Because interiority as experienced is alone normative and the inexhaustible ground of all historical expressions, any representation that occurs must express some aspect of interiority. Any statement about the experienced is objectively true in so far as it is brought into *Adäquation* with the experienced; which means, through an understanding as a re-experiencing (*nacherleben*) of the statement-as-expression, one relates the statement to the inner reality of self-presence from which it originated.[142] Thus Dilthey would indirectly show the advantages of his conceptualisation of interiority in so far as he could relate any historical expression to his conception of the totality of interiority as imagining-feeling-willing.

We have seen how Dilthey conceived of *Erleben* as recurrent structurally interrelated functions or acts in which the individual experiences impulses and information from his physical and socio-cultural environment, assimilates them in ever more complex inner patterns, and is thereby capable of ever more decisive action within and on his environment. The circular action-reaction patterns

10

progress from the automatic reflex mechanisms through elementary
learning processes up to the intricate articulation of interiority in
adulthood, where the individual's many activities in various
acquired contexts or systems (*Zusammenhänge*, e.g. family, community, profession, nation, church, etc.) are more or less unified
in the progressive effort to realise short- or long-term ideals,
values, goals. The present section has been concerned with *Ausdruck*,
with how interiority expresses itself. Objective possession, which
we could not treat, deals with spontaneous and ever more nuanced
and sophisticated expressions of emotion and conation, of aesthetic
feelings and willed projects, of values and purposes. Objective
mental comprehension explicates the patterns or structures aimed
at cognitively grasping (*auffassen*) interiority, whether on the
spontaneous level of ordinary expressions or language, or on the
level of a reflective grasp of the spontaneous level in the human
sciences' representative world of theory which culminates in the
effort to express representations of the inner patterns of interiority
itself. In this sphere of objective comprehension and possession,
the circular patterns are also present; indeed, what Dilthey was
doing was to explicate the recurrent processes operative in the
cognitive-emotive-volitional reaction of individuals within their
environments—a reaction made possible only by continuous
interacting assimilation of its cognitive-emotive-volitional
expressions.

From Interiority to History (*Verstehen*)

The next step in a critique of historical reason would be to show
how the related and recurrent functions of interiority provide a
basis for understanding the myriad expressions of itself in the
total self-mediation of interiority that is human history. For a
grounding of the human sciences must show how the objects they
deal with are in fact expressions whose meaning, value and
purpose is constituted by interiority:

The method of understanding (*Verstehen*) is correctly grounded in so
far as it takes into account that the objectifications it deals with are
really different from the objects studied by the natural sciences. The
human mind has objectified itself in history, purposes are expressed in
it, values are realised—and it is precisely such specifically human
(*Geistige*) qualities built into history which understanding grasps.[143]

There are two characteristics of the understanding which concern Dilthey's attempt to interrelate historical and scientific consciousness. First of all, understanding 'has always a particular as its object'.[144] This is because understanding involves a re-experiencing, a 'projecting oneself into' the historical expressions,[145] made possible by the similarity of cognitive-emotive-volitional patterns in all individuals. So Dilthey continues in the text quoted above:

A living relation exists between myself and historical objectifications. Their purposefulness is grounded in my choice of goals, their beauty and goodness in my evaluation, their ability to be understood in my intelligence . . . The human sciences proceed in a way that is the reverse [of the natural sciences]. They seek primarily and principally to re-transpose the ever expanding objectifications of the human-historical-social reality into the historical spontaneity (*geistige Lebendigkeit*) from which those objectifications emerged.[146]

Thus the human sciences are involved in the introrsive movement of interiority itself. This accounts for the importance of individual biography as the expression of the *Lebensverlauf der Lebenseinheiten* in historical studies.[147]

On the other hand Dilthey was aware that the majority of historical expressions were contexts or systems (*Zusammenhänge*) whose complex interrelations could never be found in any one individual's inner experience. Thus the systems of laws, the involved relationships that make up a state or nation, the sciences, periods or epochs—in understanding these the historian or human scientist is not re-experiencing the interiority of an individual but of many individuals, in none of whom the totality of the expression was present. These expressions of the *objektiven Geist* were real but they could not be inferred from the reality of the experienced self-presence of any one individual.[148] Did this mean that there could be no objectively true knowledge of them since they could not be grasped as the expression of experienced interiority?[149] Dilthey rejected any Hegelian hypostatisation of objective spirit as a solution.[150] Nor could he be content with branding them as subjective constructions of historians. Somehow they had to be related to the basic structures of interiority.[151]

Dilthey saw that understanding is always of correlations or systems.[152] History could be understood as an operational-system (*Wirkungszusammenhang*) in which there was a continual interaction between individuals and the larger contexts or systems so that in seeking to understand the individuals we are led to ever larger contexts:

> The mystery of the human person urges one on to newer and deeper efforts of understanding. And it is in such an understanding that the realm of individuality is revealed, with its centre in men and their creations. Here lies the proper contribution of understanding to the human sciences. The objectification of mind and the power of individuals together determine the world of history. History itself rests on the understanding of these [two forces].[153]

The individual is a 'cross-roads' of the many systems operative in community, profession, nation, and epoch.[154] He is the bearer and representative of these systems.[155] As a result

> understanding a single person is only possible through his making present a more common knowledge, and this common knowledge again has its presupposition in understanding. In the final analysis, the understanding of a part of the historical process reaches completion only when the part is related to the whole, and any universal-historical view of the whole presupposes an understanding of the parts united in the whole.[156]

Bismarck provided an illustration of this hermeneutic-historical circle.[157]

Dilthey thought he had found the principle for overcoming the tension between historical understanding's concern for the particular and scientific consciousness' quest for the universal—just as the basic recurrent structures did.[158] Because the individual is born and develops in a complex of operational-systems, understanding him sublates the 'Beschränkung des Individualerlebnisses'. Each of his objectifications represents or expresses something which can be understood only in reference to those operational-systems.[159] This meant that the larger systems had reality only in so far as they were related to individuals, only in this way could they be re-experienced and understood. Dilthey seemed to hesitate to go quite that far:

> The question arises as to how a larger historical context, which was not the objectification of any one mind—and so was neither directly experienced nor traced back to the experience of an individual person—can still be constructed by the historian from the expressions and statements of those living in the context. This presupposes that logical subjects of history can be posited, which are not psychological subjects. Means must exist to delimit such subjects, and grounds should exist for grasping them as units or contexts.[160]

There are new categories, patterns and forms of life, which we must appeal to, and which cannot be reduced to single lives. The individual is only the cross-roads of cultural systems and organisations, with which his being is interwoven—but how can they be understood from the starting point of his being?[161]

Dilthey's own positing of reality in the experienced self-presence of interiority made it increasingly difficult for him to answer this.

In his unfinished efforts to elaborate such categories there is no set terminology employed in designating the larger systems. It is not difficult, however, to find the basic structures of interiority in his references to meaning-systems (cognitive), value-systems (emotive) and operational-systems (volitional); although Dilthey himself never explicitly derived them in this manner and more often referred to history as an operational-system.[162] It must be kept in mind that such systems are differentiated only by the predominance of either the cognitive, emotive or volitional; in any individual all of the basic functions are operative in his participation in each of the larger systems. This is also true of his correlating the various philosophical world-views where the predominance of the cognitive as a striving for a knowledge of external reality leads to a materialism, positivism or naturalism (so e.g. Democritus, Lucretius, Hobbes, French encyclopedists, modern materialists and positivists). Where the emotive-valuational predominates, one sees all of reality as the expression of interiority, from which one has the world-views of objective idealism (e.g., Heraclitus, Spinoza, Leibniz, Schelling, Hegel, Shaftsbury, Goethe, Schleiermacher). When the volitional is ascendant the independence of man over nature is stressed and one has the idealism of freedom or dualistic idealism (as in Plato, the Christian theologians, Kant, Fichte, Schiller, Carlyle).[163] A study of the characteristics of objective idealism reveals Dilthey's own position as falling within its world-view.[164]

Although Dilthey could not account for the reality status of the larger systems he saw clearly that historical understanding was essentially a movement from part to whole and whole to part. Indeed, this was the most common characteristic of the structure of the human sciences.[165] Our knowledge of the basic structures of interiority is dependent upon the historical expressions or objectifications of that interiority, and the understanding of the expressions is possible only because of the structures: 'Thus there emerges always and at every point in human scientific study a circularity between inner experience, understanding, and representations of the human historical world in general concepts.'[166] Dilthey remarked on the presence of this circular process in the interpretation of texts, in historical criticism and scientific research.[167] It was this circular movement from individual to larger systems and back that promised to reconcile historical and scientific consciousness in understanding.[168]

The ground of this circularity lies in man's finitude which is 'tragic' because united to an insatiable desire to overcome his present limitations.[169] 'There would be a simple way out of this circularity if there existed any unconditioned norms, purposes or values on which historical study or comprehension could be measured.'[170]

The emergence of scientific and, especially, historical consciousness sounded the death-knell for any such absolutes.[171] In terms of this consciousness the unconditioned is now in the process itself of striving for an ever fuller understanding: 'The unconditioned now lies in the direction of thought progressing from one relation to another without, as far as we can see for the present, ever reaching its goal. . . .'[172] We cannot know 'the essence of life', inner experience is inexhaustible so that its explication is an 'unending task'; representations are inadequate and need ever to be corrected: these are the tensions leading the human sciences back and forth from part to whole in a continual self-correcting process of understanding.[173] The meaning of history is in the recurrent structural relationships between part and whole, between interiority and the interlocking operational-systems of history:

The meaning of history must first be manifest, and so should be sought, in the ever present and ever recurrent structural relationships, in the operational-systems, and in the elaboration of values and purposes, which, taken together in their mutual relations, constitute the inner order of history. From the structure of the individual life up to the last all-embracing unity—this is the meaning which history always and everywhere exhibits. It is a meaning grounded in the structure of the individual *Dasein* and revealing itself in the interwoven operational-systems as the objectification of life.[174]

This circular method of all historical understanding assured that the meanings, values and purposes of each individual, community, society, culture, epoch should be comprehended both in their individuality and in their interrelated generality.[175] What is present structurally in the recurrent patterns of cognitive-emotive-volitional interiority ramifies out in ever growing circles until the entire sweep of human history is anticipated.[176]

Critical Appraisal

If I am not mistaken, the importance of Dilthey's critique of historical reason for laying the foundations of vast inter-disciplinary collaboration might be summed up in four points. First, his discovery was of the factual and irreducible character of self-presence as an awareness concomitant to and constitutive of all conscious historical activity. Secondly, this interiority was not amorphous but openly and dynamically patterned in structurally recurrent and related functions or operations whose unity came from their aims of assimilating from, and contributing to, the patterns and processes of the physical and historical world. Thirdly, the world of history is effected and constituted by the interactions of many instances of interiority so that any historical objectification is the expression of that interiority and as such is understandable. Grounding the human sciences consists in thematising the basic and recurrent structures common to all men for this structured interiority is historicality. Fourthly, one has the possibility of interrelating all the manifold of contexts or systems of human activity since, in so far as they are products of consciousness, their correlation to the basic patterns of interiority would integrate them in an open and dynamically revisable way.[177] For one would have uncovered the recurrent and related operations of human creativity.[178]

Given the inherent limitations of any system or systems, mentioned in Section I of this paper, the only way to ground inter-disciplinary collaboration on a large scale is to venture a thematisation of the pre-systematic open and dynamic operations which account not only for today's systems but will also develop, correct and eventually replace them. This applies not only to scientific but also to political, social, cultural, aesthetic, philosophical and theological systems. If Dilthey offers a very fruitful starting point in such an undertaking, I should also like to point out where the new control of meaning he was trying to explicate needs to be corrected.

First of all, his notion of conscious interiority as experienced was primarily discovered in relation to feeling. Thus he attempted to correlate the cognitive and volitional structures via the emotive; as a result reality was defined in terms of an experienced 'für-mich-dasein eines Zustandes' as a self-presence prior to all questions and answers, the inner reality-itself is simply given, there. *Selbstbesinnung* aimed at articulating this there-ness of self-presence which alone could be certain and normative. Objective mental comprehension with its observations, concepts and judgements had no more than a representative function whose verification consisted in their occurrence, i.e., they must be there as self-presence is there. This implicated Dilthey in a series of dilemmas.

For, secondly, he had to admit that the representations were both expressions of the reality-itself of interiority and also transcended experienced interiority as he conceived it. Interiority itself as experienced was not self-transcending. The relation between subject and object, self and world, was ultimate. Dilthey accepted this for the natural sciences, their object's reality-itself fell under the Kantian noumenon. This did not apply to the reality-itself of interiority *as experienced*, as given, in the myriad instances of conscious human beings. Yet the expressions of this interiority were brought into *Adäquation* with this inner reality by their occurrence and not by their content. This was a norm that could apply to any, even contradictory, expressions so that in the end we cannot know the experienced reality-itself, it too falls under the Kantian noumenon. The difference is that here the noumenal is possessed, present as our immediate self-presence.[179]

Dilthey did not intend such a conclusion but he did not know how to avoid it. He saw no structural difference in objective mental comprehension between knowing external objects and knowing inner experience. Instead of working this out into a critique of Kant's notion of knowledge, applicable to the natural as well as human sciences, he simply stated that the elements, regularities and inner structural relationships of the latter are contained in inner experience itself.[180] Five years later even this relation of objective knowing to inner experience is rejected inasmuch as any scientific objectification of interiority, such as concepts-judgements-thought constructions, transcend the inner experience from which they emerge so that their understanding cannot help one in grasping the depths of interiority.[181] Ironically, in the same pages

Dilthey sees the self-transcending character of the great works of art as a truthful guide to understanding interiority.[182]

Thirdly, because interiority as experienced was not self-transcending for Dilthey he could not adequately handle the larger systems in history which could not be understood as expressing a given individual's self-presence. On the other hand, he realised how no individual could be understood apart from these larger historical systems.

Fourthly, the mere there-ness of inner experience was not able to ground a dialectic when taken as the normative moment in interiority. For the only way to falsify a conceptualisation of interiority or a world-view, according to Dilthey's criterion, would be to show that it did not occur. This is what accounts for his inability to overcome the relativism of historicism. He saw correctly that any historical activity expresses some aspect of interiority, that the meaning-values-purposes of history must be found in the recurrent basic structures of interiority, but his own formulation of those structures as centred in feeling, and normative only as given in the there-ness of self-presence, left him with no more than an interiorised form of positivism.[183] He could not effectively move from a 'Besinnung über das Leben' to a 'Besinnung über das Denken' inasmuch as he had not grasped interiority as self-transcending. Knowing was at bottom not experiencing but perceiving the experienced and representing it in concepts and judgements. These latter were not the reality-itself of interiority and their correspondence with that reality remained, for Dilthey, 'vollständig dunkel'.[184] Unwilling to impose an arbitrary conception or norm on historical spontaneity he was left with no effective criteria for determining truth and error.[185] His critique of historical reason had to sacrifice reason in the name of historicality, and, unable to overcome historicism, it tended towards the sceptical avowal of the ultimate irrationality of historical life.[186]

Does this failure mean that reason is unable to appropriate the sources of its own historical activity? I think Lonergan's meta-method has achieved what Dilthey's critique did not. Historicism is overcome, not by renouncing the claims of scientific objectivity as Gadamer proposes,[187] but by relating them to the open and dynamic structures of interiority. This is possible if the normative is not in the experienced there-ness or givenness of interiority but in the experienced operations of direct and reflective understanding. So far as I can see, this is the only way of destroying the bifurcation of phenomenon-noumenon that has haunted almost all reflections on historicality, and from which Dilthey could not escape.

B. *Lonergan's Meta-Method*

Like Dilthey, Lonergan is convinced of the fundamental importance of self-presence-in-world or conscious intentionality as the origin and starting point for adequately relating and understanding both historical and scientific consciousness. We have seen how Dilthey ultimately failed to correlate consciousness as experienced with knowing and how, as a result, the reality-itself of interiority became, so to speak, an experienced noumenon. The circle from experienced there-ness to expression to re-experience was broken and the bifurcation of phenomenal-noumenal re-emerged as that between experience and representation. This accounted not only for Dilthey's difficulties with the larger systems in history, but also for his inability to overcome historicism. Those familiar with the thought of Lonergan will see at once the relevance of his meta-method. Here I should like to discuss briefly: first, the thematisation of the basic horizon both in terms of the subjective pole of experiencing-understanding-judging-deciding and the objective pole of objectivity and reality; secondly, the amplifications of the basic horizon in universes of discourse and action; thirdly, the complexifications of the basic horizon in terms of the sciences and history. There is a certain parallel here to the three sections in my treatment of Dilthey's critique of historical reason dealing with *Verstehen*, *Ausdruck* and *Erleben*.

One will notice, however, that Lonergan does not begin his invitation to self-appropriation by differentiating the natural and human sciences. The reason is that he saw clearly how any scientific activity is an activity of conscious intentionality. Lonergan would accept the basic distinction between the natural and human sciences, although he would formulate it in terms of mediated and constitutive meaning rather than of extrorsive and introrsive experience.[188] For the normative lies not in empirical but in intelligent and critical consciousness. Hence there is no question of accepting the Kantian verdict on the unknowability of the thing-itself.[189] This is of central moment not only for the natural sciences but also for the human. For the correlation of self and world, subject and object, is set in a context that is neither one of identity nor of duality but of reality; for 'we know the real before we know such a difference within the real as the difference between subject and object'.[190] The bridge-building, which Dilthey complained philosophers had been doing since Decartes, vanishes.[191] Admittedly, the self-appropriation Lonergan invites one to is only a beginning, yet:

It is a necessary beginning, for unless one breaks the duality in one's knowing, one doubts that understanding correctly is knowing. Under the pressure of that doubt, either one will sink into the bog of knowing that is without understanding or else one will cling to understanding but sacrifice knowing on the altar of an immanentism, an idealism, a relativism. From the horns of that dilemma one escapes only through the discovery (and one has not made it yet if one has no clear memory of its startling strangeness) that there are two quite different realisms, that there is an incoherent realism, half animal and half human, that poses as a half-way house between materialism and idealism and, on the other hand, that there is an intelligent and reasonable realism between which and materialism the half-way house is idealism.[192]

The Total and Basic Horizon

Meta-method is grounded in a self-appropriation which is a heightening of consciousness, a making one aware of the basic patterns or structures operative in any instance of human conscious activity. It is a discovery neither in the world of common sense nor in the world of theory but of the world of interiority.[193] In this sense it is a discovery of the sources of truth, 'jenseits der Wissenschaft', as Gadamer requests.[194] But it is a discovery which can critically return to the worlds of common sense and theory in a methodical manner inasmuch as the self-appropriation occurs within the intellectual pattern of experience.

The experience of awareness reveals its polymorphism. The stream of conscious intentionality is directed by factors referred to as conation, interest, attention, purpose. First, there is a bio-neurological pattern of experience dominated by extroverted conation, emotion and bodily movement aimed at satisfying biological needs. Then there is the aesthetic pattern in which consciousness slips beyond stimulus-response functions to the liberation of symbolic creativity. Thirdly, the dramatic pattern emerges where the many patterns blend and succeed one another in the interest of realising the practical objectives set by one's intersubjective milieu. Fourthly, the intellectual pattern sets empirical consciousness the task of being a supple active collaborator in intelligent inquiry and critical reflection aimed at satisfying the exigencies of the desire to know. But desire outstrips achievement so that the religious pattern evolves in which man's dynamic orientation towards the known unknown finds sensitive integration in the symbols, mysteries, rituals of the religious imagination.[195] Such generic patterns admit of manifold subdivisions: the sexual, musical, poetic, literary, social, political, scientific, philosophical, theological, etc.

These patterns are operative in man's spontaneous constitution of history, he need not reflect on them any more than his own self-presence consists in a self-perception. He experiences them as he experiences his own awareness concomitant to all his conscious historical activity. Yet the conation, interest, attention, purpose of these patterns indicates that they objectify themselves in familial and community structures, in customs, works of art, societies, cultures, scientific treatises and movements, philosophical writings and schools, religious doctrines and churches. These objectifications develop and decline, flourish and are thrown into crisis.

One need not list all the glories and torments conferred by the scientific revolution in our day to see that the intellectual patterns of experience today are profoundly altering man's experiences in the other patterns as well. Historical consciousness, no less than scientific, arose within the intellectual pattern. Only through historical studies did man become aware of the relativity of all social, cultural and religious contexts. Man always constituted history, just as he always had certain biological processes, but it was only when he became aware of this historical spontaneity that the massive problems associated with historicism appeared. Spontaneous historicality can no more cope with the highly differentiated problems of man's conscious reflective constitution of history than common sense can handle the problems of, say, genetic manipulation. Of critical importance, however, is the need to mediate the sources of this spontaneous historicality within the intellectual pattern, where scientific and historical consciousness operate, in order that this creative spontaneity as methodologically mediated could provide the norms for both interrelating the many fields of specialisation within the intellectual pattern, and for dialectically criticising the interference and pseudo-problems within this pattern caused by the polymorphism of human consciousness. This would be the only way effectively to meet the problems within the intellectual pattern discussed in the first section of this paper.

Dilthey's programme of a radical *Selbstbesinnung* which would transform the Socratic *phronesis* and attain the sources of both theoretical and practical reason fell far short of its goal.[196] Lonergan has gone further than Dilthey, and, to my knowledge, further than any of the present adherents of philosophical hermeneutics, by showing how the entire classical distinction of *episteme-praktikai* can no longer be maintained.[197] As a result Lonergan has deepened the Socratic *phronesis* into a new notion of wisdom.[198] For in the measure that one is aware, not only of the patterns of experience, but of their open and dynamic sources in conscious intentionality, one has initiated a whole new control of meaning:

Thoroughly understand what it is to understand, and not only will you understand the broad lines of all there is to be understood but also you will possess a fixed base, an invariant pattern, opening upon all further developments of understanding.[199]

Operative throughout the various patterns of human experience are the basic and recurrent structures of attentiveness-intelligence-reasonableness-responsibility. I have outlined these in Figure Three.

Lonergan himself has given a short summary of these cognitional structures and they are discussed in other chapters of this volume.[200] I shall not discuss them here at any length. They form the core of the subjective pole of the basic horizon in any human historical activity. The there-ness of self-presence *as experienced* is, then, not content simply with the empirical acts and contents of consciousness. There is the *experience* of questioning, understanding, formulating this understanding in concepts, weighing the evidence, judging, deliberating, evaluating, deciding, acting. And these experiences are no less real than sensing, perceiving, imagining, feeling. In common sense no less than in the sciences it is this basic horizon with its related and recurrent operations which grounds the circular self-correcting process of learning.[201] In concrete human performance the structures are highly complex and variously differentiated; there come into play memory, the habitual contexts of insights, judgements, values, patterns of action.

In reference to Dilthey's conception of interiority it is important to notice both the incorporation of the emotive into the self-transcending movement of interiority and that the many operations coalesce into unities. What is sensed, perceived, felt and imagined is what is inquired into; what is inquired about is what is understood by insight and formulated in conceptual hypotheses; what is formulated is what is reflected on in the marshalling and weighing of evidence; this in turn is what is grasped as virtually unconditioned and affirmed or denied in judgements; these latter provide the basis for deliberating and evaluating, which in turn leads to decision and action. Consciousness, then, is a formally dynamic unity of knowing and acting which allows us to distinguish the unity from the physical, chemical, organic and neural activities occurring outside consciousness.[202]

Moreover, it is a self-mediating, formally dynamic structure. Human historical interiority is not any one level or levels taken in isolation from the others.[203] Its self-mediating character is experienced in the unavoidability of the basic structures in concrete performance. A fundamental illustration of this is in the attempt essentially to revise or reject this thematisation of interiority. Such attempts would occur inasmuch as someone's empirical attentiveness *experienced* interiority otherwise and *understood* the experiences differently, *judging* his experience and understanding to more adequately correspond to human interiority than the basic structures thematised by Lonergan, and, on the strength of this, *deciding* essentially to revise or reject Lonergan's.[204] The only way, therefore, to avoid the basic horizon is to bear witness to it negatively through inattention, stupidity, irrationality and irresponsibility.

Now such self-mediation of the basic horizon is at the same time its self-transcendence. For the self-mediation occurs in so far as one's experiencing, understanding, judging, deciding, is known, i.e. grasped in judgement as virtually unconditioned.[205] It is in judgement that the subject-as-subject mediates and constitutes the subject-as-object. The experienced there-ness of empirical-intelligent-rational-moral consciousness is known through correct judgements:

There exist subjects that are empirically, intellectually, rationally, morally conscious. Not all know themselves as such, for consciousness is not human knowing but only a potential component in the structured whole that is human knowing. But all can know themselves as such, for they have only to attend to what they are already conscious of, and understand what they attend to, and pass judgement on the correctness of their understanding.[206]

How can this transition from experiencing consciousness to knowing consciousness occur? Because experienced consciousness itself is a dynamic *intentional* unity of experiencing-understanding-judging-deciding, and as such it is a knowing and acting within the intention of being:

That intention is unrestricted, for there is nothing that we cannot at least question. The same intention is comprehensive, for questioning probes every aspect of everything; its ultimate goal is the universe in its full concreteness. Being in that sense is identical with reality: as apart from being there is nothing, so apart from reality there is nothing; as being embraces the concrete totality of everything, so too does reality.[207]

It was the oversight of this aspect of interiority which allowed Dilthey to acquiesce in the Kantian conception of knowing in the natural sciences and led him to the impasse where he could not account for a true knowledge of the reality-itself of interiority. For reality and objectivity are not known as simply experienced in empirical consciousness prior to all questions and answers. As the subjective pole of the basic horizon coalesces into a unity of experience-understanding-judgement in the intention of knowing, so the objectivity pole of that horizon is a structured unity of material-formal-actual elements.[208]

Empiricists have tried to find the ground of objectivity in experience, rationalists have tried to place it in necessity, idealists have had recourse to coherence. All are partly right and partly wrong, right in their affirmation, but mistaken in their exclusion. For the objectivity of human knowing is a triple cord; there is an experiential component that resides in the givenness of relevant data; there is a normative component that resides in the exigences of intelligence and rationality guiding the process of knowing from data to judging; there finally is an absolute component that is reached when reflective understanding combines the normative and the experiential elements into a virtually unconditioned, i.e., a conditioned whose conditions are fulfilled.[209]

Because Dilthey had placed the normative in empirical rather than intelligent and rational consciousness he could not conceive of interiority as self-transcending and so could not account for the possibility of re-experiencing the larger systems (*objektiver Geist*) in history. He was coherent; as he had misplaced the normative so he also centred the structures of interiority around feeling.

The fundamental problem in Dilthey—as in all bifurcations of the phenomenon-noumenon type—sprang from an intrusion of the extroversion proper to the bio-neurological pattern of experience into the intellectual pattern. Objectivity becomes a disguised extroversion or introversion; reality can only be either the already-out-there-now or the in-here-now, while knowing becomes taking a noetic intuition of it.[210] Truth is then either the approximation of an impoverished mental representation with that reality or remains on the generic level of the there-ness of experienced interiority. The realism of intelligent inquiry and critical affirmation, on the other hand, includes the contents and acts of empirical consciousness, but within a context where they are the data rather than the normative. For the proper object of the human mind is attained only when it knows the existence (grasp of virtually unconditioned) of the intelligibilities (insight) immanent in the empirically experienced and experiencing. Reality is not identified with the given (whether as out-there-now bodies or in-here-now presence) but with being, being as the objective of an insatiable desire to know.

Intelligibility, therefore, is intrinsic to reality. The real is neither beyond the intelligible nor separate from it; otherwise no possibility of knowledge beyond unquestioning sensations could be found. Assuredly, our knowing by experience, insight, and judgement is extrinsic to the known: the knowing is not the known. But Dilthey's dilemma (both as regards the unknowability of external objects and the immediacy of *Erleben* and *Nacherleben*) was due to a failure to advert to his own performance in experiencing-understanding-judging-deciding. For in the light of the basic horizon the distinction between knowing and the known is within being (reality) and presupposes being's intrinsic intelligibility. Otherwise our knowing would give a knowledge of the intelligible but not of reality, so that the difference between knowing and known would be a distinction within the field of the intelligible but not a distinction of two beings.[211]

Hence the entire problematic of Dilthey concerning outer and inner experience, the experiencing of outer reality as impression-resistance, the puzzlement over how one re-experienced larger systems in history that were not originally experienced in anyone's individual interiority, and the centring of interiority in feeling, misplaced the real problem of objectivity.[212] One can most certainly analyse—physically, chemically, neurologically, phenomenologically—the experiential components of objectivity but these experiential components are not the mediating and constitutive factor of the objectivity of one's analysis.[213] Anyone claiming that intelligence and reason are merely subjective appearances of yet to be determined neural events, or that they are mere sublimations of unconscious drives, or merely a representational logical superstructure to emotion and conation, such a person is overlooking the very conscious processes of his own efforts at understanding and affirming.

Universes of Discourse and Action

Having moved in the thematisation of the total and basic horizon from the patterns of experience to the basic structures of conscious intentionality, there must be a return to those patterns of experience in order to relate them to the open and dynamic structures. This return was only partially effected by Lonergan in *Insight*. The self-appropriation of the basic structures of conscious intentionality occurs within the intellectual pattern of experience, and the return to the other patterns in meta-method would be within the intellectual pattern. In *Insight* Lonergan limited himself to a brief account of the central relevance of the basic structures of interiority to an elucidation of common sense, ethics, and religious belief; the main thrust of the book is concerned to work out the implications of meta-method for the sciences and metaphysics, attempting to set things in order within the intellectual pattern before moving on to the others. Even here Lonergan's work is only a beginning, an anticipation whose realisation would require vast collaboration. Here I shall briefly discuss how Lonergan goes about relating conscious intentionality, as the ground of historicality, to the various patterns of human historical experience. In this I shall be mostly reliant on my own notes of his lectures on method at Boston College in the summer of 1968.

We have seen how for Dilthey the understanding of history was impossible because of a certain fundamental similarity of self-presence operative within the dynamic contexts of history as a complex interaction of meaning-systems, value-systems, opera-

11

tional-systems. History as an operational-system was constituted by the interplay of forces, meanings, values, purposes.[214] Yet Dilthey's incomplete notion of interiority made it difficult for him to interrelate clearly these aspects of historical process. It is not surprising that in his last period he almost entirely replaces the notion of historicality (*Geschichtlichkeit*) with that of (historical) spontaneity (*Lebendigkeit*).[215]

For Lonergan the basic related and recurrent structures of self-transcending interiority—which I here equate with historicality—led to the notion of reality as identified with intelligibility where, in proportionate being, the self-correcting process of learning corresponds to emergent probability in world-process.[216] In the transition to the historical thematisation of the basic horizon intelligibility is meaning, with the basic horizon offering the meaning of meaning, for the intelligibility of the basic horizon is a self-constituting formally dynamic intelligent intelligibility.[217]

In Figure Four I have outlined some of the chief relationships between the basic horizon and the sources, acts and terms, exigences and functions of meaning. 'Now the all-inclusive term of meaning is being, for apart from being there is nothing. Inversely, the core of all acts of meaning is the intention of being.'[218] This defines the broad sweep of the range of meaning and historical process. I should like to touch on a few of the issues outlined in Figure Four, showing their continuity with the basic horizon of conscious intentionality. First, the sources of meaning are the basic horizon itself as it articulates the transcendental intention of being in the capacity to attend, inquire, reflect, deliberate; while the categorical realisations are determinate answers reached through experiencing-understanding-judging-deciding. In the self-correcting process of learning sustained by the transcendental ability to question and the categorically limited answers there is an operational development in which the operator and integrator of genetic method is differentiated into Piaget's notions of adaptation, group and mediation.[219]

Secondly, the move from the sources to the acts and terms is simply a further differentiation of the dynamic interrelation between the transcendental and categorical. In potential acts of meaning, the meaning and the meant are not distinguished. Intersubjective feeling and meaning (e.g. a smile), have spontaneous, global, polyvalent meanings which cannot be categorised and communicated outside of the intersubjective situation where they occur. Similarly, symbolic carriers of meaning as 'images of a real or imaginary object that evokes a feeling or is evoked by a feeling' convey elemental meanings within the process of internal communication between feeling, knowledge, decision, psyche, the neural basis prior to any therapeutic or non-therapeutic interpretation of the meaning. Art as 'the objectification of a purely experiential pattern' likewise does not separate meaning and meant in its liberating, ecstatic expressions of elemental meanings. Naturally, the formative and communicative functions of meaning within potential acts of meaning can be complemented by the cognitive functions, as when the phenomenologist investigates what is meant in intersubjective meaning, or the analyst interprets the symbols within internal communication, or the art critic seeks to draw out the meanings conveyed in a work of art.[220]

Thirdly, in formal and full acts of meaning the meaning and the meant are distinguished. Formal acts of meaning are conceiving, thinking, defining, supposing, formulating, and here the meant (or term) has an uncertain status. Full acts occur in judging, where the status of the term or meant is determined and universes of discourse or spheres of being emerge.[221] Operational development with its adaptation, grouping, mediation, here finds its embodiment in linguistic carriers of meaning, for 'conscious intentionality develops in and is moulded by its mother tongue'. The development itself of language brings about the differentiation of ordinary, literary and technical languages with their corresponding differences in mediation,[222] depending on the relevant functions of meaning whose instrumental expression the language serves as.

Fourthly, performative or active acts of meaning involve judgements of value, decisions, actions. They are especially in evidence in the effective and constitutive functions of meaning where man is busy about the making of his world and himself, which are the terms of these acts of meaning. Lonergan has developed at length the notion of the human good and values, showing how operational development (adaptability, group, mediation) can aid in achieving an implicit definition of the basic constituents of the human good.[223] There are interlocked correlations between the operators and integrators in (1) individuals in their capacities and achievements, (2) cooperating groups with the divisions of tasks and roles in institutions, aimed at (3) different levels of the good.

Fifthly, in treating of the development of feelings and their relations to valuation, Lonergan seems able to assimilate the positive contributions of Dilthey's (and certainly Scheler's) more phenomenological analysis of feelings and values without falling into their intuitionism, since emotion and conation are functionally related to self-transcending interiority. Thus to the extent that elemental meaning contributes to self-transcendence it gains in value. For the normative is not on the empirical level of consciousness, and so valuation is not devalued into a matter of desires and fears. Relative to the basic horizon one has:

$$\frac{\text{consciousness}}{\text{(empirical: intelligent: critical)}} : \frac{\text{good of}}{\text{(particular: order: values)}}$$

as one can gather from *Insight*.[224] Cognitive is related to moral self-transcendence.

Sixthly, the exigences of meaning bring operational development back to the sources and core of meaning in an explicit or thematised manner (in performance one cannot 'leave' the sources). It brings about the unity of a differentiated consciousness capable of distinguishing clearly between the worlds of common sense, of theory, of interiority and of the transcendent; capable of understanding the relations between them and carrying out the transition from one to another. The systematic exigence springs from the dissatisfaction of the human mind with only a descriptive knowledge of things as they are related to empirical consciousness, providing the transition to the world of theory in which objects of knowledge are related to one another.[225] This gives rise to the critical exigence which leads one to appropriate the open and dynamic patterns of one's own interiority so that the mediation is no longer in terms of ordinary language (world of common sense) nor technical language (world of theory) but one's own operations of empirical-intelligent-critical-responsible consciousness. Then the methodical exigence effects a return to the worlds of common sense and theory in order to differentiate and relate their procedures in the light of meta-method. The transcendental exigence takes into account the unrestricted nature of the drive to self-transcendence; it is the flowering of man's cognitive and moral self-transcendence in religious transcendence. Later chapters in this book will develop this more thoroughly. Suffice it to remark that

here religion is not relegated to some pre-scientific mode of awareness; mystery is clearly differentiated from myth.[226]

History and the Foundations of Collaboration

Even this very rapid and inadequate sketch of meta-method's
approach to history through the sources, acts, functions and
exigences of meaning serves to emphasise the resemblances to
and divergences from Dilthey. Analogous to Dilthey, Lonergan does
not seek the meaning of history elsewhere than in the ongoing
historical process itself. But this meaning is not encapsulated in
the empirical self-presence of individuals requiring a re-experiencing in order to be understood. The problem with the larger contexts
or systems in history disappears once the self-transcendence of
interiority is properly thematised. Self-appropriation does involve
a circular movement from the larger contexts of society and
culture to the individual, but once this is performed there is no
difficulty in moving from system or context to other systems.
Moreover, even this concern with the individual refers to the
critical exigence of a methodical grounding of the human historical
sciences. In the actual performance of historians or exegetes within
the world of theory there is no need continually to come back to
the *Lebenseinheiten*. Finally, relativism is overcome, not by appealing to timeless concepts nor by invoking the authority of tradition,
but by adverting to the virtually unconditioned normativity of the
sources of all meaning in history.[227] These sources are the basic
horizon as historicality. Do they undergo radical historical change?
Lonergan is primarily concerned with concrete fact and not fiction.
There can be little doubt that there has been enormous development from primitive man to the present, not only in man's capacity
to be attentive-intelligent-reasonable-responsible but also in his
biased inclination to put a highly differentiated intelligence to
work for pervertedly irrational and irresponsible goals. Yet the
misuse is such because of the presence of the basic horizon;
nausea and absurdity could never be experienced were it not for
the thrust of self-transcending interiority. Although the forms of
adaptation-grouping-mediation undergo vast historical changes
there is no evidence that the heuristically defined basic structures
of interiority were ever absent from human history. And what will
be? That we can best leave to the speculators, hoping they will be
attentive, intelligent, critical and responsible![228]

The fact is that historical understanding, no less than scientific, is possible only because of the heuristically defined basic horizon. Much of the opposition of the Historical School to the claims of the sciences sprang from the classical necessitarianism and mechanistic reductionism of eighteenth- and nineteenth-century science.[229] History cannot be mastered with logic alone; now we are becoming aware that science cannot be so mastered either. Since both scientific and historical consciousness arose within the intellectual pattern of experience one would suspect that they are not as opposed as the romanticists would have us believe. The disputes over whether history was a science or an art seem cast in the shadow of the classical conceptions of *episteme* and *phronesis*. Lonergan's meta-method based on the appropriation of the basic structures of conscious intentionality has formulated a control of meaning in terms of the ongoing processes of history which effectively sublates the classical control.[230] The problems associated with historicism are solved, not by trying to reintroduce normative ideas or values in the world of theory, but by critically moving to the grounds of historicality in the world of interiority, whose appropriation allows one then to return to the world of theory in a methodical manner. Hence the new notion of wisdom found in Lonergan attains its universal ability to order, not from abstract necessities, but from its capacity for elaborating heuristic structures anticipating the concrete historical process.[231] For all historical knowledge, as well as all involvement in history (whether in the worlds of common sense or theory), is grounded in the open and dynamic structures of human historical conscious intentionality. No less in the historical sciences than in the other sciences or in the fields of common sense, the fundamental alienation of man consists in his forgetfulness of the core of all meaning, being, as it is articulated in his own intending of attentiveness, intelligence, reasonableness, responsibility.[232]

Lonergan has already given some indication of the power of this new control of meaning in his complications of the basic horizon in classical, statistical, genetic and dialectic methods, in his conception of metaphysics as the integral heuristic structure of proportionate being, and in his work on functional specialisation. All of these complications are relevant to the foundations of ongoing collaboration. From the canons of the empirical method and the complementarity of classical and statistical method, one can anticipate the general structures of world process as emergent probability.[233] A possible application of this towards a unification of the sciences is outlined in Figure Five. I have discussed this elsewhere and shall not go into it here.[234] Because the schemes of recurrence in human history are not only intelligible but intelligent 'the analogy of merely natural process becomes less and less relevant'.[235] The world-view of emergent probability, then, must be extended and deepened in genetic and dialectical methods by an explication of what Lonergan variously calls a 'universal viewpoint', 'basic context' or 'comprehensive viewpoint'.[236]

Any fully adequate dialectic for both historical performance and historical understanding must be grounded in historicality itself, i.e., the dialectic must be found in its sources within the world of interiority if it is going to be fundamental. Within historical performance one can thus relate the relative dialectics in their concrete, dynamic and contradictory interaction in terms of their furtherance of, or hindrance to, the historical unfolding of human attentiveness, intelligence, reasonableness, responsibility. As bias is the principle of decline, so the extension of effective freedom is the principle of progress.[237] Similarly, the manifold efforts to understand historical processes can be set in their genetic-dialectic relationships through a heuristically conceived universal viewpoint or basic context. Just as the fundamental dialectic operative in performative acts and terms of meaning is based on the open structured dynamism of historicality, so the many efforts at understanding history are ordered in a totality of genetic-dialectic relations grounded upon the appropriation of historicality.[238] As the heuristic character of historicality assures that historical processes are not static representations of eternal systems but ongoing successions of temporary systems, so the basic context or universal viewpoint is a heuristic notion whose totality is potential and not actual. As potential the totality is determined by the appropriation of the transcendental sources of all meanings and viewpoints; the ordering, then, proceeds according to self-transcending historicality. How is this potential totality actually determined? By the totality of successful attempts at interpretation and understanding of historical events, movements, epochs.[239] Lonergan's dialectic in functional specialisation can anticipate the totality of concrete historical efforts at understanding history just as it can the totality of efforts at making history, for each of these efforts (whether in the world of common sense or of theory) will not only stand in either a genetic or a dialectic relationship to all other efforts, but will do so in the light of the basic horizon.

As examples of the application of such a genetic-dialectic explanation one might turn to the variation in cultures arising from the variations in the relations of the functions of meaning. Thus the ancient high civilisations had highly developed communicative and effective functionalisations of meaning but myth and magic were still widespread; the cognitive functions were low in comparison with Greek civilisation. Or, in our own day, one sees—as I briefly remarked in the first section of this paper—how the cognitive functions are being challenged to thematise the constitutive functions of meaning.[240] A more specified example can be found in Lonergan's historical analysis of early Christian Trinitarian and Christological doctrines.[241] But these are only limited examples of an ongoing process which embraces all historical objectifications of any kind. This all-inclusive character does not exclude dialectic as it tended to in Dilthey, for Lonergan has been able to formulate the universal viewpoint in a specifically dialectical context based upon self-transcending historicality. As such the universal viewpoint is both factual and normative; factually men are either attentive, intelligent, critical, responsible or they are not; the observance or non-observance are facts with normative connotations.[242] The direction of dialectics, as with all the functional specialities, is towards an open, dynamic and critical collaboration in man's understanding of himself and his history.[243]

CONCLUSIONS

Lonergan's meta-method provides the foundations for an ongoing collaboration inasmuch as it has succeeded in thematising the related and recurrent operations or structures of human historical interiority. No sphere of human historical activity is foreign to its methodical interests. It has effectively appropriated the sources of both the scientific and historical revolutions in contemporary consciousness so that it is able to be both factually ongoing—not appealing to a now defunct classical normativity—and simultaneously critical. Where Dilthey has sought to attain the creative sources of all historical objectifications in an experienced interiority which, despite his own intentions, could not ground scientific objectivity or a dialectic, Lonergan succeeds by adverting to the self-transcending dynamisms of inner experience or human interiority. Dilthey had intended to work out a *Selbstbesinnung* which would issue in a *Lebensphilosophie* capable of doing justice to both theoretical and practical reason. In fact he seemed to tend more and more towards a passive contemplative stance towards history, unable to explicate a dialectic applicable to historical action.[244] Meta-method has uncovered the sources common to both theory and praxis and so is able to relate hermeneutics, history and dialectics. Dilthey's experiencing and re-experiencing was unable to offer the foundations of an extensive ongoing collaboration; meta-method's basic horizon offers a transcendental doctrine of methods proportionate to the requirements of such collaboration.

Unless I am mistaken, Lonergan's meta-method is definitely only a beginning, but a very necessary beginning. It correlates both the non-logical and the logical, the pre-systematic and the systematic. It provides for its own correction, implementation, differentiation, for these developments will occur in the measure that men are attentive, intelligent, reasonable and responsible. What is true of the method is no less true of the complexities of our historical situation. Lonergan offers no pat answers or ready-made solutions but an invitation to appropriate the sources of all one's historical activity in order, on such a foundation, to carry on the arduous task of effective collaboration. To my mind, only on such foundations could the collaboration already in progress find a basis and horizon from which to deepen and extend its efforts at securing man a worthwhile future.

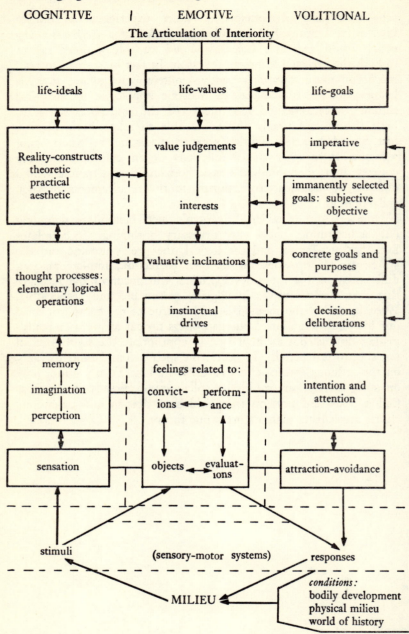

COGNITIVE | EMOTIVE | VOLITIONAL

The Articulation of Interiority

life-ideals ↔ life-values ↔ life-goals

Reality-constructs
theoretic
practical
aesthetic

value judgements

interests

imperative

immanently selected
goals: subjective
objective

thought processes:
elementary logical
operations

valuative inclinations

instinctual
drives

concrete goals and
purposes

decisions
deliberations

memory
imagination
perception

feelings related to:

convict-
ions ↔ perform-
ance

intention and
attention

sensation

objects ↔ evaluat-
ions

attraction-avoidance

stimuli

(sensory-motor systems)

responses

MILIEU

conditions:
bodily development
physical milieu
world of history

Figure I. Basic structures and functions of interiority
(*Schriften* I, 64–70; V, 90–316; VI, 139–57; VII, 3–23; VIII, 15–24)

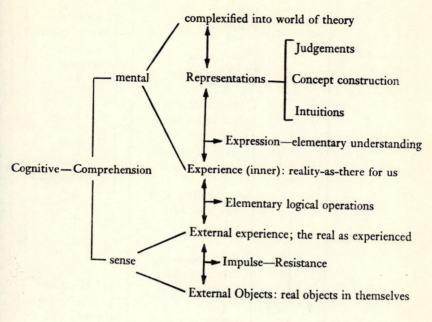

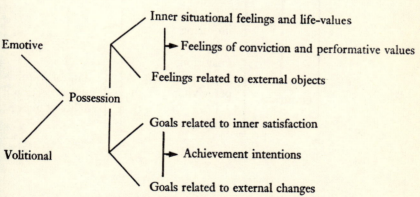

Figure 2. Objective comprehension and possession
(*Schriften* V, 90–138; VII, 3–69, 121–29, 207–13, 295-303, 307)

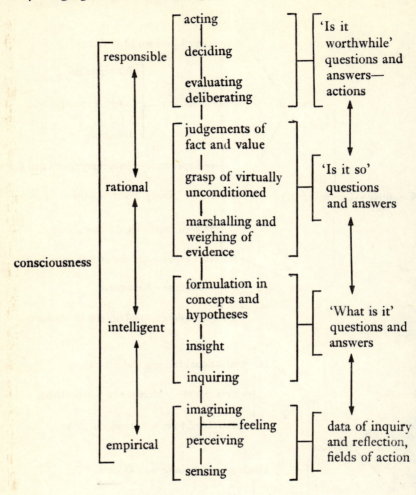

Figure 3. Basic recurrent structures of interiority

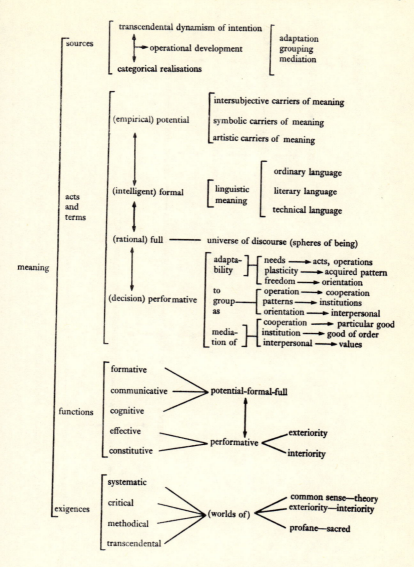

Figure 4. Basic horizon and meaning

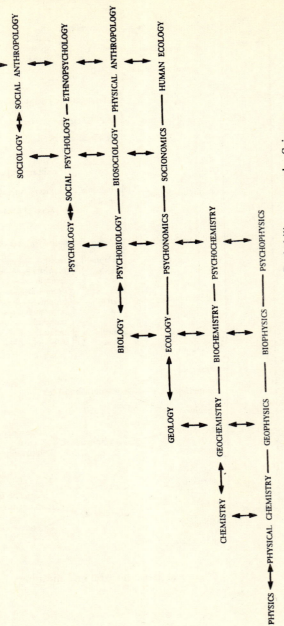

Figure 5. Generic Illustrations of Emergent Probability among the Sciences

Self-knowledge in history in Gadamer and Lonergan

F. LAWRENCE

THE following is an attempt to present the methodological orientations of Hans-Georg Gadamer and Bernard Lonergan, S.J., with regard to the problematic of self-knowledge in history. I have chosen to refrain for the most part from critical comparison and contrast— a task I hope to accomplish in a book on which I am presently at work. Hence my exposition tries to adhere rather closely to the terminologies and perspectives of the respective subjects. The minor thematisation which hopefully does occur here is genetic. For it seems to me that the direction which the hermeneutical movement since Dilthey has taken in the work of Gadamer can be characterised as heading toward what Lonergan has called fundamental inquiry in which the focal point is the integrating subject *as subject*. Finally, my decision to prescind from Gadamer's ontology of language has an important precedent in the approach he himself took in his lectures on the problem of historical consciousness at Louvain in 1957. I hope that this move makes my presentation of his argument stronger rather than weaker in the present context.

HISTORICAL SELF-KNOWLEDGE IN GADAMER

Dilthey's Epistemology of Interpretation

Perhaps no cross-section or segment of Gadamer's vast and intricate treatment of the problem of hermeneutics is as clearly indicative of the direction of his thinking on the problematic of self-knowledge in history as his running conversation with Wilhelm Dilthey. For it is the paramount influence of Dilthey's formulation of the hermeneutical problematic which forms the *terminus a quo* of Gadamer's re-grounding of hermeneutics.[1]

Dilthey's work represents the high point in what Paul Ricoeur has suggestively called the 'epistemology of interpretation'.[2] Dilthey struggled his entire academic career with the woeful lack of 'theoretical legitimation, delimitation, and articulation' in the historical sciences noted by Droysen in 1843[3] (4). In the course of Gadamer's account of that struggle[4] (205–28), an ambivalence in Dilthey's notion of self-knowledge in history is brought to light which Gadamer's own work is an attempt to set aright.

A Typology of Cartesianism

Before examining the nature of that ambiguity I would like to sketch a typology (based as much as possible on Gadamer's own assertions) of the presuppositions which vitiated Dilthey's epistemology of interpretation. Some delineation of Cartesianism is important for grasping Gadamer's entire project in *Wahrheit und Methode*, since it is a term embracing a complex of tendencies in modern thought which he had diagnosed as being a chief cause of the malaise of our time and for which his philosophical hermeneutics is intended as an antidote (XXIII, 465). 'Cartesianism' then serves Gadamer somewhat in the way 'Calvinism' served Max Weber in his famous sociological thesis. In this usage, important characteristics of Descartes' achievement are seen as coinciding roughly with a set of attitudes or climate of thought dominant in western culture since the rise of modern science. Descartes' name seems to be singled out because, as Whitehead wrote, '. . . Descartes only expressed definitely and in decisive form what was already in the air of the period.'[5]

a. *Cartesian Cognition Theory*. It is interesting to note with Gadamer that the word 'Erkenntnistheorie' came into currency in the German context at the time of the discrediting of Hegel's apriorist construction of history by the Historical School (207). But the problem intended by the word was summoned forth with special force by the emergence of modern natural science in the seventeenth century and was given its characteristically objectivist formulation by Descartes: how can subjectivity dwelling within itself (*res cogitans*) know objects existing outside (*res extensa*) itself?[6] This posing of the problem is objectivist in so far as it implies the ultimacy and the primordiality of the subject-object dichotomy (499); and within that set-up a distorted primacy of the subject who, in isolation from a world, instrumentally disposes of ideas and representations (*Vorstellungen*)[7] by means of a reflection thought of only as technical,[8] and who has therefore the problem of deciding whether or not these immanent creations have any transcendent reference to the 'real out there'. And as a final irony, the subject of this relationship ultimately knows itself as object distinguished from other objects only by being present in an immediately evident way. This same setting of the problem perdures in its essentials through the Rationalists, the English Empiricists, and Kant.[9] Moreover its application to the field of the humanities has antecedents in Pascal's distinction of *esprit de finesse* and *esprit géométrique*, and Vico's defence of the ancient tradition of rhetoric against the new *critica* of Descartes.

b. *Cartesian Model of Science.* Intimately linked with and further determining this objectivistic assumption of the subject-object dichotomy is the model or ideal of science in terms of which Descartes tried to reconcile the Galilean version of science with ancient and medieval meta-physics.[10] Significantly, Descartes seems to have discovered his model not through a detailed analysis of the operations of the new natural scientists, but in a considera-tion of the properties of the general rule or axiom in mathematics.[11] No wonder then that the Cartesian model of science is that of a *mathesis universalis*, and that the procedural ideal is basically deductive, though one deduces what follows necessarily from principles known instinctively by clear and evident intuition. On the side of the subject is the *res cogitans* which, as interiority exercising both intuition and deduction, is capable of achieving formal and abstract self-evidence; on the side of the object is *res extensa* or the sheer exteriority of spatial extension projected within the framework of the *mathesis universalis*.[12] Indeed, such a subject and object not only correlate neatly with Descartes' formu-lation of the critical problem, but are its presuppositions.[13] Cartesianism as a conception of science, therefore, posits on the one hand an object 'conceived to be something in the 3-dimen-sional space of our experience, (and yet) . . . not an object of perception in the rich, emotive personal way of everyday life . . . (And so it is) already a very abstract construction'.[14] And on the other hand it posits the disengaged knowing subject purified of every factor of subjectivity but the untainted look, perception, intuition, and the capacity to objectify mathematically what it perceives in self-evident propositions (61–2, 208, 226, 429,

12

431–2). This correlation of disincarnate subject and abstract object is supposed to import into the empirical natural sciences the same measure of apodicticity of results proper to the Greek model of science, inasmuch as the static identity of the methodical perception mathematical deduction is seen to match the immobility, necessity, and certitude of the deductive process from premises to conclusion in an expository syllogism.[15] Such is the monolithic meaning of knowing the real objectively (427–31). And because this caricature of natural science sets the standard of objectivity for the entire range of human science and wisdom, the Cartesian notion of science is monistic. For Gadamer then, something like this notion of science has been pervasive in contemporary culture (427–32),[16] and seems to be much of what he has in mind when he inveighs against 'method'.

c. *Cartesian Notion of True Knowledge.* Intermeshed with the objectivist cognitional theory and the objectivist scientific ideal is the Cartesian identification of true knowledge with the cognitional subject's possession of absolute certainty about necessary, infallible, and hence indubitable fact.[17] This is presupposed by both the cognitional theory and the scientific ideal; and together with them it culminates in Descartes' fetishism of method. Descartes' fourth rule *ad directionem ingenii* states: 'necessaria est Methodus ad rerum veritatem investigandam'. But by method he means, according to Gadamer: 'a universal procedure for any and every knowledge describable by fixed rules, controllable by set principles, and capable of sealing off the way of knowledge against prejudices and rash assumptions and in general against the unruliness of guesses and flashes of insight'.[18] Descartes' notion of true knowledge issues forth quite naturally into his famous quest for a *fundamentum inconcussum* on which he might erect in full security the edifice of science and philosophy;[19] and into the principle of universal doubt as capable of paving the way of certitude in enlightened freedom from prejudice (61, 255, 261–2).[20] This means of course not only the exclusion of 'moral' and merely believed truth from a place in the edifice of genuine knowledge, but also the elimination of the role played by the provisional in human knowing in favour of the status of formally abstract self-evidence and apodictic certainty. In summary, knowledge, certainty, and science thought of as mathematically evident are equated on the one hand (60–3, 225, 227–8); and the search for certitude is equated with devotion to understanding and truth even as hyperbolic doubt is believed to be the meaning of intelligent wonder and reasonable criticism on the other.[21] This complex of assumptions about knowledge becomes the target of Gadamer's scorn when, for example, he speaks of the fetishism of method 'in which truth becomes certitude, and where the method of knowing the truth becomes more important than the truth known—for the sake of the certainty which the method secures.'[22]

Ambiguity of Dilthey's Epistemology of Interpretation

To understand Dilthey's undertaking, it is important to grasp that just as it is one thing to have experience, and another thing to thematise that experience scientifically, so also it is one thing to perform such scientific thematisation of experience, and quite another to make explicit exactly what is happening in this performance.[23] In projecting his groundwork for the *Geisteswissenschaften*, Dilthey was expressly acting as intepreter-critic of the Historical School (186–7, 206, 477). Hence he was venturing into this third level of reflection which I shall call meta-theoretical. But inasmuch as the *Geisteswissenschaften* are thematisations of human-historical experience, man in his *specifica differentia* was at the centre of Dilthey's purview. Now it would seem obvious that if one lacks a proper conception of first-level experience, then not only will second-level thematisations fall short of the exigencies of the data, but still more fundamentally, the very *human* character of those second-level operations and the consequent exigencies of that performance will tend to be naïvely ignored. But Gadamer shows that, to Dilthey's credit, he clearly recognised both that first-level human experience is not reducible to data observable by the senses and that truly second-level thematisation of that experience does not result automatically from application of the paraphernalia of the empirical natural sciences. And so his meta-theoretical reflection brought forth the first universal hermeneutical philosophy in the twofold role of foundation for the *Geisteswissenschaften* and philosophy of philosophies (216–23). It grounded the *Geisteswissenschaften* not by establishing absolute knowledge as purely speculative, but by instituting an ideal of historical consciousness which 'methodically raises itself above the subjective contingency of its own standpoint and above the tradition accessible

to it, and thereby arrives at the objectivity of historical knowledge' (223). It was philosophy of philosophies not as 'grounding
. . . the only possible philosophy out of the unity of a speculative
principle', but as an enlightened pilgrimage to ever-increasingly
heightened historical self-awareness (223). Therefore besides being
what he conceived to be an adequate description of the ethos of
historians and human scientists, historical consciousness was for
Dilthey a general ideal of authentic human-historical experience
which is always indissolubly connected with self-knowledge[24]
(216–23).

The heart of Gadamer's critique of Dilthey consists in the
allegation that Dilthey's epistemology of interpretation represents
a concretion in the fields of historical science and philosophy of
the Cartesian typology sketched above. For Dilthey, then, meta-
theoretical reflection meant mainly Cartesian-style cognitional
theory whose prime assumption is of the aboriginal split between
subject and object. Hence, the asking of the critical question leaves
no room for also putting this prior objectivist assumption into
question: one proceeds immediately to the epistemological question
posed as one or another form of the notorious 'problem of the
bridge'. (Cf. Appendix A.) Secondly, just as the objectivist model of
natural science in terms of the abstract relation of *res cogitans* and
res extens seems to have been a genetically prior condition for
Descartes' cognitional theoretic inquiry, so also something close to
this model provided Dilthey with a touchstone for the elaboration
of a cognitional theory tailored to the *Geisteswissenschaften*. (Cf.
Appendix B.) And finally Dilthey's thinking was dominated to the
end by the Cartesian quest for certainty and the manoeuvre of
hyperbolic doubt. (Cf. Appendix C and the following.)

Gadamer, however, does not claim that nothing but Cartesian
factors enter into Dilthey's meta-theoretical reflection. Surely the
genius of Dilthey for Gadamer lies in the former's oft-expressed
intention to begin from the experience of life (62–3, 206, 210,
214–7, 222–6). For couched in this intention are his recognition
of the empirical thrust of the Historical School and of the natural
sciences generally; his acknowledgement of the constitutive
function of meaning in human-historical life; and his willingness
to confront the problems raised by historical meaning and force
as trans-subjective. Gadamer's point is rather that the symbiosis
of Cartesian and these other elements in Dilthey's meta-theoretical

reflection caused both a basic ambiguity and serious distortions in the foundations he finally managed to work out (205–28).

In Gadamer's view, the serious distortions centre in Dilthey's depiction of historical consciousness (216–7, 218–29). Both as reality and as task, Dilthey's historical consciousness appears in Gadamer's judgement to be both intrinsically contradictory and utopian (217): it is contradictory because on the one hand its inner tendency is to cut through relativity and conditionedness to absolute knowledge; and nonetheless on the other it protests that it can accomplish this feat by intending and assuming nothing but the finite and conditioned (217–24). It is utopian because it entails a superhuman infinitude on the part of man's cognitive powers: that is, it posits a universalisation of Schleiermacher's doctrine about the concrete possibility of complete and perfect reconstruction of historical contexts; and so Dilthey is affirming for man the possibility of a practically divine contemporaneity (XXI, 217–28, 505). In short, historical consciousness for Gadamer is a perversion of both the historical limitedness and the historical transcendence of man.

These serious distortions seen by Gadamer in Dilthey's notion of historical consciousness arise out of the basic ambiguity at the heart of Dilthey's orientation to a philosophy of life.[25] (221–6). What made Dilthey choose life as his point of departure was the constitutive function immanent within it of a cognitive moment, an 'immanent reflexivity', or, as Georg Misch put it (246), an original remoteness from the network of one's own actions by which the living one is able to maintain a certain distance from the pursuit of his vital purposes and an openness to meaning (222). Embedded in this original cognitive moment of life-experience is an ineluctable striving for stability and fixity (*Streben nach Festigkeit*) 'in the midst of the inconstant change of sense perception, desires and fears, which makes possible a constant and unified conduct of life'[26] (222–6). And corresponding to this immanent knowledge and striving for stability is a natural view of oneself by which one has a sense of the meaning of one's life or a feeling of self-continuity[27] (222–3). This self-image is prior to scientific objectification but can be and has been objectified both scientifically and non-scientifically as in art, custom etc. Indeed, it is constantly opened out beyond its particularity by expression and understanding into the breadth, depth, and universality of the objective spirit.

But this primordial core of Dilthey's philosophy of life where the individual and his history intersect at the deepest level has been infested by cognitional theoretic monism. For even in his description of this knowing normally immanent in life, the natural striving for stability can be satisfied only by the certitude which he deems attainable by science alone: one can affirm unconditionally only the indubitable (224, 225, 226); the anxiety, doubt, and uncertainty of ordinary life are unreally equated with the artificial and hyperbolic doubt which can be overcome by formally abstract self-evidence alone. And so the basic historical self-consciousness to which Dilthey at his best seemed to have penetrated, is concealed or weighed down with an exaggerated drive towards apodictic certitude and with an over-emphatic doubt in regard to one's historical moorings in law, ethics, religion, etc. Consequently, when this caricature of historical self-consciousness is projected into an enlightened demand for a reflexive and objectifying relation to history-as-lived, the resultant description of this thematising mediation of history is corrupted from the outset by systematically overlooking the primordial interplay between self and history. In short, Gadamer finds that the Enlightenment idea that the only objectivity valid in life is scientific on the Cartesian model is all-pervasive in Dilthey's works (222–8).

If we think of historical self-knowledge, then, in terms of a first-level mediation which is for the most part experiential, spontaneous, though not at all unintelligent; and of a second-level mediation which by technical reflection scientifically objectifies yet never exhausts the richness of this first level, then we might formulate Gadamer's pinpointing of the central ambiguity in Dilthey's work as follows: although Dilthey's work is replete with original and valid insights into either of the two levels, he never clearly distinguishes between them; rather he tends to subsume the first level without remainder into the second level. Nor can he then either assign the levels their proper autonomy or allow for their proper mutual mediation. Therefore, both with regard to furnishing a phenomenologically accurate description of human-historical experience and in the giving of a satisfactory account of the scientific thematisation of history-as-lived, Dilthey's epistemology of interpretation was a failure (244–5, 499).

GADAMER'S ONTOLOGY OF UNDERSTANDING

Overcoming of Cartesianism

Gadamer's own meta-theoretical reflection figures into the Schleiermacher-Dilthey tradition of hermeneutics as a massive change in *status quaestionis*. For if both the problematic of cognitional theory and the 'fact' of science under its rationalist-empiricist interpretations (and both of these more or less conforming to the Cartesian typology as outlined above) had monopolised the European (especially the German) philosophical tradition from the time of the breakdown of the speculative Idealist movement, through the Positivists, the neo-Kantians, and even the various philosophies of life (as in Dilthey's version),[28] a new approach was opened up by Husserl's phenomenology and followed out in Heidegger's thinking[29] (229-50, 500). The shift from the cognitional theoretic question in terms of the isolated *ego cogito* (*cogito me cogitare*) to the critique of that question as a pseudo-problem in Husserl's formulation of the intentionality of consciousness (*ego cogito cogitatum*)[30] was complemented by the relativisation of the status of so-called scientific objectivity in Husserl's step back into the *Lebenswelt*. Having laid to rest at least the objectivist ogres of Cartesian cognitional theory and Cartesian pre-eminence of natural scientific procedures, Husserl had pushed to the very brink of a phenomenology of human-historical experience. It required only Heidegger's removal of the fetters of the transcendental-subjective viewpoint of Husserl for Dilthey's most genuine philosophical intention to be set free (229): at last according to Gadamer, the fullness of human-historical life had been opened up to unencumbered and radical investigation.

No one more than Gadamer has sought to comprehend and communicate the nature of this truly emancipatory return to the facticity of life initiated by the work of Husserl and brought to a head, so to speak, by that of Heidegger, and this especially as meeting 'the radical challenge to thought set by the inadequacy of the concept of substance for historical (*geschichtliche*) being and historical (*historische*) knowing' (229). It is in the process of this comprehension-communication that Gadamer has made his important contribution to the shift of the hermeneutical tradition from an epistemology of interpretation to an ontology of understanding.

The great spur to Gadamer's contribution and an interpretative key to its general significance was provided by the gradual disengagement of Heidegger from the teleology of Husserl's philosophy. If both Heidegger and Husserl had, under the slogan, '*zurück zu den Sachen selbst*',[31] been concerned with the extralogical conditions for propositional truth, and not simply in a piecemeal but in a completely general way,[32] it was Heidegger alone who tried to re-originate '*die Frage nach dem Sein*' (240–5, 500–1).

And it was in the course of his 'conversation with the classical thought of philosophy concerning the adequate way to ask the question about being',[33] that Heidegger had clarified both for himself and for many of the post-World War 1 generation what one had to 'get over' (*verwinden*) in order to gain access to the true meaning of being; for the conceptual tools of the tradition, objectifying in the worst sense as he took them to be, were inappropriate for the question of being, let alone the answer.[34] And so radically reoriginating the question of being was for Heidegger a matter of getting beyond the ontological presuppositions of the entire philosophical tradition from the time of its Greek inception down through the transcendental philosophies of the neo-Kantians and Husserl (which were, incidentally, his immediate heritage), by asking what in fact made those assumptions possible in the first place. It was a matter of piercing through to 'what', as Gadamer describes it, 'prior to all that can become an object of knowledge, makes knowing itself, questioning itself, thinking itself possible'.[35]

For Husserl, that great critic of objectivism and metaphysics (229–37, 242), philosophy was a rigorous, even apodictic science. Accordingly, the task of a constitutive phenomenology was ultimately to demonstrate the validity of all objects as derivative from the absolute historicity of transcendental consciousness by constructing systematically the step-by-step order of evidence correlative to the layers of the constituting performances (*Leistungen*) in the transcendental ego[36] (241–2, 500). This project was, at root, although sophisticatedly beyond the 'inside-outside' formulation of the critical problem, still the Cartesian quest for certitude albeit in the form of a radicalised transcendental viewpoint.[37] Now if in *Sein und Zeit*, Heidegger had used Husserl's transcendental-phenomenological tools[38] (241–4), it was not at all for the sake of merely advancing the Husserlian programme[39] (241, note): for him the transcendental scheme was, to use the Wittgensteinian analogy, no more than a ladder. This is why his uncovery of what he considered to be the ontological prejudices latent in the 'Greek metaphysics of substance'—namely, the conception of being in terms of what is simply and statically present-at-hand, capable of being pinned-down and calculated (*Vorhandenes, Anwesendes*) (245, 247, 254, 431–2, 500, 511)—became a basis not only for his contention that Husserl's *Ur-Ich* was 'ontologically under-determined'[40] (243–4), but for his full-scale and relentless criticism of the 'objectivistic subjectivism of modernity'.[41] Implicit, there-fore, in Heidegger's move in *Sein und Zeit* from the rarefied intentionality of Husserl to factical intentionality was a critique of any and all philosophy of subjectivity or consciousness[42] (242, 245, 500, 511); and corresponding to his exposition of the ontolo-gical anticipations of ancient metaphysics (245), was an attack on the assumptions of what he took to be empirical scientific method.[43]

Whatever the manifold implication of Heidegger's raising of the question of being, this much stands out clearly: first, the demon-stration of the irrelevance of the Cartesian cognitional theoretic problem; second, the debunking of the pre-eminence of an (often Cartesianly conceived) ideal of science; and third, the coherent and profound lack of concern about the apodictic certainty of human knowledge. Husserl, on the other hand, did concur with Heidegger on the absurdity of naïve-realist cognitional theory.[44] But while he, too, had made problematic the status of obvious dominance which the fact of science had claimed, for instance, in neo-Kantian philosophies, he nevertheless shared what someone has called the scientific mythology of rigour and proof (330). For him as for Descartes, 'clarity was the criterion of all truth';[45] and so know-ledge could be grounded by self-evident reasons alone. Indeed, it was the note of apodicticity by which Husserl distinguished in principle between scientific philosophy and just another *Weltanschauung*. This relentless search for final and apodictic foundations was at the core of the radical *Selbstbesinnung* which his transcendental philo-sophy was an attempt to execute.[46] In sharp contrast to the Heidegger of *Sein und Zeit*, then, Husserl's transcendental and foundational phenomenology was very much a bearer of the Cartesian burden.[47]

If this difference between Husserl and Heidegger be true, then I believe that when Gadamer states that the whole notion of trying to find ultimate foundations underwent a complete reversal in *Sein und Zeit* (243), this can be taken to mean that the enterprise of transcendental and foundational reflection in its Idealist or its Husserlian form was both criticised and sublated. For on the one hand Heidegger's radically ontological viewpoint permitted him to purge the enterprise of the Cartesian elements mentioned above, including those that Husserl himself had never been able to see through. And on the other, when he took up the transcendental and foundational framework and applied it in *Sein und Zeit*—for he understood what he was doing here as 'transcendental' in a Kantian sense,[48] and indeed called his project a *Fundamentalontologie*—he gave these terms and that performance a new meaning precisely in so far as at least these Cartesian elements (i.e., the cognitional theoretic question based on the prior assumption of the subject-object dichotomy; the assumed normativity of an abstract-deductivist notion of science; the ineluctable quest for apodicticity) were abandoned. As Gadamer has taken pains to make clear, Heidegger's transcendental and foundational achievement in *Sein und Zeit* was neither that predicated of him by the late Oskar Becker, who thought that Heidegger had only further concretised what was still an integrally Husserlian transcendental orientation[49] (500–1); nor that of Eugen Fink, for whom Heidegger's doctrines merely serve as complementary to Husserl's at the limits of the latter's transcendental problematic;[50] nor can it be too closely associated with the moralising-existentialist reception of the 'early' Heidegger[51] (248–9, 495–7).

The point of emphasising that Heidegger's early transcendental and foundational enterprise is itself a basically new departure over against the neo-Kantian or the Husserlian is not to forget that Heidegger's famous *Kehre* is, as Gadamer interprets it, 'the recognition of the impossibility of overcoming transcendental forgetfulness of being in transcendental reflection'.[52] Rather it is to underline the implications of Gadamer's line of thought in the passage immediately preceding the statement about the *Kehre* just quoted: 'Already in *Sein und Zeit* the actual question was not in what manner can being be understood but in what way is *Verstehen* being. For understanding-of-being (*Seinsverständnis*) represents the existential distinguishing characteristic of human *Dasein*'.[53] Moreover the point is, in the light of those implications, to remark the parallel between what was going forward in the transition from

Husserl to Heidegger and what is happening in the jump from Dilthey to Gadamer. In brief, I am suggesting that the description of the discontinuity between the transcendental and foundational enterprise of Husserl and that of Heidegger in terms of greater and less taint of Cartesianism is the basic clue to the significance of the move from an epistemology of interpretation to an ontology of understanding. For Gadamer's lifework has been to 'play out' that philosophical breakthrough of Heidegger in the medium of his own personal appropriation of the humanistic heritage in art, in the *Geisteswissenschaften*, and in philosophy itself.[54]

Now it is very important both for grasping the relationship between Heidegger and Gadamer and for appreciating the radicality of their starting point, not to be misled into thinking that the word 'ontology', when used to describe Heidegger's stance or in the expression 'ontology of understanding'—particularly when it is used in the context of countering Cartesianism—denotes a lack of concern about questions of legitimation and truth, i.e., the common stock-in-trade of epistemologists and cognitional theorists. On the contrary, Gadamer stresses that 'Heidegger's own question is quite removed from . . . wishing to eliminate the question of truth in favour of the authenticity of expression . . .' (501, also 247). Gadamer holds that Heidegger was always intending, 'not an object, but something which even beforehand already determined all possibility of knowledge of objects. . . .'[55] Likewise, in his Introduction to *Wahrheit und Methode*, Gadamer states that his concern in that work is to 'seek out the experience of truth which transcends the realm of scientifically methodical control wherever it is to be encountered, and to raise the question as to its own proper legitimation' (XXV). And in the Foreword to the second edition of that work, he tells us that the question to which his investigation sought an answer is, 'Wie ist Verstehen möglich?' (XV). In the light of the fact that these concerns have such a centrality even after the 'ontological turn', it becomes evident that the phrase 'epistemology of interpretation', as I have used it up till now, refers to a transcendental and foundational problematic overwhelmed by Cartesian assumptions.

Now if these concerns on the part of both Gadamer and Heidegger are implanted in a non-Cartesian orientation, they also show what sense it makes to say that Gadamer's project and that of Heidegger as well mean to be transcendental and foundational, in spite of the fact that the later Heidegger saw fit to draw the consequence of his new breakthrough by completely disavowing the transcendental viewpoint. But it is undeniable that to raise the type of question Gadamer does in *Wahrheit und Methode* and to intend the sort of objective (if not object) which the earlier and later Heidegger in his very radicality had been intending means aiming at something irreducible to the realm of the categorial (i.e., of empirical differences, according to Gadamer's interpretation of Kant, 249). It seems justifiable, therefore, to call both the goal and the questioning transcendental and, adding the proviso that the Cartesian notion of apodictic grounding is excluded, foundational.

The cogency of this use of transcendental and foundational can, I think, be supported from another perspective. Heidegger's eventual rejection of the transcendental scheme is usually linked in Gadamer's accounts with a repudiation of the modern notion of *Bewusstsein*[56] (240–50, 500–1, 511). 'In the *Kehre* one departs from being instead of from consciousness which thinks being, or from *Dasein* who has to do with being, who understands himself in relation to being, and who is profoundly concerned with his being'.[57] Now I am convinced that it can be shown that the meaning of *Bewusstsein* in this context presumes models of intuition, perception, and reflection which bear to some extent the implication that consciousness is a matter of knowing objects, that consciousness is the same as 'objectifying' comportment.[58] It can also be shown that Heidegger was not unfamiliar with the old distinction between *actus exercitus* and *actus signatus* in which contrary assumptions about consciousness are latent.[59] It would seem, then, that the later Heidegger's rejection of transcendental pretences and/or Gadamer's interpretation of that move is at least open to the following construction in terms of formulating a hypothetical meaning for the 'ontological turn': One could gradually come to see that both Husserl (e.g., in his theories of *retentionales Bewusstsein*, of *urphänomenale Gegenwart*, and of pure *Wahrnehmung*) and the author of *Sein und Zeit* (whose transcendental analysis concentrated on the *Sichverstehen* of *Dasein*) lapsed—Husserl on a grand scale and Heidegger himself ambiguously—into equating consciousness with its objectifying function;[60] and correlatively into reducing consciousness to the status of the most immediately and obviously present of all objects.[61] In order to disassociate oneself totally from the unambiguously objectivist[62] notion of consciousness which seems to have been shared by all of modern philosophy from Descartes to Husserl, one might go on to disclaim the transcendental problematic *in the sense in which it has been practised within this modern tradition*. Thus, Gadamer notes how Heidegger's concern with the being of a work of art,[63] with poetry,[64] with language[65]—with fields then in which patterns of consciousness have nothing to do with technical-reflexive objectification—coincides with what might have been such a shift.

If this hypothetical construction of the meaning of the 'ontological turn' at all hits off the reality of the matter,[66] it also allows one to assert that just as the Idealist and Husserlian efforts do not exhaust the meaning of the terms transcendental and foundational, so also there is the notion of consciousness which does not identify consciousness with the function of knowing objects; and that the 'da' of *Dasein* in *Sein und Zeit*, when it is shorn of any objectivist ambiguity, can be closely associated with this non-idealist notion of consciousness; and, finally, that consciousness so attended to can furnish the originating focus of a transcendental and foundational reflection which is quite the opposite of a forgetfulness of being or of a 'second-level historicism'.[67] I hope to show that this notion of consciousness is the basic datum to which Gadamer's reflection continually tends to recur.

The young Heidegger used the expression *Hermeneutik der Faktizität*[68] to depict that radically non-Cartesian transcendental and foundational reflection by which I have been seeking to characterise the shift to an ontology of understanding. Gadamer, following this tack of Heidegger, uses the term 'hermeneutics' to refer directly to a project on this most basic of levels (XVI); and only indirectly to any of the types of hermeneutics which history has already brought forth. Thus his philosophical hermeneutics is not the *regional* hermeneutics as instanced by the attempt of rabbinic exegesis to formulate a set of rules for intercourse with the classical texts in order to assure both freedom from falsification and the interpretation required to actualise the normative tradition. Nor is it the special hermeneutics which made up the classical and normative sciences of theology (Christian) and law. Moreover it is neither a new *Kunstlehre* in the manner of Schleiermacher's— what Gadamer calls a system of rules covering the essential similarity of procedures of interpretation in all fields; nor a repetition of Dilthey's mission of doing for the *Geisteswissenschaften* what Kant was supposed to have done for the natural sciences. The aim of Gadamer's hermeneutics is rather to interrogate the 'totality of human experience of the world and patterns of life' (XIV), in order to thematise a 'theory of the actual experience which thinking is' (XXII). His aim embraces a universality and a comprehensiveness that is new to the hermeneutic tradition (451). Even the universal intention of Dilthey's epistemology of interpretation had been hampered by its Cartesianism from bringing the properly hermeneutical problem of understanding and presenting correctly what has been understood within the compass of a reflection on human-historical experience in all its rich concreteness.

The pivot of Heidegger's enactment of the ontological turn is his transformation of a notion which had long marked the threshold of seriously historical thought in the work of Ranke, Droysen, Dilthey, and Husserl, namely, *Verstehen*. This shift in the meaning of *Verstehen* is the aspect of Heidegger's achievement which Gadamer has made most his own.

We attach ourselves to the *transcendental* sense of the Heideggerian *Fragestellung*. Through Heidegger's transcendental interpretation of *Verstehen*, the problem of hermeneutics gains a universal scope, indeed, the increment of a new dimension (249). *Verstehen* is not an ideal of resignation for human life-experience in the old-age of the spirit, as it had been for Dilthey, nor is it however an ultimate methodical ideal of philosophy over against the naïvete of being caught up in life, as it had been for Husserl; quite on the contrary, it is the primordial form of the actuation of *Dasein*, which is being-in-the-world. Prior to all differentiation of *Dasein* into various orientations of pragmatic or theoretic interests, *Verstehen* is the mode of being of *Dasein* in so far as it is power-to-be (*Seinskönnen*) and 'potentiality' (Möglicheit') . . . (245) [Heidegger] . . . unveiled the project character of all *Verstehen* and thought out *Verstehen* itself as the movement of transcendence, of going beyond beings (*das Seiende*) (246). . . . *Verstehen* is the mode of actuation of the historicity of *Dasein* itself. Its future character (*Zukünftig-keit:* ad-ventiveness, according to William Richardson), the basic character of the project as it pertains to the temporality of *Dasein*, is limited by the other determination of thrown-ness (*Geworfenheit*), by which not only the barriers to a sovereign self-possession have been designated, but also the positive possibilities which in fact we are have been opened up and determined (KS I, 73).

Gadamer has shown how by adverting to this phenomenon, the meta-theoretical reflection of the hermeneutic tradition might be plunged into the protean sources of human-historical experience. In Gadamer's perspective, to do anything less would be a gratuitous narrowing of the hermeneutic scope. For *Verstehen* occurs throughout the range of human performance: both the first-level, spontaneous, non-reflexive and non-technical mediation of human living, and the highly specialised second-level mediations of scientific thematisation, and in meta-theoretical reflection as well. Considering the experience one has in art, in the historical *Geisteswissenschaften*, and in philosophy itself, therefore, Gadamer has sought to thematise *Verstehen* not as a methodology, not as what ought to be or might be, but simply as what as a matter of fact is concretely immanent and operative in all human experience (XXV–XXVI, 483–4).

The New Hermeneutical Focus

a. *Beyond Subject-Object*. Dilthey's transposition of the principle made famous by Vico, *verum et factum convertuntur*, according to Gadamer, amounted to a comparison of the historical subject as object with historical objects (i.e., artifacts as expressions of human life). Even in his description and expansion of the notion of the indissolubility of a pre-theoretic knowing and life, this tendency of overlooking the subject in his primordiality caused Dilthey to conceive the original connection between the self and history as that of subject to object. With this fundamental estrangement from the historical reality of the subject posited, the view of appropriation of historical self-knowledge via the resolution of hyperbolic doubt through apodictic certainty formed a coherent background for his ideal of historical consciousness whose tragic flaw, finally, was that of not taking human finitude seriously.

Gadamer's own explication of *Verstehen* (250–84), however, shatters the limits of the naïvely conceived subject-object relationship, thus laying open to view the historicity of the human horizon itself. Gadamer's central breakthrough for the hermeneutical tradition in my judgement is the degree to which he seems to recognise the historical subject not as a different type of object among a totality of other objects (however true this may also be) but *as subject*.[69] On this rendering, it pertains to the very existence of the subject in its primordiality, i.e., prior to any and all objectification of that fact,[70] and as the condition for the possibility of such reflection-objectification, *to be historically*. '. . . That we do history [i.e., research, interpret, narrate, etc.] only in so far as we ourselves are "historical" means that the historicity of human *Dasein* in its entire state of motion (moved-ness: *Bewegtheit*), of expectation and of forgetting is the condition for the fact that we re-present what has been at all' (249).

The basic epistemological problems Dilthey confronted had mainly to do with the relationship between subjective spirit and objective spirit, between the individual's perspective and the full sweep of history (294, 297). (Cf. also Appendix C.) Presupposed was of course the subject-object dichotomy. The later Husserl seemed to have made the radical break with this presupposition when he broached the theme of *Lebenswelt* for philosophical reflection: a level of experience anterior to the subject-object relationship. But the Diltheyan presupposition was matched by Husserl's predilection for pure perception and for the propositional structure of predication, which kept him from dealing adequately with the original plenitude of human-historical life; and which even, perhaps, caused him to suspect Heidegger of propounding a mere *Weltanschauungslehre*.[71] If, however, both Scheler and Heidegger had exposed pure perception as an impoverishing abstraction from the rich and cumulative contextuality of human operations, so also were the conditions for the full range of human meaningfulness shown to extend far beyond those of rigorously logical propositions and syllogistic procedure. Gadamer has tried to move beyond these false presuppositions by reflection on the significance of the more global and concrete structure of *Verstehen*, on understanding as 'thrown project' (250–90). This phenomenon manifests an ever-renewed actuation of previously structured anticipations which are being constantly adjusted: a whole of which sensations, perceptions, memories, apprehensions of meaning, judgements, decisions, beliefs, preferences, etc., as well as technical and rigorous thematisation are each only derivative parts.

Moving to the level on which human life is operative prior to the differentiation of subject and object, then, Gadamer has emphasised a primacy of the *relation* vis-à-vis the *members* (e.g., interpreter in present/subject matter of traditional text from past) of the subject-object relationship.[72] (267, 275–83). By reason of the concretely conditioned prestructures of the subject, actuation with respect to an object represents an inter-'play'[73] between the two in which *neither member* provides the fixed basis. Rather, the subject matter (object) is hit off precisely in the mediation of its identity with the difference of the present context of the subject; and, reciprocally, the knowing subject is authentically actuated in a movement of self-transcendence by which his prestructures are put into play through intercourse with the subject matter. The abstract relation of subject-object, therefore, is subsumed into the *mediation* of the concrete prestructures of the understanding consciousness with the subject matter being understood—the mediation by which history progressively unfolds.

Gadamer's emphasis on concrete relation and mediation leads him away from the terminology of subject-object to talk about the happening of understanding or of tradition. The primacy which in other vocabularies is accorded either subject or object is here translated to the dynamic *Spielraum* of history or tradition of which the subject is a part. And in its aspect of constituting the horizon of the subject, this *Spielraum* is seen by Gadamer to have the structure of a concrete (versus formal as was the case for Schleiermacher) (245, 277) hermeneutic circle. There is no intention of covering over the gap between the macro-movement of history ('the course of the battle') and the micro-movement of discrete historical individuals ('the battle plans of the generals') (353–4). On the contrary, it is his intention to illuminate the finite structure of the participation by the subject in that greater movement and hence also the concrete possibility of appropriation of historical self-knowledge as being that of a concrete hermeneutic circle. This is why for Gadamer any intuitionism or *Einfühlung* is impoverishing, all logic is simply derivative and secondary, and scientific method on the model of the natural sciences is out of place; they tend to conceal with an approximation of timelessness the fact that the actuation of the subject is a finite mediation of the present with the past (274–7, 290–323, 329–30).

On this analysis, then, the appropriation of historical self-knowledge is most intelligent and critical in the measure that it makes the finite and concrete involvement of the subject in the hermeneutic circle explicit in an achievement of what Gadamer terms hermeneutic consciousness (284–90, 329–60). Unlike the mere historical consciousness of Dilthey and the members of the Historical School, hermeneutic consciousness recognises the historicity of the primordial subject by acknowledging one of the most important if apparently paradoxical implications of the truth that the freedom of the subject is an act of self-transcendence, namely, that history does not belong to the subject so much as the subject belongs to history (261).

b. *Historical Consciousness Realised.* From Dilthey's basic ambiguity with regard to the primordiality of the historical subject flowed, in Gadamer's view of the matter, the basic distortion which is historical consciousness. As with many distortions it has much that is right about it. Indeed, the ethos of historical science would be set back immeasurably were it to discard 'the task of understanding all the testimonies of a period out of the *Geist* of that time, of removing them from the preoccupying actualities of our present life, of knowing the past without moral "know–it–all–ism" (*Besserwisserei*) even as it, too, was human',[74] as Gadamer has described the critical ideal of historical consciousness (281–2). And yet if the historian or philosopher of history fails to thematise and keep in awareness the reality of the historical subject in his primordiality, there results the methodological naïvete which, overlooking the remote and proximate conditions of realising the critical ideal of historical consciousness, makes historicists the positivists in the field of history. For authentic historical self-knowledge, Gadamer contends that not the part which is historical consciousness (282), but the whole which is hermeneutic consciousness gets things in right perspective.

The ideal of historical consciousness, i.e. of total transplantation of self into a past context or of a rehabilitation of a past context into the present, seems to have arisen both under the pressure of the Enlightenment demand that prejudices be completely expunged (the 'prejudice against prejudices')[75] (257), and out of an exigence for a practice of the Cartesian methodical doubt in all fields of scholarly endeavour (255–6, 261, 263). Propagation of the ideal was seen to be a way of counteracting a dogmatically imposed continuity of tradition which, letting nothing become problematic, excluded the possibility of free appropriation of historical self. But as the Romantic sense of the abyss between present and past solidified into objectivist epistemological schemata (276), valid reaction turned into a perpetration of a counterdogma which was also very effective in suppressing acknowledgement of the primordial historicity of the subject.

Hermeneutical consciousness, however, reinstates this primordial historicity by recalling that comprehension of any element from the past is conditioned ambivalently by the dominant influence of the prestructures of the interpreter-historian who remembers and preserves the past in the light of his future. Gadamer's central analogy for communicating this further awareness of hermeneutic consciousness is that of horizon, which he inherits from Husserl only to develop it on the level of the concrete historical subject:[76]

To have a horizon means: not to be limited to what is most proximate, but to be able to see out beyond this. One who has horizon knows how to appreciate the significance of everything within this horizon according to proximity and distance, magnitude and smallness (286). To achieve horizon always means that one learns to look out beyond what is near and most proximate, not for the sake of looking away from it, but in order to see it better within a greater whole and in the context of a more just standard of measure (288–9).

On the level of horizon Gadamer has been able, on the one hand, both to unmask the objectivist fiction of completely uprooting oneself from one's historically mediated horizon in an act of transplantation into a totally different horizon, and at the same time to uncover as equally illusory the notion of an element in history to be comprehended, which is magnificently isolated in some hermetically sealed compartment of the past.

Horizon is . . . something into which we move and which moves along with us. For one in motion, horizons shift. So also the horizon of the past, out of which all human life lives and which is present in the mode of tradition, is always already in motion. It is not historical consciousness which sets this encompassing horizon into motion. In it this movement has merely become conscious of itself. When our historical consciousness is transposed into historical horizons, this does not mean a removal into strange worlds bound by nothing at all to our world, but together they form a great intrinsically mobile horizon which reaches beyond the limits of our presently conscious perspective to embrace the historical depths of our self-consciousness. It is actually, then a single horizon which encloses all that historical consciousness contains in itself. The unique and foreign past to which our historical consciousness is turned is a component of this mobile horizon out of which human life always lives and which determines that life as its origin and tradition (288). . . . A truly historical consciousness always regards itself together with [the past situation] and indeed in such a way that it views itself and the historical other in their correct relationships (289).

And on the other hand, he has been able to exclude this sort of objectivism from his own phenomenology of the process of thematising one's historical horizon.

The key to Gadamer's distinction between historical and hermeneutic consciousness as modes of thematising historical horizon is their respective appreciation of the conditions and functions of *questioning*[77] (344–60): 'The logic of the *Geisteswissenschaften* is . . . a logic of the question' (352). Indeed, one of Gadamer's ways of defining historicity is the assertion that for finite, human *Dasein* there is no possibility of the sublation of questioning into the perfect self-transparency of full self-knowledge[78] (285).

Horizon becomes explicit at the point where new questions emerge, because questioning marks the divide between the historically pre-given determination of our horizons, which Gadamer with Hegel calls substance, and the reflexive consciousness of this substance, which he then terms subjectivity (285–6, cf. also 336–9). Hermeneutic consciousness, says Gadamer, will note that questions are provoked when the prestructures of one's horizon are challenged, for example, whenever one enters into a tension between the familiarity of one's accustomed form of life and the strangeness of some element of tradition (279, 348). Thus, the two extremities of the Cartesian doubt which precludes by its very application the emergence of the genuinely problematic, and the dogmatism which refuses on principle to entertain the truth-possibility of anything not already obvious seem, from the point of view of hermeneutic consciousness, to be equalled in practice by the mythical ideal of historical consciousness according to which one must be entirely uninfluenced by one's current presuppositions in 'reading one's answer out of' the past. In contrast to this ideal, hermeneutic consciousness will recognise that crossing the divide between substance and subject, between strangeness and familiarity, between question and answer, essentially means

reaching the correct horizon of questioning for the questions put to us when confronted by the tradition (286). In order to respond to this question put to us, we, the questioned, must ourselves begin to ask questions. We seek to reconstruct the question to which the transmitted (text, work, historical trace) would be an answer. We will not be able to do this at all without transcending the historical horizon indicated by the transmitted artifact through our questioning. The very reconstruction of the question to which the text ought to be the answer stands within a questioning process by which we seek an answer to the question set us by the tradition. For the historical horizon described in the reconstruction is not a truly comprehensive horizon. It is rather itself encompassed even now by the horizon which encloses us as questioners confronted by the word of the tradition (356; cf. also 351–60).

For Gadamer, therefore, an enlightened approach to the appropriation of self as historical entails in the first place not abstraction from personal horizon in order to open oneself up without bias to the past (280), but rather an analysis of horizon by way of an unfolding of one's own *Fragestellung*, i.e., an ongoing refinement of one's prestructured capacity to put better and better questions.[79] As Lionel Trilling once expressed it, 'Refinement of our historical sense chiefly means that we keep it properly complicated.'

Such question-sensitive analysis of historical horizon is best effected by consciously promoting one's sedimented prestructures into the 'play' of the hermeneutic circle (283, 349).

In truth the horizon of the present is apprehended in a constant learning process, in so far as we must subject all our prejudices to continuous testing. Not the least relevant opportunity for this testing is encounter with the past and understanding the tradition out of which we come. [For] without the horizon of the past, the horizon of the present would have no form at all. There is as little such a thing as a present horizon *per se* as there is a historical horizon which one might have had to attain. Rather understanding is always a process of fusion of such putative horizons existing in isolation (289).

The moment of the relationship between one's questioning and one's prejudices, then, can hardly be over-emphasised, first, because prejudices constitute, whether one intends them to or not, the *modus recipiendi* of the horizon of the subject. As Gadamer so provocatively expresses it: our being is constituted not so much by our judgements as by our prejudices (261). They are prior to any explication of historical horizon, to any questioning; they are in fact the historical condition of possibility of that thematisation and that questioning. In the second place, one's prejudices are *ipso facto* neither true nor false; they are both true and false. Hence, to pretend to erase them totally is not only to preclude the possibility of knowing which are true and which false, but to put oneself at the mercy of the false ones (282–3, 343). Third, the subject matter of past tradition has been mediated beforehand to the horizon of the interpreter-historian by the effective totality of the succeeding chain of events and interpretations (*Wirkungs-geschichte*) which become sedimented in the subject's consciousness in the form of prejudices: the historical subject is a moment in the tradition which he is appropriating. As a corollary of this, any meaning of a past context is determined, according to Gadamer's notion of effective history, not only by the immediate agents and eye-witnesses (or author and public), but also 'by the historical situation of the interpreter . . . and thus by the totality of the objective course of history' (280).

By taking these things into account, Gadamer argues, hermeneutic consciousness will also realise that the act of appropriation itself is a renovation of the tradition, a continuation of this effective history, which realises the past in the present more or less genuinely. Whereas historical consciousness, although it tends to ignore both the crucial importance of prejudice and this principle of effective history, cannot avoid either being affected by prejudice or participating actively in the effective history of tradition. It simply does so less consciously.

For what Gadamer calls a 'hermeneutically schooled consciousness', then, appropriation of historical self-knowledge is a complex, oscillating movement: on the one hand there occurs the gradual discernment by which one sifts true from false prejudices. And this happens, I repeat, not by extinguishing the prejudices that prestructure our horizon, but by throwing them into relief against the tradition one is appropriating, i.e., by putting them into question in the context of the possible truth (as contradicting or clarifying) of the tradition. And on the other hand there goes forward a gradual determination and refinement of that vague foreknowledge with which our prestructures furnish us from the outset, as more and more of the tradition is cast into relief against the background of these anticipations.

Obviously, the rigorous and self-critical work of gaining a 'past' horizon so stressed by historical consciousness is a necessary component in this movement of mutual mediation. But in a hermeneutically conscious appropriation of tradition, one enters with open eyes into a concrete enactment of the hermeneutic circle, a hermeneutic circle which, in Gadamer's words, is

. . . not of a formal nature, it is neither subjective nor objective, but describes understanding as the interplay of the movement of tradition and the movement of the interpreter. The anticipation of meaning which guides our understanding of a text is not an act of subjectivity [of a Cartesian subject vis-a-vis an abstractly isolated object] but is determined by the common affinity which binds us with the tradition. This element of community, however, is apprehended in our relation to the tradition in a process of constant educative formation (277).

Gadamer describes human living, therefore (and hence appropriation of historical self-knowledge as well) in terms of a concrete hermeneutic circle for two reasons: firstly because both the rise of questions about the meaning of reality and prospective actuation are just empty phantoms if uninformed however vaguely beforehand by a sense of meaning or direction; and this prior affinity is provided by the retrospective. And secondly because just as surely, the enriching retrospective out of which we live is not apprehended in its full clarity first, and only then applied to a particular situation; rather, Gadamer insists, both the emergence of new questions about the meaning of things and the prospective actuation of meaning are the *sine qua non* for both rightly grasping the retrospective and for bringing it to bear on the present. '. . . The essence of the historical spirit consists not in the restoration of the past, but in thoughtful mediation of the past with present life' (161).

The purpose of Gadamer's transcendental and foundational hermeneutics is to provide an extended elaboration of this basic theme in what comes to a general phenomenology of human living. It is an exposé of hermeneutic consciousness by way of contrast with derivative or stunted forms such as aesthetic or historical consciousness, in all of which forms 'the moment of effective history (*Wirkungsgeschichte*) is and remains at work in all understanding . . .' (XIX). Within the perspective of hermeneutic consciousness, the cognitional theoretic (in the sense of epistemological) question becomes: 'In what does the legitimacy of prejudice have to be grounded?' (261). And Gadamer's description of 'not what we do, not what we ought to do, but what occurs along with us but beyond our willing and doing . . .' (XIV) leads him to the assertion that true and false prejudices are discriminated progressively over time in the critico-receptive application of tradition which is ever happening both intentionally and unintentionally in the participation of succeeding generations in the circular structure of understanding. In the light of Gadamer's phenomenology, intelligent access to a non-utopian future is to be won through a critical appropriation of tradition.

Hence, hermeneutic consciousness, because it acknowledges the primordiality of the subject, is a realised historical consciousness. It never disregards the fact that the past forms one's preoccupations, gives direction to one's questions, content to one's anticipations; and it knows that the meanings and attitudes of the past depend for their unfolding on renewed question-asking and the initiating of new projects. It is the awareness that human living is a mutual mediation of retrospective and prospective, of old and new.

    c. *Consciousness as the New Focus.* One might describe the Cartesian notion of science as a case of cultural lag which persists, astonishingly enough, even after the rise of quantum mechanics in the form of a tendency among cultured people to invest modern science with some of the trappings of Aristotle's *episteme* such as certainty, absolute truth, complete logical rigour, necessity, etc.[80] (430–1). Besides the prevalence of the Cartesian myth of modern science, modern culture in the West has been dominated by science as technological, by the notion that all scientific undertaking is nothing more than accumulating and organising knowledge for the sake of 'practical' manipulation (427–30). This was the setting for the cognitional theoretic bias toward 'scientific validity' in the epistemologies of interpretation of the Enlightenment (165–72), by Romantic hermeneutics and by Historicism (341, 427–8). Somewhat in reaction to this context and to the reductive tendencies of the epistemology of interpretation, another facet of Aristotle's work is having a growing resonance now, namely, his distinctions between theoretical and practical or political science, and between practical knowing and either theoretical or technical knowing. Gadamer has especially esteemed the Aristotelian analysis of *phronesis* (511), in which he has seen '. . . a model of the problems involved in the hermeneutical task' (307). Indeed, one way of suggesting the bearing of the ontological turn in Gadamer might be to say that he has cast his philosophical hermeneutics along lines analogous to the practical philosophy of Aristotle, which was marked by its recurrent criticism of the imposition of rigorously theoretical or technical standards to a field where such requirements are absurd.

    Early in Husserl's career he contended: 'It is undeniable that what meaning (*Bedeutung*) in this sense means, embraces only ideal unities throughout which are expressed in manifold expressions and thought in manifold experiential acts (*Akterlebnissen*);

and yet just as they must be distinguished from these chance expressions, so must they be from the accidental experiences (*Erlebnissen*) of the one thinking.'[81] With this clarification, Gadamer believes, the possibility of handling transcendental and foundational problems in the realm of historicity in a strictly hermeneutical instead of psychologistic manner was established[82] (211-2). For in psychologies of understanding-of-expression, understanding gets confined to reproduction of moments of another's psychic experience within oneself. However, in the Husserlian recognition of the independence of unities of meaning from either expressions or psychic acts—although these are ever-present conditions of possibility—understanding can be seen to be a matter not so much of a reproduction of fine acts as of an apprehension of the illuminative character of immanent coherence, of a meaningfulness, that is, which is not simply dependent on (in the sense of totally subordinate to) an individual's sensitive perspective in space-time or his psychic states. This non-psychologistic theory of meaning and understanding, along with Husserl's later thematisation of 'anonymous intentionality' and 'anonymous performance'[83] (232-3, 235, 245), gave transcendental and foundational reflection phenomenologically demonstrable tools to deal with the trans-individual constellations of intelligibility which make up history.

But Husserl himself did not unravel the implications of his own insights for historicity. And Dilthey, even under Husserl's influence, was able only to formulate the 'problem of the bridge' for the context of historical knowing: How could trans-subjective patterns of meaning be known since they go beyond any individual's experience? (211). He never got beyond a 'reprivatising' solution which put all the weight on analogies drawn from the knowing which goes on in the cases of autobiography and biography (261, 477-8), from which he extrapolated to the geniality of a reproductive faculty capable of detaching itself from the limits of its own horizon to comprehend everything (historical consciousness) (218).

It is Gadamer who, exploiting Heidegger's explication of the prestructures of understanding, has gone beyond Dilthey to unfold the implications of the Husserlian breakthroughs for the problems of individual and trans-subjective meaning in history. He has defined the task of a truly historical hermeneutics in terms of taking seriously the trans-subjective structures of meaning and the relativity of particular contexts by reflecting on that tension arising between the identity (*Selbigkeit*) of the subject matter which is history's meaning and the changing situations through which that identity is apprehended and transformed (292). To begin with, there is no problem of the bridge,

. . . because the great historical realities—society and state—are in truth always determinative for every 'experience' beforehand. . . . Long before we understand ourselves in explicit retrospection, we understand ourselves as a matter of course in the family, society, and state in which we live. The focus of subjectivity is a distortion. The self-reflection of an individual is just a flash in the closed circuit of historical life. Hence the individual's prejudices far more than his judgements are the historical reality of his being (261).

The historical movement of constellations of meaning both transcends each individual and at the same time proceeds in and through the lives of individuals. By the natural and spontaneous process of socialisation (especially, Gadamer underlines, the learning of one's mother tongue), however, history deposits in the consciousness of individual participants a vague and indeterminate imprint of its evolving meaning in the form of what Gadamer refers to as the prejudices which are played out in the spiral of the individual's life.

A prime example of the tension between the identity and the difference of meaning in history is the hermeneutical problem in the narrower sense, i.e., that of understanding something presented in one context and correctly transmitting it to another.[84] Gadamer seems to distinguish three basic elements: (a) the speaker, writer, agent in his context; (b) the hearer, reader, interpreter in his context; (c) the common subject matter grasped and applied, first, in the original context, and then in any later context. Now this common subject matter to which one commonly has recourse in order to link the two contexts and which becomes concretised in them is—logically considered—analogous to the 'essence of meaning' of which Husserl said that it consists '. . . not in the experience (*Erlebnis*) bestowing the meaning, but in its "content", which presents an identical intentional unity over against the diffuse multiplicity of real or possible experiences of those speaking or thinking'.[85] But this character of 'intentional unity of meaning' is also latent in the prejudices sedimented in the consciousness of any person whether in his everyday life or in his role of scientific interpreter, although not necessarily in the univocal form which dominated the early Husserl's concerns. Hence not only the strictly hermeneutical task but all human knowing and doing is wrapped up in the tension of identity and difference of historical meaning.

In Gadamer's phenomenology of the way this tension works itself out in living or in hermeneutics proper, whenever a person either spontaneously and naturally or reflexively and technically asks questions and implements plans, the circular or reciprocal inter-action between his prejudices and the actual situation of his action is set in play: the universal (in the sense of a universality of experience versus that of science) prejudices are applied to the particular state of affairs at hand. Important to keep in mind, however, is that 'application' here means the actual grasp of the universal meaning *in* the particular situation: Although that apprehension involves the two distinct elements (one's prejudices/one's particular situation; or, the meaning of the text/the situation of the interpreter), there are not, according to Gadamer, two discrete processes of apprehension temporally succeeding one another. This structure of the application of the universal to the particular, then, is operative in both the specifically hermeneutical task and in the business of human living in general. Gadamer also stresses its parallel in formal outline to Aristotle's picture of the emergence of the knowledge of general principles (*epagoge*) in terms of the army in flight[86] (333–5).

Precisely this application-structure is overlooked in the psychologistic theory of interpretation of Romantic hermeneutics for which the point, Gadamer says, is the fathoming of the individuality of the speaker-writer-historical agent by the hearer-reader-interpreter, so that the subject matter is wholly subordinated to this end. Transposed to history and to historical life, this oversight entails, in Gadamer's critical evaluation, conceiving history not as a trans-subjective constellation of meaning (*Sinnzusammenhang*) but as a merely experiential context (*Erlbeniszusammenhang*) potentially (or in the case of fully actuated historical consciousness, actually) congruent with the limits of an individual horizon of experience, in which the relationship of historian, for instance, to the history-to-be-comprehended is that of abstract subjectivity to exterior objectivity on the Cartesian model (294, 340–4, 477–8).

In Gadamer's opposing view, the acknowledgement of both pre-judice and the application-structure entails not only the re-establishment of the primacy of the subject matter of history (hermeneutically, the point being *intelligere rem per verba* versus *intelligere verba*; cf. quote from Luther, 162) and the grasp of the fact that history runs its course beyond the self-knowledge of the individual;[87] but also, however paradoxical it may sound, the realisation that what we know historically is in the last analysis what we ourselves are.[88]

Now this configuration of knowledge-of-history (or of know-ledge in the *Geisteswissenschaften* generally) and self-knowledge on the one hand, together with the application-structure on the other, is a natural analogue of the Aristotelian notion of *phronesis* as described in the *Nichomachean Ethics*, especially the sixth book. One finds in the *Ethics* as a whole[89] a devastating critique of Plato's abstract universal idea of the Good in the course of a painstaking determination of the role of reason in ethical action. In describing how much what one knows or does in the ethical field depends on what one *is*, Aristotle scores the effective-historical point of the social and political conditionedness of the individual agent as both determining his action and determined by it (297): how the prior, imperfect incarnations of human reason in law and mores as interiorised by the moral agent provide a concrete framework for individual preferential choice (*prohairesis*) not merely as hindrances but as a support for freedom particularly when balanced as they should be by the critical function of *epieikeia* (301) and of the natural law (302-4, 490-1). Moreover, there is the incisive dis-tinction between *phronesis* and both *episteme* (e.g., mathematics) and *techne* (knowledge applied in the production of a contingent artifact).

The node of the proportion between practical knowing and the hermeneutical structure of human experience which is crucial for getting at the overall direction of Gadamer's project is that for Gadamer *phronesis* is a most lucid example of

a mode of knowing . . . which simply could no longer be related to an ultimate objectifiability in the sense of science, a knowing within the concrete situation of the conscious person (*Existenzsituation*).[90] The overwhelming alientation by the objectifying methods of modern science which distinguished nineteenth century hermeneutics and historical science appears to us a result of a false objectification. In order to see through this and to avoid it, the example of Aristotelian ethics is invoked. For ethical knowledge, as Aristotle describes it, is obviously not objective knowing, i.e., the knower does not stand over against a state of affairs which he only ascertains, but he is immediately affected by and concerned with what he knows . . . (297).

Thus, in stressing again that 'non-objectifying' knowledge of man on the analogy of *phronesis* is what the *Geisteswissenschaften* are about (298), Gadamer is once more arguing the illegitimacy of Cartesian and objectivist presuppositions in the area of historical self-knowledge. Once again he is pointing to the primordiality of the historical subject, to that intersection of subject and history on a level where the subject is constituted not so much by operation as by co-operation.

If *phronesis* provides an illuminating analogy for the immediate interpenetration of history and the subject at a level more basic than and running through the gamut of his knowing and doing, it also intimates Gadamer's sketchily and somewhat ambiguously presented notion of consciousness. Gadamer holds himself under the Husserlian demand that the structures thematised be phenomenologically ostensible within human experience[91] (XXIX, XXII). Against all psychologism and Idealism he intends to expose to our view structures which transcend the comportment of consciousness; and yet, bound as he is to the Husserlian canon of parsimony, he considers and speaks in positive terms about consciousness— for example, hermeneutic consciousness, effective-historical (*Wikungsgeschichtliche-*) consciousness—much more than his mentor in the ontology of understanding, Heidegger, has tended to. In his discussions of the distinction (first brought to his attention by Heidegger) between *actus signatus* and *actus exercitus*, are to be found the clearest expressions by Gadamer on the modest sort of consciousness which would be compatible with human finitude and historicity.[92]

The basic affirmation is that not all consciousness is objectifying consciousness. Consciousness is structured as horizon and, whatever the direct object of consciousness may be, it falls within this horizon of consciousness of which one is aware not directly or 'objectively', but indirectly or 'reflexively'. Hence the continuum of explicit direct awareness of objects running from everyday, common-sense intending to complex hypothesising, observing, and verifying in the sciences, is not the whole reality of consciousness;

a type of awareness or reflexivity *is* concomitantly with this spectrum of objectifications, but *not as object*.

The unique self of which one is reflexively conscious is not an object in the same sense in which we otherwise name an objectifying comportment of knowledge directed toward an object, which as known loses as it were its power of resistance, is dominated and becomes manipulable. [This would refer to consciousness as conceived of in a totally instrumental or technical fashion, according to Gadamer; as thought of by Descartes, Idealism, or neo-Kantian methodologies.] Rather it is in play in such a way that it accompanies lived performance. This is our proper freedom that in so accompanying vital performance choice and decision become possible; and any other freedom toward oneself, to which we raise ourselves by free resolve does not exist at all. Reflexive concomitance with performance, not objectifying standing-over-against, is the mark of an action which we call 'intelligent' (KS I, 226). [This type of reflection is] . . . a reflecting which in the exercise of an 'intention' as it were beds itself back upon its own performance . . . and in no wise reflection in the modern sense of the term. The self-actuating act is always an act already, i.e., however, it is always something wherein my own performance is vitally present to me—the transformation to explicit-direct awareness ('*Signierung*') establishes a completely new intentional object (KS I, 143–4).

This is the consciousness, then, in which history has embedded its meanings in the vague and ambivalent mode of prejudice. It is the consciousness which is 'hermeneutic', in Gadamer's sense; and which, as such, does not overlook itself.

Now Gadamer will say, for instance, that all effective-historical consciousness is more being than consciousness.[93] But this provocative and ambiguous assertion does not necessarily imply, I think, a naïvely objectivist contrast and separation of consciousness and being on his part. The consciousness set in opposition to effective-historical consciousness and compared with being, is that derivative and secondary reflection of which consciousness in the primary sense is the prior condition of possibility. It would be, then, the reflection in which some aspect of what we at first have only a concomitant awareness is moved into direct awareness. Gadamer's point—one that he is continually emphasising with regard to consciousness—is that reflection in this derivative and secondary sense can always be only partial, piece-meal, incomplete. Hence Gadamer accuses those who would locate either the general drift of history or some emancipatory steering of history within a consciousness and reflection conceived exclusively as (self-) objectification, of failing to recognise that the true wellsprings of history and freedom in history lie in that primary, not-necessarily-objectifying, but concomitant and history-laden consciousness, which in one passage he calls, 'effective reflection'.[94] This is where the subject is mediated by and mediates history in what in a broadly descriptive manner I have termed co-operation.

Certainly the secondary reflection can overlook the primary. But even when this happens, Gadamer insists, the latter is still at work—as horizon (XIX–XX). Therefore, any adequate explication of the structure of human-historical experience requires starting from and never relinquishing a massive recognition of that primary consciousness.

I have said, however, that Gadamer's explications of consciousness are sketchy and ambiguous, clearest indeed with regard to what they oppose. Gadamer does seem content to re-affirm against psychologism and Idealism that notion of concomitant awareness which he has discovered in both Plato and Aristotle, and in that degree of differentiation which they attained. Compact as this stage of thematisation is, it becomes very difficult, therefore, to distinguish the diverse grades of 'primordiality' among: (1) concomitant awareness; (2) the acts by which it mediates itself; (3) the unthematic (never totally thematisable), historical identity it receives, for example, when learning its original life-form and language. Gadamer, carrying forth and radicalising the German philosophical tradition from *Geist* through *Lebensform* to being-in-the-world, has thus far chosen to treat this matter *in extenso* only from the perspective of (3). And from this standpoint, (1) and (2) as 'effective reflection' seem to be equiprimordial with (3). Clearly, many distinctions and clarifications are still outstanding.

Now while I have found in Gadamer no elaboration of a notion of objectivity reconcilable with the radical notion of consciousness which (I am here proposing) he remains one of the few to have accorded philosophical recognition and importance; while I find his treatments of consciousness underdeveloped with regard to both the distinction and interrelationship of the operations of consciousness as they are immanent, operative, and *normative* within all the patterns of human living; while I consider his failure to distinguish clearly the paradigm-followers from the originators of the paradigms in science together with his tendency to lump the procedures of modern science under the heading of Cartesian objectivism quite inadequate, and hence short of grounding an account of the legitimate interplay of science and common sense (to which I am convinced he would not be closed); and while on the basis of the phenomenology of finite consciousness such as Lonergan has afforded, I see no reason why the philosophical affirmation of God must be relegated to the status of merely dialectical complement in the Kantian sense[95] (XXII), although I do see it as a problem which can only be handled on the level of the dialectical in Lonergan's sense[96]—all these reservations and their implications notwithstanding, I do think that Gadamer has gone decisively beyond the proponents of the epistemology of interpretation to relate history and consciousness to each other on that basic level where the subject is subject and not object. Thus he has extricated the hermeneutical tradition from myriad pseudo-problems and put it in the way of the real problems of the dialectic of self-knowledge and history. In so far as Gadamer has done this, he stands squarely in the tradition of Newmanian intellectualism (not obscurantism) when he writes: 'As understanding human beings we are implicated in a happening of truth, and we arrive, so to speak, too late when we wish to know that which we ought to believe' (465).

HISTORICAL SELF-KNOWLEDGE IN LONERGAN

As the doctoral dissertation of David Tracy[97] has made thematic, such an exemplary instance of the 'fusion of horizons' which is the work of 'hermeneutic consciousness' as that which has been occurring between the horizon of Lonergan and that of the tradition—especially Aquinas—can scarcely be found. But Lonergan's work is also the most radical and comprehensive fulfilment to date of the intentions of the 'ontological turn'. If no words better characterise the achievement of Lonergan than transcendental and foundational, so, too, no other scholar to my knowledge has reflected so diligently upon the concrete reality of the consciousness which I have called the new hermeneutical focus: the consciousness of the subject as subject.

The Shift-in-Meaning (Umdeutung) of Cognitional Theory

As an instance of this radicality and comprehensiveness, consider the shift-in-meaning Lonergan has carried out with regard to the term and exercise, cognitional theory. In the face of the misapprehensions of Emilio Betti, Gadamer had expressed the basic orientation of the ontological turn as follows: 'Basically I am proposing no method; I am only describing what is . . . I maintain that the only scientific thing to do is to *acknowledge what is*, instead of beginning from what should be or might be . . . In this sense, I try to think in its fundamental generality what *always* happens' (483–4). There is to the ontological turn, then, a criticism of the epistemological question as a quite secondary problem at best and a scandal at worst from the viewpoint of a heightened awareness which has turned its attention back to the originating experience of self as historical horizon and asks simply: What is happening here? Now the same thrust can be seen behind Lonergan's approach to the critical problem. For Lonergan has reformulated that problem 'not as the easy question whether we know but as the real issue of what precisely occurs when we are knowing'.[98]

But what for Gadamer, as a leading exponent of the ontological turn in a context until recently dominated by Positivism and neo-Kantianism, becomes a bias-as-corrective against the limited legitimacy of cognitional theory as epistemology, in Lonergan becomes a precise redefinition in which cognitional theory is distinguished from epistemology and related to it in a fashion which ensures the liberation of the epistemological question from all necessity of carrying Cartesian connotations. Thus, cognitional theory is the answer to the question: What am I doing when I am knowing? While epistemology answers the question: Why is doing that knowing? Note that the 'that' in this question does not refer to any naïve picture of what knowing should or might be like, but to the structures discovered in the radical heightening of awareness which mediates the answer to the cognitional theoretic question.[99]

From Logic to Method

Then again, Gadamer's anti-Cartesianism causes him to shy away from confronting the procedures and norms incarnated in authentic scientific inquiry (as opposed to mere rule-following). He usually confines discussion of modern science to very general treatment of historical presuppositions. But the cognitional theory of Lonergan, with its emphasis on concrete operations in the process of questioning and answering, has enabled him to differentiate clearly common sense and descriptive procedures from those heading towards scientific explanation.[100] Further, he has been able to give the shift away from the cosmocentrism of classical science a more precise meaning in his discrimination of classical from modern science: the former was a universalisation (based on sensible similarity) or classification of common sense experience whose logical ideal received its definitive formulation in Aristotelian theory of science. The latter has moved on to explanation in terms of functional correlations (based on similarities holding directly between things themselves) and has developed more subtle procedures (implicit definition, group theory, relativity, quantum theory, etc.) which subordinate deductive processes along the lines of Aristotelian logic to a greater attention to operations going on in the mind of the scientist by way of working toward a more precise control of the *movement* of generalisation.[101] Now if the Cartesian union of universal doubt with abstract deductivism approximately describes the rhetoric (what Lonergan has well termed a 'set of blunders'[102]) and activity of what Lonergan refers to as the 'hodmen of science',[103] still it may obscure the fact to which Lonergan's propensity for cognitional theory has made him so sensitive: namely, that modern science has moved from logic to method. This is why modern empirical scientific and mathematical advance allow us to understand that just as *principle*,[104] besides meaning a 'logically first proposition, an ultimate premise', can also mean simply 'first in any ordered set', and so refer to our originating power to ask and answer questions; that just as *system*,[105] besides meaning a closed 'set of definitions and axioms', can also mean 'a basic group of *operations*, that can be combined and recombined in various ways . . .' and so refer to a concrete historical subject; so also *method*[106] cannot be restricted to meaning 'a set of verbal propositions enouncing rules to be followed in a scientific investigation'. By reformulating cognitional theory's intention in consonance with the ontological turn's critique of Cartesianism, Lonergan has given the anti-Cartesian orientation the opportunity 'to acknowledge in man's developed understanding of the material universe a principle that yields a developed understanding of understanding itself, and to use that developed understanding of human understanding to bring order and light and unity to a totality of disciplines and modes of knowledge that otherwise will remain unrelated, obscure

about their foundations, and incapable of being integrated by
. . . theology'.[107]

The challenge which the shift-in-meaning of cognitional theory
has permitted Lonergan to accept, then, has been that of deriving
a notion of method adequate to the historicity and consequent
logical viciousness of the interplay of *Verstehen's* prestructures
with the world from the most conspicuously successful region of
science today, the empirical sciences of nature. Thus, he begins
with the recognition that even natural scientific inquiry does not
have to be considered under the logical conditions of the hypotheses, theories, and systems which proceed from it. Instead of
concentrating on strictly logical and paradigmatic considerations,
then, Lonergan could (from the perspective of cognitional theory)
focus on the *movement* of the inquiry process itself rather than on
results alone. In this way he could discover that what is involved
in the process from data to results is 'a normative pattern of related
and recurrent operations yielding cumulative and progressive
results'[108]—that is, *method*—in which deductive process—that is,
logic—plays only a small and relatively secondary role. In this
sense, then, Lonergan has been able to move *with* modern science
from logic *to* method.

Most significantly this preliminary notion of method has no
connotation either of the prejudice against prejudices or of con-
finement to the exigences of logical replication—despite the fact of
its derivation from empirical natural science. In brief, it is free of
Cartesianism.

The pursuit of the consequences of the ontological turn via
method radicalises rather than waters down the enterprise of transcendental and foundational reflection. The key to method for
Lonergan is the subject as subject. For method in Lonergan's
sense cannot be reduced to any canonised model or paradigm of
knowledge—whether intellectual, aesthetic, symbolic, etc. To do
'method' calls rather for a release from all logics, all closed systems
or language games, all concepts, all symbolic constructs to allow
an abiding at the level of the presence of the subject to himself,
of which Lonergan has said:

. . . It is not the presence of another object dividing his attention, of
another spectacle distracting the spectator; it is presence in, as it were,
another dimension, presence concomitant and correlative and opposite
to the presence of the object. Objects are present by being attended to:

but subjects are present as subjects, not by being attended to, but by attending. . . . [Now if a person] tries to find himself as subject, to reach back and, as it were, uncover his subjectivity, [he] cannot succeed. Any such effort is introspecting, attending to the subject; and what is found is, not the subject as subject, but only the subject as object; it is the subject as subject that does the finding. To heighten one's presence to oneself, one does not introspect; one raises the level of one's activity.[109]

We have seen how Gadamer's transcendental and foundational reflection redirects our attention to primitive (i.e., prior to all theory about it) experiences of historicity in order to explicate phenomenologically what occurs there under the broad heading of *Verstehen*. It can be said, perhaps, that Gadamer's *Verstehen* is a transcendental and yet globally compact designation of the mode of actuation of man, covering the range of human life-experience: it stands as the whole to the parts represented by, e.g., the pure perception of Husserl, the *Einfühlung* of Schleiermacher and Dilthey, the various logics of the diverse types of neo-Kantianism.

Lonergan's methodical entry into transcendental and foundational reflection seems to stand as a further question put with regard to the event of *Verstehen* as described by Gadamer: it directs our attention even more explicitly to what is occurring on the side of the subject as subject, the *noesis*, as he actuates himself and is actuated in the transitive relationship which constitutes him being-in-the-world. Not abstracting from, but heightening one's awareness *within* this transitive relationship, it asks if there is a normative pattern of related and recurrent operations yielding cumulative results on the part of what Gadamer terms effective reflection. The answer to this further question is found not in any apriorist theory or ideal of what human knowing or action might or should be; it is discovered only in that heightening of awareness mentioned above, i.e., in one's own aboriginal experience of qualitatively different levels within that awareness concomitant with the diverse levels in one's intending, not only in scientific endeavour but in the full sweep of human activity.[110]

Lonergan's generalised or transcendental method, therefore, meets the Husserlian demand for phenomenological ostensibility. And it goes beyond Husserl with Gadamer and Heidegger to take in the plenitude of *Verstehen* in a heightening of awareness which seeks to thematise the concrete structures of finite consciousness on the basis of the evidence provided by that consciousness itself rather than by proceeding by *epoche*-reduction to a non-historical *Ur-factum* which would satisfy the exigencies of Cartesian apodicticity.

Furthermore, Lonergan's transcendental method is completely general and completely concrete in a manner unparalleled in other phenomenologies: in discovering in primitive experience a normative pattern of related and recurrent operations, it moves beyond a description of the comprehensive phenomenon of *Verstehen* to an explanation. That is, it reaches the ideal of implicit definition in which basic terms and basic relations are mutually determined, thus gaining a superlative generality without sacrificing an iota of concreteness.[111]

All defining presupposes undefined terms and relations. In the book, *Insight*, the undefined terms are cognitional operations [experience, understanding, reflective understanding, deliberation] and the undefined relations are the dynamic relations that bind cognitional operations together. Both the operations and their dynamic relations are given in immediate internal experience, and the main purpose of the book is to help the reader to discover these operations and their dynamic relations in his own personal experience.[112]

Transcendental method, then, can be seen to be a matter of passing *from* a critical awareness by which we become familiar with our operations as distinct yet interrelated in their immediacy *to* a mediation of that immediacy in an explanatory formulation.

But the concrete execution of this passage brings to light the second and most significant difference between Lonergan's and other phenomenologies. Lonergan stresses repeatedly that the programme of transcendental method as he has formulated it is an invitation to authenticity, a call to a basic change in the orientation of one's conscious intentionality—because the crucial disclosure exacted by transcendental method is not merely of the basic terms (i.e., empirical, intelligent, rational, responsible consciousness), and basic relations, but of the *basic orientation*[113] which, when operative, is the dynamism behind the unfolding of the basic pattern of terms and relations:

. . . The dynamic structure of human knowing intends being. That intention is comprehensive, for questioning probes every aspect of everything; its ultimate goal is the universe in its full concreteness.[114] What is this intending? It is neither ignorance nor knowledge but the conscious intermediary between ignorance and knowledge. It is the conscious movement away from ignorance and towards knowledge. When we question, we do not know the answer yet, but we already want the answer. Not only do we want the answer, but also are aiming at the answer. Such, then, is intending and, essentially, it is dynamic.[115]

Thus, Lonergan's transcendental method pushes the discussion of the prestructures of *Verstehen* to their ultimate point of immediacy.

It is not sure that it is from sense that our cognitional activities derive their immediate relationships to real objects; that relationship is immediate in the intention of being; it is mediate in the data of sense and in the data of consciousness inasmuch as the intention of being makes use of data in promoting cognitional process to knowledge of being; similarly, that relationship is mediate in understanding and thought and judgement, because these activities stand to the originating intention of being as answers stand to questions.[116]

This point is prior to the subject-object relationship which furnished the directive theme both for Descartes and for the various schools of neo-Kantianism. And yet it is not located in some impersonal Kantian subject in the manner of Husserl's transcendental ego. It is the primordial wonder of the concrete human subject as subject. Moreover, it is what I have been suggesting that the ontological turn of hermeneutical reflection has begun to focus on.

Transcendental Method and History

Gadamer has thematised *Verstehen* in terms of its intimate and *apriori* historical conditionedness and of the consequent hermeneutically circular structure of its transitive intercourse with the world. *Verstehen* was thus shown to be the simultaneous interplay and actualisation of both prestructures and subject matter viewed in such perspectives as: fusion of horizons; the experiencing that makes one more open, more sensitive within the confines of one's insurmountable historical limits; the dialogue of question and answer where answers all serve to define a better question; the womb of language which is the dominant carrier and transmitter of one's productive prejudice. This primordial information of the subject by effective history as well as the hermeneutically circular evolution in history occurs chiefly on the level of the preconceptual, the prejudgemental, the pre-predicative, which the Cartesianism of the epistemology of interpretation could never adequately grapple with. But Gadamer's ontology of understanding had demonstrated the exigence of recognising the ever-present inter-play of prestructures and subject matter, of finite experience and infinite possibility, of answer and ever further question as inevitable features of human being-in-the-world.

Going to the very roots of the Cartesianism/anti-Cartesianism problematic, the theme of Lonergan's transcendental method is the subject's primordial 'Why?'[117] This pure question as the original fact of our openness to what-is pertains not only cognitively and appetitively, but also *constitutively* to the human affinity with being.[118] Moreover, pure question is discovered in the performance of transcendental method to unfold in a basic pattern; and this pattern gives the broad spectrum of intentionality—both the intentional pole and the multi-dimensional field of meanings—its normative (because fundamentally non-revisable) structure.[119] Hence the dynamic structure of primordial wonder is *the* original condition of possibility not only of that formation of the historical subject by effective history underlined by Gadamer, but also of the achievement of hermeneutic consciousness.

At the heart of the new hermeneutical focus, therefore, Lonergan has uncovered a *basic method*. For the dynamic pattern of operations of experience, understanding, judgement, and decision are the way effective reflection in Gadamer's sense is constituted. This dynamic pattern sets the ground-rules, if you will, for the self-transcending 'play' of the non-objectivistic subject.

I think it is safe to say that Gadamer affirms that his trans-cendental and foundational reflection has revealed a theory of *Verstehen* that has an invariability through all historical periods, although he is supremely aware of the dependence of his own explication on particular historical conditions, e.g., historical con-sciousness. For why should not his own reflection be structured as application? It is clear, then, that Gadamer wishes to convey to his readers a type of self-knowledge which has an aspect of inde-pendence from historical change. Gadamer's own explication takes its place within a historical succession of thematisations, but the subject matter becoming more explicit through the series is not itself fundamentally mutable. Rather it is the source of any such historical development.

So also Lonergan's transcendental method is a passage to a self-knowledge in this non-historical sense. For the practice of transcendental method is a matter of making the transition from self-consciousness to self-knowledge. This means that the non-revisable structure of primordial wonder at work *in actu exercito*, and experientially 'known', is known *signate* or in a second order knowing by being reflexively understood and affirmed. And this achievement, too, has its own particular historical presuppositions of which Lonergan is well aware.[120]

Now these types of self-knowledge exposed by Gadamer and Lonergan are modestly philosophical. Unlike the knowledge of self in which Hegel's *Phänomenologie* culminates, they do not claim to be full *historical* self-knowledge either in the sense of the spontaneous and natural interplay of historically sedimented pre-structures and the shifting intentional project of human lives which makes up the 'history that is written about'; or in that of the technical thematisation of that interplay which is 'history as written'.[121]

For Gadamer, the key to the problem of *historical* self-knowledge lies in the direction of the Aristotelian critique of the abstract universal and in his doctrine of *phronesis*. In the light of historical consciousness, Gadamer has explicated Aristotle's insights in terms of the interplay of the prestructures of understanding and the *Sache* of history (particularly as this happens linguistically) by which the subject is actuated within history's mysterious movement through and beyond his intentions. Lonergan's transcendental reflection, however, has illuminated the *principle* of a contemporary *phronesis*. Such a principle would need to be able to ground the distinctions capable of doing justice to the competencies, the limitations, and the modes of complementation of the differentiated potentialities that have arisen in history and of uncovering the existential and theoretic roots of distortion and perversion in a radical critique of individual and collective bias.[122] Lonergan is increasingly emphatic that no classically structured inventory of human achievement and possibility can be dogmatically posited as the nature and so criterion for man-in-history.[123] The principle which can authentically integrate and criticise the massive differentiations, specialisations, aberrations, and correctives to aberration which make up the history that goes beyond the intending of individual subjects, would not have the theoretic unity of a platonising classical ontology, but simply the unity of differentiated consciousness; the normative pattern of related and recurrent operations yielding cumulative and progressive results that is *basic*, that is *transcultural*, and that nonetheless pretends no Hegelian total self-transparency by which the subject would be elevated to a quasi-divine station outside history. Basic method, by going to the roots of protean human potentiality, has a radical if finite competence, whether it is a question of analysing the human development from global compactness through the entire field of past, present, and future differentiation; or of integrating without reducing symbolic-mythic and theoretic-systematic modes of human activity without abolishing either or substituting one for the other; or of passing judgement on human advance and regression.[124]

This radical swing back to the fundamental structures of subject as subject via transcendental method affords a factual (potentially) differentiated and normative viewpoint with regard to the concrete reality of appropriation of historical self. But the truth that application is the structure of historical causality as taught by Gadamer can be at once expanded and nuanced by basic method into an explication of the structures of scientific technical service to and co-operation in specifically historical causality. I am referring, of course, to Lonergan's 'series of normative patterns' which fall under his notion of 'functional specialisation'.[125] The power behind this conception comes principally, I think, from basic method's[126] ability to distinguish without completely isolating such things as:[127] common-sense understandings and common-sense presentations of texts from scientific or technical communications of common-sense meanings; formally hermeneutical contexts versus formally historical contexts which can be viewed in a genetico-dialectical unity; the various modes of thematisation[128] among which true meaning as *true* may also be a theme. This capacity to make valid distinctions, and to make them for the sake of a richer interplay of aspects is what enables Lonergan to get beyond the partial and descriptively classificatory distinctions of, say, an Emilio Betti (whose lack of acknowledgement of the historical subject as subject caused his distinctions to obscure the unity in the basic operations running through the diversified hermeneutical fields).[129] And so he projects a truly explanatory scheme of functionally interlocking 'hermeneutical' specialisations. Hence both the application-structure of historical causality and the dynamism of conscious intentionality are realised within Lonergan's scheme in the reciprocal interplay of the separate functions.

Furthermore, if Gadamer's argument be true, as I believe it is, that the conspicuous recognition in theology and jurisprudence of the rightful pre-eminence of the subject matter of history plus the correlative attention to the application-structure of historical causality is the widely unacknowledged but true key to the performance of all the *Geisteswissenschaften*,[130] then the structure of functional specialties emergent from Lonergan's methodological reflection upon the *Wendung zur Idee* within the Christian religion has a relevance which extends far beyond the properly theological task.

In conclusion, the same radicality of basic method which permits a specification of the scientific exactions adequate to the field of the human as constituted by meaning[131] in opposition to the reductivist tendencies of Positivists and neo-Kantians, drives it beyond Kant to uncover an exigence for a finite yet illuminating conception and affirmation of the divine *within* the thrust of the primordial question.[132] But to speak more concretely, the viewpoint and performance of basic method also underlines Gadamer's suggestion that, in the light of human historicity and finitude, belief is a condition of the possibility for true historical self-knowledge.[133] However, as the historical subject devolves his personal dialectic between 'openness as a fact' and 'openness as an achievement' within the context of a problem of evil, basic method will tend more sharply than Gadamer's hermeneutic consciousness, I would say, to deepen that awareness of the symbiosis of knowledge and belief by making 'openness *as gift*' an all-consuming issue.[134]

APPENDIX A: DILTHEY AND CARTESIAN COGNITIONAL THEORY

Dilthey pointed out the inconsistencies within the Historical School's critique of Hegel's conceptualist construction of world history from the viewpoint of Cartesian cognitional theoretic presuppositions. He not only recognised the division in the thought of the Historical School between the empirical standpoint and basic assumptions of 'Idealism from Kant to Hegel', but in his own way shared the same duality. But Dilthey, especially in his earlier days, hoped to overcome this dichotomy by means of cognitional theory, namely, by answering the call of Droysen for a Kant in the field of historical study (4, 497). In the sixth book of the *System of Inductive and Deductive Logic* (1843)[135] John Stuart Mill had attempted to carry out the enlightened programme of

Bacon and Hume by applying his version of inductive logic to the sciences of historical and social phenomena, thus grounding the 'moral sciences' by way of reductive analogy with his notion of natural scientific method.[136] Gadamer sees Dilthey's later cognitional theoretic project as a discussion with this logically reductive solution of Mill (4). Dilthey's decades-long attempt to reach foundations for the *Geisteswissenschaften*, however, aligns itself with the historical sophistication of the Historical School over against English empiricism in fighting to win the cognitional theoretic independence of these sciences (4). He expressly modelled his task on the Kantian critique: he would bridge the gap between historical experience and philosophical speculation (60–62). Whereas Kant's problem had been to legitimate (Newtonian) natural empirical science in the face of the dogmatism of metaphysics (XV), Dilthey's problem was to legitimate the sciences of properly historical experience in the face of Hegel's apotheosis of Logosphilosophy[137] (206–8, 477). Over against Hume, Kant had demonstrated the cognitional right of mathematical constructions; over against Mill, Dilthey would show the cognitional right of categories of the historical world in the *Geisteswissenschaften*. His project was a critique of historical reason which would lay the foundations not only for history as a science (which had been Droysen's aspiration), but for the entire cosmos of the *Geisteswissenschaften*.[138] Hence, most emphatically in the project outlined by his *Einleitung in die Geisteswissenschaften* of 1883[139] and in his scheme of a descriptive and analytic psychology of 1892[140] Dilthey conceived of cognitional theory along the lines established by Descartes when the latter had set out to ascertain whether or not the power of the human mind is sufficient to know the world.[141] It was the *quaestio juris*, the epistemological question formulated thus: 'With what right do we actually use concepts created by ourselves for the knowledge of things and for the description of our own experience?'[142] Cartesian as it is, the cognitional theoretic problematic in terms of which Dilthey set his epistemology of interpretation also presupposed the primacy of the subject-object split.

APPENDIX B: DILTHEY AND THE CARTESIAN MODEL OF SCIENCE

Dilthey criticises as dogmatic both the English empiricists and the neo-Kantians for their failure to distinguish adequately knowledge of nature (on the Cartesian model) from knowledge of history. But he himself participates in this dogmatism to the extent that, even in clearly differentiating the object of the *Geisteswissenschaften* from that of the natural sciences, he accepts the Cartesian model of the latter both as a point of contrast and as a standard of objectivity (5, 60–2, 499). Thus his modulation of the Cartesian cognitional theoretic problematic remains attenuated. Dilthey did move decisively beyond Descartes, Kant and the neo-Kantians in the direction of Vico in his recognition of a human *Lebenserfahrung* to be objectified in *Lebensbegriffe* (208–9), and in setting up the crucial opposition of the *Erklären* proper to the explication of the casual nexus of nature and the *Verstehen* proper to entry into the human-historical realm of experience (210). Nonetheless, his pivotal notion of *Erlebnis* not only had a cognitional theoretic function within a Cartesian framework, but was given a typically Cartesian definition (cf. Appendix C; 60–2, 209–10, 236). Later on in his development, after he had given up his attempt to provide psychological foundations for the *Geisteswissenschaften*, he was seemingly compelled by his latent Cartesianism to interpret the immanent drive of *Leben* to stability in terms of scientific objectivity *à la* Descartes (222–4, 240); and to be unnecessarily vexed by a formulation of the problem of relativity whose superficiality he would otherwise have revealed (223–4). So it was that behind his own style of Romantic hermeneutics lay his constant desire to establish the validity of the *Geisteswissenschaften* on a par with that of the natural sciences (226–7), where validity, objectivity, natural science, etc., unfortunately all coincide fairly closely with the Cartesian ideal of science discussed above[143] (223–4, 226–8, 244, 254, 259–61).

APPENDIX C: HISTORICAL CONSCIOUSNESS AS HISTORICAL ENLIGHTENMENT

Dilthey thought he could combine successfully both the empirical sensibility of the Historical School and his Romantic and Idealist heritage through a properly nuanced cognitional theory. To clearly distinguish the empiricist tendency of the Historical School from both English Empiricism and neo-Kantian dogmatism, he took care to disassociate the basic datum of the *Geisteswissenschaften* from that of the natural sciences. The key concept in this differentiation is *Erlebnis* or inner experience, which he defines as an indissoluble interiority or reflexivity[144] in contradistinction to the data of measurement and experiment. *Erlebnis*, then, is a last and elementary unit of consciousness which combines both immediacy and a sense of lasting significance and which would be irreducible into more elementary psychic units. It transcends the sensation or sensitivity which loomed so important in Positivist and neo-Kantian epistemologies.

Incorporated into the very structure of the word *Erlebnis*, moreover, is the further core notion of *Leben*, which in its turn also has a venerable history of anti-mechanist and anti-rationalist meaning (59–60). Here the Romantic-Idealist heritage of Dilthey found expression precisely as lending support to the empirical standpoint which is thus grounded in the historical reality of life versus the 'bloodlessness' of the standard cognitional theoretic subject (210). For each *Erlebnis* is related to the infinitude of *Leben* as a momentary expression (60, 62–3). *Leben* is the sheer productivity that objectifies itself into a meaningful pattern (*Lebenszusammenhang*) which is based on the meanings concretised in determinate inner experiences much in the same way as a melody is built up from a succession of motifs (62, 210).

To fill out the cognitional theoretic scheme based on *Erlebnis* and *Leben*, just as *Erklären* is suited to apprehending the temporal succession of cause-effect relationships, so *Verstehen* is fit for grasping the nexus of *Erlebnis-Leben* in historical time (210).

In order to clarify the relationship between single *Erlebnis* and the total *Lebenszusammenhang*, Dilthey applied the basic hermeneutic relationship between whole and part, especially in its Romantic version. But what might have been appropriate with respect to the unity of the lifespan of an individual subject only raises further problems when transferred to the relationship between the life-pattern actually experienced by individuals and the total pattern of history itself. For who is the subject of the latter? If the pattern of history as a whole is congruent with no single person's experience, how can it be known? (210–11).

In the earlier, more psychological attempts to answer this question, Dilthey found it helpful to speak of *Verstehen von Ausdruck*, of an understanding of expression, in order to illustrate the difference between the knowledge of the cause-effect relations in the realm of nature and the knowledge of the patterns of life which make up human history.

The basic difference, according to Gadamer, lies in the degree of the immediacy of the respective types of knowing. Thus *Verstehen* grasps the expressed in expression in a much more immediate fashion than when *Erklären* discovers a cause in its effect. In the latter instance, *Erklären* proceeds by examining with the aid of conceptual tools a succession of discrete cases to the abstraction of a uniformity or universal cause; whereas in the former, *Verstehen* penetrates the meaning of an expression by transposing it into the knower's own experience by means of empathy (*Einfühlung*)[145] However, the analogy here between the function of inner experience (*Erlebnis*) in the *Geisteswissenschaften* and that of the psychic elements in a natural scientific approach— an analogy consequent upon Dilthey's frame of reference set by Cartesian cognitional theory—was quite open to a reductive interpretation. Gadamer reports that what saves Dilthey from psychologistic reductivism and what furthermore was to be the springboard to his elaboration of a more strictly hermeneutical groundwork for the *Geisteswissenschaften*, was Dilthey's study of Husserl's *Logische Untersuchungen* (211–12). Here Husserl explicates the notion of meaning (*Bedeutung*) on the level of the intentionality of consciousness in contradistinction to any psychologism operating solely on the level of psychic components and mechanisms (e.g., association theories of the English Empiricists, etc.). Taking his clue from Husserl, Dilthey saw clearly that a psychologistic interpretation of his theory of *Verstehen* through *Einfühlung* not only would yield no solution to the question of the relationship between individual and historical *Lebenszusammenhang*; but it would leave the distinction between causal relations and relationships in the world of the spirit highly tenuous. Hence, Dilthey was provoked to emphasise that *Verstehen* of *Ausdruck* by *Einfühlung* is a work of symbolic production. In other words, Dilthey then began to concentrate on thematising the *hermeneutical* structure of *Leben* itself (477–8). Meaning (*Bedeutung*) is an expression (*Ausdruck*) by which temporally flowing *Leben interprets itself* by objectifying itself into abiding unities of meaning (211–3). In developing the hermeneutical character of *Leben*, Dilthey began to unfold for this *Geisteswissenschaften* the implications of the more permanent, impersonal supra-causal, and teleological character of meaning and structure. For example, the hermeneutical task of the *Geisteswissenschaften* cannot be to deduce and explain life-patterns from atoms of inner experience, once it is perceived that intentional consciousness is immediate to these patterns and in fact gets its very being in intending them (212). Again, Dilthey was able to pose the question of historical knowledge in a more crucial way than ever in terms of the interdependence between the individual and what lies beyond him both as meaning (*Bedeutung*) and as force (*Kraft*), i.e., between the individual subject and objective spirit.[146]

Now Gadamer claims that in the last analysis Dilthey's epistemology of interpretation becomes practically identical with a project of historical enlightenment—a search in which the Enlightenment conflict between tradition and science would reach its culmination (226, 342–3). But Hegel, too, had faced the challenge for man's historical self-knowledge set by the rise of modern science through a critique of 'extrinsic' reflection as being powerlessly detached from the concrete. Against isolated subjectivity he posited the reality of objective spirit, which is beyond reduction to or deduction from subjective intentions and reflections; and which in some sense both encompasses and constitutes them. In Hegel's scheme of enlightenment, then, the movement of self-knowledge in history is seen to be one of reconciliation of objective and subjective spirit in the absolute knowledge of Philosophy.[147] But for Dilthey, of course, Hegel's speculative resolution of the historical movement of self-knowledge was no more than a dogmatic residue from metaphysics; and, as such, it was incompatible with a truly historical world view[148] (216, 217, 219, 221–3). Nevertheless, Dilthey did begin to take a serious interest in Hegel's categories once he realised, with the aid of Husserl, that he had to disengage himself from the abstract, subjectivist, and psychologistic implications in the categories of Romantic aesthetics, metaphysics, and hermeneutics (213–28, 478). But that Romantic framework which he had long since gleaned from Schleiermacher seems to be the lodestone to which he was drawn as he fought not to surrender historical and aposteriori fact to Hegel's speculative constructions.[149]

The probable reason why Dilthey remained attracted almost in spite of himself to Schleiermacher's hermeneutics is furnished by Gadamer when he shows the consonance of Schleiermacher's fundamental presuppositions with Dilthey's aim of grounding the *Geisteswissenschaften* on an equal basis with the natural sciences

(226). For Schleiermacher, the object of hermeneutically skilled understanding is the text.

In Dilthey's reception, therefore, just as empirical natural science tries to explain the data of nature which are equally and indifferently available to any neutral observer, so the empirical *Geisteswissenschaften* will seek the intelligibility of texts which have a similar availability (227). Again, Schleiermacher held that it is possible for an interpreter to comprehend any text (i.e., the meaning of the author expressed in the text) in the same complete manner in which his monadology and what Gadamer terms his 'aesthetic consciousness' (175–6, 218) had led him to suppose that any I can understand a Thou by totally transplanting himself into the horizon of the Thou in an attainment of perfect contemporaneity (177). Now the abstract, non-historical character of this notion fits in perfectly with Dilthey's need to find for the *Geisteswissenschaften* a possibility of certitude and objectivity equal to that present in his Cartesian notion of the natural sciences. For the relationship of interpreter and interpreted (text as expression of author) in Schleiermacher's theory of totally contemporaneous reproduction of another's horizon fulfils for Dilthey all the exigences of the relation between neutral observer and data in the process of controlled observation in the empirical natural sciences. It is Dilthey's Cartesianism, according to Gadamer, that explains his continued reliance upon presuppositions of Schleiermacher (226–8).

Gadamer also brings out that this orientation towards (and way of thinking about) a Cartesian *fundamentum inconcussum* was at root an expression of the need for a bulwark for his personal passage through the phase of the crisis of culture brought on chiefly by the rise of modern science, namely, the Enlightenment *translatio imperii* from authority and prejudice to the certainly established knowledge of science (226). This is why Dilthey always demanded of the *Geisteswissenschaften* that they achieve 'results' (*Ergebnisse*) equal in universal validity (*Allgemeingültigkeit*) to the results of the natural sciences (227). Indeed, precisely because he battled so vigorously in behalf of this requisite, Dilthey established himself, in Gadamer's words, as the 'thinker of historical enlightenment'.[150]

To his own mind, coming to terms with Hegel was for Dilthey simply a matter of 'overcoming metaphysics by history' (216–7), because history for Hegel turned out to be merely 'a chapter in the

Encyclopedia of the Spirit'.[151] It was to be sublated into absolute knowledge through philosophy's speculative knowledge of *Begriff*. And so if Dilthey felt he needed Hegel—particularly his notion of objective spirit—in order to work out the implications latent in his own insight into the constitutive function of meaning which his study of Husserl (211–2) had imported into his *Lebensphilosophie*, it meant that he was obliged to perform a series of shifts in Hegelian meanings. Gadamer maintains, however, that in spite of Dilthey's determination to start from the reality of *Leben* (216) and to stay faithful to the experiential standpoint of the Historical School, Dilthey's only fundamental disagreement with Hegel concerned the latter's apriorist conceptual speculation (218–9). He was not clear, therefore, in his stance toward the exaggerated Hegelian claim of the perfectibility of self-knowledge in history (218–9). This may be because this claim corresponded all too well with Dilthey's appeal (with Vico) to the principle, *verum et factum convertuntur*, by which he intended to ground the specific identity of knower and data in the *Geisteswissenschaften* (209, 214, 217). From this perspective, it was not incoherent of Dilthey to expand the scheme of Romantic hermeneutics (226–8), to fuse it with a modified notion of the objective spirit (214–8, especially 215), and thus to relativise the Hegelian teleology of self-knowledge in history.

In the course of just this sort of a modification of both Hegel's and Schleiermacher's categories, the totality of history is thought of by Dilthey as a text (227–8) into which inexhaustible *Leben* has objectified itself (63, 216). Correlatively, the special function of philosophy for Hegel is replaced by the historically nuanced *Verstehen* exercised by Dilthey's now hermeneutical *Geisteswissenschaften*. For the 'text' of history is simply an *Ausdruck* of *Leben* to be deciphered, which of course implies, Gadamer says, that history is intelligible down to the last letter (228). And finally, instead of the total and suprahistorical self-transparency of absolute knowledge into which all that is other has been subsumed without remainder, Dilthey posits historical consciousness as the ideal of self-knowledge to be achieved by truly enlightened reason.[152]

Lonergan and the subjectivist principle

SCHUBERT M. OGDEN

I.

Since the work of Bernard Lonergan is expressly programmatic, it has seemed to me appropriate and perhaps useful to discuss it as such. Accordingly, this paper aims at a general criticism of the basic structure and direction of Lonergan's philosophical-theological proposals. The drawback, of course, is that this aim requires one to abstract from the particular reflections of an unusually subtle thinker and to risk giving a very one-sided impression both of his achievement and of one's own appreciation for it. But Lonergan would be the first to agree, I think, not only that a comprehensive programme is the only 'correct strategy', but that the main question facing anyone undertaking such a strategy is whether his has been a 'successful campaign'.[1] In any event, this is the question which my own encounter with Lonergan has sharply raised and which, with whatever risks, I here intend to pursue.

The classic statement of Lonergan's programme is given in the well-known words with which *Insight* begins and ends: 'Thoroughly understand what it is to understand, and not only will you understand the broad lines of all there is to be understood but also you will possess a fixed base, an invariant pattern, opening upon all further developments of understanding'.[2] What is striking about this statement is its identification of the task and method of philosophy as precisely self-understanding, or, as Lonergan puts it, the 'personal appropriation of one's own rational self-consciousness'.[3] Presupposed by this identification is the view that there is a 'duality' in human knowing in that 'in each of us there exist two different kinds of knowledge'.[4] There is the kind of knowledge whose basis is 'the data of sense' and whose most refined and fully developed form is empirical science. But there is also the kind of knowledge whose primary object is not the known but the knowing subject and which is based, therefore, on the 'data of consciousness'. According to Lonergan, it is this second kind of knowledge which is the proper objective of philosophy as self-distinguished from the special sciences. For while to be human at all is to be conscious of one's own consciousness, this still is not to have self-knowledge, which can be achieved only in so far as one's consciousness itself becomes the datum of understanding and judgement. Furthermore, even though the primary object of such self-knowledge is our own knowledge and ourselves as its subjects, 'knowledge of knowledge is, in a certain sense, knowledge of the objects of knowledge'.[5] It is so in the sense that there is an 'isomorphism that obtains between the structure of knowing and the structure of the known', so that the 'affirmation of oneself as a knower also is an affirmation of the general structure of any proportionate object of knowledge'.[6] In knowing ourselves, we know vastly more than ourselves, in that we know, not the contents of scientific results, but 'the general structure' of all such contents, 'the invariant form for which the sciences provide the variable matter'.[7] Thus philosophy as full self-understanding comprises not only 'cognitional theory' but also 'metaphysics'; it begins as 'an understanding of all understanding' only to move on to 'a basic understanding of all that can be understood'.[8]

It is essential to Lonergan's programme to insist, however, that philosophy properly develops in just this order, with cognitional theory coming first, metaphysics second. He thus holds that metaphysics is 'derived from the known structure of one's knowing' and describes cognitional theory as 'a base of operations for the determination of the general structure of the concrete universe'.[9] At stake in this insistence is the possibility of something rather like what Emerich Coreth calls 'a methodical-systematic laying of the foundations' of metaphysics.[10] Whereas Aquinas, according to Lonergan, offers an analysis of cognitional activity that presupposes a whole metaphysical system, 'what we want is to take the same fact, the same psychological fact and express it without the metaphysics'.[11] The reason for this is that we can thereby provide critical support for our metaphysical superstructure. 'We'll be able to build up our metaphysics critically on the basis of an exact account of what our knowing is if we don't mix in the metaphysics with the account of the cognitional process'.[12] But if Lonergan insists that one must 'begin from knowledge and reach metaphysics only as a conclusion',[13] he certainly does not think that metaphysics is somehow doubtful or unnecessary. On the contrary, he speaks confidently of the 'inevitability' with which the movement toward full self-understanding carries one to the highest reaches of traditional metaphysical knowledge—and beyond.[14] 'The self-appropriation of one's own intellectual and rational self-consciousness begins as cognitional theory, expands into a metaphysics and an ethics, mounts to a conception and an affirmation of God, only to be confronted with a problem of evil that demands the transformation of self-reliant intelligence into an *intellectus quaerens fidem*'.[15] Thus, in Lonergan's view, there are really only two alternatives to an integral theistic metaphysics that is open to its 'sublation' in Christian faith and theology: either the philosophical movement towards full self-understanding is arbitrarily arrested at some stage by 'obscurantism', or else it entangles itself in the incoherence of 'counterpositions', which explicitly deny the very positions they implicitly affirm.

The end towards which Lonergan's programme is directed, then, is nothing less than the re-establishment of the *philosophia perennis*. Because the main lines of this philosophy, at least, can be shown to follow inevitably from an exact account of human knowing, which they presuppose but are not already presupposed by, they can receive the kind of 'critical' justification that the present state of philosophical development demands. As results now obtained 'not by strokes of genius but by method', they are also obtained 'without any appeal to authorities', and 'without deductions from principles that claim to be self-evident yet, in fact, are not self-evident to everybody'.[16]

Now I should suppose no one would doubt Lonergan's contention that he has, in fact, developed 'a metaphysics with a marked family resemblance to traditional views'—that, specifically, his metaphysics of proportionate being 'bears an astounding similarity to the doctrines of the Aristotelian and Thomist tradition', and that his 'conception of God as the unrestricted act of understanding coincides with Aritotle's conception of the unmoved mover as νόησις νοήσεως'.[17] But just because Lonergan's results are so strikingly similar to those originally obtained otherwise, without benefit of his novel method, one may well ask to what extent it is really the method that accounts for the results. As a matter of fact, this is evidently a crucial question if one is to come to terms with Lonergan's programme. If his understanding of understanding is sound, and if the metaphysics he says he derives from it is, in fact, derived from it, instead of being (however unintentionally) imposed upon it, then he has undoubtedly re-established the perennial philosophy in the very way he claims. So far as I can see, however, there is ample reason for doubt about both points— about the soundness of Lonergan's cognitional theory and about the derivation from it of his metaphysics of proportionate and transcendent being. Thus my question as to the success of his programme arises from doubts about the results of his philosophy as distinct from his identification of self-understanding as its proper task and method.

It should already be clear, however, that I am not disposed to ask whether Lonergan shares in his own way in 'the subjective turn' of modern Western philosophy. He is unequivocal in stressing 'the priority of the concrete reality that is the experiencing, intelligent, rational subject', and he himself singles out 'neglect of the subject' as 'the root difficulty' of the present philosophical-theological situation.[18] Still, the more I have studied his work, the more I have been struck by yet a further confirmation of Whitehead's statement that 'the difficulties of all schools of modern philosophy lie in the fact that, having accepted the subjectivist principle, they continue to use philosophical categories derived from another point of view'.[19] In other words, my doubts about Lonergan have to do not so much with whether he accepts the subjectivist principle as with whether it is from this principle that his philosophical categories are derived. Just what this means and why there are reasons for such doubts I must now try to explain.

II.

The first step is to sharpen up what is meant by 'the subjectivist principle'. Since I intend to use this phrase in essentially the way Whitehead himself uses it in the statement just quoted, we may proceed by considering its meaning in that statement taken in context. In doing so, however, we should note that this is not the only meaning Whitehead assigns to the phrase. In the very chapter of *Process and Reality* in which this statement occurs and which also bears the phrase as its title, he evidently makes use of it in two quite different senses.[20]

The clue to its sense in the statement is the sentence that immediately follows: 'These categories are not wrong, but they deal with abstractions unsuitable for metaphysical use'.[21] From this we may infer that the difficulties of modern philosophy of which Whitehead speaks are not the purely immanent difficulties of an incoherence, which he supposes to result from acceptance of the subjectivist principle, on the one hand, and continued use of categories derived from a different point of view, on the other. His reference, rather, is to the difficulties that arise from continuing to use these particular categories, which, just because they are derived from a viewpoint other than the subjectivist principle, involve abstractions that are metaphysically inappropriate. If we ask, then, what these categories are, Whitehead's answer is presumably indicated by the succeeding sentences in the paragraph:

The notions of the 'green leaf' and of the 'round ball' are at the base of traditional metaphysics. They have generated two misconceptions: *one* is the concept of vacuous actuality, void of subjective experience; and the *other* is the concept of quality inherent in substance. In their proper character, as high abstractions, both of these notions are of the utmost pragmatic use. In fact, language has been formed chiefly to express such concepts. It is for this reason that language, in its ordinary usages, penetrates but a short distance into the principles of metaphysics.[22]

Assuming that Whitehead is speaking here, even if not by name, of the 'categories' responsible for the difficulties of modern philosophy, we may conclude that these categories either are or include what he calls earlier in the chapter 'the substance-quality categories'. The warrants for this conclusion are evident from the earlier context, which, because of its importance for our whole concern, I quote at length.

Speaking of Descartes, Whitehead says:

He also laid down the principle that those substances which are the subjects enjoying conscious experiences, provide the primary data for philosophy, namely, themselves as in the enjoyment of such experience. This is the famous subjectivist bias which entered into modern philosophy through Descartes. In this doctrine Descartes undoubtedly made the greatest philosophical discovery since the age of Plato and Aristotle. For his doctrine directly traversed the notion that the proposition, 'This stone is grey', expresses a primary form of known fact from which metaphysics can start its generalisations. If we are to go back to the subjective enjoyment of experience, the type of primary starting point is 'my perception of this stone as grey'. Primitive men were not meta-physicians, nor were they interested in the expression of concrete experience. Their language merely expressed useful abstractions, such as 'greyness of the stone'. But like Columbus who never visited America, Descartes missed the full sweep of his own discovery, and he and his successors, Locke and Hume, continued to construe the functionings of the subjective enjoyment of experience according to the substance-quality categories. Yet if the enjoyment of experience be the constitutive subjective fact, these categories have lost all claim to any fundamental character in metaphysics.[23]

It is clear, I think, that there is a close parallel between what is said here and the meaning of the statement with which we began. The difficulties that Whitehead sees in all schools of modern philosophy are evidently one and same with those that are implied to have beset Descartes, who, missing the import of his own discovery of the primacy of the experiencing subject, continued to philosophise in the substance-quality categories of traditional metaphysics. But if this is so, there no longer need be any question about the sense of 'the subjectivist principle' in the original state-ment. It can only mean the same thing that Whitehead here and elsewhere variously refers to as Descartes' 'principle' and 'dis-covery', and explicitly identifies with 'the subjectivist bias' that Descartes introduced into modern philosophy. It thus means, as Whitehead expresses it in yet other formulations, that 'subjective experiencing is the primary metaphysical situation which is pre-sented to metaphysics for analysis' and that 'the whole universe consists of elements disclosed in the analysis of the experiences of subjects'.[24] This interpretation is confirmed, then, by Whitehead's point in the concluding sentence, that, as he puts it elsewhere, 'with the advent of Cartesian subjectivism, the substance-quality category has lost all claim to metaphysical primacy'.[25] This is clearly the same point he makes in the original statement, when he asserts that categories derived from a point of view other than the subjectivist principle are, even if not wrong, unfit for metaphysics.

If this is so, however, we are able to understand more clearly what Whitehead must mean in saying that all schools of modern philosophy have accepted the subjectivist principle. Since logically this principle can imply nothing less than what he speaks of as the 'deposition of substance-quality', the continued use of substance-quality categories must in turn be an implicit rejection of the principle. Hence anyone continuing to use these categories, as all the modern schools of philosophy are said to have done, can have accepted the subjectivist principle only verbally. That this is, in fact, Whitehead's meaning is more than obvious from his detailed discussion, in this chapter and elsewhere, of the philosophy of Descartes and his successors.[26]

There is another phase of Whitehead's discussion in this chapter that deepens the meaning of 'the subjectivist principle'. I refer to his argument for the conclusion that 'the order of dawning, clearly and distinctly, in consciousness is not the order of metaphysical priority'.[27] By this he means that 'those elements of our experience which stand out clearly and distinctly in our consciousness are not its basic facts; they are the derivative modifications which arise in the process'.[28] The reason for this is that 'consciousness only arises in a late derivative phase of complex integrations', and consequently 'only illuminates the more primitive types of prehension so far as these prehensions are still elements in the products of integration'.[29] Employing the distinction, so crucial for his own cognitional theory, between the two pure perceptive modes of 'presentational immediacy' and 'causal efficacy', Whitehead also says that 'consciousness only dimly illuminates the prehensions in the mode of causal efficacy, because these prehensions are primitive elements in our experience', while 'prehensions in the mode of presentational immediacy are among those prehensions which we enjoy with the most vivid consciousness'.[30] Thus he speaks of the 'law, that the late derivative elements are more clearly illuminated by consciousness than the primitive elements' and contends that 'the consequences of the neglect of this law . . . have been fatal to the proper analysis of an experient occasion. In fact, most of the difficulties of philosophy are produced by it. Experience has been explained in a thoroughly topsy-turvy fashion, the wrong end first'.[31]

Keeping in mind the statement with which we began, which also proposes to explain the 'difficulties' of philosophy, one cannot but be struck by this argument. It suggests that Whitehead is speaking of the same difficulties, only now attributing them not to the continued use of inappropriate metaphysical categories but to a faulty analysis of experience which mistakenly assumes that what is clear and distinct in consciousness is also fundamental. What is here only a suggestion is more than confirmed, then, by the larger context of Whitehead's discussion, and most especially by the following:

> The current accounts of perception are the stronghold of modern metaphysical difficulties. They have their origin in the same misunderstanding which led to the incubus of the substance-quality categories. The Greeks looked at a stone, and perceived that it was grey. The Greeks were ignorant of modern physics; but modern philosophies discuss perception in terms of categories derived from the Greeks.
>
> The Greeks started from perception in its most elaborate and sophisticated form, namely, visual perception. In visual perception crude perception is most completely made over by the originative phases in experience, phases which are especially prominent in human experience.[32]

From the connection Whitehead makes here, it is apparent that we need to take account of yet another dimension of the meaning of 'the subjectivist principle.' For if it is the '*same* misunderstanding' which gives rise both to the inappropriate categories of traditional metaphysics and to accounts of experience that explain it from the wrong end first, then no principle could imply the deposition of the first without implicitly overcoming the second as well. In other words, included in what Whitehead means by 'the subjectivist principle' is the further 'principle' that 'consciousness presupposes experience, and not experience consciousness'.[33]

Summarising this discussion, I can now formulate in somewhat different terms how I myself make use of Whitehead's phrase. I use it to mean, first of all, that the primary object of philosophical reflection is my own existence as an experiencing self and that, therefore, philosophy's only proper task and method is integral reflective self-understanding. But I also mean by the phrase that the experiencing self is vastly more than understanding, especially the fully reflective understanding properly sought by philosophy, and that it most seriously misunderstands itself when, forgetting this, it supposes that its sense perception is its only direct experience of reality beyond. In other words, as I use it, 'the subjectivist principle' serves to assert not only that the subject is indeed the key to philosophical understanding, but also that the subject can be understood only by breaking out of the limits within which understanding tends to move, even in understanding itself. It follows that a real acceptance of the subjectivist principle would have the same negative implication for traditional philosophical positions that Whitehead envisages, namely, the rejection both of a metaphysics for which substance is the primary reality and of a cognitional theory which, starting from what is clearly and distinctly given in consciousness, concludes that sense perception is our only mode of experiencing what is other than ourselves. Conversely, to take up either of these traditional positions would be implicitly to reject the subjectivist principle, and, to that extent, to make any supposed acceptance of it unreal, merely a matter of words.

III.

Returning to Lonergan, I am going to argue that in his work, too, there are difficulties which lie in the fact that, whatever may be supposed from his method, he continues to use philosophical categories derived from another point of view than the subjectivist principle, as that principle has now been defined. Actually, my argument for this conclusion will do little more than indicate some of those kinds of things that could and should be done to establish it. But as I have said, this paper aims at no more than a general criticism of Lonergan's programme, and I must be content with showing only that my doubts about its success are not entirely unfounded.

The first point about which I expressed such doubts is the soundness of Lonergan's account of cognition. Given what has now been said, I can locate the difficulty I see here very simply: Lonergan fails to understand understanding in so far as he continues to make the traditional categorical distinction between 'sense' and 'intellect' central to his cognitional theory.

The reason this distinction leads to misunderstanding is the point of view from which it derives—namely, one which starts from understanding to understand experience, instead of starting from experience to understand understanding. At first glance, it may be thought inexcusable that I should suppose this to be Lonergan's point of view. Does not his whole account of understanding manifestly start from experience, in that he distinguishes 'levels of consciousness', of which he expressly holds the experiential level to be primary? The point is well taken, but it does not affect the issue I am raising. I am not at all questioning that Lonergan holds experience to be presupposed by human understanding, at least to the extent that it extrinsically conditions such understanding. My point is simply that the experience of which he holds this to be true is not the experience we actually enjoy and undergo, but only so much of it as is focally understood, because it is given clearly and distinctly in consciousness. In this sense, I maintain, Lonergan follows the long philosophical tradition, perpetuated by empiricists as well as rationalists, of starting from understanding to understand experience, rather than the other way around.

Of course, the evidence for this judgement is not only or even primarily that Lonergan continues to use the terminology expressive of this procedure. I am well aware that a careful analysis of his work could conceivably show that he uses such terms as 'sense' and 'intellect' with meanings significantly different from those traditionally assigned them. But so far as I have been able to make such an analysis, the indications are clear that Lonergan not only speaks in the traditional terms but also thinks in the traditional categories.

One indication of this is his characteristic account of experience as either 'outer' or 'inner', and hence as either 'sense' or 'consciousness'. By this account, any experience we have of beings other than ourselves consists entirely in what we are able to perceive of them by our five senses. As for experience of ourselves, it is one and the same with the consciousness immanent in our various activities, practical as well as cognitional. Thus Lonergan maintains, for instance, that our experience of ourselves as experiencing is our consciousness of ourselves as sensing, which, as such, is identical with our sensitivity itself 'coming to act'.[34] But this means that, as he explains it, our only experience is *conscious* experience, which is precisely the traditional position that experience presupposes consciousness, instead of what I take to be the correct position, that consciousness presupposes experience.

There is another indication that the real difficulty in Lonergan's thinking is his understanding of sensation and, following from this, his conception of the place and function of intellect. Typically, he speaks of 'the stream of sensitive consciousness', or of 'the mere flow of outer and inner experience', occasionally shifting the metaphor slightly by speaking of experience as a 'kaleidoscopic flow', or of 'the cinematographic flow of presentations and representations'.[35] In much the same vein, he can also refer to 'the sensible manifold of juxtapositions and successions', assert that 'the given is residual and, of itself, diffuse', and, in at least one notable passage, even characterise sensation as 'the Humean world of mere impressions'.[36] Small wonder, then, that, with this understanding of sense as simply the 'residual and diffuse materials for inquiry and reflection', he is led to the conception that 'all objectivity', even that belonging to experience itself, 'rests upon the unrestricted, detached, disinterested desire to know'.[37] 'By our senses we are given, not appearance, not reality, but data'.[38] Therefore, 'it is not true that it is from sense that our cognitional activities derive their immediate relationship to real objects; that relationship is immediate in the intention of being; it is mediate in the data of sense . . . inasmuch as the intention of being makes use of data in promoting cognitional process to knowledge of being; similarly, that relationship is mediate in understanding and thought and judgement, because these activities stand to the originating intention of being as answers stand to questions'.[39] In other words, Lonergan's position is not simply that there could be no *knowledge* of objects apart from intellectual functioning; he holds that there could not even be an *experience* of objects, as distinct from mere data, unless intellect had already constituted them by directly intending being itself. But once again, this is a familiar position of the philosophical tradition—in this case, the position which, construing experience as mere 'sense data' or 'impressions', wrongly looks to intellect for the objectivity that experience as we actually live it quite adequately provides for itself.

Finally, the limits of Lonergan's thought are indicated with particular clarity by the range of alternatives he considers in defining his cognitional theory. To my knowledge the only other theories he ever carefully criticises are those which, exactly like his own, assume that sense and intellect exhaust the possible first principles of cognition and, accordingly, develop accounts of knowing as involving either one or the other, or, in some way, both. At any rate, he most carefully works out his own so-called 'critical realism' over against two other views for which knowledge somehow involves both intellect and sense—in the one case, the 'naïve realism' of a contemporary Thomist like Gilson, and, in the other, a Kantian-type 'critical idealism'.[40] Significantly, the only point really at issue between these three views is how to conceive the *intellectual* component in knowledge. So far as their theories of experience are concerned, they agree so extensively as to explain expressions of complacency such as the following: 'We have sense experience which is fairly easy to identify. The whole problem in cognitional analysis is to discover that there is something else there besides sense. What are we looking for when we are looking for intellect? We are usually looking for something like a sensation and it is nothing like a sensation'.[41] Such statements make clear that Lonergan's categories as well as his terms are derived from a point of view other than the subjectivist principle. For wherever that principle has been accepted more than merely verbally, the main problem of cognitional analysis has been held to be, not to discover intellect, but to rediscover experience. Thus, from Bergson and James to Dewey and Whitehead, the point has been made and remade that an adequate understanding of experience as itself something else besides sense removes the whole basis of traditional cognitional theories, and so relativises *all* the alternatives that Lonergan takes into account.

So much for doubts about the soundness of Lonergan's cognitional theory. The second point I find doubtful is the logically different one focused by his claim to establish his metaphysics methodically and critically by deriving it entirely from this same theory of cognition.

Let us be clear that there is no way in the nature of the case whereby the issue here can be finally decided. This follows both from what Lonergan calls the 'isomorphism' between the structure of our knowing and the structure of reality itself and, in a somewhat different way, from my own view that, if one assumes consistency in thought, cognitional theory and metaphysics may be presumed to be correlative. Just because, or in so far as, there is such an ismorphism or correlation, it must always seem about as plausible that a thinker's metaphysics has been derived from his cognitional theory as that his cognitional theory has been derived from his metaphysics—the truth being that both derive from the same understanding, or, as the case may be, misunderstanding, of the nature of our existence as experiencing selves. Moreover, I am quite prepared to grant that Lonergan's metaphysics of proportionate being raises no particular questions as to its derivation. The correlation between it and his cognitional theory is close, and to that extent there seems reason enough to allow his claim. But in the case of his metaphysics of transcendent being, especially his conception of God, I have been unable to discern any such correlation and, therefore, suspect that at this point, at least, his metaphysics is imposed on his cognitional theory, rather than based on it. In short, the difficulty here, as I see it, is this: Lonergan fails to establish his metaphysics critically in so far as he continues to use the traditional category of 'unrestricted understanding' without deriving it from his cognitional theory.

Before elaborating this judgement I recall Lonergan's basic position that all first principles, including those required for knowledge of the transcendent, are grounded in 'invariant structures of human knowing and human doing.'[42] The *reductio ad principia* of Aquinas, he argues, is really a *reductio* to the subject, 'because the first principles lie in the subject as empirically, intellectually, rationally and responsibly conscious'.[43] From which it follows that, in a broad sense, 'all human knowledge is empirical', since, if one takes account of 'the data of consciousness', as well as 'the data of sense', one may say that 'all human knowledge proceeds from data'.[44] Accordingly, even though 'there are no data on the divine', in that 'God is not among the data of sense and he is not among the data of human consciousness', still our knowledge of him is empirical and subject to verification in so far as it follows from facts and in accordance with principles that *are* given in experience.[45] By Lonergan's own account, then, assertions about the transcendent, like metaphysical assertions generally, can be shown to be meaningful and true only by deriving them methodically from an understanding of understanding. My question is simply whether what he himself asserts about God can claim to be derived in this way.

The argument for a negative answer begins with his key assertion that 'God is the unrestricted act of understanding, the eternal rapture glimpsed in every Archimedian cry of Eureka.'[46] Like all knowledge, Lonergan holds, 'knowledge of transcendent being involves both intelligent grasp and reasonable affirmation.'[47] Yet such knowledge is peculiar in that we can grasp the transcendent intelligently only by extrapolating from what we otherwise know, which is to say, 'by proceeding on the side of the subject from restricted to unrestricted understanding and on the side of the object from the structure of proportionate being to the transcendent idea of being'.[48] Only in this way can we arrive at the concept of an unrestricted understanding which, in understanding itself, also understands everything else and therefore has as its content the idea of being as such. In arriving at this concept, however, we undoubtedly reach the notion of God; for 'our concept of an unrestricted act of understanding has a number of implications and, when they are worked out, it becomes manifest that it is one and the same thing to understand what being is and to understand what God is'.[49] Hence Lonergan's key assertion and his further contention that 'all other divine attributes follow from the notion of an unrestricted act of understanding'.[50]

We need not recapitulate Lonergan's reasoning in 'working out the implications of an unrestricted act of understanding in itself and in its relations to the universe'.[51] Suffice it to say that, by this procedure, he deduces a conception of God having the following prominent characteristics: God is invulnerable, in that his understanding is beyond the possibility of correction, revision, or improvement, even as his being is utterly without defect, lack, or imperfection; consequently, God is also unconditional, necessary, and simple, as well as timeless and eternal and incapable of change or development; finally, as the self-explanatory being, God is also the explanation of everything else, and so is the creator and conserver of the universe, its omnipotent efficient cause, omniscient exemplary cause, and ultimate final cause. Since all this, according to Lonergan, follows from the insight that 'what man is, through unrestricted desire and limited attainment, God is as unrestricted act',[52] the implication of his reasoning is that, were any or all of this false, it would also be false that God is unrestricted understanding. But this implication, in my judgement, is open to question, and, by pressing this question, one can expose the difficulty in Lonergan's work.

The basis of the question is the fact, or what I take to be the fact, that the presupposed contrast between restricted and unrestricted understanding is, in itself, ambiguous. To be sure, there is no ambiguity in the distinction between an understanding that understands only *some* of the things that conceivably could be understood and another understanding that understands *all* such things. The difference between 'all' and 'some' is perfectly clear-cut, just as are the differences between each of them and the third term of the division, 'none'. Nevertheless, when one considers human understanding as each of us exercises and experiences it, there are evidently two very different senses in which it might be said to be a restricted understanding. This might be said in one sense because we always understand as actual only some of the things that are *actually* the case, which means that we are more or less ignorant both of the past and the present and of the future as well, so far as the future is objectively determined by what is already actual. But our understanding might also be said to be restricted in the quite different sense that we never understand as actual more than some of the things that are *possibly* the case, where the criterion of possibility is simply the absence of self-contradiction in the conceptions of the things. I submit that, if we are to judge solely from an understanding of ourselves, the difference between these two senses of the phrase, 'restricted understanding', is clear and unmistakable. We continually have the two quite different experiences of coming to know what, but for our ignorance, we most certainly could have known already and of learning yet other things that we most certainly could not have known before, because they have only just now become actual. Because this is so, however, the contrasting phrase, 'unrestricted understanding', must be correspondingly ambiguous, so far, at least, as its meaning is extrapolated from our own self-understanding. Either it means an understanding as actual of all of the things that are actual, and as possible of everything else; or else it means an understanding as actual even of all the things that are possible, and thus an understanding to which the distinction between actual and possible simply cannot be applied. Yet different as these two meanings are, they are both able to give a sense to 'unrestricted understanding'. They each imply the same distinction between 'all' and 'some', and, therefore, so conceive understanding that it differs not just in fact but in principle from all merely human understanding.

Obviously, the conception of God that Lonergan works out, with its assertions that God is utterly timeless, necessary, and immutable, could be validly deduced only if 'unrestricted understanding' is taken in the second of these two meanings—just as, conversely, it is only in this meaning that unrestricted understanding would be denied were one to deny Lonergan's assertions.

The question, therefore, is how Lonergan manages thus to resolve the ambiguity that an understanding of human understanding itself apparently leaves open. By what right does he infer from the key insight that God is unrestricted understanding, that God is also 'non-temporal', that he 'must not be contingent in any respect', and that he is 'intrinsically the same whether or not he understands, affirms, wills, causes this or that universe to be'?[53]

It certainly will not do to reply that Lonergan here exercises the right bestowed by the axiom, *Deus est quo maius cogitari nequit*, of preferring maximal to a minimal conception of unrestricted understanding. For aside from begging the question of which of the two conceptions is really maximal, this reply must face the objection that the second conception involves a self-contradiction and so, strictly speaking, is not even a conception. This is the case, one may argue, because the distinction between actuality and possibility is an ultimate or transcendental distinction, which must apply somehow to all beings, not excluding the eminent being God. Because possibility by its very nature is inexhaustible by actuality, there being incompossible possibilities, even the greatest conceivable actuality must of necessity be limited and thus distinct from limitless possibility. Accordingly, one may contend that to speak of God as Lonergan does, as wholly timeless, necessary, and unchanging, is either intentionally to deny that God is anything actual, or else unintentionally to deny it by asserting what is, in fact, self-contradictory, and hence no conception at all, much less a maximal conception.

At the moment, however, I am less interested in contending that Lonergan's conception of God is a pseudo-conception than in questioning his claim to have derived it methodically from an understanding of understanding. The truth seems to be that here, even if nowhere else, he arrives at his metaphysical conclusions, not by following his own method, but by uncritically employing a traditional category, which is to say, by in effect appealing to authorities and treating as self-evident what is by no means so to everyone. This is not to imply, of course, that it would be impossible to derive Lonergan's traditional conception of unrestricted understanding from the positions established by his own cognitional theory. I mean simply that, if one considers what Lonergan does and does not do in developing this conception, there is no reason to suppose that this is how he himself derives it. On the contrary,

16

the very thing that prompts one to doubt that Lonergan's theory of cognition is sound also creates doubt that his metaphysics is critically based in an exact account of human knowing—namely, his continued use of philosophical categories which, despite his acceptance of self-understanding as the method of philosophy, are evidently not derived from the subjectivist principle.

IV.

Clearly, it is easy to find fault with this whole argument. Even if the preceding reasoning is correct, and based on a fair interpretation of Lonergan's intentions, it still is no more than an indication of the kinds of criticism that his work both requires and deserves. But probably the most obvious objection is more basic: all that the argument shows, finally, is that Lonergan is vulnerable to criticism from the standpoint of a subjectivist principle defined in essentially Whiteheadian terms. So far from in any way showing that he neglects the subject, it simply establishes that he does not attend to the subject in the manner or with the results of someone following Whitehead. Therefore, to counter the argument, it is sufficient to make the point, which is readily made, that Lonergan has, in effect, a subjectivist principle of his own, which can challenge, as well as be challenged by, the Whiteheadian one presupposed by the argument.

I have little hesitation in conceding this objection. As a matter of fact, I have already made every effort to acknowledge the limitation of the argument in just the respects to which it calls attention. I have not in the least questioned that Lonergan does, in some way, accept the subjectivist principle; and I have tried to make clear that my own definition of this principle does essentially agree with Whitehead's. But in conceding the objection, I would also note the implication of the counter-argument supporting it. If one is to make the point that Lonergan asserts and follows his own subjectivist principle, one can hardly doubt the usefulness of what has been attempted in this paper. For one acknowledges thereby the very fact whose recognition has prompted the attempt— namely, that we have here two philosophical-theological approaches which are strikingly parallel in their respective principles, and yet, at point after point, from cognitional theory to the metaphysical conception of God, directly challenge each other's positions. If this fact were generally recognised, so that thinkers sympathetic to the two approaches were already aware of their mutual challenge, there would hardly be any use in pointing it out. But as it is, there has seemed to me every reason to call attention to it and to insist on its acknowledgement as the minimal response to what I have tried to show.

From problematics to hermeneutics: Lonergan and Ricoeur

DAVID M. RASMUSSEN

I

The task of comparison is one which is desired neither by those compared nor by the one who is assigned the task; the blame, however, is reaped by him whose task it is to compare. In situations like this I am reminded of Alfred North Whitehead's statement that contemporary actual entities do not influence one another. Of course Whitehead did not intend persons, but it has often occurred to me that the statement could be extended beyond his immediate intention. I suppose every thinker shares with the poet the vision of writing 'for the lovers' whose minds after all are not yet made up, or in Lonergan's terms, those who have experienced, understood and judged, but alas, have not yet decided. In the case of both Lonergan and Ricoeur, intellectual innocence has been lost for decisions have been made, 'freedom has consented to necessity' and the result has been the creation of a style of thinking that is distinctive, unique and in some ways incomparable.

The manners in which comparability is possible are in themselves a matter of interpretation, in some ways a thematic construct, in others illustrative of a historical *geist*, the thrust of which has registered in both thinkers. It is in this latter sense, not simply because of physical or intellectual encounter, but because of a common participation in the ambiguities of a cultural and philosophical heritage, that the comparison can be made. Hence, when we suggest that comparison can be organised around a theme, the implication is not that it accounts for the totality of either point of view, or worse that the theme itself is actually a higher viewpoint into which the two points of view can be welded, tempting though the latter thought may be.

Reflections on our respective thinkers have led me to the assumption that this essay can be organised around the theme: from problematics to hermeneutics. There are reasons for this choice. As a considerable portion of this paper will illustrate, this theme is central to the methodological side of Paul Ricoeur's work. I conceive this interpretative task as essential for it will establish the foundation for the concluding critique. Further, the theme is central to the work of Bernard Lonergan in the sense that the use of a hermeneutic has become increasingly central to the overall direction of his thought. Like Ricoeur, Lonergan's methodological problematic informs his hermeneutics. The guiding question of this essay will be this: how is it possible to characterise Lonergan's use of hermeneutics when understood in the context of the original hermeneutic work of Paul Ricoeur? The critical problems will emanate from this question.

II.

Freedom, the subject of the final discussion of the first volume of Paul Ricoeur's *Philosophy of the Will*, is defined as solely human, the telos of his philosophical anthropology. Under the methodological rubric of the qualified phenomenological reduction which characterised this work, freedom is presented as a 'radical paradox' which balances uneasily in deciding, moving, and consenting . . . the three distinct movements of the will as 'incarnate', 'contingent', and 'motivated', emerging 'ceaselessly out of indecision', a 'kind of process' arising as a 'risk and not from a decree', 'gracious' and 'spontaneous'. Although the thematic properties of Ricoeur's thought are not confined to considerations of freedom alone, this subject presents the reader with the first clue to the emerging combination of issues which coalesce to illustrate the direction and scope of his work.

The struggle to transcend the modern existential vision of man as condemned to finitude provides a second predominant theme. *Fallible Man* opts neither for finitude nor infinitude as the predominant anthropological norm selectively illustrated in a Cartesian paradox, the Platonic myth of the melange, and Pascal's description of man situated between two infinites. Epistemologically, immediate perception is always transcended by language about the thing perceived. The argument concludes with the contention that understanding man as limited to finitude is narrow because language functions in such a way that the finitude of perception is always transcended.

In the concluding essay of *History and Truth*, Ricoeur employs a *dialectical method to circumvent the French philosophers who make negativity the primary 'ontological' characteristic of man*. As with finitude, so with negation, Ricoeur furthers the drive towards fundamental affirmation by locating in the original act of negation, *a negation of a negation*, and therefore a movement toward primary affirmation. He states:

> . . . negativity is the privileged road of the climb back to foundation; . . . to discover human transcendence in the transgression of point of view, and negativity is transcendence; then to discover in this negation a double negation, the second negation of point of view as primary negation, and then to discover this primary affirmation within negation.[1]

In the original act of consciousness one may discover negation, but negativity can be overcome through a transgression of the finitude of point of view, the primary fact of experience. Negation thus leads to affirmation through the quasi-Hegelian process of a double negation culminating in affirmation. Herbert Spiegelberg has called Ricoeur's phenomenology essentially a philosophy of 'affirmation': wherein 'the central motif is that of a reconciliation, a reconciliation of man with himself, his body and the world'. According to Spiegelberg, Ricoeur's philosophy represents a movement beyond Sartre's philosophy of freedom which is 'essentially negation'. Erazim Kohak has described Ricoeur's philosophy as an example of the 'French materialism and idealism in an existentialist garb'. Although the term 'idealism' is perhaps too strong, Ricoeur shares with Gabriel Marcel the desire to affirm man's being-in-the-world as well as his idealistic tendency to emphasise affirmation and transcendence.

Ricoeur's thought may be characterised by a drive towards the *concrete* involving the methodological shift from the techniques of eidetic phenomenology, eidetic reduction, to a concrete hermeneutic programme. Abstract considerations of will are replaced by concrete confessions of evil in symbol and myth. The abstract mode of conscious reflection is replaced by concrete considerations of language involving a choice of symbol and myth as the subject matter for philosophic investigation. In symbol and myth the human experience of rupture is presented while the hermeneutic method explicates that experience. In this sense, the investigation of language represents the final aim of Ricoeur's philosophical anthropology. In his programmatic article, 'The Hermeneutics of Symbols and Philosophical Reflection', Ricoeur illustrates the possibilities illuminated through this orientation.

In the very age in which our language is becoming more precise, more univocal, more technical, better suited to those integral formalisations that are called precisely 'symbolic' logic . . . it is in the age of discourse that we wish to recharge language, start again from the fullness of language.[2]

Ricoeur's contention is that man's most significant confrontation with evil can be discovered through a hermeneutic consideration of man's actual confession of evil.

What ties the work of Ricoeur together is not any one of these themes, but their combination in his overall quest for a global philosophical anthropology. This search for an understanding of man is sufficiently comprehensive to include both finite and infinite, the voluntary and the involuntary, freedom and necessity, mind and body, abstract and concrete, perception and signification, symbol and reflection. The primordial image which illustrates best Ricoeur's entire phenomenological work is the vision of man as 'situated', situated between the polarities of his reflection and active experience. A study of Ricoeur's thought brings this vision into realistic focus.

This central concern originally stimulated my interest in Ricoeur and, of course, it is basic to this presentation. The problematic of this essay, the interrelation between mythic-symbolic language and the nature of man, is given form by this key issue in Ricoeur's thought. Ricoeur poses an answer to that problematic by demonstrating that a mythic-symbolic language is *necessary* for global understanding of man. But a consideration of mythic-symbolic language, not an early issue in Ricoeur's thought, occurs as a means of furthering the development of philosophical anthropology, for it is by recourse to symbol and myth that the adventure of human freedom confronted by radical limitation is made explicit. In the original volume of *The Philosophy of the Will* the possibility for that development is latent, although the necessity for it emerges subsequently. I shall try to capture the dynamic movement of Ricoeur's thought by considering the 'anthropological problematic' as it is centred in his earlier work and the emergence of mythic-symbolic language later. The first interpretive problem is methodological while the second concerns the development of a philosophical anthropology. I will attempt to discover (a) what hermeneutics has to do with philosophy, and (b) how hermeneutics may be incorporated in an avowedly phenomenological philosophic programme.

Global Philosophical Anthropology

No doubt every philosophical position has within it a certain model or image of an exemplary type which illustrates its aim and direction. Such a model may serve as a starting point which clarifies the later developments in such a way that it provides a key to give the interpreter of that position a fundamental sustaining insight into the direction of that orientation. The term global anthropology is taken most directly from *Fallible Man*, the general concern of which is to further a discussion already begun in *Freedom and Nature* on the central human problem, the will. As a book, *Fallible Man* attempts to make more concrete the reality of the basic internal rupture of the will revealed initially through the discussion of the relations of the voluntary and involuntary processes of the will. It is out of this dichotomy that the global image emanates.

The problematic of *Fallible Man* consists in an attempt to find a way to reflect upon a double hypothesis: first, 'that man is by nature fragile and liable to err', and second, that the 'ratio' of fallibility comprises a 'certain non-coincidence of man with himself'. A moment ago it was indicated that Ricoeur depends primarily on the 'Cartesian paradox of the finite-infinite man', the Platonic myth of misery, and Pascal's reflections on the dual nature of man for illumination. For Ricoeur, the central meaning of the three references is that they all conceive man as 'situated' or 'intermediate' between the diverse elements which make up his being: 'Man is not intermediate because he is between angel and animal; he is intermediate within himself, within his selves.'[3] This self-perception by man himself is called a 'pre-comprehension' to be conceived not as an ontological reflection, but as a foundation for reflection. Hence, the initial discussion is to be understood as an exercise in pre-philosophy which will establish a foundation for the actual philosophic elaboration of man's situational dilemma.

At this point, the Platonic discourse on the soul is apt. 'Unable to speak of it (the soul) in the language of Science, that is, in the discourse on immutable Being, the philosopher expresses it in the language of allegory, and then in the language of myth.'[4] Plato's concept of *thumos* designates dynamically the central human issue Ricoeur wishes to stress. 'The soul appears as a field of forces undergoing the double attraction of reason called "that which urges" and of desire which is characterised as "something which holds back". '[5] In *thumos* one encounters a dangling man image wherein the suspended human subject 'undergoes the double attraction of reason and desire'. A correlate view is found in the Pascalian vision of the man who exists as a being intermediate between the very great and the very small, between infinity and nothingness, a man who is 'a nothing in comparison with the infinite, and all in comparison with nothing'. So Descartes, Plato, and Pascal have constructed a common view of man, suspended between a set of conflicting forces—a mixture.

Ordinarily the term 'global' denotes a comprehensiveness that designates the unification of diverse elements which overcome the narrowness of perspectival views. On the level of modern moral investigation the dominant tendency has been to stress perspectival models, the major characteristic of which has been finitude. The global view conceived and developed by Ricoeur may be understood as something of a polemic against such perspectival views of man. 'By allowing ourselves to begin with the Cartesian theme of finite-infinite man—even though we may have to reinterpret it completely—we disassociate ourselves to some extent from the contemporary tendency to make finitude the global characteristic of human reality.[6]

But the term does not eliminate the situational perspectives that have been so predominant in contemporary investigations of the human dilemma. Rather the global notion attempts to present a more complex vision, hopefully a more adequate view of the matrix of human options that find their consequence in the evolution of contemporary radical limitation as a moral perspective. Hence a global view is something of a postulate, a hypothesis about the structure of human experience which presupposes a unity of that structure, but only as a possibility. To be suspended between a totality of options eliminates neither perfection nor limitation; rather it is the ontological characteristic which leads to the possibility of fallibility. Man's 'ontological characteristic of being-intermediate consists precisely in that his act of existing is the very act of bringing about mediations between all the modalities and all levels of reality within him and outside of him'.[7]

The global vision of man need not be a moral vision if the situational image is merely presented as a descriptive analysis of man without moral valuation. But the global view is pre-eminently moral because it allows for the possible emergence of the concept of fallibility. The situational view of man incorporates duality within totality in such a way that suspension is between polar opposites. In themselves, neither duality nor polar opposition constitutes a moral perspective. Only when the human is conceived as suspended between the most radical of the human polarities, the possibility of transcendence and the possibility of fault, does the global view become a moral view. The global view is conceived as a problematic vision because instead of presenting easy resolutions to the basic dichotomies of human experience, these dichotomies are revealed in such a way that their solution will be the critical issue which the philosophical system will attempt to resolve adequately.

The global view of the human dilemma is most directly the problematic in the book *Fallible Man*; indirectly the image appears elsewhere. For example, the problem of *Freedom and Nature* is to overcome an understanding of self and consciousness which fails to incorporate a realistic understanding of the role and function of the body involving the primary role of involuntary processes. In *The Symbolism of Evil* considerations of the extremes of the global view are given concretely through incorporation of the language of avowal (confession) in primary symbols and myths reincorporated through a hermeneutic method into philosophic discourse. In *De l'interpretation* an encounter with the works of Freud is undertaken to bring a more adequate (global) view of man into both psychological and philosophical discourse. The attempt to construct a global philosophical anthropology therefore will be understood as an originary starting point for the interpretation of Ricoeur's philosophical thought.

The process of thinking from global image is a problem for the transformation of phenomenological methodology as well as for the substantial issue of this philosophical anthropology, namely the will with its correlate polarities, freedom and limitation. Under the rather broad rubric, phenomenology, Ricoeur has chosen to transform the phenomenological method from one grounded in classical Husserlian eidetics to one which finds hermeneutic interpretation as primary. No one methodology is sufficient to comprehend fully, describe adequately, and understand properly the multitude of issues to be included in a philosophical anthropology. With this method and its transformations, Ricoeur has attempted to struggle with the dialectic of freedom and limitation. Our approach will be to consider the methodological issues first, content issues second, and finally correlation of method and content in Ricoeur's later work.

The Eidetic Method and its Limitations

Whatever Ricoeur's final judgement on the eidetic method, it sets the context for his original constructive work, *Freedom and Nature*. Classical phenomenology plays a central role in Ricoeur's thinking for he is concerned to retain his own version of Husserl's eidetic method, refusing to begin this constructive work on the basis of existential signification alone, as did many late post-Husserlian phenomenologists. The eidetic method which Husserl employed to constitute transcendentally acts of consciousness functions in a similar way for Ricoeur, although the primary datum is the willing subject cognizant and becoming cognizant of its activities. Therefore, the eidetic method functions at the most elemental level as a method of description which attempts to unfold the fundamental structures of the voluntary and the involuntary under the rubric, will, as they are articulated in decision, bodily motion, and consent.[8] In this sense the description that the eidetic method undertakes is a 'triadic interpretation of the act of the will',[9] for 'To say "I will" means first, "I decide", secondly, "I move my body", thirdly "I consent" '.[10]

Eidetic, the adjective derived from *eidos*, Plato's alternative term for idea, was utilised originally in the phenomenological movement to designate essences. For Ricoeur, essence is too strong a term. The eidetic method describes, lays open, basic structures within a particular region; it is this function that distinguishes eidetic description from explanation. Explanation means 'to move from the complex to the simple'.[11] It is this orientation that dominates empirical psychology and the natural sciences. In contrast, the key term relating to description is 'reciprocity', for here with the relation of the voluntary and the involuntary, the informing principle of each is the other. Ricoeur sees the relationship between the voluntary and the involuntary as the presentation of a reciprocity that transcends equality. The voluntary is always that which occurs as the primary and most immediate phenomenon. 'I understand myself in the first place as he who says, "I will".'[12] It is this centrality of the willing self, what 'the Stoic called the directing principle'[13] that caused what Ricoeur believes to be the first Copernican revolution in philosophy.

The striking characteristic of Ricoeur's version of the phenomenological method is his attempt to apply it to the area ordinarily thought to be most distant from the eidetic sphere of pure consciousness, namely the bodily involuntary. The basic assumption is that description is constituted by reciprocity so that the mutual interrelations of the voluntary and the involuntary will lead to understanding and intelligibility. The methodological benefit of descriptive orientation is that illumination is brought to the opaque and often incomprehensible realm of the involuntary by viewing it as reciprocal with the voluntary, while the voluntary, which is often conceived as in its non-complexity, is given richness through description in relation to the involuntary.

Ricoeur shares with classical phenomenology, and to a certain extent with the later or second generation phenomenologists, the use of the concept of intentionality to recover and constitute the subjective world of meaning. Generally the more technical members of this group hold that ordinary uncritical perception and cognition is false, and that it is necessary to establish a reversal of attitudes involving a movement from a 'natural attitude' to a phenomenological, or truly subjective attitude in order to discover the foundations of noetic meaning. Consequently consciousness is not associated with phenomenalism or sensationalism, but rather with intentional fields synthetically given to the realm of the subject.

Ricoeur's interpretation of intentionality is distinctive; while the difference between Ricoeur and Husserl is a subtle one. 'Any function is constituted by its type of object, or as Husserl says by its intentionality. We express it differently by saying that consciousness constitutes itself by the type of object to which it projects itself.'[14] The centrality of the notion 'project' distinguishes Ricoeur's interpretation of intentionality from Husserl's because Husserl associated the notion with the reflective acts of pure consciousness instead of the dynamism of the will. From his, Ricoeur's point of view, the project is formulated in decision, becoming processively an action associated with bodily motivation leading to complete formulation and execution. Viewed teleologically from its status as completed act, the project is defined as 'acquiescence to necessity' because at that point the project can no longer be changed. The notion of project could be designated as a simple volitional task, voluntarily initiated and voluntarily achieved. However, such a view cannot account for the complexities of voluntary-involuntary correlations and reciprocities. Rather, the involuntary side of bodily motivation presents 'reasons' for voluntary action. The action (voluntary motion) which occurs as a consequence of a voluntary act (decision) reveals the involuntary organs of willing, habit, etc.—that is, those things which make voluntary action possible but also place upon it its most radical limitation. Therefore, the range of volition incorporates necessity.

This doctrine of intentionality shares with traditional phenomenology the attempt to overcome a dualism between ordinary physical experience and psychological or mental experience. Ricoeur's argument bears within it Franz Brentano's original insight with regard to the distinction between genetic and descriptive psychology, an insight which, because of its focus on intentionality, was thought to be one of Husserl's most significant insights. Brentano wanted to find a fundamental characteristic which separates psychological perception and cognition from non-psychological ordinary perception and cognition of physical objects. The positivistic criticism of psychological experience has assumed that only those perceptions that could be tested were valid, perceptions of physical objects, whereas psychological experience, memories, judgements, dreams, etc. were untestable and therefore invalid. As far as Brentano was concerned the insight into the intentionality of psychic phenomena established their validity against the positivistic criticism inasmuch as psychic acts of consciousness retain an intentional relationship to an object. Consciousness is never empty. Consciousness is always intentional in the sense that it has reference to an object. 'No hearing without something heard, no believing without something believed, no hoping without something hoped, no striving without something striven for, no joy without something we feel joyous about.'[15]

Although Husserl was overwhelmed by Brentano's insight, calling it the key to phenomenological investigation, he went far beyond his one-time mentor by generalising the notion of intentionality to apply to consciousness generally and universally. For Husserl all consciousness, not simply psychological perception, is intentional. Consequently, throughout his life Husserl sustained a polemic against empirical psychology, arguing that empirical psychology always grounded itself in an epistemologically uncertain physical model which reduced all perceptions to a physical scale. Ricoeur, sustaining this same phenomenological bias with regard to empirical psychology, finds the disturbing factor in such a psychology to be the 'reduction of *acts* (with their intentionality and their reference to an Ego) to facts'. Hence, the centrality of the human subject constituted in conscious acts is lost. But, the difference between Husserl and Ricoeur is worth noting. Ricoeur acknowledges the legitimacy of the so-called empirical disciplines finding that they have relevance to a phenomenological investigation because the knowledge obtained by such analysis may contribute to knowledge of the subject. Hence, the data derived from empirical disciplines may be reintegrated into a phenomenological context by a diagnostic method, essentially an eidetic analysis.

Ricoeur's interpretation of the eidetic method includes more than the repossession of consciousness to which Husserl directed the method; rather, Ricoeur seeks to enlarge the method to include consciousness of the body. To speak, therefore, of 'becoming receptive to the Cogito's *complete* experience'[16] implies the extension of the eidetic method to include the involuntary structures, the bodily constitution, of one's experience. This is a difficult task for the tendency of consciousness is to exclude bodily experience by dismissing it to be classified with the realm of objects. Ricoeur, not the first to find this insight into the splitting of the Cogito from itself in Descartes, finds the Cartesian genius in 'having carried to the limit this intuition of thought which returns to itself in positing itself and which takes into itself only an image of its body and an image of the other.'[17]

In other words, consciousness tends to exclude consciousness of the body resulting in the conclusion that the 'Cogito is broken up within itself'.[18] Conscious reflection objectifies the body, an objectification which has led to treatment of the body in empirical psychology, biology, and the natural sciences generally as a natural object. Ricoeur, not wanting to reject the contributions of the natural and empirical sciences, wishes to make a transition from the objective view of the body to a subjective view wherein the involuntary can be understood in relationship to the voluntary and the Cogito can be restored to its rightful position.

Such an enterprise is carried on in the name of freedom; 'Freedom has no place among empirical objects; it requires a reversal of viewpoint and a discovery of the Cogito.'[19] This methodological process of freeing the body from empirical description where it appears as bound to a scheme of cause and effect, and the process of recovering the true subjectivity of the body and relating it to the thinking self, has the consequence of restoring to the Cogito that which is lost internally because of the splitting up of reflection and lost externally because of the treatment of the body as an object. The Cogito, arrived at through an eidetics of the will, is complete in the establishment of a proper balance between freedom and nature.

At the juncture of the phenomenological recovery of the body—that is, the bringing back of the body into the realm of subjectivity, the eidetic method is itself altered to meet the demands peculiar to bodily existence. The tendency of the self to posit itself (Descartes) and therefore to exclude bodily spontaneity is broken by what Ricoeur calls 'my incarnation as mystery'. This means that the objectivity of description is deepened at each level of description by a movement towards a discovery of bodily spontaneity. 'I need to pass from objectivity to existence.' As the voluntary provides an opening for the discovery of the involuntary, so pure description of the structures of willing provides an opening for the recovery of bodily spontaneity. The two motifs attempt to balance and overcome the possible dualism between the subjectivity of mental operations and the objectivity of bodily descriptions.

If one evaluates Ricoeur's usage and application of the eidetic method against the backdrop of classical phenomenology, it is possible to conclude that he has expanded that method to include bodily regions often thought to be inaccessible to the methodologies of classical phenomenology. In another way however, Ricoeur places his own restrictive limits on the method. A moment ago the claim was made that the most radical form of Ricoeur's global philosophical anthropology occurs as the vision of man 'situated'

between the extremities, transcendence and fault. Surprisingly for
Ricoeur, the eidetic method occurs not only as a means of internal
bracketing of the structures of the voluntary and the involuntary,
but also as a means of excluding certain types of phenomena from
the range of eidetic description. Transcendence and fault, so
important for the overall understanding of Ricoeur's work, are
excluded here. The process itself may be called one of double
bracketing, suspending certain phenomena within brackets while
excluding other phenomena which would ordinarily appear.

Ricoeur believes that if one begins the philosophical discussion
with the immediate focus on fault and transcendence, the fundamental possibilities which can be illustrated by the eidetic method
are thereby obscured. 'The greatest error we could make with
respect to a fundamental ontology of willing and nature is to
interpret it as an actual, immediate ethic.'[20] In order to avoid the
possible obscurities that transcendence and fault would bring to a
pure description of the will under the eidetic method, they are
bracketed out momentarily only to be brought back in at a later
point—in *The Philosophy of the Will*, Volume II, to be exact.
Valuation of an ethical kind is excluded thereby on the ground that
ethical prejudgement, although ultimately necessary, is a mode of
immediate falsification. The inclusion of fault will simply distract
from an eidetic attempt to describe man's volitional nature in the
sense that the Cogito's complete bodily experience which it is the
task of the eidetic method to clarify, is lost. Fault, with its correlates
of radical evil and the rupture of the will, obscures the possible
by illuminating the limitations of the actual. The full moral
significance of the reconciliation between mind and body can be
understood only after a neutral description of the voluntary and
the involuntary is given. Finally, a total understanding of fault
can be given on the basis of an analysis of myth and symbol, and
that requires a hermeneutic method for elucidation, intelligibility
and understanding.

But, if the eidetic method does not hold the prospect of a global
recognition of that ultimate 'suspension' between transcendence
and fault or the prospect of the ultimate reconciliation of these
extremes in the human subject, it does hold the prospect of another
kind of reconciliation. Through opening up the realm of the body,
through understanding thereby the unity of the voluntary willing
self in reciprocity with the mysterious realm of the body, the

eidetic method contains the possibility of sustaining and achieving on this abstract level the fundamental reconciliation of freedom and nature. 'The study of the voluntary and the involuntary is a limited contribution to a far broader scheme which would be the reconciliation of a paradoxical and a reconciled ontology.'[21] In its broadest sense, the paradox is between freedom and nature in the context of an eidetic phenomenology. 'There is no logical procedure by which nature could be derived from freedom (the involuntary from the voluntary) or freedom from nature.'[22] If, from an understanding of nature one could derive freedom, then the question of paradox would not arise. Yet, Ricoeur's contention is that the thematic term is reciprocity and paradox and not logical derivation. The actuality of paradox directs itself toward reconciliation, while the discovery of the reciprocity between freedom and nature will contribute toward that reconciliation. But a full concrete reconciliation is beyond the scope of the eidetic method.

One must conclude that Ricoeur's use of the eidetic method is based on the assumption that *an eidetics is necessary but not adequate*. The implicit necessity for an eidetic method is contained within each of the defining characteristics listed above. From the perspective of global philosophical anthropology each defining characteristic has its own implicit limitation. First, if the eidetic method can be applied to the development of the voluntary and the involuntary, it is necessary to go beyond the voluntary and the involuntary to deal adequately with the Cogito not only as perceived neutrally, but as experienced realistically. Second, to achieve this movement, it is necessary to break out of the brackets established originally to attain a neutral view of the basic structures of the will. Third, the very attempt to recover the complete experience of the Cogito requires that the eidetic method be transcended so that the complete experience of the Cogito be related to the actual experience of the Cogito. Fourth, and perhaps most important, if the fundamental requirement of the eidetic method is that it is necessary to bracket out the actualities of transcendence and fault, and if, as Ricoeur says, transcendence and fault are fundamental to an accurate elaboration of global anthropology, then the eidetic method must be dispensed with so that one can find a means for the reincorporation of transcendence and fault. Finally, if the ultimate direction of a global anthropology is towards the achievement of a full reconciliation of man with himself and the world,

17

the eidetic method can suggest only the direction of such a movement; it cannot present the solution.

For all of these reasons it is in the name of an adequate global anthropology that the eidetic method is broken. The anthropological problematic is incorporated within the very structure of the eidetic method. Eidetics can present neutral structures, abstract possibilities. Eidetics cannot deal with man who, as fallible, stands before the possibility of evil, nor can it appropriate fault as an actual immediate experience. *The introduction of a criterion of adequacy is itself the occasion for the demise of the eidetic method.* It is this problematic that drives Ricoeur to a method of existential description.

Existential Description and Its Limits

The debate among phenomenologists involves the relation of the eidetic (Husserl) to existential signification (Sartre, Heidegger). Perhaps there is no better testimony to Ricoeur's desire to bridge the various alternatives within the phenomenological movement, incorporating its best insights into his own thought, than his methodological movement from eidetic to existential description. One may conclude that neither eidetic nor existential description is adequate for a full global philosophical anthropology. Both are necessary for a full description. It is the *quest for adequacy* that gives to this mode of thinking its direction, drive and orientation.

Methodologically conceived, existential description requires a transition from the ideally possible to that which is possible in actuality. As Husserl thought of them, eidetic structures are to be associated with the ideal realm of pure possibility, and not connected with the radical limitations confronted by the human subject in his concrete day-to-day existence. As Ricoeur conceives of it, the transition from the realm of eidetic description to the realm of existential description may be understood as a transition from ideal to actual possibilities. This does not mean that one can transform the eidetic method into a kind of essentialism; rather, a functional definition is intended. Eidetic description reveals functional possibilities. The eidetics of the will presents a distinct advantage over the empirics of the will in the sense that the eidetic method of bracketing can suspend structures, taking them out of their ordinary context, with the consequence that they are understood thereby apart from the possible objectification that might occur in ordinary existential experience. In this sense the distinction between that which is possible ideally and that which is possible actually is immense. But no complete description of the human subject is possible without a movement from the ideal to the actual. Hence a transition must be made from that which is possible ideally to that which is possible actually in order to introduce those things which qualify man's actual experience, limiting thereby his fundamental possibilities to the realm of 'concrete description'.

So it is logical that existential description breaks the brackets in which the actuality of human fault was suspended originally. As we have seen, global philosophical anthropology understood on the most inclusive level is a philosophical anthropology which understands man as 'situated' between transcendence and fault. Existential description provides a means to begin to reincorporate the realm of fault previously excluded. Fault was bracketed, Ricoeur suggests, because 'fault . . . is not a feature of fundamental ontology similar to the factors discovered by pure description. . . . Fault remains a foreign body in the eidetics of man'.[23]

The inclusion of fault at the level of existential description poses a series of difficulties. Like eidetic description, existential description, fundamentally rational in orientation, is dominated by the motif of reflection upon acts of consciousness. Fault can begin to be reincorporated at this juncture on a conceptual level. The original brackets whereby fault was excluded, now discarded, do not allow for the complete presentation of fault and its correlate human evil in its full empirical actuality.

Existential description methodologically approaches not the full actuality of fault but fallibility as a possibility. The contention is that for evil and fault to be confronted in their full actuality it is necessary to deal with the concrete individual confessing his confrontation with evil. Such a confrontation requires another methodological revision, namely, the transition to hermeneutics. So the methodological task of the work, *Fallible Man*, is to locate evil as a possibility within man through the application of a descriptive method which does not elucidate fault and evil *per se*, but the concept of fallibility. This is both the possibility and the limitation of existential description.

Under these carefully specified limitations of existential description the concept of fallibility can be approached in terms of a type of description which uses a transcendental, practical, and affective form of reflection. The prospect of fallibility is that finally it can locate the possibility of evil within man. The descriptive method in this existential form is able to trace the derivation of the concept of fallibility by discovering through the knowing, acting, and affective aspects of the will, the confirmation of that original double hypothesis about the nature of man concerning his fragility and liability to err and his global disproportion with himself. The final meaning derived from existential description is 'that the *possibility* of moral evil is inherent in man's constitution'.[24] One may conclude: the function of existential description is to place global philosophical anthropology *before* the possibility of human fault and rupture.

Because the notion of fallibility has been introduced, the transition from eidetic description to existential description provides the basis for the development of an ethic. As we have seen in *Freedom and Nature*, Ricoeur cautioned against the immediate plunge into an ethic, claiming that the eidetic method with its neutral perspective and its necessary abstraction provided only the foundation for the latter possibility. The moral significance of the reconciliation between soul and body remained suspended requiring a long detour in order to be perceived'.[25] This restriction disappears in *Fallible Man* and instead of offering caution, Ricoeur suggests that *Grandeur and Limitation of an Ethical Vision of the World* might have made a 'subtitle of this book'. Ethical considerations are not limited to existential description, for it is by the method of hermeneutics that the actuality of freedom, evil and their interdependent relations are revealed. But existential description functions as the method which opens the door to ethics by preparing the way for the possibility of fallibility within the heart of man. This advance to ethical considerations is correlated with the movement towards the reinclusion of fallibility (*Fallible Man*) and the actuality of fault (*The Symbolism of Evil*). It is possible to conclude that simultaneous with the movement from eidetics to existential description is the movement from the abstract and neutral to the concrete and ethical.

As with eidetic description so with existential description, the limitations of method make necessary a further movement if a global philosophical anthropology under the rubric of the will can be attained. Each of the premises of the existential description orientation is not only an affirmation of the actual power and ability of that method; each has within it a fundamental limitation. If it is true that existential description requires a transition from the ideally possible to that which is possible in actuality, it is also true that existential description is limited—in fact, confined—to the realm of evil as a possibility. It can only locate evil; it cannot fully probe its meaning. If it is true that existential description breaks the brackets in which the actuality of human fault was suspended, it is also true that existential description cannot fully understand fault in its depth as that which is experienced and conferred as the source of evil. If existential methodology can only locate the fallible within man through a global description of the knowing, acting, and feeling subject, it cannot approach the consequences of that discovery. Finally, if existential description begins to work toward the foundation of an ethics, it is also the case that this method can only constitute a preliminary stage in that construction because it has only pointed to the source of evil as a possibility. It has not dealt with the concrete man who has committed an evil act. To overcome the limitations of existential description, it is necessary to turn to hermeneutics.

Hermeneutic Phenomenology and Language

Ricoeur's contention is that the limitation of a philosophical method which begins conceptually with fallibility is that it can confront fault only as a possibility. The case for hermeneutic phenomenology is sustained in the name of a desire to recover a direct experience of fault, for the question confronted is whether or not it is the lot of the philosopher to remain outside the actual experience of evil, condemned to the realm of purely possible considerations. Here we are at the boundary between existential description and the development of a hermeneutic. Either philosophy must remain with the realm of possibility or it must plunge into the slippery and opaque realm of statements about man's actual experience of evil. If philosophy confines itself to the realm of pure description, it can both locate the possibility of evil within man and show how man is liable to err simply because of the constitution of his being. Philosophy at that level can show that man is fallible; but it cannot deal with the fault that is the consequence of experienced fallibility. This is that 'point of no return' where one questions whether or not philosophy can go beyond the realm of the immediacy of man's conscious experience. The advantage of remaining at this boundary is the advantage of clarity, that is, of remaining in the realm of clarity, in the sphere of univocal concepts and meaning. But the making of the 'wager' results in the plunge into the realm of symbols and myth, the opaque realm of man's confession of evil. The problem is whether or not philosophy is capable of moving into this new milieu.

The term 'wager' implies that there is a leap from fallibility to fault accounting for a movement into discourse on symbols and myths implying a movement from rational philosophical problems. This is deemed a wager because it is done on the assumption that the transition will enrich the discourse on freedom and limitation. Ricoeur makes the wager. He risks the possible loss of clarity for depth. He risks the loss of a clear but narrow vision of man for a global view of man. The hermeneutic occurs at this juncture not simply as an experiment in method but in the name of an attempt to recover the actual human experience of fault and the consequent quest for freedom. While fallibility is confined to the possible, it is in the name of this quest for the concrete that a hermeneutic phenomenology is established. In this sense, the wager marks the beginning of hermeneutics.

The realm in which the actual experience of evil is encapsulated is that confessional 'language of avowal', a language the characteristics of which are a hermeneutic method of interpretation. This language speaks for fault and evil to the philosopher, and what is noteworthy in it is that it is symbolic through and through.[26] It is because the meaning of that language is hidden, opaque, and obscure that a new method is required to bring that language into the realm of philosophical reflection. The case for hermeneutic phenomenology then is predicated upon the assumption that the experience of evil can be encountered directly in a particular kind of language, that is, symbol and myth. Let it suffice to note here that the characteristics of that kind of language, to be considered later in detail, are to be distinguished from language which has as its aim and prerogative transparent conceptuality. At this point the methodological significance of this 'turn to hermeneutics' requires consideration.

Ricoeur's argument with regard to this particular kind of language is not that it can be described by philosophy but that it actually functions as a pre-philosophical basis for philosophical reflection.

Given the particular methodological context within which Ricoeur's thought is set, the departure is radical because it actually requires philosophy to give up temporarily reflection on the constitutive acts of consciousness (eidetic phenomenology) in order to turn to an explication of experience as it is given in pre-philosophical materials. Given this conception of the function of language, the constitutive foundation of philosophy is not to be found within the realm of philosophy at all but in that pre-philosophical language which provides the basis for philosophical reflection. It must be acknowledged consequently that the hermeneutic conception of phenomenology alters the Husserlian conception of philosophy in the sense that it departs radically from considerations of the constitution of the transcendental Cogito, to considerations of pre-philosophical givens for later philosophical consideration and integration. As we shall attempt to show later, this does not mean a total departure from a phenomenological tradition, rather it means a transformation of phenomenology.

The key question raised by the use of symbols and myths, the language of avowal, is, if philosophy is required to turn to a pre-philosophical source for its fundamental data, how is it to bring that material back into the realm of philosophy? Ricoeur's reply is given in the hermeneutic thesis 'the symbol invites thought'. This is a distinctively non-reductionistic hypothesis with regard to the methodological analysis of symbolic language. Relying on the achievements of the phenomenology of religion, particularly those of Mircea Eliade, Ricoeur assumes that the status of the symbol in relationship to reflective analysis is one that construes the correlation between the symbolic form and philosophical reflection to be a non-positivistic one. Philosophy does not get behind the symbol with the explicit intention of eliminating that form; rather philosophy assumes that the symbol gives meaning. Mircea Eliade presented the case for the special function of the religious symbol well when he stated:

A religious phenomenon will only be recognised as such if it is grasped at its own level, that is to say, if it is studied as something religious. To try to grasp the essence of such a phenomenon by means of physiology, psychology, sociology, economics, linguistics, or any other study is false; it misses the one unique and irreducible element in it—the element of the sacred.[27]

Such a starting point, avowedly anti-reductionistic, allows the symbol to present its own meaning as a resource for philosophical reflection, while philosophical reflection attempts to bring that meaning into the realm of intelligibility, albeit not to exhaust the symbol but to understand it. It was then from the phenomenology of religion that Ricoeur derived an initial insight pertaining to the interpretation of symbols, namely, that the symbol must be interpreted on its own level with its own special set of rubrics and rules.

Methodologically speaking one is confronted with the problem of the construction of a theory of the symbol which attempts to define the symbol adequately while not submitting it to a false reduction. In order to do this Ricoeur constructs a theory of symbol which distinguishes between the symbol and the sign, making the contention that all symbols have a sign element within them while signs are not symbols. Signs find their primary identification in their one-dimensional conceptually clear identity, being transparencies which strive for univocal meaning with singular intention. In contrast to the sign, the symbol is composed of polar dimensions to be identified not by univocity but by double intentionality. The significance of this notion of double intentionality is that in contrast to a conceptually clear language which is perhaps the aim of science, the language of the symbol is multivalent, designating, in phenomenological terms, an intentional field of meaning.

The definition of the symbol as a doubly intentional phenomenon does not clarify the manner in which the intentionalities are presented, a problem most crucial to both the notions of the symbol and their later elaboration. The correlation between intentionalities settled upon by Ricoeur is this: that which constitutes the symbol has both a literal meaning and a symbolic meaning, the latter constituted by the former. Phenomenology of religion would suggest, for example, that the meaning of sky symbolism, sky gods, ascension symbolism, etc. always has a set of characteristics given by the sky, namely, the qualities of transcendence, infinity, eternality, etc. Thus the literal signification of the sky as an appearance is given through its various manifestations as sacred. In the context of *The Symbolism of Evil*, the symbol of stain may have an abstract, opaque reference to a feeling of psychic impurity, but this second intentionality is known through and constituted by a primary intentionality of stain which is the literal signification of stain, that is, a spot. Hence, the primary intentionality is that of literal signification, the spot, while the secondary intentionality of the symbol probes beyond the literal form to manifest the feeling of psychic impurity which is derived from that primary form. It follows that the symbols of stain, sin, and guilt, the three basic symbols analysed in *The Symbolism of Evil*, will find their methodological elaboration through the clues given by this intentional elaboration of the characteristics of symbols.

Ricoeur's theory of myth follows directly from this view of symbol. Myth is conceived as a secondary elaboration of symbolic material, in this context the application of a primitive hermeneutic to the primary symbols of stain, sin and guilt. The symbols of stain, sin and guilt find their original mythic context in the 'myths of evil', a set of myths which composes two typological groups. The first group includes those myths which contain the drama of creation, the tragic myths in which the hero is subject to a fatal destiny, and myths of the soul in exile (the Orphic myth). The second group of myths contains the 'anthropological myth proper' which is defined by our author as the 'biblical narrative of Adam's fall'. As we shall discover in greater detail later, Ricoeur attempts to find the methodological solution to the correlation between the different typologies through a consideration of their content, evil. Essentially 'the world of myth is . . . polarised between two tendencies: one takes evil back beyond the human; the other concentrates it in an evil choice from which stems the pain of being man'.[28] The hermeneutic task then is to conceive these myths in a comparative way, discovering thereby the basic elements or structures within them which in turn illuminate the meaning of myth. A comparative or structural hermeneutic is employed to illuminate, in this case at least, the phenomenon at hand.[29] Again, Ricoeur has drawn heavily upon the phenomenology of religion to solve a primary hermeneutic problem, namely, the task of moving from a set of data present but uninterpreted to the interpretation of that data. The basic problem of such a methodology is that understanding occurs through comparison. The symbols stain, sin, and guilt are placed beside one another in order to understand their mutual testimony to the fact of evil. In a similar way the myths are compared to uncover their meaning and their correlate structures. The conclusion of the analysis illustrates the double character of evil.

So again we come across, at a higher level of elaboration, the polarity of the primary symbols, stretched between a scheme of exteriority, which is dominant in the magical conception of evil as stain, a schema of interiority which only fully triumphs with the painful experience of the guilty and scrupulous conscience.[30]

In other words, evil illustrates two tendencies most clearly: the tendency to see evil as prior to man's experience of it, and the tendency to posit evil within man and make him the cause. It is the Adam myth, Ricoeur argues, which tends to include both aspects because it 'has in fact two faces'. In its most elemental form it is both the myth which asserts the priority of evil, like the symbol of stain, and yet it also locates evil within man as in the case of the symbol of guilt. From Ricoeur's perspective, the Adam myth is the anthropological myth proper because it is inclusive of the entire symbolism of evil.

Having elaborated briefly the theory of symbol and myth, it is possible to develop Ricoeur's theory of hermeneutics based upon the proposition 'the symbol invites thought'. The invitation to hermeneutic reflection occurs on two levels, argues Ricoeur: the level of comparison and the level of wager. This movement may be considered circular inasmuch as thought from the symbol finally returns to its origin, namely, the rediscovery of the symbol. The comparative level is the first level, that of bringing the various symbols and myths together and discovering their essential and structural relations. Ricoeur, however, wants to extend the hermeneutic method beyond the comparative level to include the question of truth which is suspended by the comparative method.

Symbols are given: they are also decided upon. There is a level beyond the comparative level wherein one has to make, on religious grounds at least, a decision for or against a particular set of symbols. Hence in contrast to the hermeneutic of the phenomenology of religions, Ricoeur extends his hermeneutic to include the problem of truth, that is, to the level of a truth which one can affirm. This notion of truth is associated closely with the concept of faith inasmuch as it is not given as an objective certainty but, as Pascal and Kierkegaard have shown, it is the correlate of a wager. At this point the hermeneutic circle includes personal involvement for 'you must understand in order to believe, but you must believe in order to understand'.

A hermeneutic procedure is informed by a choice, which

instead of being the result of pure autonomy is associated with one's culture, tradition and history. Hence our author has chosen to opt for that tradition of thought on evil, both western and Christian, which is situated in that circular movement between faith and understanding. But the dialectic that has ensued in western thought between that which is understood and that which has been believed is at best a tenuous one. Ricoeur, aware of the rational demands of philosophic understanding on the one hand and the multivalence of symbolic forms on the other, tries to clarify the problem both historically and methodologically. In general philosophers attempt to use necessary and universal concepts to attain an understanding of reality. The symbol, however, presents a multiplicity of meaning; it is not universal and necessary in a univocal sense. Often, and this is the tragic story of the interpretation of symbols in the west, interpretation has meant demythologisation in the sense that a false reduction of the symbolic form has been accomplished. So the process of philosophical reflection on symbols and myths is not an easy one. As we have seen, the two poles of the symbolism of evil are the designation of evil as a matter of human responsibility and the feeling that evil is 'already there', prior to one's experience of it. Ricoeur finds that the history of reflection on the problem of evil has incorporated these two tendencies; inasmuch as it has, western thinkers have chosen either to allegorise or to gnosticise the problem of evil. To allegorise is to rationalise, to divorce the literal signification of the symbol from its symbolic signification. The gnostic interpretation of the symbolism of evil has centred upon the experience of evil as an experience prior to human responsibility, making that interpretation into a kind of 'dogmatic mythology'. Consequently the history of reflection upon evil tends to simplify the problem, making it either into a simple matter of human responsibility or a matter of that which is prior to human responsibility. Of course rationality and rational reflection has had little difficulty in dealing with the first option, for if evil is simply a matter of human responsibility, then it is easily understood and quite resolvable, at least as a problem on an abstract plane. But if one interjects the other side of the problem of evil, its priority to human experience, it becomes absurd, something which reason cannot fathom. So reason and reflection can account for evil as a matter of human responsibility, but thought reaches a limit when evil is experienced as tragically present. This is of course a dilemma, in many ways a hermeneutic dilemma. But perhaps it illustrates the significance of a hermeneutic investigation with its circular dialectic, radically inclusive of both what is easily accessible to reflection and the point at which reflection reaches its limit. When one understands evil as something that transcends one's personal acts, then evil exists as something that precedes man. The consequence of this insight is a return to the tragic which defies rationalisation. At this point the hermeneutic circle is complete. Thought reaches its limit and it must return to the symbol.

We are now in a position to probe the question of the contribution of hermeneutics from the perspective of phenomenological method. What does phenomenological hermeneutics contribute to philosophical reflection that is not already given in eidetic and existential description? Here we touch again upon the perilous question of the proper interpretation of symbols without their destruction, that is, an interpretation that avoids gnosis and allegory.

The symbol gives a richness and consciousness to what otherwise has had an abstract character. To confront the experience of fault on the level of its immediate confessional utterance in all its variety in symbols and myths is to introduce a symbolic richness to reflection that would be otherwise unattainable. The question remains, what is actually and specifically contributed to thinking by this orientation?

'The riddle of the slave-will, that is, of *a free will which is bound and always finds itself bound*, is the ultimate theme that the symbol gives to thought'.[31] On the one hand, this is what the symbol and the myth signify, which is another way of stating that evil is understood in terms of freedom. Although Ricoeur wished to avoid the possibility of gnosis and allegory, he realised that philosophy temporarily falls into this trap with the ultimate hope of returning to the symbol. Reflection, itself, is a form of 'demythologising'[32] and its risk is allegory, that is, to break the symbolic aspect of the symbol from its literal ground.

Reflective thought is essentially demythologising, it interprets mythology by reducing it to allegory. The problem of evil is in this regard an exemplar: *reflection upon the symbolism of evil reaches its peak in what we shall call the vision of evil*.[33]

It is significant that Ricoeur finds Augustine to be the one who first elaborated this allegorical interpretation of evil most fully in his protest against the Manichaean doctrine of evil. Augustine attempted to show that evil was its own cause; he saw evil at the heart of freedom and therefore not derived from a source or cause outside man. For Ricoeur it is Kant who carries this reflection to a place of utmost clarity by showing that freedom itself is the power of deviation,[34] a form of subversion. If reflection, by its departure from the symbol, can show that evil lurks at the very heart of freedom and has no other cause than freedom, one has reached a point of utmost clarity but at the price of depth. What is lost by this departure from the symbolism of evil is the other side of evil, its tragic aspect.

The tragic aspect of evil first expresses itself in the literal character of stain, the spot, something already there, prior to the exercise of freedom 'evil as tradition'.[35] It is this side that allows for the gnostic interpretation of evil, the temptation to put evil in a framework, to express it independently of freedom. Again Ricoeur calls upon Augustine and Kant. The expression of this theme par excellence is the Pauline–Augustine interpretation which places guilt *in Adam*; therefore evil is understood to be prior to each individual existence. Augustine tried to work this out in the Pelagian controversy by relying on themes of reprobation and of biological generation. Intellectually, Augustine found evil prior to man and then made him responsible for it. In terms of logic and clarity, Pelagius was essentially right in the perspective of his argument. But for Ricoeur, Pelagius is the perfect example of clarity without depth. 'Although Pelagius was right intellectually, Augustine was right experientially when he turned to the pseudo-concept of original sin.'[36] For Kant this view was developed in terms of his notion of *a priori*, that is, the *a priori* possibility of evil as ground of actual evil. Ricoeur finds Kant as complement to Augustine since he alleviated most of the 'dogmatic mythology' from this side of evil by simply showing its *a priori* condition as possibility.

To what conclusion can the reflection following the symbol come? On the one hand it can elaborate evil as contingent, at the heart of freedom, present in every free act. On the other, it can see evil as necessary, prior to every individual act, ethical in the former sense, tragic in the latter. But that is the problem, is there any rational way to include both the necessity and the contingency of evil in a single reflection? Ricoeur's answer is that every attempt to include the 'totality' has failed. 'For either the thought of necessity leaves contingency aside, or it so includes it that it entirely eliminates the "leap" of evil which posits itself and the "tragic" of evil which always precedes itself.'[37] It either takes the gnostic (dogmatic mythology) or the allegorical path opting for clarity at the loss of depth. We reach the point where reflection is driven to its limit. There is no purely rational way of synthesising the contingency and necessity of evil and this is precisely the point where the hermeneutic circle is completed, for reflective thought is driven back to the symbol because the symbol can retain this multivalence while reflective thought cannot. Reflective thought is driven back to evil in two ways. First, understanding has reached its limit and one is driven back to faith. The symbol is simply reaffirmed. Second, the return to symbolism is motivated by an attempt to recover in symbols a reconciliation, a renewal of thought that has reached its limit in symbols of evil.

It remains to evaluate both the claims and the consequences of a phenomenological hermeneutic. The argument for turning philosophy towards the language of avowal was sustained on the assumption that through a confrontation with this language of symbol and myth it would be possible to confront concretely the experience of fault which had always hitherto remained an abstraction, a possibility.

It seems that hermeneutic phenomenology based upon the language of avowal contributes to the elaboration of global anthropology in the following ways. Hermeneutic phenomenology, given the pre-established basis and orientation of Ricoeur's thought, may be understood to advance the quest for global anthropology by finding in language a *concrete ground* for fault, the disturbing problem and central issue of the global view of man. The question is, is this a more adequate way of reflecting on man than the reflection under the previous methodologies? The case for hermeneutics providing a more adequate mode for reflection can be established by Ricoeur in two ways: internally, the drive in Ricoeur's thought is directed towards man's concrete and elemental experience. Thought from the symbol has a concrete basis. It is grounded in an actual experience of evil and it does not go beyond that actual experience. The methodological concern for adequacy is complemented by the development of a hermeneutic. On the external side—that is, the relation of hermeneutics to other possibilities, it is possible to indicate the options that Ricoeur wishes to dismiss. Not only does symbol provide a concrete ground for global anthropology, it is in fact *a guide*. The symbol invites thought; it shapes the character of hermeneutics but it also functions as a guide to thought. Not only does the symbol stimulate thought, it also provides a criterion for reflection. The gnostic and allegorical alternatives are cases in point. The attempt to place evil in the context of either a reflective or an ethical system wherein the symbolic dimension is lost is itself to be resisted. Ricoeur is adamant in his desire not to make evil into a principle of negativity nor to give it the status of pure *necessity*.

Thus, thought from the symbol is judged by the symbol. Thought which moves from the symbol can contribute to global anthropology by itself providing a *limit* for reflection. The symbolism of evil is instructive in this regard, for the confession that evil precedes man and is therefore prior to freedom provides a hiatus which cannot be bridged by reflection. The interruption of reflection drives one back to the symbol wherein the original faith stance is affirmed. Consequently, the concreteness of this hermeneutic position may be affirmed over speculative idealism or journalistic moralism. Ricoeur's thought does not reduce an understanding of man to a narrowness which sacrifices depth for clarity. The hermeneutic method contributes to that end. The advantage of this perspective is that accomplished by seeking a philosophical resource in a particular kind of language. Ricoeur's hermeneutics is not derived *de novo*, but is in fact the result of his confrontation with the issues of phenomenological methodology—that is, the advantages and limitations of eidetics, the methodological problems of man's actual experience of evil and issues of language. Any adequate interpretation of Ricoeur's hermeneutic position requires a consideration of the total methodological struggle and accomplishment that dominates his thought. Further, in achieving the first aspect of the correlation which is the subject matter of this discussion, it has been necessary to go back to the original consideration of methodology in Ricoeur's constructive work.

In brief, the classical mediation of meaning has broken down. It is being replaced by a modern mediation of meaning that interprets our dreams and our symbols, that thematises our wan smiles and limp gestures, that analyses our minds and charts our souls, that takes the whole of human history for its kingdom to compare and relate languages and literatures, art-forms and religions, family arrangements and customary morals, political, legal, educational, economic systems, sciences, philosophies, theologies, and histories. New books pour forth annually by the thousands; our libraries need ever more space. But the vast modern effort to understand meaning in all its manifestations has not been matched by a comparable effort in judging meaning. The effort to understand is the common task of unnumbered scientists and scholars. But judging and deciding are left to the individual and he finds his plight desperate. There is far too much to be learnt before he could begin to judge. Yet judge he must and decide he must if he is to exist, if he is to be a man.[38]

The area of potential and fruitful confrontation between Lonergan and Ricoeur lies not in polemic, nor in superficial comparison, but in the designation of critical areas of common interest productive of 'insight', hopefully inviting reflection. Like Ricoeur, Lonergan's thinking emanates from a cultural and philosophical crisis so pervasive that it has necessitated a methodological reconstruction sufficient to provide the foundation for new modalities of thought. Like Ricoeur, Lonergan has attempted through the establishment of that foundation to repossess the possibility of being religious in the modern context of secularity. Indeed, both have seen religion as a kind of anthropological necessity. Like Ricoeur, Lonergan has been a critic of the phenomenological method in its classical form. Finally, the Lonergan who began his reflections on a cognitional framework which grounded the process of human knowing has turned, like Ricoeur, to the concrete to probe the mediation of meaning, a paramount hermeneutic problem. So perhaps we are entitled to claim that as Ricoeur moves from the problematic of a global anthropology to the concrescence of mediated meanings, so Lonergan has moved from the problematic of human knowing to the concreteness of a human science which in some sense demands a hermeneutic foundation.

The critical set of questions arising out of the foregoing study of Ricoeur in relationship to Lonergan is the nature and status of hermeneutics particularly as it relates not only to cognitional structure *per se* but to the function and character of the symbol. I state this because Ricoeur's distinctive contribution to the hermeneutic discussion has been to relate hermeneutics to a theory of language grounded in the theory of double meaning. The theory of double meaning is in turn grounded in the discovery of the distinctive function of the symbol which, as we have said, finds its ground in the notion of double intentionality. The function of the symbol in symbolic logic is to develop univocal meanings while symbols in their religious, oneric, and poetic contexts are multi-valent. The recognition of this difference in symbols leads to the recognition of difference in the manner in which language is used. The scientific model, which attempts to exclude the subject, is based on the necessary relationship of things to each other which aims at univocity. Hence language in a scientific context tends to become ideal, modelled on a desire for clarity. The problem is this: when such a model has been applied to mythic-symbolic phenomena the consequence has been to eliminate the multival-ence, to argue for univocity, and in fact to eliminate double mean-ings. Hence, interpretation analogously hermeneutics, has found itself in the precarious position of having to reject a scientific or logical model in favour of 'something else'. The specification of this so-called other foundation seems to be one of the central issues facing contemporary hermeneutic discussion. Significantly, this issue is not only shared by Paul Ricoeur, it seems in one way or another to be central to Mircea Eliade and his history of religions school, the later Heidegger and Gadamer, as well as those who have taken their hermeneutic cue from the later Heidegger.

Two historical examples may suffice to indicate the scope of the problem. Major approaches to the data of the history of religions and anthropology in the nineteenth and early twentieth centuries tend to presuppose that religious myths and symbols were repre-sentative of a false consciousness, unscientific in nature, the products of a pre-logical mentality. As a consequence, the student of such data was forced to eliminate the false presumptions of his data through a reduction to a superimposed model of meaning. The turning point in this type of analysis came with the discovery of the complexity of myth and symbol (Otto, Eliade, Levi-Strauss), a discovery that came to mean that mythic-symbolic language, for example, is as complex as any other type of language, as well as the discovery of the category of the sacred. The consequence of these developments in the history of religions has been to devise a 'special hermeneutics' appropriate to symbolic data in order to avoid the mistake of interpretation as elimination.

18

The other example may be taken from Ernst Cassirer's monumental work, *The Philosophy of Symbolic Forms*. In that work Cassirer establishes a theory of mind which has as its basic category symbolic transformation of experience. The negative consequence of this approach has been to understand the mythic-symbolic, the original or 'primitive' manifestation of symbolic transformation, as only a stage in the evolution of symbolic transformations. In other words one of the results of this approach was to sacrifice the mythic, the original stage of symbolic transformation, to the scientific, the last stage of symbolic transformation, in terms of a historical evolutionary theory which makes the ultimate elimination of the original mythic stage necessary.

The way out of this problem is to find a non-reductionistic foundation for hermeneutics which does not have, as a necessary implication, the destruction of the very data which must be retained in some sense. Let us return to the theory of symbol for a moment. It was the discovery of the double intentionality of the symbol that led Ricoeur to the generalisation that there are two types of hermeneutic positions presently available. In the first type the aim of hermeneutics is to demystify, in theological terms to demythologise. In the second instance, the object of hermeneutics is informed by the category of recollection of meaning wherein the myth and the symbol are not only granted the legitimacy of an authentic expression of meaning, but the claim is made for a hermeneutic foundation which illuminates the basic characteristics of the modality under study.

With these two alternatives in mind it is possible to turn directly to the work of Bernard Lonergan. The critical problem is this: much of Lonergan's thought about hermeneutics falls into the category of a hermeneutic of demystification. Certainly, the ideal of science, with its pejorative assumptions about the qualitative distinctions between the primitive and the scientific mentality is one of the foundational principles of *Insight*. To quote:

The primitive cannot begin to distinguish accurately between what he knows by experience and what he knows inasmuch as he understands. His understanding of nature is bound to be anthropomorphic and his understanding of man is fettered by his own inability to conceive other men with a mentality different from his own.[39]

In a sense one uncovers the problematic here. How is it possible to save the religious orientation when the very method chosen to understand it destroys the mentality which has produced it? That is the dilemma.

In this essay I have spent considerable time with the somewhat tortuous route taken by Ricoeur in order to show how a hermeneutic phenomenology is possible. One of the consequences for Ricoeur was a series of transformations of the phenomenological method. I do not mean to imply here that Lonergan take a similar route, neither am I suggesting that the method of insight be revised totally. I am suggesting that the kind of reduction implicit in the cognitional theory of insight be paralleled by a correlate hermeneutic of recollection or reintegration.

In order to make this point clear let us turn for a moment to Fr Lonergan's approach to the relationship of metaphysics and myth. He states: 'Mythic consciousness is the absence of self-knowledge, a myth is a consequence of mythic consciousness and metaphysics is a corollary of self-knowledge.'[40] Initially this means that there is an opposition between myth and metaphysics. But the relationship is also 'dialectical in the sense that myth has within it the foundation for the possible emergence of metaphysics. As myth recedes, metaphysics advances. The assumption is that behind both myth and metaphysics there is a unitative theory of cognition implying that both manifestations are grounded in man's ultimate desire to know. However, what is unexamined is the unqualified assumption that the advance of one is the decline of the other. In other words, both myth and metaphysics must be accounted for in the context of a development theory. So, we have here another instance of the Cassirer type methodology leading to a reductionistic theory of myth. It is in this sense that we are confronted with a hermeneutic of demystification.

Another aspect of the problem is illustrated by the primacy given in Lonergan's thought to categories of explanation over those of description. The judgement made is this: 'As long as interpretation remains on the descriptive level, it may happen to be correct but it cannot escape the relativity of a manifold of interpretations to a manifold of audiences; in turn, this relativity excludes the possibility of scientific collaboration, scientific control, and scientific advance towards commonly accepted results.'[41] At this point are we not confronting one of the more open judgements made by the hermeneutic of demystification? The problem is twofold: first, to what extent is the object of hermeneutic study open to explanatory considerations, and second, does not the primacy of explanatory orientations over descriptive ones presuppose an integration of hermeneutic data that is simply too easy?

In order to illustrate this problem, let us return to Ricoeur's phrase 'the symbol invites thought'. As we have seen the hermeneutic orientation presupposed here assumes that it is impossible to get behind the symbol, that is, to explain it in a scientific sense. Symbols, whether poetic, literary or oneric, are primal manifestations which require no explanation, rather they require a sophisticated hermeneutic of description. The symbol invites reflection rather than reduction to an explanatory scheme. This means that it is necessary to allow for the 'relativity of manifold interpretations' if one is to account for the *authenticity of the hermeneutic object*. Certainly, the case can be made that in later hermeneutic discussions greater emphasis has been placed on the manifestation of the object of investigation to consciousness rather than on the constitution of consciousness. If we consider this shift in the context of the interpretation of symbolism, primacy is given to the object interpreted while the hermeneutic task is conceived as that of developing categories of understanding which will allow the symbol to manifest itself. In a phenomenological sense this is the attempt to discover the authentic intentionality of the symbol.

Consequently it is too easy to fit such interpretation into an explanatory scheme, inasmuch as this attempt inevitably results in the distortion of the symbol. Invariably the predilection for a scientific model as the foundation for hermeneutic inquiry results not in the attempt to think through the symbol in correlation with the recurrence of a cognitional structure but rather such a hermeneutic wants to bring to consciousness that range of sedimented meanings latent in the symbolic manifestation.

For the moment I have confined my considerations to the hermeneutics of symbols; however, the case for the hermeneutic of recollection could be generalised in two ways: firstly, in terms of the transitions of phenomenological methodology, and secondly in terms of the implications of the definition of hermeneutics for hermeneutic study generally. As phenomenology has made the linguistic turn with the later Heidegger, Merleau-Ponty, Ricoeur, and others, it has seen language in correlation with experience in such a way that it has *attempted to understand how language mediates experience*. In Heidegger's discourse on poetry the issue is *one of discovery of how the poet mediates being through language*. In the case of Merleau-Ponty the issue is one of discovery of *how speaking mediates consciousness*, while in the case of Ricoeur the *investigation of language has been carried on in the name of the distinction between the literal and the symbolic*. Significantly in the case of each, language has been given a special significance in terms of the hermeneutic problem. This points to the second issue—namely, the function of language in relationship to the new definition of hermeneutics. If more attention is placed upon the special character of the object of hermeneutics and if that object is linguistic, then it is apparent that the task of hermeneutics will be the investigation of special languages which have their own characteristics, rubrics, properties, etc. The point of such an investigation will be less to show how one linguistic mode is an extension of another linguistic modality, rather the purpose of such a hermeneutic analysis will be to allow the special intentions of the specific language under investigation to manifest themselves in such a way that it is possible to grasp the claims of their various manifestations.

I have raised the questions that appear to me to be the most serious ones emerging from Lonergan's approach to hermeneutics when understood in relationship to more recent approaches to hermeneutics, characterised particularly by the work of Paul Ricoeur. One can summarise the limitations of this approach by understanding it as a hermeneutic of demystification based upon a uniform theory of cognition which has as its aim the reduction of mythic-symbolic manifestations to lower order significations in order to account for so-called higher significations. Negatively, the consequence of sustaining this approach may be the elimination of the mythic-symbolic (the foundation of religion) the very thing the system wishes to preserve.

Personally I consider the kind of criticism just made to be serious but I do not conceive of it as devastating. The question is, *can a hermeneutic of demystification engage a hermeneutic of recollection?* It is with this question that our discussion will conclude.

One may question the necessity of engaging in the battle between myth and metaphysics. The juxtaposition that occurs between the two modalities of thinking is not essential to the system of thought under study. Indeed, if more attention were given to the special character of the mythic-symbolic dimension, demystification need not be the consequence of the interpretation of myth. In fact, it seems quite possible to argue that the system is open to the kind of transformation that allows a different hermeneutic style on the basis of a consideration of a few key notions within the system.

The polymorphism of human consciousness as Fr Lonergan conceives of it could be constructed in such a way as to allow the mythic-symbolic to be expressive of a more authentic dimension of human consciousness. Certainly, Lonergan has taken great care to show that consciousness differentiates itself in terms of distinctive modalities of expression. Hence, there is the correlate acknowledgement that literary and poetic manifestations of consciousness are essentially different from scientific modalities, while a philosophic expression of consciousness is essentially different from a political one. In this sense the mythic-symbolic is to be understood as a distinctive expression of consciousness. It seems a construct like the polymorphism of human consciousness is one step in the process of freeing myth from the general tendency to conceive of it as a moment in the history of consciousness rather than as an element in the structure of consciousness. If more attention were paid to the consideration of the peculiar structure of the mythic-symbolic rather than conceiving of it in an evolutionary scheme this transition might be possible.

This possibility is dependent upon the manner in which Lonergan's uniform theory of cognition is to be understood. The theory of cognition, the foundation of Lonergan's system, illustrates, with regard to the problem at hand, the way in which the category mind orders modalities of human expression. In order to make the case for the uniformity of cognition it has been *deemed necessary to develop a hierarchical ordering of values, that is, theoretical versus practical, scientific versus common sense*, etc. Consequently the direction of *Insight* is cumulative as one moves from the world of common sense to the world of theory. The correlate judgement has been one which gives primacy to evolutionary categories, to transitions from the world of common sense to the world of theory. Significantly, it *does not seem that the evolutionary categories derived from scientific orientations need to be universalised to account for all the data of cognition*. Further, it does not seem that the theory of cognition is necessarily dependent upon the theory of evolution. It seems evident that whereas *evolutionary categories function well in the field of the natural sciences*, they *function rather poorly in aesthetic fields.* The *symbolic products of cultures*, myths, artistic creations, literature, etc. simply cannot be explained in evolutionary categories, instead they have an integrity of their own. Hence we are left with the question, is the theory of evolution essential to the theory of cognition? I think the answer must be one which gives a greater status to non-scientific modes of cognition. Evolution should be essential only to those areas where it functions most usefully. The theory of cognition should be universalisable without associated theories of evolution.

Finally, if there is a possibility for the correlation of the hermeneutic of demystification with the hermeneutic of recollection within Lonergan's system, one of the most intriguing areas for investigation might be the establishment of a foundation for the theory of symbol. It is possible that an investigation of Lonergan's category of the known-unknown may be the source for the development of such a theory. Significantly, this notion has within it potentialities for dealing with the dualities and opacities associated with psychic, poetic, and religious symbolism inasmuch as it could account for both the literal and the symbolic elements of the symbol without distorting them.

Being for Lonergan: a Heideggerean view

WILLIAM J. RICHARDSON

THE pretensions of this brief reflection are less grandiose than its title. It does not pretend to be exhaustive. It seeks only to resume briefly Fr Lonergan's treatment of the problem of being and to indicate the type of reserve that one is bound to make about it if one takes account of Martin Heidegger's fundamental philosophical experience. Only in this modified sense does it represent a 'Heideggerean View'—not in the sense that it summarises Heidegger's attitude toward Fr Lonergan's work (to which he has apparently never addressed himself), nor in the sense that it represents a beetle-browed critique of this work by a thoroughgoing, uncompromising disciple of Heidegger.

In the simplest terms, being, for Fr Lonergan, is no more and no less than the 'objective of the pure desire to know'.[1] This desire to know is the dynamic orientation of the human spirit which constitutes the drive '. . . that carries cognitional process from sense and imagination to understanding, from understanding to judgement, from judgement to the complete context of correct judgements that is named knowledge . . .'[2] Hence being is all that is known and all that remains to be known, and '. . . since a complete increment of knowing occurs only in judgement, being is what is to be known by the totality of true judgements . . .'[3]

But the judgemental act (or totality of judgemental acts) by which being is known is the culmination of the cognitional process. Preceding the judgement and helping to make it possible is first of all the *notion* of being. This may be taken in a 'pure' sense, by which the author means simply the unrestricted desire to know that antecedes and permeates all the other elements of cognition. He identifies it with Aristotle's 'wonder' that is the driving force of all intelligent inquiry.[4] Moreover, the notion of being not only permeates all elements of the knowing process but it anticipates somehow the content of the to-be-known. '. . . Prior to every content (the notion of being) is the notion of the to-be-known through that content . . .'[5] Taken in this way, it is described as a 'heuristic' notion (indeed, the 'supreme' one) i.e., a notion that anticipates what is to be discovered and to this extent both prepares and facilitates discovery. The notion of being, thus understood, is to be distinguished clearly from a 'concept' of some sort, i.e., an act of understanding, that grasps and formulates an 'essence' that, after reflection, can be affirmed or not affirmed (in a judgement) to exist. Inasmuch as the notion of being precedes and makes possible the *concept* of the understanding and the *affirmation* of reason, it is considered the 'ground of intelligent inquiry and critical reflection'.[6]

Now, the notion of being, thus understood, is to be distinguished not only from the 'concept' but from the 'idea' of being. For an 'idea' is the *content* of the act of understanding. Hence, the idea of being will be being as grasped by the understanding. Whereas the notion of being as 'pure' raises all questions but answers none and as 'heuristic' envisages all answers but determines none, the idea of being includes all answers to all questions as these are grasped by the understanding. This means that it comprehends universal concrete being—universal in so far as being extends to the entire universe of the to-be-known, and concrete in so far as it includes everything to-be-known about everything in such a universe.[7] An act that understands everything about everything will obviously be 'unrestricted'. '. . . Being is the objective of the unrestricted desire to know. Therefore the idea of being is the content of an unrestricted act of understanding . . .'[8]

Fr Lonergan comes to the discussion of the idea of being when his method brings him to consider the possibility of transcendent knowledge, i.e. knowledge of something beyond the universe of 'proportionate' being—being as proportioned to man's capacity to know. Fr Lonergan maintains that such knowledge is possible and, indeed, a fact.[9] He argues the point by what fundamentally is a process of 'extrapolation'. Once the human knower, driven by his unrestricted desire to know, raises the question 'What is being?', he can attain at best a restricted answer. Yet the drive compels him to keep on asking. Hence, the author's extrapolation:

. . . While man cannot enjoy an unrestricted act of understanding and so answer the question, What is being? still he can determine a number of features of the answer by proceeding on the side of the subject from restricted to unrestricted understanding and on the side of the object from the structure of proportionate being to the transcendent idea of being.[10]

Fr Lonergan proceeds to describe what such an idea would be like—an immaterial, non-temporal, non-spatial unity[11]—maintaining that the primary component (or 'intelligible') of such an idea would be the unrestricted act's understanding of itself, i.e. intelligence in act, and the secondary component (or 'intelligible') would be the unrestricted act's understanding of everything else inasmuch as it understands itself.[12]

Given the idea of being thus conceived, Fr Lonergan is led, by an appeal to the notion of causality, to affirm that there is such an act of understanding. The argument here is based upon the intelligibility of being—i.e. upon the principle that what is unintelligible is not being (nothing). For Fr Lonergan, sheer contingence (mere matters of fact that admit of no explanation) is unintelligible (nothing). Thus the argument runs: '. . . The universe of proportioned being is shot through with contingence. (But) mere contingence is apart from being, and so there must be an ultimate ground for the universe. . . .'[13]

We understand him to mean that: contingent being is unintelligible of itself and therefore requires some other (non-contingent) being to account ultimately for its intelligibility; the non-contingent being that accounts ultimately for the intelligibility of contingent being must also account for the intelligibility of itself (otherwise it would be neither non-contingent nor ultimate); non-contingent being that accounts for the intelligibility of itself would be being in which intelligible and intelligence are identified, i.e. intelligence in act; such a being may be considered 'an ultimate ground of the universe' since it is the ultimate principle of all intelligibility.

From here, the going is easier. Lonergan elaborates the implications of the unrestricted act of understanding into a rather full-blown notion of what 'God' is—at least as an object of thought.[14] The final step is to pass to the affirmation *that* God is, which, in effect, is a further explication of the fact that the idea of being *is*. We resume the argument in its briefest form: 'If the real is completely intelligible, God exists. But the real is completely intelligible. Therefore, God exists.'[15] Fr Lonergan begins with the minor premise and the argument, in outline, is as follows: being is completely intelligible, the real is being, therefore the real is completely intelligible. As to the major, he proceeds thus: if the real is completely intelligible, then complete intelligibility exists. If complete intelligibility exists, the idea of being exists. If the idea of being exists, God exists. Therefore, if the real is completely intelligible, God exists.[16]

It should be clear that in resuming the argument as schematically as this, we make no pretence of capturing either its subtlety or its depth. Our purpose is merely to recall to those already familiar with it the general route by which Lonergan arrives at the affirmation of God.

Before we try to evaluate all this in the light of the Heideggerean experience, it will be well to recall briefly what that experience is. In a letter written in 1962, Heidegger describes the initial moments of that experience:

. . . The first philosophical text through which I worked my way again and again from 1907 on, was Franz Brentano's dissertation: On the Manifold Sense of Being in Aristotle (1862). On the title page of his work, Brentano quotes Aristotle's phrase: *to on legetai pollachōs*, I translate: 'A being becomes manifest (i.e., with regard to its Being) in many ways'. Latent in this phrase is the *question* that determined the way of my thought: what is the pervasive, simple, unified determination of Being that permeates all of its multiple meaning? . . . How can they be brought into comprehensible accord? This accord can not be grasped without first raising and settling the question: whence does Being as such (not merely beings as beings) receive its determination?[17]

Heidegger's initial and enduring question, then, is about the meaning of Being (*Sinn des Seins*). Being, to be sure, is always the Being of beings, but is nonetheless different from them. As time goes on, the question focuses more and more on the sense of Being as different from beings, and eventually on this difference (the 'ontological difference') as such. In any case, it is perfectly clear that Heidegger is not concerned with the problem of beings (*Seiendes*) at all. Still less with the manner of knowing them.

It is metaphysics that concerns itself with beings—*on hei on* in Aristotle's phrase. The Being, whose sense Heidegger interrogates, is the 'ground' of beings, i.e., is the source that lets them 'be' (manifest), hence Heidegger conceives of his task as laying the groundwork for metaphysics (a 'fundamental ontology', as he called it in the early days), without itself being metaphysics.

Moreover, *on hei on* can be understood as investigating beings in their most general characteristics *as* beings, and the result is what the tradition has come to call 'general metaphysics', or 'ontology'. On the other hand the phrase can suggest the consideration of beings as what they are by reason of their grounding in some supreme being, frequently called 'God', and then it becomes 'theology'. But this double orientation derives from the basic ambivalence of the phrase *on hei on*—i.e., from the fundamental structure of metaphysics itself. That is why Heidegger claims that the structure of metaphysics is 'onto-theo-logical' of its very nature.

In Heidegger's earlier periods, characterised especially by *Being and Time* (1927), the focus of his interrogation of the sense of Being (as different from beings) fell in *Dasein* (man in his very essence) and its privileged comprehension of Being (*Seinverstandnis*). Beginning with 1930, however, the focus of the interrogation shifts to Being itself as it reveals itself in and to *Dasein*. From this point on, Being is conceived as revealing itself to *Dasein*, and, indeed, in different modes through different epochs of history. Being sends or 'e-mits' itself (*sich schickt*) to *Dasein* and *Dasein* reciprocally is com-mitted (*Schicksal*) in the process. Correlation of e-mitting (by Being) and com-mitting (of *Dasein*) constitute a 'mittence' (*Geschick*) of Being, and a combination of mittences (*Ge-schick-e*), taken in the ensemble or inter-mittence (*Ge-schick-e*) constitute history (*Geschichte*), i.e., Being-as-history. Different mittences constitute the epochs of history, whether this be taken in a strict sense, as in the mittence to an individual person (e.g., to Descartes), or in a broader sense, as in the mittence to a given philosophical period (e.g., to German Idealism), or in the broadest sense as in the mittence of the entire history of metaphysics (as Heidegger understands it) from Plato to Nietzsche. Metaphysics, then, with its whole onto-theo-logical structure is for Heidegger no more than an epoch of Being-as-history. In his most recent years, the drift of Heidegger's thought has been more and more in the direction of exploring the ontological difference as such in terms of the original e-vent (*Ereignes*) out of which such a mittence arises.

In the light of such an experience, how would Fr Lonergan's experience of being look to the Heideggerean view? To begin with, it seems clear that Fr Lonergan's concern for being is a function of his interest in the nature of human understanding and not vice versa. Indeed, being is *defined* in terms of human understanding, i.e., as the 'objective of the pure desire to know'. Hence it is always conceived as *that-which-is-*(knowable), i.e., as *Seiendes*, in so far as this is addressed to intelligence. To be sure, what-is is not simply the individual being but the concrete universe, the totality of all that is—beings in their totality (*Seiende in Ganzen*).[18] It would seem, then, that Fr Lonergan is in no way interrogating Being as *different* from beings, indeed (as far as the present writer can see) there appears to be no indication that he takes account of such a difference at all. A beetle-browed Heideggerean would probably say, then, that Fr Lonergan is a victim of the 'forgetfulness of Being' (*Seinsvergessenheit*), or, more precisely, of a 'forgetfulness of the ontological difference'.

For this reason, the Lonergan enterprise is clearly a 'metaphysical' one and, no matter how subtly elaborated, needs in turn further grounding in some foundation for metaphysics.[19] Moreover, as metaphysics it manifests strikingly the onto-theo-logical structure of this discipline. To be sure, Fr Lonergan's own insistent concern is with concrete being, but he does admit the legitimacy of dealing with the 'general character of the concrete universe' in an abstract way and thus suggests what Heidegger would call the 'ontological' character of metaphysics.[20]

More significant, however, is Fr Lonergan's move from 'proportionate' to 'transcendent' being or, more precisely, from contingent being to God. The outline of this move has already been delineated. What is important here is not the intricacies of the argument but its general direction. The argument is based on the principle that the ensemble of beings is intelligible. Now it should be remarked in passing that when one begins the discussion of being by simply declaring that it is the 'objective of the pure desire to know', it does not take a very subtle analysis to infer that being is intelligible.[21] But that is beside the point at the moment. The argument proceeds, as we have seen, by saying that proportionate, contingent being is ultimately intelligible only in terms of non-contingent, self-explanatory being that is an ultimate ground of the universe.[22] In other words, beings are intelligible only when grounded[23] in a supreme being that is unique[24] and eventually called 'God'.[25] Here, then, is metaphysics in its theological dimensions. Metaphysics for Fr Lonergan is clearly onto-theo-logical in structure.

And this is exactly what Heidegger claims to be the very nature of metaphysics. For the Heideggerean view, the Lonergan conception is not suspect because there is some fault in the metaphysical stance or in its fundamental argument (e.g., its culmination in the affirmation of God's existence) but rather because it is metaphysics at all, i.e., because it is oblivious of the ontological difference. What he questions is not whether, or how, metaphysics legitimately comes to God, but rather how God comes to metaphysics, i.e., how it comes to pass that metaphysics *has* this onto-theo-logical structure—how such a structure arises out of the e-vent of the ontological difference.[26]

We might add, for the sake of clarification, that a committed Heideggerean would not only find fault with Fr Lonergan's experience (or non-experience) of the Being question but also with his conception of God, whom Heidegger would describe by the classical formula: *Causa sui.* No matter how elaborately Fr Lonergan develops his own notion of God (e.g., 'in the twenty-sixth place, God is personal'),[27] it remains, in Heidegger's terms, a metaphysical notion, for it conceives of God as (Ultimate) cause inasmuch as he is the principle of all intelligibility.[28] Now, whatever is to be said for such a God as the term of a philosophical exercise, this is not the true God of valid religious experience: '. . . This is the (Ultimate) Cause as *Causa sui.* Such is the appropriate name for God in philosophy. To such a God man can neither pray nor offer sacrifice. Before God as *Causa sui* man can neither fall on his knees in reverence, nor in His presence make music and dance.'[29]

Does Heidegger have a better God to offer? No. He is interested in Being, not God, and to this extent his thought is a God-less thought. But his quest for the meaning of Being has led him to an attitude of attentive openness to revelation that may indeed leave him free to respond to God's call, should he hear it as coming from God: 'Accordingly, a god-less thinking that must forego the god of philosophy, god as *Causa sui*, is perhaps all the nearer to the divine god. That means in this case: it is freer for him than onto-theo-logic would pretend.'[30]

One may presume that the disciple of Fr Lonergan will not take kindly to the reproach that this effort has apparently overlooked

the Being-question that has been Heidegger's unique preoccupa-
tion, and will be inclined to ask whether there is not nonetheless a
genuine affinity between the two thinkers in so far as each admits
that man is opened up towards a horizon within which beings are
encountered. Do they not at least share a common experience of
'horizon?'

The notion of horizon is important for Lonergan. He defines it
as follows:

Literally, a horizon is a maximum field of vision from a determinate
standpoint. In a generalised sense, a horizon is specified by two poles,
one objective and the other subjective, with each pole conditioning the
other. Hence, the objective pole is taken not materially, but like the
formal object *sub ratione sub qua attingitur* (under that aspect which the
activity specifically regards); similarly, the subjective pole is considered
not materially, but in its relation to the objective pole.[31]

Now in the present case, the objective pole of the horizon of
being for Lonergan (as we understand him) is the universe of
concrete being (*Seiendes*) in so far as it is knowable, i.e., accessible
to man's intelligence in the act of knowing.[32] The subjective pole
would be presumably man's intelligence itself under the guise of
its unrestricted desire to know. Hence, the notion of being may be
said to disclose a horizon for Lonergan in so far as it is the incho-
ative moment of all human knowing in its basic orientation toward
the sum total of beings-to-be-known, in so far as they are knowable.

Now in the early Heidegger, too, one can find the suggestion of
'horizon' for man but it is not at all polarised by the correlation of
the totality of beings-as-knowable on the one hand and the human
capacity to know on the other. On the contrary, the horizon is
rather the condition of possibility that permits knower and known
to encounter each other in the first place. In *Kant and the Problem
of Metaphysics*, Heidegger immerses himself in a Kantian context
and finds his own problematic there.[33] Perhaps this is where the
student of Lonergan can most easily gain access to his basic
perspective.

As Heidegger reads Kant, the purpose of the *Critique of Pure
Reason* was not to construct a theory of knowledge but to lay the
foundation for metaphysics (i.e., the *metaphysica specialis* of the
Leibniz-Wolff tradition). Insisting on the finite character of
human knowing, according to which the knower does not create the
objects of his knowledge but must receive them, Kant probed the

a priori (i.e., pre-experiential) conditions of possibility of this knowing. Now if, for the finite knower, the givenness of beings-to-be-known is itself conceived *a priori*, then there must be built into the structure of the knower himself a pre-experiential comprehension of their structure as beings, i.e., of their Being, which may be conceived as a sort of domain, or horizon, within which these beings *can* be encountered and known. This *a priori* horizon of encounter is what Heidegger in Kant's name calls 'transcendence'.[34] Heidegger's own explanation can hardly be improved upon:

A finite knowing essence can enter into comportment with a being other than itself which it has not created, only when this already existing being is in itself such that it can come to the encounter. However, in order that such a being as it is can come to an encounter (with a knower), it must be 'known' already by an antecedent knowledge simply as a being, i.e., with regard to its Being-structure. . . . A finite (knower) needs (a) fundamental power of orientation which permits this being to stand over in opposition to it. In this original orientation, the finite (knower) extends before himself an open domain within which something can 'correspond' to him. To dwell from the beginning in such a domain, to institute it in its origin, is nothing else than the transcendence which characterises all finite comportment with beings . . .[35]

In the Kant-book, then, transcendence is fundamentally the structure (rooted in the finite knower) of an open domain within which other beings can be encountered. At other times, it is called a 'horizon of objectiveness', or of 'objects'—i.e., within which beings may reveal themselves as objects—which must from the very beginning be open.[36]

How Heidegger justifies his interpretation of Kant's endeavour need not concern us here. At the moment it is important only to see how the word 'transcendence', thus understood, is transposed into his own problematic. '. . . Man is a being who is immersed among other beings in such a way that the being that he is not as well as the being that he is himself have already become constantly manifest to him . . .' So far, this is nothing but what in Kant he calls 'transcendence'. But he adds immediately: '. . . This manner of Being (proper to) man we call existence . . .'[37]

In *Being and Time* 'existence' is described as the Being of *Dasein*. *Dasein*, of course, is the name chosen by Heidegger to designate the nature of man in so far as he is characterised before all else as endowed with a special comprehension of Being that permits him to discover and name beings as what they *are*. Existence, thus understood, is later on written as 'ek-sistence', to suggest more clearly its fundamental nature. In other words, by reason of its Being *Dasein* stands (-*sistit*) outside of (*ek-*) itself and towards Being, the lighting-process by which beings are revealed. We may add, too, that in the phenomenological analysis of *Being and Time*, Being reveals itself as the horizon of the World, so that *Dasein's* openness towards Being can be described as to-be-in-the-World. In any case, it becomes perfectly clear that whatever the justification of its Kantian antecedents, transcendence for Heidegger means the same thing as existence, *Dasein*, and to-be-in-the-World: it designates *Dasein's* structural comprehension of Being by reason of which *Dasein* can pass (-*scendit*) beyond (*trans-*) all beings, including itself, to the Being of beings by which they are revealed to it. It is this passage that characterises Dasein as a self and accounts for the fact that its fundamental structure is not that of a substance but of a process (*Geschehen*).

If 'horizon' is understood in this fashion, then it is far broader and deeper than the correlation between knowable and knower. Its 'objective pole' (to the extent that this language is acceptable for Heidegger) is not a being nor the ensemble of beings but the World as such, the matrix of Total Meaningless within which beings have meaning and are accessible to man. Its 'subjective pole' would be not human intelligence as such but the entire structure of *Dasein* as disclosure (*Erschlossenheit*) of the World. The phenomenon of knowledge *presupposes* this correlation and is only one mode of *Dasein* that is derived from, or rather founded in, its essence as to-be-in-the-World.[38]

One would expect Heidegger to say that the intelligibility of beings, which, like the phenomenon of knowledge, implies a relationship between beings and intelligence, is equally derived from, and founded in, something prior. The fundamental polarity that institutes a 'horizon' for Heidegger is not between knowable and knower but between World and *Dasein*.

It might be worth remarking that the word 'horizon' appears with relative rarity in *Being and Time*, and when it does it is usually in conjunction with the problem of temporality. For example:

The unity of the horizonal schemata of future, past (as having-been) and present is grounded in the ecstatic unity of temporality. The horizon of all temporality determines that whereunto [*Dasein*] is *disclosed* . . .[39]

19

To explain the full import of a text such as this would take us too far afield at present. Let it suffice to cite the text in passing so as to indicate the unannounced importance of temporality in all that has been said heretofore.

The mention of temporality in this context is important because it serves to highlight the fact that even though in *Being and Time* Heidegger uses the language of the transcendental tradition, still the experience he is trying to articulate is very different from the traditional transcendental one.[40] Eventually he would renounce the language entirely.[41] Moreover, the focus of his interrogation shifted from *Dasein* to Being, when, beginning with *Vom Wesen der Wahrheit* (1930), Being begins to be experienced not merely as World that is disclosed in and through *Dasein* but as the Open to which *Dasein* is open.

In 1944–5, when Heidegger was well into the later period, a conversation took place in which he repudiated the notion of horizon as not sufficiently basic for his purposes.

The dialogue as recounted takes place between a scientist, a servant and a master whom we take to be Heidegger himself. When the issue of 'horizon' arises, the author says (we abbreviate):

Horizon and transcendence are experienced in terms of objects and our manner of representing object, and determined only with regard to objects and our representing [of them]. . . . In this fashion we still do not experience in any way what lets the horizon be what it is. . . . We say that we look into the horizon. The scope of vision is therefore an Open to which openness does not come simply because we look into it. . . . Hence, the horizontal is only the side turned toward us of an Open that surrounds us. It is filled by a vision into the shining forth of what appears to our representing as an object. . . .[42]

From this it will appear that the very conception of horizon is tainted by the subject-ist, representational thought that he is trying to overcome. The task is to think the Open itself of which the horizon is only the side turned towards us. It is the Open that lets the horizon be what it is. What is clear is that Heidegger is trying to probe into that domain that is different from the beings encountered within the horizon, and, indeed from the horizon itself. None of these perspectives is to be found, at least for the present writer, in the work of Fr Lonergan.

In sum, the devout student of Heidegger would probably say of Fr Lonergan's experience of being that it suffers from the limitation of the most obvious virtue of his thought—i.e., its intense effort at 'a study of human understanding' as this functions in the phenomenon of knowing. Important and valuable as such a study is, its focus is upon beings and their relation to human intelligence. Hence it overlooks the question about Being as different from beings—i.e., about the ontological difference as it emerges out of the e-vent of *A-letheia*. Even when Fr Lonergan speaks of a 'horizon' of knowledge, this appears to be the horizon of transcendental knowing, not the World as such (the matrix of Total Meaningfulness), still less the Open to which *Dasein* is open, of which the horizon of knowing is but 'the side turned towards us'.

But is such a critique decisive? What would happen if Fr Lonergan *did* take account of the Being-question as Heidegger poses it? Would such a stance impose any essential changes in his thought? Would it expose it to a new light that might disclose in it a new depth? Such are the questions that would arise at this point for the devout Heideggerean. Indeed he might see the very raising of such questions as indicative of Heidegger's chief legacy to other philosophers. In any case, he would feel that the answering of them belongs not to him but to Fr Lonergan and his disciples.

The new context of the philosophy of God in Lonergan and Rahner

BERNARD TYRRELL

In his talk 'The New Context of Theology' Lonergan indicates that the shift from a classicist world-view to historical-mindedness or awareness has profound implications for philosophy as well as for theology.[1] Rahner likewise from the period of *Hearers of the Word* right up to the present has not ceased to emphasise the importance of the 'turn to the subject' for any viable 'natural theology' as well as for theology as understood in the sense of a direct reflection on the data of revelation.

The present essay attempts to sketch in a tentative fashion certain basic characteristics of the new context of the philosophy of God as envisaged by Lonergan and Rahner respectively. Now attention should be given to our use of the expression 'tentative fashion' in the last sentence and this for two reasons. First, the aim of our ongoing collaboration is in this participant's view more the raising of questions than an attempt to reach definitive answers. Answers have as their condition of possibility a clear understanding of the questions involved and the goal of achieving a common understanding of certain basic questions can be quite lofty and ambitious in itself. Secondly, the author of this essay is at present involved in a study dealing in part with the discussion to be raised in this paper. This study will treat in detail much that can only be touched upon here.

The approach in this paper is formal rather than material. Its fundamental interest is not the content of 'natural theology' such as, for example, the nature of Lonergan's or Rahner's proof for the existence of God, but rather the context or cultural ambience in which such things as 'proofs', etc. are developed. Further, the concern here is more skeletal and global than concentrated and specialised. Finally, the overall motion in our discussion will be from the more all-encompassing structural issues to the more specific and delimited problematics and developments.

The discussion in this paper will begin, therefore, with a consideration of the relationship between grace and nature as Lonergan and Rahner conceive this relationship. The next section will involve the more specific consideration of the relationship between philosophy and theology as envisaged respectively by the two theologians and, of course, the problem of 'Christian philosophy' will be intimately involved. The discussion of the meaning and significance of a 'Christian philosophy' will lead immediately into what we choose to call the existential context of the philosophy of God. Here the concentration will be on certain existential conditions of possibility required respectively by Lonergan and Rahner for the proper working out of a philosophy of God. Attention will be given to Lonergan's notion of conversion and to Rahner's notion of conversion and mystagogy. Finally, a few comments will be offered regarding the recent *praxis* of Lonergan and Rahner in their operations as 'natural theologians' and possible pedagogical implications of this praxis. Clearly, any one of these divisions could well constitute a book in itself but so could the study of one aspect of the eye of a fly. The aim here, however, is the study of formal structure, of context and of contexts within contexts. It is suggestive and probing rather than conclusive and probative.

THE GRACE-NATURE DISTINCTION IN LONERGAN AND RAHNER

Lonergan's position on the grace-nature distinction is straightforward and consistent. In his 1949 article 'The Natural Desire to see God'[2] he deals with this problem and his position remains basically unchanged as is clear from such articles as 'Openness and Religious Experience'[3] and the very recent 'Natural Knowledge of God'.[4] It should be noted however, that in his more recent writings Lonergan has moved out of the orbit of traditional scholastic categories and expressions and has undergone a substantial development in his thought. The interpreter of Lonergan, therefore, must consequently be acutely aware of this shift and be able to recognise the transpositions from scholastic categories to the historico-existential modes of expression which characterise Lonergan's later thought.

Now, in the view of this interpreter—and here the word 'tentative' should be operative, at least as regards the grace-nature distinction—Lonergan has not contradicted his earlier views in the context of his more recent writings but rather has moved to a higher view-point. Indeed, it might be generally stated that 'the new context of the philosophy of God in Lonergan' involves either certain constants in his thought or else movements to higher viewpoints rather than contradictions. The term 'new context of the philosophy of God in Lonergan' is consequently applicable both to the Lonergan of *De Verbo Incarnato*[5] and to the Lonergan of 'Functional Specialities in Theology'[6] though in the latter case in a somewhat more nuanced fashion.

In his article 'The Natural Desire to see God' Lonergan makes the following succint comment: 'I would affirm that world-order is prior to finite natures, that God sees in his essence, first of all, the series of all possible world orders each of which is complete down to its least historical detail, that only consequently inasmuch as he knows world-orders does God know their component parts such as his free gifts, finite natures, their properties, exigencies, and so on.'[7]

What is most important for our purposes in the preceding statement of Lonergan is that in his analysis grace and nature, though distinct as 'free gift' and 'finite nature', are not related to each other in some vague extrinsicist fashion but rather are enfolded in the unity of a world-order which is known by God prior to the distinct components of this particular world order.

On a cognitional rather than metaphysical level Lonergan in his later 'Openness and Religious Experience' speaks of openness as (i) fact, (ii) achievement and (iii) gift.[8] His distinctions illuminate in an implicit but clear fashion his conception of the meaning and validity of the distinction between grace and nature. For Lonergan openness as fact is the pure desire to know. It is what Aristotle was referring to when he spoke of the wonder which is the origin of all science and what Aquinas meant when he spoke of man's natural desire to know God through his essence. Secondly, there is openness as achievement. Openness as achievement is basically the self in its self-appropriation and self-realisation. Finally there is openness as gift. Man by nature wants to know everything about everything. Yet, to know everything about everything one would have to know the essence of God. Man can, of course, by nature constantly enlarge his horizon perspectives. The differentiation and even higher integrations which have occurred and are constantly occurring within human consciousness bear eloquent testimony to this fact. Yet, here a distinction must be made. There are possibilities of horizon enlargement endemic to the very structure of human consciousness (finite nature). But there is also an ultimate enlargement which lies beyond the limits of any horizon-enlargement available to the native resources and capabilities of natural intelligence. This enlargement is the face-to-face encounter with God, knowledge of God not through the mediation of any created medium but through God himself. This ultimate horizon-enlargement can only come as a personal free gift from above, descending from the Father of Light and the God who is Love.

What is most important for this study is Lonergan's stress on the fact that these three aspects of openness are to be interrelated but not in any extrinsic or accidental fashion. Thus, in the concrete universe which is the world-order of our experience 'openness as fact is for openness as gift'. [9] Likewise, 'openness as achievement rises from the fact and conditions and, at the same time, is conditioned by the gift'. [10] These three forms of openness are linked together in the concrete historical development of the human spirit and it is this intimate linkage which explains the primacy of religious experience in the world of man and hence the non-extrinsic quality of the relationship between grace and nature.

Openness as fact, therefore, is an *a priori* of the possibility for openness as achievement. If there was not the fact of the existence of the natural desire to know there would be nothing in which achievement or self-appropriation could occur. Likewise, openness as fact is an *a priori* condition of the possibility for openness as gift. For, if the pure desire to know were not unrestricted or in other words correlative to the totality of being in its complete universality and concreteness, there would be nothing for the Gift to communicate itself to in a face-to-face intercommunion of knowing and loving.

A final reference should be made to Lonergan's lecture entitled 'Natural Knowledge of God'. There will be occasion to refer to this talk in more detail later on but here two points should be noted. First, Lonergan firmly maintains against his critics that his proof for the existence of God in *Insight* is valid. 'If human knowing consists in asking and answering questions, if ever further questions arise, if the further questions are given honest answers then, as I have argued elsewhere at some length (in *Insight*), we can and do arrive at knowledge of God.'[11] Lonergan also adds that it is only in a grace-context that one can achieve a philosophical knowledge of the existence of God but, as he puts it, although 'I do not think that in this life people arrive at natural knowledge of God without God's grace . . . what I do not doubt is that the knowledge they so attain is natural'.[12] For Lonergan accordingly grace and nature are not simply abstractions but ontological 'realities',[13] as distinct as are body and soul and of real existential import and significance in their distinction and interrelationship.

Rahner's many discussions of the nature-grace problem are well known as is their complex and controversial character. In the present context, however, the area of discussion is largely limited to certain of Rahner's more recent articles on this issue.

It should be noted from the first, however, that the meaning of Rahner's 'supernatural existential' has been subject to intense scrutiny. William C. Shepherd, for example, in his study *Man's Condition*[14] considers at length the nature-grace problem as it has evolved in Rahner's thought and as it is related to the famed 'supernatural existential'.

Among other things Shepherd avers that Rahner evolved the conception of the 'supernatural existential' to solve the problematic of nature and grace as it was developed in the context of the post-Tridentine tradition.

In that context it [the supernatural existential] . . . referred to a part of man's constitution, while the other part was purportedly made up by 'pure nature'. But within Rahner's own framework of thought, and within his own system, the supernatural existential refers to the activity of God, not at all to man's makeup.[15]

In Shepherd's view, however, Rahner's 'doctrine of nature and grace'[16] or, put in other words, his more delimited and traditional treatments of the subject, are considerably mitigated in emphasis in his 'theology of nature and grace'[17] or 'in Rahner's system as a whole where the emphasis is on God's presence to the human condition taken in its entirety'.[18]

Now the present writer is inclined to agree with Shepherd that a historical study of Rahner's views on the nature-grace relationship in terms of the 'supernatural existential' reveals at least certain ambiguities if not incompatibilities. Rahner's most recent articles, however, in *Sacramentum Mundi*, for example, seem at least open to the interpretation that the supernatural existential is not a certain *tertium quid* or ontological reality distinct both from man as obediential potency for the vision of God and from grace (as actualising and sanctifying) but is rather employed as a descriptive existential category which is identifiable basically with various aspects of God's saving grace.

With these preliminary observations in mind it will be helpful to briefly consider some of Rahner's more recent observations on the grace-nature problematic in order to then make some tentative comparisons between his views and those of Lonergan.

In his article 'Man (Anthropology)' in *Sacramentum Mundi* Rahner brings out that a true distinction between grace and nature should be acknowledged but that this distinction should be derived from a theological starting-point and employed as a concept regulated by theology without 'having antecedently to assume the purely natural concept of *pure nature* as fixed philosophical norm'.[19] The distinction between grace and nature would have its ground and unity in the recognition that man is a created personal subject who is a limitless receptivity to God. Man, however, although open to a revelation of God does not demand this and God is free either to reveal or conceal himself. For Rahner grace is, then, to be described as 'the condition of the possibility of the capacity for connatural reception of God's self-manifestation in word . . . and in the beatific vision'.[20] Nature, on the other hand, 'is the constitution of man which is presupposed by, and persists in, this capacity to hear'.[21] Rahner thus speaks of both supernatural and natural existentials.[22] The light of faith, for example, is a supernatural existential and such terms as absolute transcendence, eternal validity (immortality), freedom, personality, etc. pertain to the nature of man as spirit or *potentialis obedientalis* for supernatural grace.[23]

Rahner, however, still in effect speaks of nature as a 'remainder concept' and is careful to insist that 'the strictly *theological* concept of nature . . . does not mean a state of reality, intelligible in itself and experienced by us separately . . . on top of which . . . an additional reality would be superimposed'.[24] Nature thus is conceived as an element in a higher synthesis which is not experienced apart from the graced situation.[25] Rahner does indeed grant that the concept of pure nature as a limit concept is useful and 'justified as a means of elucidating what actually exists'.[26] Man is not able, however, in Rahner's view, to form 'any positive and unmixed idea, full, definite and certain in content of what would still be found in a *natura pura* and what would not'.[27] This is so because 'our cognition always occurs within the order of grace and we cannot really escape from the dynamism of grace even in cognition, whether we are consciously aware of it or not'.[28] It is thus impossible for us to tell with absolute precision what in a purely natural order would remain of what we experience as freedom, guilt, etc.

Now the question might be raised as to what similarity or dissimilarity exists between Lonergan's and Rahner's positions on the nature-grace question. Certainly both acknowledge that the distinction does have a validity. Nature and grace for both indicate distinct interrelated elements in the concrete universe of our experience. There is also a similarity between Rahner's attempt to ground the grace-nature distinction within the unity of a theological anthropology which in its first moment envisages man as a created personal subject who is a limitless receptivity to God and to whom God can freely communicate himself as Gift, and Lonergan's implicit distinguishing of nature and grace in man in his 'Openness and Religious Experience' where he speaks of man in terms of openness as fact, achievement and gift.

The present writer would like to ask, however, whether in Lonergan's overall system nature does not enjoy a more positive and richer role than it does in Rahner's systematic? Certainly, Lonergan would grant with Rahner that the concept of 'pure nature' is a marginal theorem which should not be magnified into a doctrine of central concern.[29] Moreover, Lonergan would no doubt agree with Rahner about the impossibility of saying exactly what human freedom, etc. would be like in a state of 'pure nature'. Lonergan is quite careful, for example, to emphasise in *Insight* in the chapter which deals with the self-affirmation of the knower that 'as I might not be, as I might be other than I am, so my knowing might not be and it might be other than it is. The ultimate basis of our knowing is not necessity but contingent fact, and the fact is established, not prior to our engagement in knowing, but simultaneously with it'.[30] Likewise as was noted above, Lonergan clearly acknowledges that 'openness as achievement rises from the fact and conditions and, at the same time, is conditioned by the gift'.[31] Such is the uniqueness of the present order of the universe as Lonergan conceives it and hence such is the futility and uselessness of attempts to extrapolate from this concrete world-order to detailed content possibilities of other possible world orders.

It remains doubtful, however, in this writer's mind that Lonergan would choose to speak of 'nature' as a 'remainder concept'. In this context Rahner in both his earlier and his more recent writings is at pains to emphasise that it is very difficult to detail in terms of our necessarily graced experiences exactly what is of grace and what is of nature. Lonergan, however, as was observed above, while acknowledging that without grace it would be *de facto* impossible to come to certain knowledge of God, nonetheless insists that man can and does come to this knowledge and that it is natural knowledge. In fact, Lonergan claims to have reached this knowledge in the elaborate proof for the existence of God in *Insight*. In Rahner's works, however, although a proof for God's existence is articulated in diverse manners, the knowledge of God which is achieved is far less detailed and this would appear to be almost by deliberate choice. There is far less stress in Rahner on God as Meaning than there is on God as Mystery whereas the opposite has been the case, overall, in Lonergan's works. Finally, these rather fundamental differences in stress would appear to be rooted ultimately in different views on the import which should be attributed to the respective roles of nature and grace in the phenomenon of man in his encounter with God.

THE PHILOSOPHY-THEOLOGY DISTINCTION IN LONERGAN AND RAHNER

Christian Philosophy

Both Lonergan and Rahner are quick to point out the close connection between the nature-grace problematic and that of the relationship between philosophy and theology. The problem of a Christian philosophy is the inevitable outcrop of these dialectically interrelated dual polarities.

Lonergan in his 'Dimensions of Meaning' article in *Collection* indicates the connection of the above polarities when he remarks that 'once philosophy becomes existential and historical, once it asks about man, not in the abstract, not as he would be in some state of pure nature, but as in fact he is here and now in all the concreteness of his living and dying, the very possibility of the old distinction between philosophy and theology vanishes'.[32]

Now, as is apparent from the preceding section, Lonergan does not consider that the distinction between philosophy and theology has in every sense vanished. He clearly affirms in his article on the natural knowledge of God that such natural knowledge is not only possible but actual. He states that he has offered an adequate 'proof' for the existence of God in *Insight*. What Lonergan would then appear to be opposing in his 'Dimensions of Meaning' statement is an abstract deductivism which would separate rather than distinguish the philosophic and theological moments in the reflections of the concrete person. Indeed, in his *Gregorianum* review of two books dealing with the problem of Christian philosophy Lonergan clearly opts for a distinction but not a separation between philosophy and theology and ends by stating that

the issue which goes by the name of a Christian philosophy . . . is basically a question on the deepest level of methodology, the one that investigates the operative intellectual ideals not only of scientists and philsophers but also since Catholic truth is involved, theologians. It is, I fear, in Vico's phrase a *scienza nuova*.[33]

In this writer's view what Lonergan is referring to in the quotation just cited would appear to closely approximate what he is attempting in his work.

Method in Theology

The problem of the relationship between philosophy and theology leads immediately to the problematic of Christian philosophy as is evident from what Lonergan has to say about the *scienza nuova*. Now, although the ultimate foundational explanation of the nature of Christian philosophy no doubt remains to be given there are certain inquiries which may be made about Lonergan in his function as 'Christian philosopher' and about his views to date regarding the nature of a Christian philosophy.

First, then, the context in which Lonergan has philosophised and is still philosophising should be considered. In the *Gratia Operans* articles,[34] which constituted the nucleus of Lonergan's doctoral dissertation, Lonergan's primary concern was to do a proper hermeneutic of Aquinas' thought on operative grace. This study culminated in an acute analysis of Aquinas' notion of the relationship between human freedom and divine transcendence. Clearly, the Lonergan of the *Gratia Operans* articles may be termed a Christian philosopher both because the context in which he worked was Christian and because the central problematic with which he dealt originated in reflections on Christian revelation and yet evoked the most profound metaphysical considerations.

Again, the Lonergan of the *Verbum*[35] is a Christian philosopher. In *Verbum* Lonergan's principal concern was to articulate a proper human analogy for understanding—in a necessarily imperfect yet fruitful fashion—the divine processions. To this end Lonergan concentrated on the development of the *Verbum* in Aquinas. He pointed out, of course, that Aquinas in his working out of the concept of *Verbum* was attempting to fit an Augustinian creation into a framework which was Aristotelian and that the basic context in which Augustine developed his thought on the *Verbum* was Trinitarian and its fundamental impetus anti-Arian.[36] Lonergan's function here as a Christian philosopher or as one who operated philosophically within the context of Christian revelation is manifest.

Insight, of course, appears to be more purely secular in nature than *Gratia Operans* or *Verbum*. Yet, *Insight* involves a highly creative and nuanced extension of the seminal implications of *Verbum* into a full-blown study of the noetic operations of contemporary scientists and men of common sense alike. Moreover, Lonergan retains in the 19th chapter of *Insight* the theory of the relationship between human freedom and divine transcendence which he affirmed in *Gratia Operans* to be an authentic interpretation of the view of Aquinas. *Insight*, therefore, in a *radical* sense may be affirmed to be as 'Christian' as are Lonergan's two major earlier works.

Finally, it need not be stressed that the Lonergan of 'Openness and Religious Experience' and the very recent 'Natural Knowledge of God' is a Christian philosopher in the historical contextual sense just indicated.

Yet, the objection might be raised that Lonergan is a Christian philosopher in the sense that he was a Christian who philosophised within a Christian context but that this is an extrinsicist, contextual, *de facto* rather than intrinsic, *de jure* type of 'Christian philosophising'.

The second question to be asked, accordingly, is whether or not Lonergan holds that there is any validity in speaking of a 'Christian philosophy' in any other than an accidental extrinsicist or, at best, historical sense.

In point of fact, Lonergan does explicitly use the term 'Christian philosophy'[37] and has both spoken and written about what he calls the 'origins of Christian realism'.[38] Lonergan clearly holds that there is an epistemology and a metaphysics implicit in Christian revelation. He does not maintain, however, that the philosophy implicit in revelation is so unique that it could not be known at least *in principio* or *de jure* by reason unaided by grace. Lonergan does insist, however, that there is a quality about revelation and man's response to the word in faith which involves a certain type of realism and hence implicitly an epistemology and metaphysics.

Tersely expressed, it is Lonergan's view that in man's graced assent in faith to God's word there is a spontaneous intellectual motion to rise above sensism and idealism toward a 'dogmatic realism'[39] in which truth is implicitly acknowledged to be known through correct judgement and not properly in any prior stage of cognitional process. Finally, Lonergan envisages what he terms 'critical realism'—the aim of *Insight*—as being the explication of what is implicit in 'dogmatic realism'. Such is the intimate connection between philosophy and theology in Lonergan's thought and such is the depth of meaning he attributes to the expression 'Christian philosophy'.

Rahner, like Lonergan, sees the problem of the relationship between philosophy and theology as rooted in the grace-nature distinction. Rahner, however, unlike Lonergan, is known more for his essays and lectures than for his major systematic works. In the last thirty years Rahner has addressed himself to practically every major and, if you will, minor theological problem. In fact, he even wrote a short 'theological' preface for a study done on the religious significance of the songs of the Beatles.[40] The task of the Rahner interpreter is accordingly a highly complex and difficult one. Thus, as was noted at the outset of this paper, it is the intention here to offer suggestive tentative analyses rather than definitive interpretations and conclusions.

For Rahner, then, just as 'the concrete reality of grace includes nature within itself, so also . . . philosophy is an inner moment of theology'.[41] Rahner insists very much on this point that philosophy is an inner moment of theology and emphasises that the *separation* of the two which evolved in the past few centuries was due to the—in his view—highly questionable baroque-scholastic conception of the grace-nature distinction.[42] Indeed, Rahner states quite flatly in his fairly recent 'Theology and Anthropology' that '*natural* theology is from first to last not an occupation carried on alongside theology based on revelation, as if the two could be carried on independently of one another: natural theology is an inner element in revelation theology itself'.[43]

Rahner, therefore, is at least as insistent as Lonergan in that the *distinction* between philosophy and theology should not be transformed into a *separation*. Rahner does, however, wish to preserve a certain distinction between philosophy and theology, although it should be recognised that there is a certain dialectic of emphasis in regard to this distinction operative in various essays by Rahner.

In a 1962 article entitled 'Philosophy and Theology' Rahner argues that 'grace, understood as the absolute self-communication of God himself, must always presuppose as a condition of its own possibility (in order to be itself) someone to whom it can address itself and someone to whom it is not owed'.[44] Rahner proceeds to develop the point that just as grace in a sense presupposes nature as a condition of its own possibility even though nature is ultimately for the sake of grace and not vice versa, so theology requires philosophy for its own proper development, although philosophy is radically a moment within theology and for the sake of theology:

God has willed the truth of philosophy only because he willed the truth of his own self-revelation. . . . He could, however, only will precisely this divine truth which is given out and away from himself, as the truth which is a gratuitous grace and is expressed in and out of love. For this reason he had to create the one from whom he could keep this truth a secret, i.e. the philosopher who, because he himself experienced God as the one who conceals himself, could accept revelation from him *as a grace*.[45]

Now in his more recent writing Rahner emphasises the *de facto* existence of a philosophical pluralism or 'gnoseological concupiscence' which is more or less here to stay.[46] Rahner further comments that

there no longer exists today a single philosophy which is finished and already adapted to the needs of theology, a philosophy which theology could simply presuppose, *and this holds also for Catholic Christians*. In this sense there is no longer a neo-scholastic philosophy if we understand by this a relatively finished 'system'.[47]

Rahner concludes that in the present state of philosophical pluralism 'there is no alternative but to *philosphise* within theology itself'.[48]

Here it is important to note that Rahner still acknowledges the value and importance of philosophy as systematic transcendental reflection but he pushes the point that 'there are so many different themes, starting-points, terminologies, relationships to other sciences, and to philosophical tradition that no individual or small (efficient) team can take in the whole of philosophy, though they know that other philosophies exist besides their own'.[49] This means for Rahner that although there still does exist a 'stock of standard philosophy'[50] in the Church and 'it is necessary in a theology which is demanded by the oneness of the confession of faith',[51] nonetheless 'this ecclesiastical teaching philosophy cannot close its mind to outside factors or claim to call itself the *philosophia perennis* in the manner of the neo-scholasticism of the last century'.[52]

Rahner himself in his own most recent articles and lectures continues to employ transcendental method in his theologising. This is quite clear not only from such an article as 'Theology and Anthropology'[53] but also from his Münster lectures of the past two years entitled *Einführung in den Begriff des Christentums*. Rahner, therefore, while acknowledging the fact of 'gnoseological concupiscence' perdures in his use of transcendental reflection within his theologising, and in a very recent article remarks that in so far as philosophy does not attempt to be systematic transcendental reflection it is to be placed under the heading of a non-philosophical discipline.[54]

Now implicit in what has been said is the problem of 'Christian philosophy' in Rahner. First of all, there is no need to belabour the point that Rahner is a *de facto* Christian philosopher. The whole aim of Rahner's early *Hearers of the Word*[55] for example, is to determine the metaphysical structure which constitutes the human spirit as an obediential potency for revelation. The Christian context of the problematic is clear. Moreover, in Rahner's massive *Schriften* the philosophising is so integrated into the theological framework of the articles that most average readers of Rahner do not tend to think of him as a philosopher at all. The fact then that Rahner is a *de facto* Christian philosopher is manifest.

There is, however, the further question regarding Rahner's

understanding of the nature of 'Christian philosophy'. Now in his very recent discussion of the problem of 'Christian philosophy' in *Sacramentum Mundi* Rahner is rather negative and extrinsicist in comparison to earlier treatments of the same subject. Rahner begins by saying that 'if such a thing exists at all, it must remain philosophy in principle and method, and aim at being nothing else'.[56] Rahner further remarks that philosophy must be free, that the Christian philosopher can accept revelation as a negative norm, that 'a philosophy can be called Christian inasmuch as it received impulses from Christianity to do its own work',[57] that 'a philosophy will . . . be Christian when the philosopher who is a Christian strives for the greatest possible convergence between his philosophy and his faith'[58] and finally that a 'philosophy can also be Christian when it uses philosophical methods—with the help of history of religion—to analyse Christianity as a *de facto* phenomenon in the philosophy and phenomenology of religion'.[59]

As is clear, the above comments of Rahner about 'Christian philosophy' all deal with the *de facto* historical type of Christian philosophy but not with a philosophy as in some way intrinsic to revelation and implied in it. This does not necessarily mean, however, that Rahner does not acknowledge that there is a philosophy intrinsic to revelation and hence a 'Christian philosophy' in the *de jure*, intrinsic sense. The intent of these comments is simply to indicate the caution which must be employed in attempting to do a hermeneutical analysis of Rahner's conception of the nature of 'Christian philosophy'.

Now Rahner, as was observed earlier, emphasises in his more recent essays that philosophy and specifically 'natural theology' is a moment within theology and must not be carried on independently of theology. Moreover, in this context Rahner stresses that 'as soon as man is understood as that being which has absolute transcendence toward God . . . then anthropocentricity and theocentricity in theology are not contradictories but strictly one and the same thing seen from two different aspects and each aspect is unintelligible without the other'.[60] The goal of the philosophy of God or 'natural theology' for Rahner, however, is precisely to discover in the transcendence of the human spirit man's openness to God as the absolute mystery and to make man aware that he is a possible hearer of the word of the living God.[61] Here then the depth and scope of Rahner's *operative notion* of 'Christian philosophy' clearly emerges. Not only is there a mutual interdependence of philosophy and theology in Rahner's system but for him it is impossible 'to speak theologically about God without saying something about man, and vice versa'.[62] Rahner accordingly, in this writer's opinion, in his stress on the role of transcendental anthropology in theology speaks his most profound heuristic word about the possibility and actuality of a 'Christian philosophy' or what Lonergan would seem to refer to as a *scienza nuova*.

The Existential Context of the Philosophy of God in Lonergan and Rahner

Up to this point the discussion has centred more on philosophy in general than on 'natural theology' or the philosophy of God. Within the wider problematics of nature-grace and philosophy-theology, however, 'natural theology' finds it contextual location and it is now possible to discuss certain aspects of the philosophy of God in its more specific existential dimensions.

In his *De Methodo Theologiae*[63] Lonergan remarks that

the major texts, the classics in religion, letters, philosophy, theology, not only are beyond the original horizon of their interpreters but also demand an intellectual, moral, religious conversion of the interpreter over and above the broadening of his horizon. In this case the reader's original knowledge of the thing is just inadequate. He will come to know the thing only in so far as he pushes the self-correcting process of learning to a revolution of his outlook. He can succeed in acquiring that habitual understanding of the author that spontaneously finds his wave length and locks on to it only after he has effected radical change in himself.[64]

Lonergan refers to the above comments on the development of the interpreter as 'the existential dimension of the problem of hermeneutics' and states that 'its existence is at the root of the perennial divisions of mankind in their views on morality, on philosophy, on religion'.[65]

Lonergan's emphasis on the importance of conversion for enabling an interpreter to enter into the horizon-perspective of a given author or philosopher, etc. and hence to be able to move freely within the latter's world remains a constant in his more recent discussions. Thus, in reply to a question put to him at the theological assembly held in Toronto regarding foundational theology Lonergan

pointed out that acceptance of the truths of faith pertains to religion, but not all who accept (that is, are converted to) the truths of faith possess that 'reflection upon conversion' which is the foundation for theology. This he went on to say leads to the further question of whether one who does not accept the truths of faith can be a theologian. There is no room for such a theologian in theology in this technical sense of finding its foundations in accurate reflection upon conversion.[66]

Now, *mutatis mutandis* Lonergan's comments about the need for conversion in the theologian also apply to the philosopher and most especially to the philosopher whose field is the philosophy of God.

In his lecture 'Natural Knowledge of God' Lonergan indirectly indicates the need for various conversions in a person who wishes to function authentically as a 'natural theologian':

Natural knowledge of God is affirmed if one holds that there is a valid argument (for God's existence) and if one holds that apprehending the argument is intrinsically natural. One goes beyond the *quaestio juris* to the *quaestio facti*, when one turns from conditions of possibility to conditions of actual occurrence. Such conditions are always very numerous. In the present instance men must exist. They must be healthy and enjoy considerable leisure. They must have attained sufficient differentiation of consciousness to think philosophically. They must have succeeded in avoiding all the pitfalls in which so many great philosophers have become entrapped. They must resist their personal evil tendencies and not be seduced by the bad example of others. Such are just a few very general conditions of someone actually grasping a valid argument for God's existence.[67]

Lonergan in the above statement implicitly indicates the need for intellectual, moral and religious conversion in an individual who hopes to operate fruitfully as a philosopher of God.

For Lonergan, intellectual conversion is intimate, radical, conscious and deliberate because it involves a personal grappling with the self in which the spontaneous tendency to conceive of the *really real* in terms of body must be overcome through a type of self-transcendence in which the individual moves out of the *aesthetic sphere* in Kierkegaard's use of this term—as interpreted by Lonergan—into the world of the intelligible and being where the *really real* is understood and affirmed to be what is known through the mediation of the inner words of understanding and judgement.[68]

Again, intellectual conversion in the context of natural theology is an existential, *de jure*, intrinsic condition of possibility for understanding and affirming the validity of Lonergan's approach to the God-problem because Lonergan's whole proof for the existence of God hinges on the validity of his affirmations of the identity of the *real* with being and of the complete intelligibility of the real. And, to arrive at these affirmations the individual must first have succeeded in affirming himself as a knower in the sense indicated in chapter eleven of *Insight* and also in affirming the validity of the notions of being and objectivity as articulated by Lonergan in chapters twelve and thirteen.

Moral conversion, unlike intellectual conversion, is not an intrinsic *de jure* condition of possibility for grasping and affirming the existence of God in Lonergan's sense. It is, however, of equal importance and may thus be properly described as a *de facto* existential condition of possibility for achieving actual philosophical knowledge of the existence of God. Thus, in moral conversion there is involved a real self-transcendence or a moving beyond the objects of desire and fear, all merely personal satisfactions and tastes and preferences, into the world of objective value.[69] The real self-transcendence involved in moral conversion enables one to be truly objective and hence to approach the God-problem in a proper manner.

Religious conversion like moral conversion is a *de facto* existential condition of possibility for any profitable approach to a natural reflection on God. Religious conversion, however, is not simply the intentional self-transcendence involved in intellectual conversion or the real self-transcendence which defines moral conversion but the complete self-transcendence of being in love with God through his grace. Religious conversion accordingly involves the deepest fulfilment of man and so above all frees man to do natural theology in an authentic fashion.

What we have tried to indicate in the above comments about the various conversions is the existential context in which Lonergan situates his philosophy of God. For Lonergan 'natural theology' is most properly viewed not in splendid isolation but rather in a broad hermeneutical context which takes cognizance of the central role of conversions not only in man's concrete living but also in his existential thinking and above all in his thinking about God.

The existential context of the philosophy of God in Rahner is evident in his insistence that natural theology is a moment within theology, that conversion is crucial to the successful performance of any natural theology and that a certain 'mystagogical approach' must be operative in the individual who attempts to understand 'proof' for the existence of God, etc.

First, as was observed earlier, it is Rahner's view that 'natural theology' must not be carried out in total independence of theology. Indeed, Rahner stresses in his proposal dealing with the reform of the theological curriculum of German seminarians that philosophy and theology be studied together and be related to each other in a direct intrinsic manner.[70] Rahner thus sees philosophy as posing certain basic questions about man and God to which theology gives the ultimate answers. The important thing to note, of course, is that Rahner clearly locates the solution of the problem of the relationship between transcendental philosophy and theology within a theological context. Rahner views it as abstract and non-existential to isolate 'natural theology' from the realm of theology in which alone 'natural theology' discovers its autonomy and yet its intrinsic relatedness to theology.

Again, Rahner, like Lonergan, stresses the importance of conversion in any individual who would hope to engage in 'natural theology' in a successful manner. Rahner does not concentrate on the phenomenon of conversion in the same way Lonergan does but its central importance for Rahner is clear both in his earliest and more recent writings.

In his 'What is Heresy?' Rahner speaks of a radical circuminsession of truth and love. He implicitly indicates the importance he ascribes to conversion or spiritual transformation for the attainment of truth:

There is a basic fulfilment of human existence, a depth of human existence . . . in which knowledge and decision, truth and goodness are no longer separable, but where only the true possesses goodness and where only the good cannot land outside truth. Yet precisely this original basic act (in which knowledge achieves its full nature by saving itself, and thus preserving itself, within the decision of love, just as the converse is also true) is still an act of knowledge of truth and significant for salvation, in so far as this act is (also) precisely this because the truth itself belongs to the highest moral goods and hence morality . . . fails itself if it does not find the real truth.[71]

This statement of Rahner on the circuminsession of knowing and loving in man is paradigmatic of the thrust of Rahner's entire intellectual enterprise and indicates the radically unitary existential character of his thought. In *Spirit in the World*, Rahner stressed that the diversity of powers in man had to be explained in terms of a prior unity—'what is multiple is not united of itself'.[72] This type of emphasis has been in Rahner's thought ever since and explains his stress on the close interrelationship of philosophy and theology and the existential context in which a philosophy of God should be developed and studied.

More specifically, in *Hearers of the Word*, Rahner explicitly speaks of 'conversion' and the role of love in an authentic doing of 'natural theology'. For example, he states that

free decision is not merely a consequence of knowledge, but itself helps to determine that knowledge. This means that the most profound truth is also the most free. The truth of the knowledge of God, in the way in which one understands his God, always rests upon the order of his love or its disorder. It is not as though man first of all knew God in a *neutral* fashion, subsequently considering whether to adopt a loving or hating attitude towards this God. Such a neutral knowledge, such 'objectivity', is a dangerous abstraction of the philosophers. . . . The concrete knowledge of God is always determined from the start by the way in which man loves and treasures the things presented to him.[73]

For Rahner, therefore, it is meaningless to speak about 'natural theology' or 'proofs' for God's existence apart from the context of love. Rahner does, of course, hold that metaphysical knowledge of God is possible. Moreover, he emphasises that this form of knowledge is 'no less rigorous, objective, and logical'[74] than other forms of knowledge. He insists, however, that this type of knowledge is 'in its essence . . . at the same time an effort made by the whole person in free decision'.[75] Indeed, for Rahner 'any alteration in knowledge is, in this context, always a "conversion".'[76] Rahner thus in *Hearers of the Word* neither denies the validity of a certain type of natural theology nor does he minimise its importance. He does emphasise, however, that it cannot and must not be carried out in an abstract or non-existential context: 'That one might convince a villain of a mathematical truth but not of a proof of God's existence is no indication of the strength of the one and the weakness of the other, but an indication of the degree to which a "proof" of God's existence demands an effort from man.'[77]

Finally, Rahner states quite clearly in a recent article that

the proofs for God's existence themselves and the 'mystagogy' that is the absolutely necessary condition of their success must from the outset approach the absolute mystery which pervades our existence. They must confront both theoretical knowledge and the existential experience of life with this mystery, and then say: Precisely this is what we mean when we speak of 'God'.[78]

Two points should be made in terms of the quotation just cited. First, Rahner acknowledges, though in a nuanced fashion, that 'proofs' of God do have a role. Secondly, Rahner makes it clear that God as Mystery must be the ultimate quest of 'natural theology' and that 'mystagogy' is an absolutely essential condition for the success of any proofs.

It should be observed that Rahner has never written an article on mystagogy. He does, however, use the term in his Munich and Münster lectures which do not yet exist in a finished published form but hopefully soon will.[79]

For Rahner, approaching God through 'mystagogy' would appear to mean that any given individual should attempt to discover the Mystery which is God at the core of his most existential experiences, i.e. in his experience of love, loneliness, dread, commitment, hope, etc. The path of mystagogy is intimately personal and differs for each individual. Basically, what Rahner would seem to be getting at in his stress on the mystagogical approach is that a philosophical approach to the existence of God can only succeed in its transcendental aspirations if it roots itself very deeply in a concrete existential context. Here the classic distinctions between grace and nature, philosophy and theology, etc. are subsumed in a higher existential unity. For Rahner diversity has its roots in unity and the search for the unity within diversity has been one of the major quests of his entire career.

PEDAGOGICAL QUESTIONS AND CONCLUSIONS

A basic pedagogical question which arises from this discussion is how philosophy and theology should be interrelated in a curriculum. The question is unfortunately somewhat provincial since it arises within a Roman Catholic context. It may be hoped, however, that it possesses dimensions or aspects which are trans-credal, but these must still be worked out.

Rahner, in his critique of a proposed curriculum for German seminarians, argues that philosophy and theology should not be taught in chronologically distinct phases but together. Further, he is at pains to emphasise that they should not be arbitrarily inter-related but intrinsically. He is, of course, speaking in the context of seminary education but the issue is broader since it involves the adoption of fundamental views on the part of a Christian as to what the proper interrelationship between philosophy and theology should be.

Lonergan has not addressed himself to this problem in a specific fashion. However, in his *Method in Theology* he does have a chapter on religion in which he articulates his latest views on 'natural theology'. He is, of course, doing this within a theological context and in a methodological work. Lastly, Lonergan's thought certainly involves an implicit view of the manner in which philosophy and theology should be pedagogically interrelated. Also, Lonergan has lectured on education and articulated a view of the role of the Catholic university in which theology is the ultimate, necessary existential unifying factor in the curriculum. [80]

Throughout this essay many comparisons of an either explicit or implicit nature have been made in regard to Lonergan and Rahner. In each section of the discussion similarities and dis-similarities have emerged. It is not our purpose here to make critical judgements about the excellence or non-excellence of the diverse emphases in the thought of both. Instead, this essay will end where it began, i.e. in the context of questioning:

(1) Does Lonergan in fact assign a more independent role to philosophy as a science than Rahner does? If so, is this due to principle or simply to practice?

(2) Is there a convergence or a divergence of viewpoint on the part of the two thinkers regarding the problem of Christian philosophy?

(3) There is—or at least has been—a fundamental stress in Lonergan's thought on God as Meaning whereas Rahner for some time now has stressed God as Mystery. Is this difference in stress due to a difference in understanding of the grace-nature, theology-philosophy problematics?

(4) In the context of the views of Lonergan and Rahner what should a 'philosophy of God' be today?

Final Note

Since this article was written Lonergan has completed and published his *Method in Theology*. In the light of recent lectures in Dublin which Lonergan has given on his *Method in Theology* there are certain nuances I would add if I were to write this type of article again. I would, for example, indicate that for Lonergan God is *Mystery* in a most singular and primal sense and this means that my contrast between Lonergan's stress on God as *Meaning* and Rahner's emphasis on God as *Mystery* would be subject to certain modifications. I would still maintain, however, that there is a certain fundamental validity in the contrast.

Again, in *Method in Theology*, Lonergan indicates that in his view the separation of natural theology from systematic theology was an error and that now with Rahner he would urge that natural theology be carried out within systematic theology. It should be noted, however, that Lonergan does not deny that a true distinction exists between natural theology or what can in principle be known about God through reason and systematic theology which involves a reflection upon the data of revelation. Yet, for Lonergan such things as 'proofs' for the existence of God are not generally worked out by the unconverted but by those who are already believers and are seeking a deeper understanding of what they believe and an intelligent grasp of the meaningfulness, reasonableness and worthwhileness of their religious commitment. It is then conversion rather than proof which is all-important and the separation of natural theology from systematic theology has tended to obscure and even threaten this basic truth.

With the above observations in mind, however, I believe that what I wrote about Lonergan and Rahner in the present article remains basically and heuristically in the right direction. Indeed, Lonergan's emphases on the primal reality of God as *Mystery*, on the need to distinguish but not separate natural theology and systematic theology and on the need to put the primary emphasis on conversion rather than proofs tend to confirm the basic thesis and thrust of the article, namely the crucial importance of envisaging natural theology in its new and proper Christian and existential context.

Bernard Lonergan responds

I MUST begin by thanking the contributors whose work is enlightening without calling for any reply. Then I shall attempt a partial answer to the questions Bernard Tyrrell raised at the end of his paper. Finally, I shall discuss three pairs of papers: Garrett Barden and David Rasmussen are concerned with myth; Schubert Ogden and Robert Johann are concerned with experience; Emerich Coreth and William Richardson are concerned with being.

First, then, two former students, Matthew Lamb and Frederick Lawrence, have related my thought to that of Wilhelm Dilthey and Hans-Georg Gadamer respectively to give us the benefit of their years of study in German-speaking universities. Joseph Flanagan has done a pertinent piece of work by contrasting my methodical approach to knowledge and language with a purely logical or conceptualist approach. Patrick Heelan has employed the tools of linguistic analysis to offer a coherent account of a recalcitrant aspect of quantum theory and, at the same time, to point to other areas where similar problems arise.

Next, Bernard Tyrrell ends his paper by asking for a comparison between Karl Rahner's views and my own on four topics: the independence of philosophy as science; Christian philosophy; God as meaning and God as mystery; and the philosophy of God. I shall indicate my own opinion on these topics without venturing to pronounce on Karl Rahner's.

With regard to philosophy as science, I must distinguish. Philosophy is not science in any rationalist sense; it is not the work of some pure reason or some speculative intellect; it is not a set of self-evident and necessary truths from which follow necessary conclusions; it is not some precisely defined and permanent system of eternal verities; and so it does not enjoy the independence that would be claimed by any rationalist stand. At the same time, philosophy is not science in the sense that the natural sciences are sciences. Their immediate goal is not truth but an ever fuller understanding of phenomena. Their advance is an ever greater approximation to truth. But such approximations are ever subject to radical revisions that, as it were, change the whole aspect of things. For me, then, philosophy occupies an intermediate position. It is primarily concerned with the three questions: What am I doing when I am knowing? Why is doing that knowing? What do I know when I do it? The answer to the first question is derived from the data of consciousness. The answer to the second is derived from the answer to the first. The answer to the third is derived from the answers to the first and the second. The answer to the first question is a cognitional theory. The answer to the second is an epistemology. The answer to the third is a metaphysics.

It will be noted that we have inverted the Aristotelian procedure. Aristotle's basic terms and relations are metaphysical. His physical concepts add further determinations to his metaphysical concepts, and his psychological concepts add still further determinations. On the contrary, our basic terms and relations refer to elements in cognitional experience. From the analysis of cognitional activity there is derived an epistemology. From the analysis and the epistemology there is derived a metaphysics.

Such a metaphysics is, in a sense, empirical. It contains nothing that does not find a corresponding and grounding element in cognitional activity. Again, it is in a sense critical, for any alleged aspect of metaphysics that does not possess a corresponding and grounding element in cognitional activity is to be eliminated.

Philosophy in the primary meaning we have been outlining is an ongoing process. It will always be possible to learn more about cognitional activity and, consequently, further refinements in epistemology and metaphysics are also possible. On the other hand, philosophy in this sense is not subject to the radical revisions to which the natural sciences are subject. For the conditions of the possibility of a revision have to be admitted by any reviser and, when they are, they are found to coincide with the already proposed cognitional theory.

There remains the question of the independence of such a philosophy. In the first place, then, it is not independent of conscience, of man's ability to deliberate on what truly is good, to evaluate how good it is, to decide accordingly. On the contrary, the whole of philosophic investigation has been guided and ruled by a deliberate and conscientious pursuit of truth. Indeed, it is through total dependence on such guidance that philosophy attains what is meant by its independence.

I have been speaking of philosophy in what I believe to be its primary concern. But that primary concern is only a beginning. It provides a basic tool that has very many applications. It provides a nucleus to which further elements from other sources can be added. So there arises philosophy with a roving commission. If its various applications and the sundry additions are arranged in some order, philosophy becomes defined not by a fixed but by a moving viewpoint.

The significant order, I find, is reached by conceiving a horizon as a line of ongoing development, by conceiving a conversion as the repudiation of a less adequate and the acceptance of a more adequate horizon, and by distinguishing intellectual, moral, and religious conversion. By intellectual conversion I understand the elimination of blindspots with regard to human cognitional activity, its objectivity and the reality it knows. It is the goal of what I have already called the primary concern of philosophy. By moral conversion I understand the shift of motivation from satisfactions to values. Such a conversion is the ground of ethical philosophy. For just as philosophy in its primary concern is guided and grounded by a conscientious pursuit of truth, so ethical philosophy is guided and grounded by a conscientious pursuit of value. By religious conversion, finally, I understand God's gift and man's acceptance of God's love (*Rom.* 5: 5; 8: 38f.).

Now from a rationalist or deductivist viewpoint it may seem of great importance to determine just what is presupposed and just what is implied by any of the meanings attributed to the word philosophy. But I believe such importance to be greatly reduced, if not to vanish, when the rationalist or deductivist viewpoint is rejected, when procedures are, not from premises to conclusions, but from data through understanding to judgements and decisions, when significant decisions are the highly personal and indeed existential matter of conversion, and when conversions are not logical consequences of previous positions but rather notable rejections of previous positions.

So with regard to Christian philosophy my views are rather humdrum. There is no philosophy that sets up an exigence for

God's gift of his love, or that constitutes a sufficient preparation for that gift. There is a philosophy that is open to the acceptance of Christian doctrine, that stands in harmony with it, and that, if rejected, leads to a rejection of Christian doctrine.

With regard to God as mystery and God as meaning, I think the simplest answer is to refer to Aquinas' five ways of proving the existence of God. The article concludes with the statement that what has been proved to exist is what everyone means by God. But what is this meaning known by everyone? Is it that everyone in some fashion or other does prove the existence of God? Or is it that God gives sufficient grace to everyone, that the one sufficient grace is the gift of charity without which nothing else is of avail (1 Cor. 13), that that gift orientates one to what is transcendent in lovableness, that that orientation can occur without any corresponding apprehension, that it can be, in Rahner's phrase, a content without a known object, that such a content is an orientation to the unknown, to mystery? Such an orientation to mystery, in my opinion, is a main source of man's search for God. As Pascal quoted in his *Pensées*: 'You would not be seeking for me unless you had already found me.'[1]

Finally, by a philosophy of God I would understand knowledge of God achieved by man as man. It is a nice theoretical issue that does not arise when thought becomes existential and personal. Then discourse on religion takes many forms of which the fullest is theological.

I think that the papers by David Rasmussen and Garrett Barden are complementary. The intention of truth in myth, which is Barden's topic, is concerned with the object that a hermeneutic of recollection, desired by Rasmussen, would uncover. At the same time, Barden's account of a contemporary student's advance from mythic to critical consciousness is a case in which deserting the myth constitutes a liberation. My own contention in *Insight* that as metaphysics advances myth recedes is not to be taken out of context. For Professor Rasmussen a myth is a symbolic narrative. In *Insight* there are two kinds of symbolic narratives: mysteries and myths. I did not contend that as metaphysics advances, mysteries recede, and so I see no difficulty in finding room in my position for symbolic consciousness or for a hermeneutic of recollection.

At least from my viewpoint, the papers by Robert Johann and

by Schubert Ogden are also complementary. The former relates me to John Dewey, the latter to A. N. Whitehead, and both question my use of the word experience. I employ it, not in the sense intended when one speaks of men of experience, but in the sense of a distinct type of cognitional activity which, however, does not normally occur without the occurrence of other types. Now I do not think that distinction presupposes separation, but it will be more helpful to avoid abstract argument and to draw attention to Professor Johann's claim that what I call an ongoing, self-correcting process of learning is just what Dewey means by experience. If Professor Ogden were to discover that Whitehead meant something similar when he took his stand on experience, the distance that separates us would in some measure be reduced.

Professor Johann proposes that I should borrow something from John Dewey's pragmatism. He finds a basis for this view in my own recognition of the subordination of experiencing, understanding, and judging to the fourth level operations of deliberating on what truly is good, evaluating how good it is and deciding what to do about it. Now this does imply that a moral decision should lie at the root of cognitional enterprise. But it is a further point to claim that the grounds for a sound moral decision have been set forth by Dewey's pragmatism. If it is pragmatism to hold that men individually are responsible for their own lives and collectively they are responsible for the world in which they live, I have no hesitation about agreeing.

At the same time, I cannot regret the way I wrote *Insight*. My purpose was not a study of human life but a study of human understanding. My strategy was a moving viewpoint that gradually moved from simpler to more complicated types of understanding. My goal was to prepare the way for working out a method for theology.

Professor Ogden finds that I use the traditional term, unrestricted understanding, without deriving it from my cognitional theory. I suggest that the derivation at least is indicated by the statement: '. . . such a procedure (from restricted to unrestricted understanding) not only is possible but also imperative. For the pure desire (to know) excludes not only the total obscurantism, which arbitrarily brushes aside every intelligent and reasonable question, but also the partial obscurantism, which arbitrarily brushes aside this or that range of intelligent and reasonable questions that admit determinate answers.'[2]

I cannot directly discuss Professor Ogden's argument about possibility and actuality, for his precise meaning most probably has roots with which I am not familiar. In my own terms, however, I would distinguish possibility as something conceptual and potency as something real. Further I would distinguish active and passive potency. I would grant that potency and act are relevant categories for the whole of reality, that all finite beings are constituted by really distinct passive potency and act, and that God is constituted by really identical act and active potency. I do not conceive God as the actuation either of the totality of passive potency or of some notable part of passive potency. I conceive him as simply act, as identical with unrestricted active potency, and so as the ground of the possibility of all passive potency. Finally, I see no difficulty in an unrestricted act of understanding grasping that certain *possibilia* are not *compossibilia*.

However much Emerich Coreth and William Richardson differ from each other, they make a similar complaint about my position. I recognise a notion of being, a concept of being, theories of being, knowledge of being, and the idea of being. But I do not show proper concern for the Aristotelian topic of being as being. I speak of being not in terms of being but only in terms of the cognitional activities by which being is known or to be known. I analyse finite being into central and conjugate potencies, forms and acts, but the meaning of these elements is reached not by profound metaphysical intuition or reflection but simply by their isomorphism with the structure of cognitional activity. If I am asked about the being of beings, the ontological difference, I take refuge in the adequate real distinction between central act and, on the other hand, central potency and form or alternatively in the inadequate real distinction between central act and the subsistent being it actuates. If I am pressed to say what is the sense, the meaning, the intelligibility of being as being, I am content to reply that to understand being is to understand everything about everything, that such understanding is unrestricted, and that unrestricted understanding pertains only to God. In brief, I hold that different beings have different essences, that only one being has being itself (*ipsum esse*) as its essence, and that to understand that being as being is to understand that essence.

The display of medieval metaphysics in these last paragraphs may lead the reader to suspect that really I do take over traditional concepts that have no place in my own explicit thinking. The fact is that my aim is *vetera novis augere et perficere.* Nor is my procedure haphazard. Basically it is a matter of deriving basic terms and relations from the data of consciousness, of accepting traditional metaphysics in the sense that is isomorphic with these basic terms and relations, and of rejecting traditional metaphysics in any sense that is not the to-be-known of human cognitional activity. Nor is this procedure gratuitous. It is the one way of systematically avoiding the verbalism to which the Aristotelian 'as such' is open and even prone.

Notes

INTRODUCTION (pp. 1–3)

[1]Cf. B. Lonergan, *Doctrinal Pluralism*, Milwaukee, 1971, 48.

[2]'An Interview With Fr Bernard Lonergan', edited by Philip McShane, S.J., *The Clergy Review*, LVI (1971), 428–9.

[3]For the same point in another relevant context cf. *Method In Theology*, London, 1972, 260; and p. 7, footnote 2.

[4]For a survey cf. S. P. Grossman, *A Textbook of Physiological Psychology*, New York 1967.

[5]P. McShane, 'Zoology And The Future of Philosophers', *Philosophical Studies* XXI.

[6]F. E. Crowe, 'The Exigent Mind', *Spirit as Enquiry* (identical with *Continuum*, Autumn 1964), 27. Fr Crowe has made similar points elsewhere, e.g. *Collection*, edited by F. E. Crowe, S.J., Herder and Herder, New York, 1967, xix–xx; 'The Origin and Scope of Bernard Lonergan's *Insight*', *Sciences Ecclésiastiques*, IX (1957) 265 ff.

[7]Cf. A. R. Aresteh, *Final Integration In The Adult Personality*, Leiden 1965. On p. 18 Aresteh remarks, 'Unless the psychologist has himself experienced the state of quest of final integration in the succession of identities he will hardly acquire an understanding or incentive for doing research on it.'

[8]Cf. A. Maslow, *Towards A Psychology of Being*, New York 1968. On p. 204 Maslow remarks that 'though in principle self-actualisation is easy, in practice it rarely happens (by my criteria, certainly in less than one per cent of the adult population).'

[9]A dimension mediated by interiority in self-appropriation on the level of feelings. Cf. *Method in Theology*, 33–4, 39–40.

[10]From a letter of Edmund Husserl to Franz Brentano, 15 October 1904, quoted in H. Spiegelberg, *The Phenomenological Movement* I, The Hague 1965, 89.

THE INTENTION OF TRUTH IN MYTHIC CONSCIOUSNESS
(pp. 4–32)

[1]B. J. F. Lonergan, *Insight: a Study of Human Understanding*, London 1957, 531. Later references to this book will use the abbreviation *Insight*.

[2]This view was advanced by T. S. Eliot and is taken up by Northrop Frye in *The Anatomy of Criticism*, Princeton 1957. It is implicit in critical procedure but few have investigated the idea accurately.

[3]Binary divisions are now popular from the writing of Claude Levi-Strauss and his followers; but the majority of the suggested classifications focus on content and ignore the source of the division. Gilbert Durand in his monu-

mental *Les Structures anthropologiques de l'imaginaire*, Paris 1960, assigns a place to this symbolic image in his 'régime diurne' associated with the balancing reflex and the separating tendency of vision. The division of the intellectual universe into known and to-be-known may be consonant with dualistic imagery but it is not confined to these symbols, and does not exclude other equally significant and widespread structures; the issue is not the grammatical analysis of the expression but the semantic analysis of the intending subject.

[4]Objectification occurs in the transition from consciousness of self to the initiation of knowledge of self when the subject becomes the object of his own consideration. Still, the consideration of self can and does occur in many modalities and the primitive objectification is a far cry from theoretic understanding or even from the purely theoretic venture. Jean Piaget's paper 'Pensée egocentrique et pensée sociocentrique' in the *Cahiers Internationaux de Sociologie* (1951) is an excellent short account—to be completed by his other writings—of the emergence in the child of the possibility of the objectification of self. Since this objectification takes place in the person's intersubjective universe in the first place, it will be an interpretation of self as appearing in the company of family and friends. Harry Stack Sullivan's *Interpersonal Theory of Psychiatry*, London 1953, is theoretically an exploration of the genesis of this objectification from infancy to adulthood and therapeutically an effort to encourage the distorted subject away from an unreal evaluation to one in which his self system may be able to survive and expand.

[5]*Insight,* 532. Psychically the unknown translates as the unfamiliar; the loss of symbols of the unfamiliar reduces man's psychic image of his meaning and his dimensions are seriously restricted. Cf. on this Rollo May's paper in *Symbolism in Religion and Literature*, edited by Rollo May, New York 1960. Jung when he refers to the need for religion; Durand when he calls for the reintroduction of the imagination; Ricoeur when he notes that the symbol of guilt engages the total subject, seem to be discussing basically this loss of human resonance.

[6]Sacred and profane are not always utterly opposed; for the Profane may be the field in which the Sacred emerges and once it has emerged may validate the Profane.

[7]Professor Evans-Pritchard has questioned the usefulness of the division. He is correct inasmuch as the division is presumed to demand a definitive content. In fact, perhaps a more important criticism would be to note that in contemporary anthropological writings there is verbal agreement about the terms but no idea of the kind of analysis required to go beyond words.

[8]E. E. Evans-Pritchard, *Witchcraft, Oracles and Magic among the Azande*, Oxford 1937. I have developed this discussion in an essay 'Method and Meaning' published in a *Festschrift* for Evans-Pritchard, edited by André Singer, Oxford 1971.

[9]*Insight,* 533.

[10]Cf. Paul Ricoeur, *De l'Interpretation*, Paris 1965.

[11]It is crucial to recognise the difference between meaning, the symbol, and analysis of the meaning. The data of the human scientist is not the material image merely but the image already meant. V. W. Turner in his *The Forest of Symbols*, Cornell 1968, when he writes that all ritual has meaning, seems to

fail to make this essential distinction; all ritual has meaning but not necessarily analysed theoretic meaning, just as all dreams are meaningful though not always theoretically understood—or even understood in a common-sense way by the waking subject, for the subject is mysterious to himself and his actions only faintly reveal to him his being.

[12]Cf. G. Durand, *op. cit.*, in which he notes the immediate semanticity of the symbol. The mere image is not immediately semantic but the image as expressed by the symbolising subject is already meaningful for it appears in a common semantic field; Durand's work is an effort to discover more accurately the properties of the field.

[13]*Insight*, 533. This interpretation is not theoretic—although it may be mystery linked to a theoretic meaning—but the spontaneous activity of intelligence operating within mythic consciousness.

[14]As Rollo May notes (*op. cit.* see note 5) the dream does not merely refer to something other than itself but provides the dreamer with the existential context of his living for the moment. Myth does not represent the real world which is reached in some other way; it at once manifests and is the real world; the subject's effective world is not discoverable by physics and chemistry, though these must eventually be invoked if his meaningfully constituted world is to be fully understood, but by discovering his meaning in which he lives.

[15]Acknowledgement of the possibility of ethnocentric interpretation reveals at least minimal advertence to a problem; but for the most part there is little sign of anything beyond this minimum.

[16]Of course the link has been made in different ways among authors as different as Freud, Jung, Sullivan, May, Turner, Eliade. Besides the question of the intention of truth there is the question that emerges from its consideration: is the function of the image the same in dreaming as in waking consciousness? The intention of truth is not merely an addendum to the image; it so penetrates the imagination of the waking subject as to invest his consciousness with a new modality. As James Joyce once wrote—'And the conscious mind? What do they know of that?'

[17]There is in dream an ambiguous liberation from conscious control which includes a liberation from rationality.

[18]Cf. Sullivan, *op. cit.*, 339; see also my paper 'Modalities of Consciousness', *Philosophical Studies*, Dublin 1970.

[19]Cf. Rollo May, *op. cit.* The dreamer's psychic orientation may be different from the orientation imposed in waking life; the dream then becomes not merely a release but also the symbol of psychic suggestion. Imagination—in dreaming and other modes—can exert on the subject a pressure to spontaneous expansion which calls for intelligent appreciation and incorporation in conscious control.

[20]So Mircea Eliade in *Mythes, Rêves et Mystères*, Paris 1957, correctly notes that myths are recounted and rites enacted at special times and in special places; commonly these times and places are interpreted by the actors as sacred and linked with the events of the sacred history; their prior symbolic meaning which underlies all interpretation is to provide a context as sleep provides the context of the dream and the theatre that of the drama. This is the basic symbol of separation which is variously thematised.

[21]Cf. M. Eliade, *op. cit.*

[22]The restriction may be associated with E. Durkheim's collective representations as determining communal meaning.

[23]*Insight*, 538.   [24]*Ibid.*, 541.   [25]*Ibid.*, xxiii.   [26]*Ibid.*, xxviii.

[27]*Ibid.*, 537–8.   [28]*Ibid.*, xxviii.

[29]*Collection* edited by F. E. Crowe, New York 1967, 219–36.

[30]*Insight*, xviii.

[31]A significant phase in the operation of art as expansion is that it can break through barriers of distortion to reveal, if only in passing, the possibilities of the subject. Thus all art is political inasmuch as it interrogates every system which would offer a premature and restricted definition and consequent context of man.

[32]*Insight*, 432.

[33]*Ibid.*, 600.

[34]*Ibid.*, 473; cf. also Lonergan, *Collection*, 243.

[35]*Insight*, 534; 549.

[36]*Ibid.*, 543; *Collection*, 219.

[37]The consequences of overlooking the inherent dynamism of mythic consciousness are revealed in contemporary confusion over the notion of development, the direction of progress and the meaning of a comparative method.

[38]Professor Evans-Pritchard frequently—for instance in *Theories of Primitive Religion*, Oxford 1967—criticises Frazer for imputing to primitives a mentality similar to that of the investigator; but in other places he is equally clear that an anthropologist is not competent to judge the conceptions of another people. The crucial questions of course are, Should he become competent? and Is such competence possible?

[39]That ideas, images and expressions vary is, needless to say, agreed; but the manner in which these different expressions etc. emerge from viewpoints or mentalities gets hardly more than verbal attention.

[40]Pedagogically the critic will attempt to show that the meaning of the words is more intricate than is generally recognised.

[41]*Insight*, Ch. xvii, 'Metaphysics, Mystery and Myth'.

[42]*Collection*, 246ff.   [43]Cf. *ibid.*, 176–7.   [44]*Insight*, 535.

[45]*Insight*, 474.

[46]Cf. Paul Ricoeur, *Finitude et Culpabilité*, Paris 1960, Vol. II, the chapter entitled 'Le Symbole donne a penser'.

[47]*Insight*, 475–6.

[48]Cf. 'De Ex-sistentia' in *De Constitutione Christi*, Rome 1956.

[49]*Insight*, 547.

[50]This position may be contrasted with Durand's theory of the place of symbolism in living (*op. cit.* and *L'imagination Symbolique*, Paris 1964). I differ from him in that I do not consider that theoretic meaning in which the intention of truth achieves its critical and directive role is to be placed in a particular category on the same level as other symbolising. It may be true that classical insistence on rationality carried with it a stress on a certain symbolic scheme which reinforced this tendency to the exclusion of other equally important symbolic expressions and integrations. But in the contemporary

effort to achieve a new control of meaning it would be disastrous to fail to distinguish between the intention of being and its proper unfolding and admittedly partial symbolisations of man as a rational animal. Durand's own effort is to discover and implement the discovery in education of the human symbolic fields; he does not intend that his own work be merely a partial symbolic expression.

[51]*Collection*, 245.   [52]*Ibid.*, 245–6.
[53]*Insight*, 543; *Collection*, 114–20; cf. also note 50.
[54]*Insight*, 546–8; *Collection*, 136–7.   [55]*Insight*, 548.
[56]*Collection*, 136   [57]*Insight*, 548.
[58]On this development see R. G. Collingwood, *The Principles of Art*, Oxford 1937; S. K. Langer, *Mind: a Study of Human Feeling*, Baltimore 1967; H. Read, *A Concise History of Modern Sculpture*, London 1964. It is worth noting that in her idea of art as a development from earlier virtualities Mrs. Langer differs from E. Cassirer for whom myth seems to have been a completed symbolic form; as indeed, though in different terms, it was for Lévy-Bruhl.
[59]Cf. my 'Modalities of Consciousness', *Philosophical Studies*, 1970.
[60]Recently there is a greater acknowledgement of the meaning subject particularly perhaps in the criticism of painting but he often remains obscure and ill-defined. In philosophical hermeneutics, of course, the signifying subject is the theme of much investigation. Already in C. S. Pierce the meaning relation is considered triadic not dyadic (cf. S. K. Langer, *The Practice of Philosophy*, New York 1930, 122), and H. J. Pos in an issue of the *Revue Internationale de Philosophie* in 1939 remarks that Husserl came to the view that 'the chief task of linguistic philosophy, or phenomenology, is to regain an awareness of the speaking subject' cf. M. Merleau-Ponty, 'Phenomenology and the Sciences of Man', E. tr. John Wild, in *The Primacy of Perception*, ed. James M. Edie, Northwestern University Press 1964, p. 82 (The date of the original is 1961.) It is interesting to note a rejection of the dyadic account of the meaning relation in Roland Barthes' 'Historical Discourse', in *Structuralism: a Reader* ed. M. Lane, Jonathan Cape, London 1970, p. 154: 'Like all discourse with pretensions to "realism", historical discourse believes it need recognise no more than two terms, referent and expression, in its semantic model.'
[61]*Insight*, 198.   [62]*Collection*, 257–8.
[63]*Carnets de Lucien Lévy-Bruhl*, ed. M. Leenhardt, Paris 1949. For a fuller discussion of this point see my 'Method and Meaning' in *Essays Presented to E. E. Evans-Pritchard* edited by Singer, Blackwells, Oxford 1971.
[64]Concentration has been on the fact that a statement was untrue but little attention was paid to the equally salient fact that it was thought to be true or intended to be true.
[65]*Insight*, 638.   [66]*Collection*, 257–8.   [67]*Insight*, xxix.
[68]*Insight*, 548.

IMMEDIACY AND THE MEDIATION OF BEING: AN ATTEMPT TO ANSWER BERNARD LONERGAN (pp. 33–48)

[1]B. J. Lonergan, 'Metaphysics as Horizon', *Gregorianum* 44 (1963) 307–18; reprinted in *The Current* 5 (1964) 6–23; also in E. Coreth, *Metaphysics* (E. tr. J. Donceel) New York 1968, 197–219, which I shall quote in the following.

²E. Coreth, *Metaphysik. Eine methodisch-systematische Grundlegung*, Innsbruck 1961. In what follows I shall be referring to the 2nd German edition of 1964.

³'. . . I should not equate metaphysics with the total and basic horizon, the *Gesamt-und Grundwissenschaft*. Metaphysics, as about being, equates with the objective pole of that horizon; but metaphysics, as science, does not equate with the subjective pole', 'Metaphysics as Horizon', 218. 'The critique, accordingly, has to issue in a transcendental doctrine of methods with the method of metaphysics just one among many and so considered from a total viewpoint. For latent in the performance of the incarnate inquirer not only is there a metaphysics that reveals the objective pole of the total horizon but also there is the method of performing which, thematised and made explicit, reveals the subjective pole in its full and proper stature', *ibid.*, 219.

⁴*Ibid.*, 218 f. and *Insight, passim.*

⁵Even in Lonergan, however, the phenomenological basis remains very 'formal' in so far as he limits himself to the common structures of understanding, particularly of scientific understanding, and does not try to embrace the concrete, socially and historically moulded world of experience and understanding of man's, as of an 'incarnate inquirer's' ('Metaphysics as Horizon', 218f.).We shall come back to this point.

⁶In this connection, cf. my book: *Grundfragen der Hermeneutik: Ein philosophischer Beitrag*, Freiburg 1969, especially 82f. and 104ff.

⁷'Metaphysics as Horizon', 218f.

⁸See *Insight*, 375f.

⁹*Ibid.*, 375. Cf. also O. Muck, *Die transzendentale Methode in der scholastischen Philosophie der Gegenwart*, Innsbruck 1964, 253.

¹⁰For the differentiation between 'Subject as Subject' and 'Subject as Object', cf. my *Metaphysik* par. 18 (150f.) and par. 19 (193ff.).

¹¹Concerning the overcoming of the Subject-Object-split, cf. *Grundfragen der Hermeneutik*, especially 104–15.

¹²Cf. *Metaphysik* par. 13 (134ff.).   ¹³Cf. *ibid.* par. 14 (140ff.).

¹⁴A very thorough discussion of this point is to be found in: G. B. Sala, 'Seinserfahrung und Seinshorizont nach E. Coreth und B. Lonergan', *Zeitschrift fur Katholische Theologie* 89 (1967) 294–338, especially 298ff.; for this reason I take this opportunity to express my position briefly on the matter.

¹⁵These words originate from Hegel's sharp criticism of Schelling's *absoluter Identität*. 'Dies Eine Wissen, das im Absoluten alles gleich ist, der unterscheiden-den und erfüllten oder Erfüllung suchenden und fordernden Erkenntnis entgegenzusetzen, oder sein Absolutes für die Nacht auszugeben, worin, wie man zu sagen pflegt, alle Kühe schwarz sind, ist die Naivität der Leere an Erkenntnis': G. W. F. Hegel, *Phänomenologie des Geistes*, ed. J. Hoffmeister, Hamburg 1952, 19. The same holds analogically for a knowledge about 'being as being', which could not be further differentiated and concretised.

¹⁶See E. G. Gilson, *Réalisme thomiste et critique de la connaissance*, Paris 1939, to which also Lonergan particularly refers, see his 'Metaphysics as Horizon', 204ff.

¹⁷'. . . l'apprehension de l'être par l'intellect consiste à voir directement le concept d'être dans n'importe quelle donnée sensible': Gilson, *ibid.*, 215.

[18]Cf. *Metaphysik* par. 83 (456ff.).

[19]'Being . . . is the objective of the pure desire to know': *Insight*, 348. 'Being, then, is (1) all that is known, and (2) all that remains to be known': *ibid.*, 350. Cf. O. Muck, *op. cit.*, 252.

[20]This kind of definition is not called 'operative definition' by Lonergan himself, but by O. Muck, *op. cit.*, 252, in view of Lonergan's method.

[21]'This definition assigns, not what is meant by being, but how that meaning is to be determined. It asserts that if you know, then you know being; it asserts that if you wish to know, then you wish to know being; but it does not settle whether you know or what you know, whether your wish to know will be fulfilled or what you will know when it is fulfilled', *Insight*, 350; cf. O. Muck, *op. cit.*

[22]'. . . for Professor Gilson being (p. 225) or the concept of being (pp. 215, 226) is "seen" in the data of sense. But for Fr Coreth being is what is asked about with respect to the data of sense. So far from being seen in data, being, for Fr Coreth, is what is intended by going beyond the data. For questioning goes beyond an already known to an unknown that is to be known: for Fr Coreth the already known is the datum, and the unknown to be known is being', 'Metaphysics as Horizon', 214.

[23]*Metaphysik,* par. 31, Zusatz (221), par. 39 (254), par. 62, 2 (358), par. 70 (395).

[24]'Metaphysics as Horizon', 218f.

[25]*Ibid.*

[26]Cf. my article, 'Die Welt des Menschen als Phänomen und Problem'; *Neue Erkenntnisprobleme in Philosophie und Theologie* (Festschrift für Josef de Vries), Freiburg 1968, 39–63; also: *Grundfragen der Hermeneutik* especially 72–82.

[27]I have tried to show this more in detail in the article: 'Hermeneutik und Metaphysik', *Zeitschrift für Katholische Theologie*, 90 (1968) 422–50; also in *Grundfragen der Hermeneutik* especially 184–99.

[28]Cf. *Grundfragen der Hermeneutik*, 197ff.

LONERGAN AND DEWEY ON JUDGEMENT (pp. 79–92)

[1]John Dewey, *Experience and Nature*, New York 1958, 135.

[2]*Ibid.*, 21.   [3]*Ibid.*, XII.   [4]*Insight*, 348.

[5]Lonergan, 'Cognitional Structure', *Continuum* 11, 3 (Autumn 1964), 540.

[6]*Insight*, 350.   [7]*Experience and Nature*, 15.   [8]*Ibid.*, 7.   [9]*Ibid.*, 5.

[10]*Ibid.*, 151.   [11]*Ibid.*, 23.   [12]'Cognitional Structure', 531.

[13]Dewey, *The Quest for Certainty*, New York 1960, 86.

[14]*Experience and Nature*, 163.

[15]Cf. Dewey, *Problems of Men*, New York 1946, 343.

[16]'Cognitional Structure', 535.   [17]*Insight*, 552.

[18]Cf. Dewey, *Logic: The Theory of Inquiry*, New York 1938, 129.

[19]*Ibid.*, 104.   [20]*Ibid.*, 66.   [21]*Ibid.*, 105.   [22]*Ibid.*, 120.

[23]*Ibid.*, 121.   [24]*Ibid.*   [25]*Ibid.*   [26]*Insight*, 287.   [27]*Ibid.*

[28]*Ibid.*, 284.   [29]*Ibid.*   [30]*Ibid.*, 286.   [31]'Cognitional Structure', 534.

[32]*Ibid.*, 542. Italics mine.

[33]Dewey, 'Qualitative Thought', *The Symposium* i (1930), 5–32. This article can also be found in *John Dewey on Experience, Nature and Freedom,* ed. Richard Bernstein, New York 1960, 176-198.

THE LOGIC OF FRAMEWORK TRANSPOSITIONS (pp. 93–114)

[1]Published here with kind permission of the *International Philosophy Quarterly* in which this paper appeared in the Fall issue of 1971.

[2]Wilfred Sellars expressed his view in *Science, Perception and Reality* (London 1963), chap. i and in a more developed form in *Science and Metaphysics* (London 1968).

[3]*Insight*, 392 and *passim.* See also my 'Horizon, Objectivity and Reality in the Physical Sciences', *International Phil. Qrtly*, vii (1967), 375-412.

[4]For example, N. R. Hanson, *Patterns of Discovery*, London 1961; P. K. Feyerabend, 'Problems of Empiricism', in *Beyond the Edge of Certainty*, ed. R. G. Colodny, Englewood Cliffs, N.J. 1955, 145–60.

[5]See Rudolf Luneburg, *Mathematical Analysis of Binocular Vision*, Princeton 1947.

[6]See my 'Toward a New Analysis of the Pictorial Space of Vincent van Gogh' (to be published).

[7]See my 'Horizon, Objectivity and Reality in the Physical Sciences', *op. cit.*

[8]*Ibid.* The term is also used by Lonergan who defines it as 'the maximum field of vision from a determinate standpoint', 'Metaphysics as Horizon', *Cross Currents* xvi (1966), 489.

[9]I am using 'descriptive statement' for any statement of fact whether it uses experiential or explanatory conjugates.

[10]This has been shown by the author in 'Complementarity, Context-dependence and Quantum Logic', *Foundations of Physics,* I (1970), 95–110.

[11]Bohr would hardly have endorsed the claim that $L_{A \oplus B}$ is a new kinematic language that neither contains nor is contained by the descriptive language of classical physics. Cf. my 'Complementarity . . .', *op. cit.*

[12]For the properties of lattices, see G. Birkhoff, *Lattice Theory*, 2nd edn. Rhode Is. 1948.

[13]See, for example, E. Gilson, *The Christian Philosophy of St Thomas Aquinas*, London 1957; L. B. Geiger, *La participation dans la philosophie de St Thomas d'Aquin*, Paris 1942; C. Fabro, *Participazione e causalita*, Turin 1960.

[14]Mario Bunge, *Scientific Research II*, New York 1968, 47.

[15]Antonio de Nicolas has found an illustration of this lattice in the implicit philosophy of the Rigveda, cf. his *Four-dimensional Man* (to be published by Chapman, London).

[16]See A. Eddington, *The Nature of the Physical World*, Cambridge 1920, xi-xiii.

[17]Lonergan, *Insight*, 79.

[18]W. Sellars, *Science, Perception and Reality*, chapter 1.

[19]Lonergan, *Insight*, 303-4.

[20]For instance, in their contributions to *Criticism and the Growth of Knowledge*, ed. Lakatos and Musgrove, London 1970.

²¹Thomas Swing is using a 'dialectic of incommensurables' that may well exemplify the description given above, as the theme of his study of medieval and post-medieval cultural history.

WILHELM DILTHEY'S CRITIQUE OF HISTORICAL REASON AND BERNARD LONERGAN'S META-METHODOLOGY (pp. 115–66)

¹In discussions within the German context I have found it helpful not to refer to Lonergan's method as transcendental but as meta-method. The differences between Lonergan's method and *Transzendentalphilosophie* (Kant or Husserl) are rather basic. Perhaps of equal significance are the differences between meta-method and the transcendental Thomist trend initiated by Maréchal. So, for example, on Lonergan's differences from Coreth, cf. Lonergan, *Collection*, 202–20; and G. Sala, 'Seinserfahrung und Seinshorizont', *Zeitschrift für Kath. Theologie*, 89 (1967) 294–338. Also instructive are the misunderstandings which arise when Lonergan is grouped into this trend, cf. the misinterpretations of Lonergan's position in Muck, *Die transzendentale Methode*, Innsbruck 1964, 235, 247–9, 251; and in Holz, *Transzendentalphilosophie und Metaphysik*, Mainz 1966, 97–9, 134, 161. Hence it is not surprising that J. Donceel hesitates in identifying Lonergan with the Maréchal trend, see *Continuum*, 7 (1969).

²*Spirit as Inquiry*, New York 1964, 26.

³*Gesammelte Schriften*, Stuttgart 1956-,V, 12. Henceforth roman numerals with page references will be to this authoritative edition of Dilthey's works, the roman numerals referring to the respective volume.

⁴Cf. *Der Junge Dilthey*, Stuttgart 1960, 79–80; also I, xviii, 36, 116, 402–3, 418–19; V, 45, 317–18, 144, 196; VII, 10, 117, 278; VIII, 174–5. Of the secondary literature cf. Bollnow, *Dilthey*, Stuttgart 1966, 18–20; H. Diwald, *Wilhelm Dilthey. Erkenntnistheorie und Philosophie der Geschichte*, Göttingen 1963, 16–17, 26–30, 34–6, 43–6; P. Hünermann, *Der Durchbruch geschictlichen Denkens im 19. Jahrhundert*, Freiburg 1967, 134, 147–8; P. Krausser, *Kritik der endlichen Vernunft*, Frankfurt 1968, 60–65.

⁵See Dilthey's 'Breslauer Ausarbeitung' from his *Einleitung in die Geisteswissenschaften*, published in Krausser, *op. cit.*, 224–5.

⁶Cf. pp. 123, 127, 145. Krausser is especially convinced of the need to reinvestigate Dilthey in the light of modern systems-analysis, *op. cit. passim*; and see also Krausser's 'Dilthey's revolution in the theory and structure of scientific enquiry and rational behaviour', *Rev. Metaphysics*, 22 (1968), 26off.

⁷*Der Junge Dilthey, Briefe und Tagebücher*, 79–80.

⁸Cf. V, 275: 'Der Mensch ist geschichtlich durch und durch'; and so in history 'der Mensch sich selbst erkennt'. See also VII, 224, 250, 279.

⁹Dilthey was convinced of the importance of the genetic method of Fichte, cf. XIV/2, 661–2. But he corrected this profoundly by insisting on the independent existence of the object. As we shall see, he had difficulties with this 'objektiver Geist', cf. p. 139ff. above.

¹⁰Thus Dilthey transformed the three-faculty doctrine on man's interiority (*Verstand, Gemüt, Wille*) into dynamically correlated functions. Correlative to this, history was not understood in reference to a transcendent: 'Das Wesen

der Geschichte ist die geschichtliche Bewegung selber, und wenn man dieses Wesen Zweck nennen will, so ist sie allein der Zweck der Geschichte.'(*Der Junge Dilthey*, 190; see also VII, 172).

[11]Cf. Dilthey's 'Ideen über eine beschreibende und zergliedernde Psychologie', V, 139–240; see also Habermas, *Erkenntnis und Interesse*, Frankfurt 1968, 185–7.

[12]Cf. Gadamer, *Wahrheit und Methode*, Tubingen 1965, 210–13; and Mohanty, *Edmund Husserl's Theory of Meaning*, Hague 1969.

[13]Cf. pp. 133–7, 143–5 above.

[14]Cf. Lonergan, *Insight*, 135, 250–54, 375–84, 671–2.

[15]Cf. V, 144, 136–7, 151, 198, 238; VII, 3–23, 26–7.

[16]Cf. Bollnow, *op. cit.*, 18–23; also M. Riedel, 'W. Dilthey und das Problem der Metaphysik', *Philosophisches Jahrbuch*, 76 (1969), 339–40.

[17]Cf. Diwald, *op. cit.*, 145–53.

[18]Cf. his *Poetics*, VI, 103–287; the interrelating of philosophical world-views, V, 400–404; VIII, 15–24; on his intentions to apply this also to religion, cf. L. Renthe-Fink, *Geschichtlichkeit*, Göttingen 1968, 102–10.

[19]Cf. I, 351–85; VII, 173, 335–45; VIII, 190–96.

[20]Cf. V, 145, 356–63; VII, 137–38.

[21]Cf. C. P. Snow, *The Two Cultures*, London 1959; F. Matson, *The Broken Image*, New York 1964; J. Habermas, *Technik und Wissenschaft als 'Ideologie'*, Frankfurt 1968, 104–19.

[22]Cf. Habermas, *Theorie und Praxis*, Berlin 1963, 231–57; G. Picht, *Wahrheit Vernunft Verantwortung*, Stuttgart 1969, 343–407; H. Albert, *Traktat über kritische Vernunft*, Tübingen 1968, 1–79.

[23]Cf. V, 356–63, 406–13; VIII, 206–19.

[24]Cf. V, 361–6; I, xv–xx, 116–20; V, 146–53, 406; VII, 88–120.

[25]Cf. McLuhan, *Understanding Media: The Extensions of Man*, New York 1965, 38. I do not mean to suggest that the natural sciences are transforming themselves into human sciences but that from two directions the natural sciences are being forced to take into account (in a way they previously did not) the constitutive meaning of subjectivity. First, in the intrusion of the subject into the observation process, or rather the recognition that the subject must be taken into account. Secondly, the vast extent of the natural sciences' effective control and transformation of natural processes increases the need to find the norms for this transformation, not in nature, but in mind or constitutive interiority. Cf. my short essay 'Science' in *Prophetic Voices*, New York 1969, 202–5.

[26]Cf. Heelan, *Quantum Mechanics and Objectivity*, Hague 1965: A. Bucholz, *Die grosse Transformation*, Stuttgart 1968; H. Frank (ed.), *Kybernetik— Brucke zwischen den Wissenschaften*, Frankfurt 1966.

[27]Cf. Habermas, *Tecknik und Wissenschaft als 'Ideologie'*, 48–103; N. Wiener, *The Human Use of Human Beings*, New York 1954, especially pp. 250 and 280; also Matson, *op. cit.*, 161ff.

[28]Cf. Wolf-Dieter Narr, *Theoriebegriffe und Systemtheorie*, Stuttgart 1969; G. Radnitzky, *Contemporary Schools of Metascience*, Göteburg 1968, vols. I and II on the Anglo-Saxon and Continental schools of meta-science respectively. Cf. also on the sociology of knowledge, e.g. P. Berger, *The Social Con-*

struction of Reality, New York 1966 and Wolff, *Versuch zu einer Wissenssoziologie*, Berlin 1968.

[29]Cf. note 25 above; note the convergence of the two in the growing need experienced for planning and coordination in terms of rationally constituting the present in the light of the future, e.g. the studies of the Hudson-Institute; cf. also my 'Towards a Synthetisation of the Sciences', *Phil. of Sciences*, 32 (1965) 182–91; and K. Deutsch, *The Nerves of Government*, New York 1963.

[30]Cf. V, 26f., 175, 180, 195, 355–6; IV, 217–28; VII, 148–52. On the tetradic character of Hegel's dialectic with its implicit recognition of the impossibility of total synthesis, cf. J. van der Meulen, *Hegel. Die Gebrochene Mitte*, Hamburg 1958, and T. Koch, *Differenz und Versöhnung*, Gütersloh 1967.

[31]Cf. V, 200–240, 400–406; VII, 3–23, 228–45; VIII, 171–84, 188–9.

[32]Cf. VII, 146–88, 205–207; VIII, 78–80.

[33]Cf. V, 364–5; VIII, 3–9.   [34]VIII, 172.

[35] On Godel's theorem cf. J. Ladrière, *Les limitations internes des formalismes*, Louvain 1957; H. Hermes, *Aufzählbarkeit, Entscheidbarkeit, Berechenbarkeit*, Berlin 1961, and the interesting applications to theological hermeneutics by H. Peukert, 'Zur formalen Systemtheorie und zue hermeneutischen Problematik einer politischen Theologie', *Diskussion zue politischen Theologie*, Mainz 1969, 82–95. On General Systems Theory, cf. Narr, *op. cit.*, 170–82; and Kuhn, *The Structure of Scientific Revolutions*, Chicago 1962. On the debates between Structuralism and Marxism, as well as Existentialism, cf. L. Sebag, *Marxisme et Structuralisme*, Paris 1964; L. Althusser, *Pour Marx*, Paris 1965. On the Popper-Frankfurt debate, cf. E. Topitsch (ed.), *Logik der Sozialwissenschaften*, Cologne 1965; also Narr, *op. cit.*, 45–83.

[36]In this connection note Krausser's remarks on the possible contribution of Dilthey in *Kritik der endlichen Vernunft*, 210-19. As will be seen, Krausser's interpretation of Dilthey is one-sided and completely overlooks the problem which Dilthey himself saw so clearly: if all systems are temporary or (scientifically) hypothetical, still the recurrent patterns operative in their formation-correction-replacement are not basically revisable.

[37]Cf. V, 378–98; VI, 144–57, 288–305; VIII, 172–3.

[38]Cf. VIII, 172–3; XIV/1, 100–47; cf. also on his projected analysis of dogmas, Renthe-Fink, *op. cit.*, 99–110.

[39]Cf. VI, 185–8; VIII, 172–3.

[40]Cf. the theologies of secularisation, death of God, de-hellenisation of dogma; and also the theologies of hope, of revolution, and political theology.

[41] Cf. J. B. Metz, *Zur Theologie der Welt*, Mainz 1968, 99–146, and *Diskussion zur politischen Theologie*, Mainz 1969, 217–301; also G. Picht, *Mut zur Utopie*, Munich 1969, 131–54. The significance of meta-method lies in its ability to appropriate both modern scientific-historical consciousness and religious consciousness; the question is how intellectual and moral conversion is related to religious conversion and how all three are ongoing processes.

[42]Cf. W. Hofmann, *Grundlagen der modernen Kunst*, Stuttgart 1966, 243–496; T. Adorno in *Aspekte der Modernität* edited by Steffen, Göttingen 1965, 129–49.

[43]See *Wahrheit und Methode*, 221-8, especially 225. Far from being the motive force in empirical science, a method of universal doubt would destroy such science although it would leave the existential subject untouched. Cf.

Lonergan, *Insight* 408–11; on belief in science, *ibid.*, 427–8, 704–5, 712–13.

⁴⁴Cf. *Sein und Zeit*, Tübingen 1963, 10th edn., 356–64, especially 363. Cf. also E. Tugendhat, *Der Wahrheitsbegriff bei Husserl und Heidegger*, Berlin 1970, 2nd edn., 292–8.

⁴⁵For Dilthey the reality-itself of interiority is the given there-ness of *Selbigkeit* or *Innerlichkeit* and any statement about this experienced is 'objektiv wahr' in so far as it utters the occurrence of the experience (*Erlebnis*)—i.e., any expression is true in so far as either through experience or re-experience (*Nacherleben*) it manifests the given there-ness of interiority, the 'für-mich-dasein eines Zustandes'. Cf. pp. 134–7, 144–6 above. This meant that all expressions, in so far as they occur, must express some aspect of interiority and therefore be understandable through re-experience (cf. p. 137 above). Now Heidegger's ontological radicalisation of understanding and disclosure seems to curiously reflect a similar pattern. In *Sein und Zeit* ¶44 the main concern of Heidegger is *not how* truth discloses but *that* it discloses, so that *any* manner of disclosure is related to truth and the luminosity of 'there' is seen as the 'ursprünglichste Phänomen der Wahrheit'. But when all understanding is characterised as truth one no longer inquires into the truth of understanding since as disclosure it already is truth. Cf. Tugendhat, *op. cit.*, 350, 356–62, 399. Compare Tugendhat's complaint that Heidegger gives no concrete formal regulatives (*op. cit.*, 360, 376, 399) with Diwald's remarks on the lack of criteria for veracity in Dilthey (*op. cit.*, 157, 69–71, 76–7, 156–8).

⁴⁶There is the question of whether or not Gadamer, in taking over Heidegger's notion of truth (cf. *op. cit.*, 463–4), comes closer to Dilthey than he suspected, cf. Tugendhat, *op. cit.*, 358 note 35, and C. V. Bormann, 'Die Zweideutigkeit der hermeneutischen Erfahrung', *Phil. Rundschau*, 16 (1969) 92–119.

⁴⁷Cf. *Erkenntnis und Interesse*, 224–6.

⁴⁸Cf. *ibid.*, 252–7, 262–300; *Wissenschaft als Ideologie*, 146–68. On the need for Habermas to clarify his notion of 'Erkenntnisleitende Interesse' cf. N. Lobkowicz, 'Interesse und Objektivität', *Phil. Rundschau*, 16 (1969) 249–73; also R. Bubner, 'Was ist kritische Theorie?' *ibid.*, 213–49, especially 243–7.

⁴⁹Cf. T. Prufer, 'A Protreptic: What is Philosophy?', *Studies in Philosophy*, Washington, D.C. 1963, 1–19; and also W. Oelmüller, *Die unbefriedigte Aufklärung*, Frankfurt 1969, 9–34.

⁵⁰On horizon, cf. D. Tracy, 'Horizon Analysis and Eschatology', *Continuum*, 6 (1968) 166–79; Heelan, 'Horizon, Objectivity and Reality in the Physical Sciences', *I.P.Q.* (1967) 375–412. That the basic horizon is historicality, cf. Lonergan's *Hermeneutics* (privately circulated lecture copy) 14–16. If it were not historicality then Lonergan would not be able to explicate functional specialisation as he has, cf. *Gregorianum*, 50 (1970) 2ff.

⁵¹Cf. Lonergan's notion of 'a transcendental doctrine of methods' in *Collection*, 219–20. Also *Insight*, 393.

⁵²Cf. Prufer, *op. cit.*, 13–16; Richardson, *Heidegger—Through Phenomenology to Thought*, Hague 1963, 634–5. Note also Bormann's question to Gadamer, *op. cit.*, 118: 'Doch wie erfahren wir diese Verbindung von Objekt und Subjekt, von Sein und Verstehen?' and G. Bauer's remarks in *Geschichtlichkeit, Wege und Irrwege eines Begriffes*, Berlin 1963, 160.

[53]Cf. *Insight*, 566.

[54]Cf. Tracy, *op. cit.* and Lonergan, *Insight*, 380–81, 393, 685–6, 222–42.

[55]Cf. Habermas' critique of Marx for conceiving 'Reflection nach dem Muster der Produktion', *Erkenntnis und Interesse* 59–87. Thus the sources of the dialectic must be sought elsewhere if one is to critically guide the transition from industrial to post-industrial society, cf. H. Kahn and A. Wiener, *Ihr werdet es erleben*, Vienna 1967, 40, 175ff. on the increase of tertiary and quartiary professions and the transition to a 'Lerngesellschaft'. Also relevant to the transition is Heilbroner's thesis on the dialectic between capitalism and science, see his *The Limits of American Capitalism*, New York 1965, and the qualifications made by F. Lundberg in his *The Rich and the Super-rich*, New York, Bantam ed. 1969, 930–33.

[56]*The Human Use of Human Beings*, 250, 280.

[57]Cf. F. Matson, *The Broken Image*, 247: 'When man is the subject, the proper understanding of science leads unmistakably to the science of understanding'. See also M. Polanyi, *Personal Knowledge*, New York 1958, and Habermas, *Wissenschaft als Ideologie*, 113, on the need for a scientifically explicated *Weltverständnis* for guiding practical decisions.

[58]Cf. Narr, *op. cit.*, 63–5, 79–83; Radnitzky, *op. cit.*, Vol. II.

[59]*Wahrheit und Methode*, 224–5. Dilthey was as strong as Gadamer on the impossibility of presuppositionless thought (cf. Krausser, *op. cit.*, 228; VIII, 182) but he did not identify *Voraussetzung* with *Vorurteil*. On the Enlightenment, cf. H. Blumenberg's more positive presentation of theoretical 'curiositas', in *Die Legitimität der Neuzeit*, Frankfurt 1966, 203–432.

[60]Cf. VIII, 192–3, 204, 225; I, xv, 351–9; III, 210–68; V, 352–63; VII, 89–117, 335–8; *Briefwechsel zwischen W. Dilthey und Grafen Paul Yorck von Wartenburg*, Halle 1923, n. 1104. Henceforth this will be known as *Briefwechsel*.

[61]V, 31–73 especially 31–6, 189; *Briefwechsel*, n. 104; VII, 79–88, 148: here Dilthey refers to the *Geisteswissenschaften* as those sciences dealing with what is constituted by the human spirit or directly constitutive of it: descriptive-analytic psychology, sociology, law, history, political science, economics, aesthetics, philosophy, religion, etc. Hence I have translated *Geisteswissenschaften* as 'human sciences'. For Dilthey human biology, physiology, neurology, etc. are *Naturwissenschaften* even though they deal with man, cf. VII, 81–2.

[62]Cf. I, 8–14, 14–21; VII, 3–19; Renthe-Fink, *op. cit.*, 107.

[63]I, xvii.

[64]I, xvii–xix, 9, 15, 37; VII, 26, 252, 255, 261–2; VIII, 186.

[65]I, 38, 42, 49, 51, 61, 64–6, 68; V, 136, 196, 265–6; VI, 62, 188–90, 228–41, 288–305; VII, 3–23, 79–88; Renthe-Fink, *op. cit.*, 106–13, 120–29.

[66]VII, 229, 228, 256, 261–2; Renthe-Fink, *op. cit.*, 82, 90, 107, 115–17, 120–5.

[67]VIII, 171; also I, 86–115.

[68]*Der Junge Dilthey*, 80; V, 88–9, 339–416; VIII, 171, 206–19.

[69]V, 136–7; VIII, 172.

[70]Cf. I, 14–21; V, 169, 237; VII, 88–93, 125; V, 223, 245–6, 242–58.

[71]I, 394; cf. also p. 198.   [72]Cf. V, 242–5; 434.   [73]V, 248.

[74]Cf. V, 249.   [75]Kant, *Kritik der reinen Vernunft*, B 275–9.

[76]*Ibid.*, A 117.   [77]*Ibid.*, B 156.

[78]Cf. Krausser, *op. cit.*, 46, 224–5; I, xviii, 418; VIII, 174–5.

[79]I, xvii–xviii, 10; V, 11, 145, 171–2, 238, 362; VI, 314–15; VII, 26–7.

[80]Cf. Krausser, *op. cit.*, 34, 42, 60–65; V, 171–5, 210, 238, 253–4.

[81]VII, 32–5; V, 95, 98–105, 108–11, 114–17.

[82] V, 95, 133, 98–105. On p. 133 Dilthey thought that this interpretation had removed the opposition between 'Spekulation und Leben oder Handeln', but on p. 198 of I he holds that the notion of correspondence between perception and thinking, between reality and being 'ist vollständig dunkel'. The reason for this may be found in V, 198, where he maintains that 'wir können niemals den Denkakt selbst mit Aufmerksamkeit auffassen'. Note Heidegger's critique of this in *Sein und Zeit*, 202–11.

[83]I, 363–73, 392–5, 404; V, 91–2, 242–58; VII, 32–5, 275, 295–303.

[84]I, 369; VII, 275: 'Vielmehr sind die ersten Wahrheiten als die nächsten Ausdrücke für eine Tatsache am wenigsten hypothetisch; je weiter die Allgemeinheit vorwärts schreitet, desto starker ist das Moment des Hypothetischen in ihr.'

[85]V, 153, VII, 125.

[86]Cf. notes 62 to 64 above; also V, 265, 332; VII, vii, 19, 146–7, 157, 191, 237, 309; VIII, 178.

[87]V, 136–7, 151–2, 156–7, 170–3, 175–9, 191–5; VIII, 15f.

[88]V, 5; also V, 195–6; VIII, 182; Diwald, *op. cit.*, 48.

[89]V, 145, 171–5, 363; VIII, 180–82, 15–19.

[90]Cf. V, 151–2, 197–201, 180; VII, 3–23, 82–3, 135, 279: 'Der Mensch erkennt sich nur in der Geschichte, nie durch Introspektion.' (Cf. Diwald's objection, *op. cit.*, 152–3); VIII, 13, 39, 176ff., *Briefwechsel* n. 58; on basic structures and acquired contexts: V, 176–84, 200–26.

[91]VII, vii, 152, 255–8; 262–3, 277; V, 228–9.

[92]V, 136–7, 142–5, 173, 175, 178–9, 189–90, 193–4, 197–200, 206, 237–40; VI, 145.

[93]Cf. VII, 79–88, especially 82–3.   [94]Cf. V, 90–138.   [95]I, 394–5.

[96]V, 197; cf. also V, 190, 196: one need not be aware of the processes in one's spontaneous living. See also VII, 26–7.   [97]V, 197.

[98]V, 200–1; VIII, 10–18; VII, 191; cf. Diwald, *op. cit.*, 38.

[99]Cf. Krausser, *op. cit.*, 229–33; V, 207–11; 98–100.

[100]V, 310, 328; VII, 23.

[101]Note that Dilthey took this classical doctrine over from Trendelenburg in terms of the typical world-views, cf. Trendelenburg, *Uber den letzten Unterschied der philosophischen Systeme*, Berlin 1955. Here one notes again the circular character of Dilthey's procedure: he experiences the cognitive-emotive-volitional structures, and not only individually but in historical contexts. Cf. J. Wach, 'Die Typenlehre Trendeleburgs und ihr Einfluss auf Dilthey', *Philosophie und Geschichte* II (1926).

[102]Cf. V, 11, 200, 263–5.   [103]V, 200, 95; VIII, 257–8.

[104]For detailed account of this, cf. Krausser, *op. cit.*, 95–100, 229–35.

[105]V, 204–5. This is important as it made it increasingly difficult for Dilthey to incorporate or relate the cognitive functions of knowing to his inner experienced there-ness of self-presence.

[106]Cf. pp. 131–2 above and V, 197.   [107]V, 206.

[108]V, 112; VII, 42–3. Note how the two-headed arrows indicate the growing complexification of the circular process from stimuli to response from reflex-mechanisms through elementary learning processes to the gradual articulation of an individual's ideals, values, goals.

[109]V, 177–83, 217, 226–37, 241–316.   [110]V, 185–90, 214–17.

[111]Cf. V, 215–19; VII, 8–9, 324–31.

[112]Compare Dilthey's remarks in 1880 (Krausser, *op. cit.*, 224–5) with those in 1896–7 (VIII, 182). Krausser totally overlooked the intention of Dilthey to overcome the hypothetical basis of the *Geisteswissenschaften* in his descriptive-analytic psychology. Put in terms of Krausser's own elaboration of the recurrent structures of finite reason—are these structures themselves *aufhebbar*? For Dilthey they were not.

[113] V, 171–6, 206, 221, 223–4. These three basic structures are not reducible to one another, cf. V, 212–13; VII, 137–8.

[114]VII, 309; also V, 226–37.

[115]Cf. I, 395; V, 226, 223–30, 251; also Diwald, *op. cit.*, 145–53.

[116]VII, 210–16, 225, 237–9, 257, 262–4.   [117]VII, 7; VIII, 13.

[118]VII, 26–7; V, 190, 196–7.

[119]VII, 3, 103, 295, 304–5, 309, 313–14; VIII, 233.

[120]VII, 6–9, 22–3, 121–9.

[121]IV, 219ff.; VII, 3, 31, 150, 157, 258, 271; VIII, 12.

[122]VII, 194–5; 29.   [123]VII, 6–7, 331.

[124]VII, 300, 307; V, 45; VII, 146, 219, 254. Note that Dilthey was ultimately unable to ground the transition from spontaneous historicality to the world of theory since, while *Erleben* was not perceptualist (not of the Subject as Object but the Subject as Subject), *Erkennen* and *Wissen*, as representative, were.

[125]VIII, 51; cf. I, 150–350.   [126]VII, 332–3; VIII, 174–5.

[127]Cf. V, 21, 341; VII, 160, 164, 316.   [128]VII, 316–17.

[129]VII, 30–31, 326; V, 319, 332.   [130]VII, 37.   [131]VII, 38.

[132]VII, 38, 42–3.

[133]VII, 38–9; cf. 25: 'Dass hier nicht nur eine Inhaltlichkeit im Erlebnis enthalten ist, sondern diese in einer Bewusstseinsart . . . (zeigen die Gegebenheit) wie sie die Wahrnehmung charakterisiert, oder die Annahme eines Tatbestandes . . . oder die Setzung von Realität im Urteil. Gleichviel welche Unterschiede zwischen einer Phantasievorstellung und einer Wahrnehmung bei gleichem Gegenstand, psychologisch angesehen, bestehen mögen . . . strukturell angesehen ist die *Art des Bewusstseins inbezug auf das Gegenständliche keine verschiedene.*' Thus perceptions, imaginative representations and judgements are structurally similar in objective comprehension.

[134]VII, 38, 316–17. Note also the influence of Schleiermacher here, XIV/1 p. 133: 'In der Ordnung der Begriffe drückt sich das Beharrliche und Wesentliche aus. Dagegen bezient sich das System unserer Urteile darauf, wie an diesem Beharrlichen und Wesentlichen der Wechsel der Bedingungen, das Spiel von Ursachen und Wirkungen die zufälligen und veränderlichen Zustande hervorbringt.' Thus concepts and judgements presuppose one another in circular fashion (121–2) but concepts themselves have an 'ursprüngliche Identität' with the objects (122) and knowing occurs both in the form of

concept and of judgement (125). Concepts dominate speculative knowing and judgements empirical and historical knowing (133). On Dilthey's interpretation as a whole, cf. XIV/1, 105–35

[135]VII, 38, 41.   [136]VII, 32.

[137]VII, 19, 194. Here one notices the perceptualism of knowing as contrasted with the awareness of feelings as experienced.

[138]VII, 30.

[139]VII, 30–1, 125, 244, cf. note 142 below.   [140]VII, 31–2.

[141]Cf. VII, 32, 139–40. On p. 9 Dilthey did formulate a principle of selection in terms of better and more conscious representations of the total *Zusammenhang*, but his own further elaboration reduced the principle of selection to one of classification.

[142]VII, 13, 18: 'Die Notwendigkeit der Beziehung zwischen einem bestimmten Erlebnis und dem entsprechenden Ausdruck des Psychischen wird unmittelbar erlebt. Es ist die schwierige Aufgabe der Struktur-psychologie, Urteile zu vollziehen, welche die strukturellen Erlebnisse mit dem Bewusstsein der Adäquation wiedergeben, die in einem Deckungsverhältnis zu bestimmten Erlebnissen stehen. Als unentbehrliche Grundlage dienen ihr dazu die in tausendjähriger Arbeit ausgebildeten und verfeinerten Ausdrucksformen . . .' Also 26–7: 'Jede Aussage über Erlebtes ist objektiv wahr, wenn sie zur Adäquation mit dem Erlebnis gebracht ist . . . sie sagt (als wahr) nur das Stattfinden des wahrnehmenden Verhaltens selber aus. Und dieser Bewusstseinstatbestand ist mir als Realität gegeben.' Also 125–7, 213–16, 38, 44. Now the 'Wesensbestimmungen' in judgements cannot as such be brought into adequation with experience since they transcend experience (note 139 above) but, Dilthey seems to maintain, in so far as they occur within the there-ness of self-presence, they are brought into adequation with experience not as determining the objectivity of their content (cf. p. 26) but simply as occurring. Five years later he was a bit more nuanced, cf. VII, 125: 'bei Ruckkehr zum Gegenstande dieser [Gegenstand] in der ganzen Fülle seines anschaulichen Daseins das Urteil oder den Begriff bewährt, verifiziert. Gerade für die Geisteswissenschaften ist es besonders wicntig, dass die ganze Frische und Macht des Erlebnisses dann direkt oder in der Richtung vom Verstehen zum Erleben hin zurückkehrt.' Here the object as being-there in its intuitive fullness verifies the judgements or concepts if it preserves them. In any case, the important point is that for Dilthey the reality-itself of inner experience consisted in that experience itself prior to any objective mental comprehension. The result is obvious: since he could not conceive of knowing as immediately given experience the experience itself takes on a noumenal character (cf. notes 121–2 above) to such an extent that Dilthey cannot brand other conceptualisations of this inner experience as false. Because it is *Unerschöpflich* and the normative is only in the empirically given, any expression must reveal something of interiority. On a certain similarity to Heidegger's more ontological notion of truth, cf. notes 44 and 45 above. Also Tugendhat, *op. cit.,* 344: 'Bei Heidegger selbst fehlt freilich die Unterscheidung zwischen dem faktischen Akt des Entdeckens und dem Entdecken *in specie* . . . [und es] ergibt sich eine Auffassung, derzufolge die Wahrheit nicht ein angemessenes Aufzeigen von einem unangemessenen unterscheidet, sondern ein aufgezeigtes Seiendes von

einem verborgenen: das Seiende *wird* wahr, wenn es faktisch aufgezeigt wird'. Cf. also 331–56.

[143]VII, 118; also 3, 71, 79, 82–3.

[144]VII, 212. Note that Dilthey was not advocating what is known as a strictly psychological interpretation of expressions in understanding, cf. VII, 19 and 85.

[145]VII, 213–16.   [146]VII, 118–20.   [147]VII, 196–204, 246–51.

[148]VII, 163–88, 251.   [149]VII, 308.   [150]VII, 150–52, 271.

[151]VII, 150, 308, 251.   [152]Cf. VII, 257.   [153]VII, 212–13.

[154]VII, 135.   [155]VII, 151.   [156]VII, 152.   [157]VII, 141–3.

[158]Cf. p. 133 above and compare with VII, 137–8, 141.

[159]VII, 141, 146–7.   [160]VII, 282.

[161]VII, 251. The 'Formen des Lebens' indicates that the *Realitätscharakter* of *Leben* extends also to *Lebensverlauf* (VII, 140) but beyond this individual sphere Dilthey is very vague.

[162]VII, 152–88, 228–45; cf. Diwald, *op. cit.*, 221–48.

[163]On the types of world-views, cf. V, 402–3; VIII, 75–118, 140–56. On their methodological presuppositions, VIII, 3–25, 157–62. Note that as Dilthey could only classify the many representations of interiority, so his effort to overcome the antinomies of the many philosophical systems could only achieve a classification of the antagonists without any hope for a lessening of the conflict, cf. VIII, 75–6, 220–35.

[164]Cf. E. Rothacker, *Logik und Systematik der Geisteswissenschaften,* Munich 1927, 52–67; Diwald, *op. cit.*, 210–11. This is evident in so far as Dilthey centred his entire analysis of interiority upon the emotive-valuational experience.

[165]VII, 153.   [166]VII, 145, 152.

[167]VII, 161–2; XIV/2, 657–9, 708; Krausser, *op. cit.*, 73–92.

[168]Cf. notes 154–8 above.

[169]VII, 244, 187; V, 225. Hence the importance of religion or metaphysics or the unconditioned for Dilthey's critique of historical reason, cf. VIII, 172. On Dilthey's ambiguous attitude in regard to metaphysics, cf. Hünermann, *op. cit.*, 192–206, 214–5, and the article of Riedel cited in note 16 above.

[170]VII, 262.   [171]VII, 173, 335–38.   [172]VII, 300; VIII, 172.

[173]VII, 9, 32, 38, 81, 128, 142–3, 145, 150, 153, 157, 161–2, 191, 211, 331. Note that one has here a parallel to Gadamer's dialectic of finitude and infinitude, cf. *Wahrheit und Methode,* 434, 449–9; and also *Kleine Schriften* I, Tübingen 1967, 111, where Gadamer sees the move to unlimited possibilities as through finitude.

[174]VII, 172, also 232–6.   [175]VII, 154–5, 191.

[176]VII, 171: 'Diese Regelmässigkeit bestimmte auch die bisherige Entwicklung und ihr ist die Zukünft unterworfen.' Cf. also 191, 72–3, 268ff.

[177]Cf. Dilthey's own attempts to ground the human sciences in this way (volumes I, VII, VIII *passim*), to interrelate all systems of philosophy (volumes V and VIII), to work out a poetics and aesthetics (vol. VI), a pedagogics and ethics (vol. VI, IX), and his desire to apply the method to religion (Renthe-Fink, *op. cit.*, 94–110).

[178]Cf. G. Picht, 'Die Kunst des Denkens' in *Wahrheit Vernunft Verantwortung,* 427–34.

[179]Cf. VII, 32–3.   [180]VII, 32.   [181]Cf. VII, 205–6.

[182]VII, 207; cf. also 19 and 85.

[183]Here, then, we find the criticism of Habermas in *Erkenntnis und Interesse*, 224–6 validated from a horizon diverse, yet related to his own.

[184]Cf. I, 198; VII, 206; VII, 18 and note 142 above.

[185]Cf. references to Diwald in note 45 above.

[186]Cf. VII, 151, 288–9, 359; Bollnow, *op. cit.*, 26–33; Diwald, *op. cit.*, 160, 185, 187, 222; and G. Lukács, *Von Nietzsche zu Hitler*, Frankfurt 1966, 113–35.

[187]Cf. *Wahrheit und Methode*, 218–28, 477–512.

[188]While the natural sciences mediate a meaning (or intelligible relationships) immanent in natural processes, the human sciences mediate the meanings which man himself constitutes, cf. Lonergan's 'The Absence of God in Modern Culture' (manuscript form, 1968) p. 5; also *Insight*, 235–6, 508–9; and *Collection*, 252–67.

[189]Cf. *Insight*, 253–4, 339–42; also G. Sala, *Das Apriori der Erkenntnis bei Kant und Lonergan* (Bonn, doctoral thesis, 1970).

[190]*Verbum: Word and Idea in Aquinas*, Notre Dame 1967, 88.

[191]Cf. *Briefwechsel* n. 48.   [192]*Insight*, xxviii.

[193]On the worlds of common sense, theory, interiority, cf. *De Methodo Theologie* (Rome, mss. 1962), 7–14. Also Tracy, 'Horizon Analysis and Eschatology', *Continuum*, 6 (1968), 166–79 and D. Tracy's doctoral dissertation, *The Development of the Notion of Theological Methodology in the works of B. J. Lonergan*, Rome 1969, 378–97.

[194]Cf. Gadamer, *Kleine Schriften*, 51–54. On pp. 49–51 Gadamer reiterates his notion of the sciences as seeking a Cartesian type of certitude. Cf. note 43 above.

[195]Cf. *Insight*, 181–89, 530–49.

[196]Cf. M. Riedel, 'Das Erkenntniskritische Motiv in Diltheys Theorie der Geisteswissenschaften', *Hermeneutik und Dialektik* I, Tübingen 1970, 233–9. Also the references in note 90 above.

[197]See *Collection*, 252–67; also the lectures: 'Theology and Man's Future', and 'The Absence of God in Modern Culture'.

[198]Cf. *Insight*, 306, 407.   [199]*Insight*, xviii, 748.   [200]Cf. *Collection*, 221–39.

[201]Cf. *Insight*, 174–5, 286–93, 300, 303–4, 397–8, 448–9, 558, 622–3, 713–18.

[202]*Collection*, 224–7, *Insight*, 326–8.

[203]*Insight*, 324ff. and *Collection*, 222–4.

[204]Cf. *Insight*, 335–6; also my article, 'Ascent from Human Consciousness to the Human Soul', *Insight, Review of Religion and Mental Health*, 3 (1964), 18–28.

[205]On judgement and the virtually unconditioned, cf. *Insight*, 271–316, 331, 340–41, 343–5, 366, 372, 377–8, 517–19, 549–52, 610, 653, 707–13.

[206]*Collection*, 227; *Insight*, 319–47.   [207]*Collection*, 228.

[208]Cf. *Insight*, 431–51; also Heelan, *Quantum Mechanics and Objectivity*, 8, 81–6, 109–11, 150–55, 156–66.

[209]*Collection*, 229f.

[210]*Insight*, 250–54. Also the references in note 208 above.

[211]Cf. *Insight*, 499–501.

[212]Cf. note 73 above and compare the references there with VII, 83.

²¹³Any analysis of the experiential components in objectivity is only via the structures of understanding and judgement. Cf. Heelan, 'Horizon, Objectivity and Reality in the Physical Sciences', *International Philosophical Quarterly*, (1967), 375ff.

²¹⁴Cf. VII, 152–88; also Diwald, *op. cit.*, 221–48, and Bollnow, *op. cit.*, 114–66.

²¹⁵Cf. Renthe-Fink, *op. cit.*, 120-30.

²¹⁶Cf. *Insight*, 448–9; on emergent probability, 115–28, and this in human history, 209–11 and references in note 201 above.

²¹⁷Cf. *Collection*, 223–4; *Insight*, 319–24, 348–64, especially 357–9 on being as the core of meaning.

²¹⁸*Insight*, 358.

²¹⁹Cf. *Insight*, 458–79, and *De Methodo Theologiae*, 1–4.

²²⁰Cf. *Insight*, 184–5.

²²¹Cf. *Insight*, 293–9, 304–309, 357–9. Here I have not included the important notion of instrumental acts of meaning, which apply to the expression of the other acts, cf. *Insight*, 553–8, 568–73.

²²²Cf. *Insight*, 176, 177, 292, 426–7, 544–5, 554–5. On the genetic development of language and its relation to consciousness, cf. L. S. Wygotski, *Denken und Sprechen*, Stuttgart 1969.

²²³On implicit definitions, cf. *Insight*, 12–13, 392, 435, 437, 491–2.

²²⁴Cf. *Insight*, 595–633. On the function of therapy, *ibid.*, 191-206.

²²⁵On the transition from description (relations to empirical consciousness within the common-sense mode) to explanation (relation of things to one another) cf. *Insight*, 247, 291–2, 295–6, 345, 415, 436, 504–5, 538–9, 546–7. Note that Lonergan's thematisation of the basic horizon is explanatory, *ibid.*, 332–5.

²²⁶Cf. *Insight*, 530–49. For Lonergan, then, religion is not relegated to the realm of *vorstellen* but linked to man's cognitive and moral self-transcendence.

²²⁷Cf. Lonergan's contrast with relativism, *Insight*, 342–7, and hermeneutics as ongoing, 562–97.

²²⁸On heuristic notions, cf. *Insight*, 36–7, 63, 298, 312–13, 392, 461, 522–3, 577–8, 580–81, 586–7. In relation to being, 356, 371–2, 394, 642.

²²⁹Hence Dilthey's criticisms of 'erklärende Psychologie' inasmuch as it reduces consciousness to causal relationships after the manner of the natural sciences, cf. V, 158–68. Cf. also Matson, *op. cit.* for abundant illustrations; also R. G. Collingwood, *The Idea of History*, Oxford 1963, 165–83.

²³⁰Cf. references in note 197 above, also Lonergan's 'The Dehellenisation of Dogma', *T.S.* (1967), 336ff. The curious fact is that Dewart in trying to separate or distinguish being and reality in fact seems to be attempting to avoid the classical control of meaning while not really confronting the obvious parallels such a distinction has with the noumenal-phenomenal bifurcation spoken of above. Cf. Dewart's *The Foundations of Belief*, New York 1969.

²³¹Cf. *Insgiht*, 564–8.

²³²*Ibid.*, 191–206, 214–44, 401–30, 558–62, 619–24.

²³³Cf. *ibid.*, 103–39, 245–70, 458–87.

²³⁴Lamb, 'Towards a Synthetisation of the Sciences', *Phil. of Science* (1965), 182ff.

[235]*Insight*, 210–11.

[236]*Ibid.*, 564–8; unpublished article 'Hermeneutics' (1962); 'Functional Specialties in Theology', *Gregorianum*, 50 (1969), 489.

[237]Cf. *Insight*, 217–44; *Collection*, 244–5.

[238]*Insight*, 565 on how the universal viewpoint has its base in an adequate self-knowledge.

[239]Cf. Lonergan's 'Hermeneutics', 14. It is also of note that Karl-Otto Apel seeks a methodically relevant regulative principle beyond that found in Gadamer's *Applikation* and he finds this principle in the idea of an unlimited 'Interpretations-gemeinschaft, die jeder, der überhaupt argumentiert (also jeder, der denkt!), implizit als ideae Kontrollinstanz voraussetzt'; cf. *Hermeneutik und Dialektik* I, 140–44. Note how Lonergan's universal viewpoint envisages this concrete potential totality.

[240]This was briefly touched on in the Boston College Lectures. There is the problem of relating the many efforts at explanatory history e.g., Sorokin's or Toynbee's or Voegelin's, to the basic context or universal viewpoint, cf. Lonergan's 'Introductory Lecture on the Philosophy of History' (manuscript, 1960).

[241]Cf. *De Deo Trino* I, Rome 1964, and *De Verbo Incarnato*, Rome, *ad usum auditorum*, 1964.

[242]Cf. Lonergan's 'Hermeneutics', 14–15.

[243]Cf. *Insight*, xvii–xxx, 568; 'Functional Specialties in Theology', *Gregorianum*, 50 (1969), 485ff.

[244]Cf. Riedel, *op. cit.*, in *Hermeneutik und Dialektik*; and Habermas, *Erkenntnis und Interesse*, 224.

SELF-KNOWLEDGE IN HISTORY IN GADAMER AND LONERGAN
(pp. 167–217)

[1]Hans-Georg Gadamer, *Wahrheit und Methode: Grundzüge einer philosophischen Hermeneutik*, Tübingen 1965 (1st edn. 1960), 157–8. Hereafter cited in the text by page numbers only; and in the notes abbreviated WM.

[2]Paul Ricoeur, 'Existence et Hermeneutique', *Interpretation der Welt*. Festschrift for Romano Guardini, eds. H. Kuhn, H. Kahlefield, K. Forster, Würzburg, 1965, 32–51.

[3]Hans-Georg Gadamer, *Le Probleme de la conscience historique*, Chaire Cardinal Mercier, no. 2, 1957, Louvain 1963, 19. Hereafter abbreviated PCH.

[4]Cf. also PCH 21–37.

[5]Alfred North Whitehead, *Science and the Modern World*, Lowell Lectures, 1925, New York 1964, 129.

[6]Hans-Georg Gadamer, 'Verstehen', in *Die Religion in Geschichte und Gegenwart* (hereafter abbreviated RGG) VI, 3rd edn. Tübingen, 1962, 1381–3; also Gadamer, *Kleine Schriften I. Philosophie: Hermeneutik*, Tübingen 1967, 139–40. This will be hereafter abbreviated KS I.

[7]KS I, 18–19, 24–5, 140, 221.   [8]KS I, 224–5.

[9]Hans-Georg Gadamer, 'Denken', in RGG II, 3rd edn. Tübingen 1958, 84–5.

[10]Hans-Georg Gadamer, *Philosophisches Lesebuch II*, Frankfurt a.M. 1967, 72. Hereafter abbreviated PLb II.

[11]PLb II, 72–3.   [12]*Ibid.*

[13]Ernst Cassirer, *An Essay on Man. An Introduction to a Philosophy of Human Culture,* Garden City, New York, c. 1944, 71. Whether or not Gadamer would claim that these Pythagorean overtones in Descartes adequately describe the range of modern scientific procedure since the seventeenth century—it is certain that he often tends to do so—his references to Cartesianism also seem to be conveying a point not dissimilar to that of Patrick Heelan in *Quantum Mechanics and Objectivity,* The Hague 1965, when he wrote: 'The classical notion of what constituted a real physical thing and object of physics was founded upon a Cartesian Mind-Body Parallelism in which Mind was thought to "reflect" Matter as in a "Mirror". . . . The classical physicist oriented himself to the construction of idealised and objectifiable phenomenal objects, i.e. concretely, to an explanation in terms of classical particles, spatially constructed models and classical fields' (27–8); in further testimony to the pervasive influence of Cartesianism, Heelan stated: 'Cartesian Dualism, under the influence of the Kantian Critique, becomes transformed into a psychophysical parallelism, then assumed by Bohr in the formulation of the principle of complementarity' (57–8).

[14]P. Heelan, *Quantum Mechanics and Objectivity,* 27–8. Cf. preceding note.

[15]KS I, 48–50.   [16]KS I, 22–3, 161–78, 211, 219.   [17]KS I, 17, 49–50.

[18]PLb II, 72.   [19]Gadamer, '*Denken*', RGG II, 84–5; KS I, 224.

[20]KS I, 22–3. On Descartes' own lack of consistency with this principle, WM 263.

[21]Hans-Georg Gadamer, 'Tradition 1. Phänemologisch', RGG VI, 966–7. Cf. also, PCH 33; KS I, 224.

[22]KS I, 17.

[23]KS I, 85–6. Cf. also, Bernard Lonergan, 'Theology in its New Context', *Theology of Renewal* Vol. I: Renewal of Religious Thought, New York 1968, 34–46; and Patrick Heelan, 'Horizon, Objectivity, and Reality in the Physical Sciences', *International Philosophical Quarterly,* VII (1967), 375–412, especially 377–9.

[24]KS I, 6–7.

[25]On the contribution of Georg Misch, who was the first to underline the importance of Dilthey's life-philosophical orientation: WM 202, 222, 478; PCH 26–7.

[26]Wilhelm Dilthey, *Gesammelte Schriften* VII, 3; cited by Gadamer, WM 224.

[27]PCH 26–7.

[28]Hans-Georg Gadamer, *Philosophisches Lesebuch III*, Frankfurt a.M. 1970, 289. Hereafter abbreviated PLb III.

[29]PLb III, 289–92.

[30]Hans-Georg Gadamer, 'Die phänomenologische Bewegung', *Philosophische Rundschau,* II (1963), 31–2. Hereafter abbreviated PB. Cf. also, KS I, 139–40.

[31]Edmund Husserl, *Ideen zu einer reinen Phänomenologie und phänomenologischen Philosophie, Jahrbuch für Philosophie und phänomenologische Forschung I,* Halle 1922, 35.

[32]KS I, 53.   [33]PLb III, 292.

[34]Hans-Georg Gadamer, 'Martin Heidegger', *Neue Sammlung,* 5 (1965), 8. Hereafter cited as MH. Cf. also, PLb III, 292.

[35]MH 8; WM 242, 500.

[36]PB 7–8, 21–32; also, Gadamer, 'Geschichtlichkeit', RGG II, 1496–8.

[37]PB 7, 29.   [38]KS I, 74.   [39]PB 24–5, 37–9.

[40]Hans-Georg Gadamer, 'Nachwort' zu: M. Heidegger, *Der Ursprung des Kunstwerks*, Stuttgart 1960, 105–6. Hereafter cited as UK.

[41]KS I, 74; WM 94–5.   [42]KS I, 140.   [43]KS I, 48–51; WM 431–2.

[44]PB 7–9, 32–6; PLb III, 289–90.

[45]E. Husserl, *Ideen*, 151; cf. note 31.   [46]PB 20–39.

[47]PLb III, 289–90; UK 105.   [48]PB 8–9, 36; KS I, 74–87.

[49]Cf. Gadamer's disagreements with Becker in PB 24; and in Gadamer, 'Anmerkungen zu dem Thema "Hegel und Heidegger" ', *Natur und Geschichte. Karl Löwith zum 70. Geburtstag*, Stuttgart 1967, 123–31. They are significant for determining the make-up of Heidegger's transcendental and foundational undertaking in *Sein und Zeit* in relation to that of Husserl.

[50]PB 37–8. Cf. remark in the preceding note.

[51]KS I, 88–9, 145; PLb III, 291.

[52]KS I, 74. Cf. also PB 9; PLb III, 292; MH 5.

[53]KS I, 74; WM 94–5.

[54]Cf. WM, 2nd edn., 'Einleitung', XXV–XXIX; and 'Vorwort', XIII–XXIV.

[55]PLb III, 292; WM 94–5.   [56]KS I, 73–4, 83–8, 140–7, 208; MH 5–9.

[57]MH 5.

[58]KS I, 74, 85–7, 140, 143–5; PB 20–40, especially 20, 23–4, 37–8.

[59]KS I, 86, 140, 145, 223–6, especially 226; PB 23–4.

[60]KS I, 74.   [61]Cf. especially PB 35–9.

[62]I am using the word, 'objectivist', here to denote: (a) the contention that consciousness=knowing objects; (b) a perspective which possesses no means of distinguishing the substance of, say, classical metaphysics from the conscious subject, since subject (e.g., for Descartes) is simply that metaphysical substance with which we happen to have the most contact.

[63]UK 102–125.   [64]MH 5–9.   [65]KS I, 89–90; MH 5–9.

[66]Suggestive evidence in support of my clearly 'extrapolating' interpretation is to be found in Otto Pöggeler's work, *Der Denkweg Martin Heideggers*, Pfullingen 1963, 67–80, in the section entitled, 'Transzendentale und hermeneutische Phänomenologie'. Most notable are: (a) The contrast between Husserl's departure from *Anschauung*, and Heidegger's early decision to begin from *Verstehen*; (b) how *Anschauung* of objects may be correlated with Heidegger's notion of being-as-*Vorhandensein*, or what Pöggeler also explicates as a *Vor-Augen-Sein*, *Vor-Augen-Stephendes*, which is, of course, the original sin of the metaphysical tradition. Cf. Pöggeler, 31–3, 42–5, 51–3.

[67]This expression is used by Gadamer to describe, for example, the position of O. Becker, cf. WM 500–501.

[68]Martin Heidegger, *Sein und Zeit*, Tübingen 1967, 72.

[69]This is my interpretation of Gadamer's meaning when he writes: 'Understanding-of-being represents the distinguishing characteristic of Dasein. Already here (in *Sein und Zeit*), then, being is not understood as the result of the objectifying performance of consciousness, as was still the case in Husserl's phenomenology. Rather the question about being penetrates into another dimension entirely, in so far as it envisages the being of the very *Dasein* which

understands itself. Here the transcendental scheme [I interpret: as Cartesian-objectivist] must in the end shatter. The infinite counterpart (*Gegenüber*) of the transcendental ego has been assumed into an ontological [I interpret: transcendental and foundational in a non-Cartesian sense] *Fragestellung*' KS I, 74; cf. also, WM 243.

[70]'That *Dasein* has to do with its being, that it is singled out before all other beings by understanding-of-being, does not represent, as it appears to in *Sein und Zeit,* the ultimate basis from which a transcendental *Fragestellung* [read: Cartesian-objectivist] ought to depart. Rather there is discussion in this work about a completely other ground, which first makes all understanding-of-being possible: and that is, that there is a "da", a lighting-process in being (*Lichtung im Sein*), i.e., the difference between beings and being' WM 243. For a further clue to what I mean and am taking Gadamer as meaning about the being of the subject as subject, compare the following quotation with the above and the quotation in the preceding note: 'Being oneself is being, and by being is not meant the abstract but the concrete. It is not the universal concept "not nothing" of Scotus and Hegel but the concrete goal intended in all inquiry and reflection. It is substance and subject: our opaque being that rises to consciousness and our conscious being by which we save or damn our souls. That conscious being is not an object, not part of the spectacle we contemplate, but the presence to himself of the spectator, the contemplator. It is not an object of introspection, but the prior presence that makes intro-spection possible. It is conscious, but that does not mean that properly it is known; it will be known only if we introspect, understand, reflect, and judge. It is one thing to feel blue and another to advert to the fact that you are feeling blue. It is one thing to be in love and another to discover that what has hap-pened to you is that you have fallen in love. Being oneself is prior to knowing oneself. St Ignatius said that love shows itself more in deeds than in words; but being in love is neither deeds nor words; it is the prior conscious reality that words and, more securely, deeds reveal. That prior opaque and luminous being is not static, fixed, determinate, once-for-all; it is precarious; and its being precarious is the possibility not only of a fall but also of fuller develop-ment. That development is open . . .' Bernard Lonergan, '*Existenz* and *Aggiornamento*', *Collection*, 248–9.

[71]PB 37–8; KS I, 141–3. Cf. also note 66.   [72]KS I, 75.

[73]For Gadamer's phenomenology of *Spiel,* cf. WM 97–105; KS I, 76–80.

[74]KS I, 103.

[75]For Gadamer's very penetrating and original contribution on the topic of prejudice: WM 256–69, especially 256–61.

[76]Gadamer's account of the notion of horizon in Husserl: WM 231–5; for his own use: WM 286–90.

[77]KS I, 107.

[78]On the nexus between experience as human and finitude, cf. WM 335–40.

[79]Gadamer sets his phenomenology of the appropriation of self as historical in opposition to the formal, universally valid method of *Verstehen* first elabor-ated fully by Schleiermacher (158–61, 174–5, 178–80; also 165–9), and later adopted in somewhat modified form by Dilthey (227–8). By its application, the interpreter-historian was thought capable of equating himself temporally with

his object, of transplanting himself into the other's situation, and of reproducing the original creative act by inverting the process, going from objectification-expression to act (280).

⁸⁰On the Aristotelian notion of science vis-a-vis the modern notion, cf. Lonergan, *Collection,* 259–67; and, 'The Absence of God in Modern Culture', *The Presence and Absence of God,* ed. C. F. Mooney, New York 1969, 54–69; cf. also Lonergan citation, note 23.

⁸¹Edmund Husserl, *Logische Untersuchungen* II: Untersuchungen zur Phänomenologie und Theorie der Erkenntnis, I Teil, 3rd edn., Halle 1922, 92.

⁸²Hans-Georg Gadamer, 'Geisteswissenschaften', RGG II, 1304–8; cf. also, 'Verstehen', RGG VI, 1381–3; and KS I, 143.

⁸³KS I, 186–91.

⁸⁴I might mention here that Gadamer speaks clearly about the intention of understanding within any interpreter as having a drive towards being correct; and he emphasises the need for a continual *mensuratio ad rem.* But I do not see that he clearly explicates, as would, say, Lonergan, the distinct exegetical operation of judging the correctness of one's understanding. Certainly such a distinction does not necessarily exclude an appreciation of 'productive misinterpretation'.

⁸⁵E. Husserl, *Logische Untersuchungen* II, *op. cit.,* 96-7.

⁸⁶*Post. An.* II, 19. Cf. KS I, 109–10.

⁸⁷KS I, 186–91.   ⁸⁸KS I, 42–5.

⁸⁹For Gadamer's estimation of Aristotle's *Ethics* for the ethical problematic itself: KS I, 186–91.

⁹⁰KS I, 85; cf. also, KS I, 221–3, 167–70, 186–91.   ⁹¹PB 39.

⁹²KS I, 85–6, 125–9, 143–5, 224–7; PB 22–4.   ⁹³For instance, KS I, 127.

⁹⁴KS I, 125.   ⁹⁵PB 39–40.

⁹⁶On Lonergan's notion of dialectic, cf. his 'Functional Specialties in Theology', *Gregorianum,* 50 (1969), 4–6, 10–11, 16, 18–19.

⁹⁷David William Tracy, *The Development of the Notion of Theological Methodology in the Works of Bernard J. Lonergan, S.J.,* Dissertatio ad Lauream in Facultate Theologica, Rome 1969.

⁹⁸Lonergan, *Collection,* 141.

⁹⁹Bernard Lonergan, 'Response', *Proceedings of the American Catholic Philosophical Association,* 41 (1967), 256–7. It would be an interesting chapter in the comparative history of ideas to trace the reasons why Gadamer's philosophic hermeneutics is characterised by an out-and-out reprehension for cognitional theory as expounded in a philosophical context under the sway of Cartesian-Idealist objectivism; while Lonergan, having spent years getting behind the *verba* to the subject matter of Aquinas when the latter wrote: *Anima humana intelligit seipsum per suum intelligere, quod est actus proprius ejus, perfecte deomstrans virtutem ejus et naturam* (*S.T.* Ia, q.88 a.2 ad 3m, cited in '*Insight:* Preface to a Discussion', *Collection,* 153), was able rather to re-articulate both the cognitional theoretic and the epistemological question, thereby confronting them head on. On the record of Lonergan's encounter with Aquinas on this issue, cf. the articles, 'The Concept of *Verbum* in the Writings of St Thomas Aquinas', *Theological Studies* 7 (1946), 349–92; 8 (1947), 35–79, 404–44; 10 (1949), 3–40, 359–93; or the recently revised form

of the same entitled, *Verbum, Word and Idea in Aquinas*, ed., David Burrell, Indiana 1967.

[100]On common-sense understanding, cf. Lonergan, *Insight*, chapters VI and VII, 173–244; on scientific understanding cf. chapters II–V, 33–172. For a later explication in terms of 'mediations of meaning', cf. 'Dimensions of Meaning', *Collection*, especially 255–8.

[101]On classification versus correlation, cf. *Insight*, 37–8, 44–6. For Lonergan's elucidation of the shift from classical to modern science, I am quite dependent on his *De methodo theologiae* (Notes from lectures at the Gregorian University), as well as on the works mentioned in notes 23 and 80.

[102]Lonergan, *Insight*, 434.   [103]Cf. reference to Lonergan, note 23.

[104]Bernard Lonergan, 'The Natural Knowledge of God', *Proceedings, Catholic Theological Association of America*, 23 (1968), 62.

[105]Bernard Lonergan, 'Notes from the Introductory Lecture in the Philosophy of History', Thomas More Institute, 23 Sept. 1960, 9.

[106]For a basic contrast of method as a set of rules and method as horizon, cf. reference to Lonergan, note 23.

[107]Lonergan, *Collection*, 155. Cf. also 'Isomorphism of Thomist and Scientific Thought', *Collection*, 142–51.

[108]Cf. Lonergan, 'Functional Specialties in Theology', *op. cit.*, p. 1, footnote.

[109]Lonergan, 'Cognitional Structure', *Collection*, 226–7. Cf. also, *Collection*, 175–92, 248–9; as well as, *De Constitutione Christi ontologica et psychologica*, Rome 1956, 83–99; and, *The Subject*, Aquinas Lecture, Milwaukee 1968.

[110]Lonergan, *Insight*, vii–xxx.

[111]On the notion of universality by reason of potential concreteness as opposed to sheer abstractness, cf. Lonergan, *Insight*, 566; and on the similar difference between abstraction as enriching and abstraction as impoverishing, cf. 87–9.

[112]Lonergan, 'Response', *op. cit.*, 254–5. Cf. also, *Insight*, 392; *Collection*, 198–9.

[113]Lonergan, *Collection*, 199.

[114]Lonergan, *Collection*, 228; cf. also 228–31, and *Insight*, 348–74.

[115]Lonergan, 'The Natural Knowledge of God', *op. cit.*, 59. Cf. also, *Insight*, 352–6.

[116]Lonergan, *Collection*, 235–6.

[117]Lonergan, *Insight*, 4, 9–10, 74, 220–22, 231, 474.

[118]Lonergan, *Collection*, 173–92.   [119]Lonergan, *Insight*, 395–6.

[120]Lonergan, *Insight*, 385; also, 747–8.

[121]Lonergan 'Introductory Lecture in the Philosophy of History' (cf. note 101). On 'history that is written' or 'history as a scientific subject', cf. 1–7; on 'history that is written about', especially 9–11.

[122]Lonergan, 'Introductory Lecture in the Philosophy of History', *op. cit.*, 8–14.

[123]Bernard Lonergan, 'The Transition from a Classicist World-View to Historical Mindedness', *Law for Liberty: The Role of Law in the Church Today*, ed. James E. Biechler, Baltimore 1967, 126–33.

[124]On the need for discriminating between 'the liberty that generates progress and the bias that generates decline' (236), cf. *Insight*, 217–44. On the notion

of a universal viewpoint compatible with human finitude, cf. 564-8, 594.

[125]Lonergan, 'Functional Specialties in Theology', *op. cit.,* 1-20.

[126]On the general implications of basic method or universal viewpoint for the problems of interpretation, cf. *Insight,* 586-94.

[127]I am dependent on the formulation of Bernard Lonergan in 'Hermeneutics' (Notes for lectures during Theology Institute, Regis College, Toronto, 16 pages), for the salient issues mentioned here.

[128]Bernard Lonergan, 'De argumento theologico ex sacra scriptura', (Notes for lecture to professors at Gregorian University and Biblical Institute, Gregorian University, Rome, 1962). Cf. also, Lonergan, *De Deo Trino I. Pars Dogmatica,* 2nd revised edition, Rome 1964, 5-14; and II. *Pars Systematica,* 3rd revised edition, Rome 1964, 7-64.

[129]WM 264, 293, 308-11, 482-4, XVIII, XIX.   [130]WM 290-5, 307-23.

[131]Lonergan, 'Dimensions of Meaning', *Collection,* 252-67.

[132]Lonergan, *Insight,* Chapters XIX and XX, 634-730. Cf. also his, 'The Natural Knowledge of God', *op. cit.,* and 'The Natural Desire to See God', *Collection,* 84-95; as well as *Collection,* 248-51.

[133]Lonergan, *Insight,* 703-18; also his, 'Belief, Today's Issue', *Canadian Messenger* (June 1968), 8-12.

[134]Lonergan, 'Openness and Religious Experience', *Collection,* 198-201. Cf. also, *Insight,* 687-748.

[135]PCH 15; WM 4, note.

[136]Hans-Georg Gadamer, 'Geisteswissenschaften', RGG II, 1304-8.

[137]KS I, 2-10.

[138]Peter Hünermann, *Der Durchbruch geschichtlichen Denkens im 19. Jahrhundert,* Freiburg-Basle-Vienna 1967, 169. Cf. also PCH 23; KS I, 2-10; WM 206, 477.

[139]P. Hünermann, *Der Durchbruch, op. cit.,* 169-209.

[140]P. Hünermann, *Der Durchbruch, op. cit.,* 210-39.

[141]KS I, 139; PLb II, 73.   [142]KS I, 35; WM XV, 483-4.

[143]KS I, 4, 49-50, 167, 213-14, 216.

[144]WM 60-63, 209; on the history of the word, *Erlebnis* see WM 57-60.

[145]KS I, 4, 5; WM 211.

[146]Hans-Georg Gadamer, 'Geschichte und Geschichtsauffassung III. Geschichtsphilosophie', RGG II, 1488-96. Cf. also KS I, 5.

[147]KS I, 132-7.   [148]KS I, 6, 138.

[149]On Schleiermacher's 'aesthetic' presuppositions, WM 175-81, especially 177-8; on his hermeneutics, 172-85; for an overview of his limitation in Gadamer's estimation, 157-61.

[150]KS I, 6; WM 226, 505.   [151]PCH 23; WM 217.

[152]KS I, 73; WM 198, 216, 218-19, 505.

LONERGAN AND THE SUBJECTIVIST PRINCIPLE (pp. 218-35)

[1]*Insight,* xxx. Lonergan admits here to sharing the view of Hume that 'one does not conquer a territory by taking here an outpost and there a town or village, but by marching directly upon the capital and assaulting its citadel'. To

which he immediately adds: 'Still, correct strategy is one thing; successful execution is another . . .'

[2]*Ibid.*, xxviii, 748. [3]*Ibid.*, 748. [4]*Ibid.*, xvii.

[5]'Insight', transcription (typescript) of five lectures delivered at University College, Dublin 1961, 11.

[6]*Insight*, 399, 523. [7]*Ibid.*, 498, 733.

[8]*Ibid.*, xxviii. I prescind here from the distinction commonly made in Lonergan's more recent writings between 'cognitional theory' and 'epistemology'. See, e.g., *The Subject*, Milwaukee 1968, 32f.; and 'Theology and Man's Future', lecture (typescript) delivered at St Louis University, 1968, 4.

[9]*Insight*, xxix, 361.

[10]*Metaphysik, Eine methodisch-systematische Grundlegung*, Innsbruck, 2nd edn., 1964.

[11]'Insight', 17. [12]*Ibid.*, 20. [13]*Insight*, xxvii. [14]*Ibid.*, 744.

[15]*Ibid.*, 731. [16]*Ibid.*, 521.

[17]'Response', *Proceedings of the American Catholic Philosophical Association*, XLI (1967), 258; and *Insight*, 521, 677.

[18]'Insight', 40; and *The Subject*, 33.

[19]*Process and Reality: An Essay in Cosmology*, New York 1929, 253.

[20]Cf., e.g., these two formulations, which in form are all but identical: (1) 'The subjectivist principle is, that the datum in the act of experience can be adequately analysed purely in terms of universals.' (2) 'The subjectivist principle is that the whole universe consists of elements disclosed in the analysis of the experiences of subjects' (*ibid.*, 239, 252). As I go on to argue, it is in the sense expressed by the second of these formulations that 'the subjectivist principle' is used in this paper.

[21]*Ibid.*, 253. [22]*Ibid.*, 253f. [23]*Ibid.*, 241. [24]*Ibid.*, 243, 252.

[25]*Ibid.*, 243. [26]Cf., e.g., *ibid.*, 116ff., 208ff., 219f. [27]*Ibid.*, 246.

[28]*Ibid.*, 245. [29]*Ibid.* [30]*Ibid.*, 246. [31]*Ibid.*

[32]*Ibid.*, 179. Cf. *Adventures of Ideas*, New York 1933, 281 where Whitehead argues that 'the exclusive reliance on sense-perception promotes a false metaphysics'.

[33]*Ibid.*, 83. [34]*Collection*, 226. [35]*Insight*, 330, 348, 357, 383.

[36]*Ibid.*, 514, 382, 324. [37]*Ibid.*, 383. [38]*Collection*, 235.

[39]*Ibid.*, 235f. [40]Cf., e.g., *ibid.*, 206–19, 231–6. [41]'Insight', 17f.

[42]'Response', 257. [43]'Insight', 39f. [44]'Response', 256.

[45]'Natural Knowledge of God'. Contribution to the 23rd Annual Convention of the Catholic Theological Society of America, 1968 (typescript), 4.

[46]*Insight*, 684. [47]*Ibid.*, 641. [48]*Ibid.*, 644. [49]*Ibid.*, 657f.

[50]*Ibid.*, 677. [51]*Ibid.*, 668. [52]*Ibid.*, [53]*Ibid.*, 651, 655, 661.

FROM PROBLEMATICS TO HERMENEUTICS (pp. 236–71)

[1]Paul Ricoeur, *History and Truth*, E. trs. Charles A. Kelbley, Evanston, 1965, 327.

[2]Paul Ricoeur, 'The Hermeneutics of Symbols and Philosophical Reflection', *International Philosophical Quarterly*, II 2 (1963), 192–3.

[3]Paul Ricoeur, *Fallible Man*, E. trs. Charles Kelbley, Chicago 1965, 6.

[4]*Ibid.*, 13. [5]*Ibid.* [6]Ricoeur, *Fallible Man*, 6. [7]*Ibid.*

[8]Paul Ricoeur, *Freedom and Nature: The Voluntary and the Involuntary*, E. trs. Erazim V. Kohak, Evanston 1966, 6.

[9]*Ibid.*   [10]*Ibid.*   [11]*Ibid.*   [12]*Ibid.*   [13]*Ibid.*

[14]Ricoeur, *Freedom and Nature*, 6.

[15]Herbert Spiegelberg, *The Phenomenological Movement*, I, 2 vols., 2nd edn., The Hague 1965, 39.

[16]Ricoeur, *Freedom and Nature*, 13

[17]Ricoeur, *Freedom and Nature*, 14.

[18]*Ibid.*   [19]*Ibid.*   [20]Ricoeur, *Freedom and Nature*, 22.

[21]Ricoeur, *Freedom and Nature*, 19.   [22]*Ibid.*

[23]Ricoeur, *Fallible Man*, xvii.   [24]Ricoeur, *Fallible Man*, 203.

[25]Ricoeur, *Freedom and Nature*, 22.

[26]Ricoeur, *Fallible Man*, xviii.

[27]Mircea Eliade, *Patterns in Comparative Religion*, Cleveland 1963, xiii.

[28]Ricoeur, 'The Hermeneutics of Symbols and Philosophical Reflection', *op. cit.*, 199.

[29]David Rasmussen, 'Mircea Eliade: Structural Hermeneutics and Philosophy', *Philosophy Today*, XII, No. 2/4 (Summer 1968), 138–47.

[30]Ricoeur, 'The Hermeneutics of Symbols and Philosophical Reflection', *op. cit.*, 199.

[31]Ricoeur, *Fallible Man*, xxiii.

[32]Ricoeur, 'The Hermeneutics of Symbols and Philosophical Reflection', *op. cit.*, 204.

[33]*Ibid.*   [34]*Ibid.*, 208.   [35]*Ibid.*, 209.   [36]*Ibid.*, 211.   [37]*Ibid.*, 215.

[38]Bernard Lonergan, *Collection*, 265–6.

[39]Bernard Lonergan, *Insight*, 541.   [40]*Ibid.*, 542–3.

[41]Lonergan, *Insight*, 587.

BEING FOR LONERGAN: A HEIDEGGEREAN VIEW (pp. 272-83)

[1]Bernard Lonergan, *Insight*, 348.   [2]*Ibid*, 348.   [3]*Ibid.*, 350.

[4]*Ibid*, 356.   [5]*Ibid.*, 356.   [6]*Ibid.*, 642.   [7]*Ibid.*, 363, 643.

[8]*Ibid.*, 644.   [9]*Ibid.*, 640.   [10]*Ibid.*, 644.   [11]*Ibid.*, 644–6.

[12]*Ibid.*, 646–51.   [13]*Ibid.*, 656.   [14]*Ibid.*, 657–69.   [15]*Ibid.*, 572.

[16]*Ibid.*, 672–3. See entire section, 667–77.

[17]M. Heidegger, 'Preface' to my *Heidegger: Through Phenomenology to Thought*, The Hague 1963, x.

[18]*Insight*, 360; cf. 361, 363.

[19]For a fuller treatment of how Heidegger conceives the grounding of metaphysics, see 'Introduction to *What is Metaphysics?*', E. trs. W. Kaufmann, in *Existentialism from Dostoievski to Sartre*; ed. W. Kaufmann, New York 1957, 207–21.

[20]*Insight*, 362.   [21]*Ibid.*, 388, 652.   [22]*Ibid.*, 654–5.

[23]*Ibid.*, 656.   [24]*Ibid.*, 659.   [25]*Ibid.*, 657–69.

[26]See 'Die onto-theo-logische Verfassung der Metaphysics', *Identität und Differenz*, Pfullingen 1957, 66–73.

[27]*Insight*, 668.   [28]*Ibid.*, 651–7, especially 655; cf. 672.

[29]'. . . Dies ist die Ursache als die Causa sui. So Lautet der sachgerechte Name für den Gott in der Philosophie. Zu diesem Gott kann der Mensch

weder beten, noch kann er ihm opfern. Vor der Causa sui kann der Mensch weder aus Scheu ins Knie fallen, noch kann er vor diesem Gott musizieren und tanzen.' (*Identität und Differenz,* 70, my translation.)

³⁰'Demgemass ist das gott-lose Denken, das den Gott der Philosophie, den Gott als Causa sui preisgeben muss, dem gottlichen Gott vielleicht naher. Dies sagt hier nur: es ist freier für ihn, als es die Onto–Theo–Logik wahrhaben möchte.' (*Identität und Differenz,* 71, my translation.)

³¹Lonergan, 'Metaphysics or Horizon'. *Cross Currents* XVI (1966), 481–94: quotation from p. 489.

³²*Ibid.,* 494; cf. *Insight,* 348–50.

³³M. Heidegger, *Kant and the Problem of Metaphysics,* E. trs. J. Churchill, Bloomington, 1962.

³⁴Heidegger finds his warrant in Kant's explanation of the word 'transcendental': '. . . I call that knowledge transcendental which concerns itself in general not so much with objects *as with our manner of knowing objects in so far as this must be a priori possible* . . .' (I. Kant, *Kritik der reinen Vernunft,* ed. R. Schmidt, Hamburg 1952, B 25; Kant's italics.)

³⁵'Ein endlich erkennenedes Wesen vermag sich zum Seienden, das es selbst nicht ist und das es auch nicht geschaffen hat, nur dann zu verhalten, wenn dieses schon vorhandene seiende von sich aus begegnen kann. Um jedoch als das Sciende, das es ist, begegnen zu konnen, muss es im vohinein schon uberhaupt als Seiende, d.h. hinsichtlich seiner Seinsverfassung, "erkannt" sein. . . . Endliches Wesen bedarf dieses Grundvermögens einer entgegenstehenlassenden Zuwendung-zu. . . . In dieser ursprünglichen Zuwendung halt sich das endliche Wesen überhaupt erst einen Spielraum vor, innerhalb dessen ihm etwas "korrespondieren" kann. Sich im vorhenein in solchem Spielraumhalten, ihn ursprünglich bilden, ist nichts anderes als die Transzendenz, die alles endliche Verhalten zu Seiendem auszeichnet. . . .' (M. Heidegger, *Kant und das Problem der Metaphysik,* 2nd edn. Frankfurt 1950, 69–70, my translation.)

³⁶E.g., *Kant und das Problem der Metaphysik, op. cit.,* 82 (*Horizon von Gegenständlichkeit*); 128 (. . . *der Gegenstände*); 110 (*im vorhinein offen*).

³⁷'. . . Der Mensch ist ein Seiendes, das inmitten von Seiendem ist, so zwar, das ihm dabei das Seiende, das er nicht ist, und das Seiende, das er selbst ist, zumal immer schon offenbar geworden ist. Diese Seinsart des Menschen nennen wir Existenz . . .' (*ibid.,* 205).

³⁸See M. Heidegger, *Sein und Zeit,* 9th edn., Tübingen 1960, 59–60.

³⁹'Die Einheit der horizontalen Schemata von Zukunft, Gewesenheit und Gegenward grundet in der ekstatischen Einheit der Zeitlichkeit. Der Horizont der ganzen Zeitlichkeit bestimmt das, *woraufhin* das faktisch existierende Seiende wesenhaft erschlossen ist . . .' (*Sein und Zeit,* 365, my translation, author's italics.)

⁴⁰See, for example, the extremely radical interpretation in *Kant und das Problem der Metaphysik* of the transcendental imagination as original time, 156–84.

⁴¹See M. Heidegger, Platons *Lehre von der Wahrheit mit einen Brief über den Humanismus,* Berne 1954, 72.

⁴²'Der Horizont und die Transzendenz sind somit von den Gegenständen und von unserem Vorstellen aus erfahren und nur im Hinblick auf die Gegen-

 stände und unser Vorstellen bestimmt. . . . Auf solche weise dasjenige, was den Horizont das sein lasst, was her ist, noch keineswegs erfahren wird. . . . Wir sagen, dass wir in den Horizont hineinsehen. Der Gesichtskreis ist also ein Offenes, welche Offenheit ihm nicht dadurch zukommt, das wir hineinsehen . . . Das Horizonthafte ist somit nur die uns zugekehrte Seite eines uns umgebenden Offenen, das erfüllt ist mit Aussicht ins Aussehen dessen, was unserem Vorstellen als Gegenstand erscheint.' (M. Heidegger, *Gelassenheit*, Pfullingen 1959, 39, my translation.)

THE NEW CONTEXT OF THE PHILOSOPHY OF GOD IN LONERGAN AND
RAHNER (pp. 284–305)

[1]'Theology in its New Context', *Theology of Renewal I*, New York, 1968· (The terms 'classicist world view' and 'historical consciousness' are not used in this talk but they express its general orientation and are used elsewhere by Lonergan.)

[2]*Collection*, 84–95.

[3]*Ibid.*, 198–201.

[4]*Proceedings of the Catholic Theological Society of America*, 1968, 64–9.

[5]*De Verbo Incarnato*, 3rd revised edn. Rome 1964.

[6]'Functional Specialties in Theology', *Gregorianum*, 50 (1969).

[7]*Collection*, 88.　　[8]*Ibid.*, 199.　　[9]*Ibid.*, 200–1.　　[10]*Ibid.*, 201.

[11]'Natural Knowledge of God', 63.　　[12]*Ibid.*, 69.

[13]The term 'realities' is used here to indicate that 'grace' and 'nature' are real and distinct but we wish here to prescind from the whole substance-accident problematic.

[14]*Man's Condition*, New York 1969.　　[15]*Ibid.*, 171.　　[16]*Ibid.*, 238.

[17]*Ibid.*　　[18]*Ibid.*, 241.　　[19]*Sacramentum Mundi*, III, 369.

[20]*Ibid.*　　[21]*Ibid.*　　[22]*Ibid.*　　[23]*Ibid.*, 368–9.

[24]*Sacramentum Mundi*, II, 417.　　[25]*Ibid.*

[26]*Sacramentum Mundi*, IV, 298.　　[27]*Ibid.*　　[28]*Ibid.*

[29]'The Natural Desire to See God', *Collection*, 94.

[30]*Insight*, 332.

[31]*Collection*, 201.　　[32]*Ibid.*, 266.

[33]Review of *Saint Augustin et le neoplatonisme* by M. F. Sciacca, and *Existe-t-il une philosophie Chretienne?* by Nedoncelle, in *Gregorianum*, 40 (1959), 183.

[34]*Gratia Operans. A Study of Speculative Development in the Writings of St Thomas Aquinas* (dissertatio ad lauream in facultate theologica Pontificiae Universitatis Gregorianae), 1940. Cf. 'St Thomas' Thought on *Gratia Operans*', *Theological Studies*, 2 (1941), 289–324; 3 (1942), 69–88, 375–402, 533–78.

[35]*Verbum: Word and Idea in Aquinas*, London 1968.　　[36]*Ibid.*, x.

[37]*De Deo Trino: Pars Dogmatica*, Rome 1964, 154.

[38]'The Origins of Christian Realism' (lecture at Regis College, Toronto, 8 Sept. 1961; text from tape-recording).

[39]*De Deo Trino: Pars Dogmatica*, 108.

[40]Georg Geppert, *Songs der Beatles,* Munich 1968.

[41]'Philosophy and Theology', *Theological Investigations* VI, 72.

[42]'Zur Neuordnung der theologischen Studien', *Stimmen der Zeit*, 1 (1968), 15.

[43]'Theology and Anthropology', *The Word in History*, New York 1966, 9.

[44]*Theological Investigations* VI, 75.   [45]*Ibid.*

[46]'Philosophy and philosophising in theology', *Theology Digest* (February 1968), 21.

[47]*Ibid.*, 18.   [48]*Ibid.*, 19.

[49]'Philosophy and Theology', *Sacramentum Mundi* V, 20.

[50]*Ibid.*, 24.   [51]*Ibid.*   [52]*Ibid.*

[53]Cited above from *The Word in History*.

[54]'Philosophy and Theology', *Sacramentum Mundi* V, 21.

[55]*Hearers of the Word*, E. trs. Michael Richards, New York 1969.

[56]'Philosophy and Theology', *Sacramentum Mundi* V, 22–3.

[57]*Ibid.*, 23.   [58]*Ibid.*   [59]*Ibid.*   [60]*The Word in History*, 1.

[61]*Sacramentum Mundi* V, 21–2.   [62]*The Word in History*, 1.

[63]*De Methodo Theologiae.* Hermeneutics (Notes for lectures during Theology Institute, Regis College, Toronto, 20 July 1962), 7.

[64]*Ibid.*   [65]*Ibid.*

[66]*Congress on the Theology of Renewal of the Church*, Toronto 1968, 7.

[67]*Proceedings of the Catholic Theological Society of America*, 68–9.

[68]*The Subject*, Milwaukee 1968, 19–29.

[69]*Insight*, 624. (Lonergan makes use of Kierkegaard's term *aesthetic* to designate in a general way what he often refers to as naïve realism.)

[70]*Stimmen der Zeit*, 1 (1968), 16–17.   [71]*Theological Investigations* V, 473.

[72]*Spirit in the World*, New York 1968, 253.

[73]*Hearers of the Word*, 106.   [74]*Ibid.*   [75]*Ibid.*   [76]*Ibid.*

[77]*Ibid.*, 107.

[78]'Atheism and Implicit Christianity', *Theology Digest* (February 1968), 53.

[79]*Einführung in den Begriff des Christentums* exists as a set of student notes.

[80]'The Role of a Catholic University', *Collection*, 114–20.

BERNARD LONERGAN RESPONDS (pp. 306–12)

[1]*Pensées*, vii, 553.   [2]*Insight*, 644.

73-514

International Lonergan Congress,
St. Leo College, 1970
Language truth and meaning